Painting
Clouds and Skies
in Oils

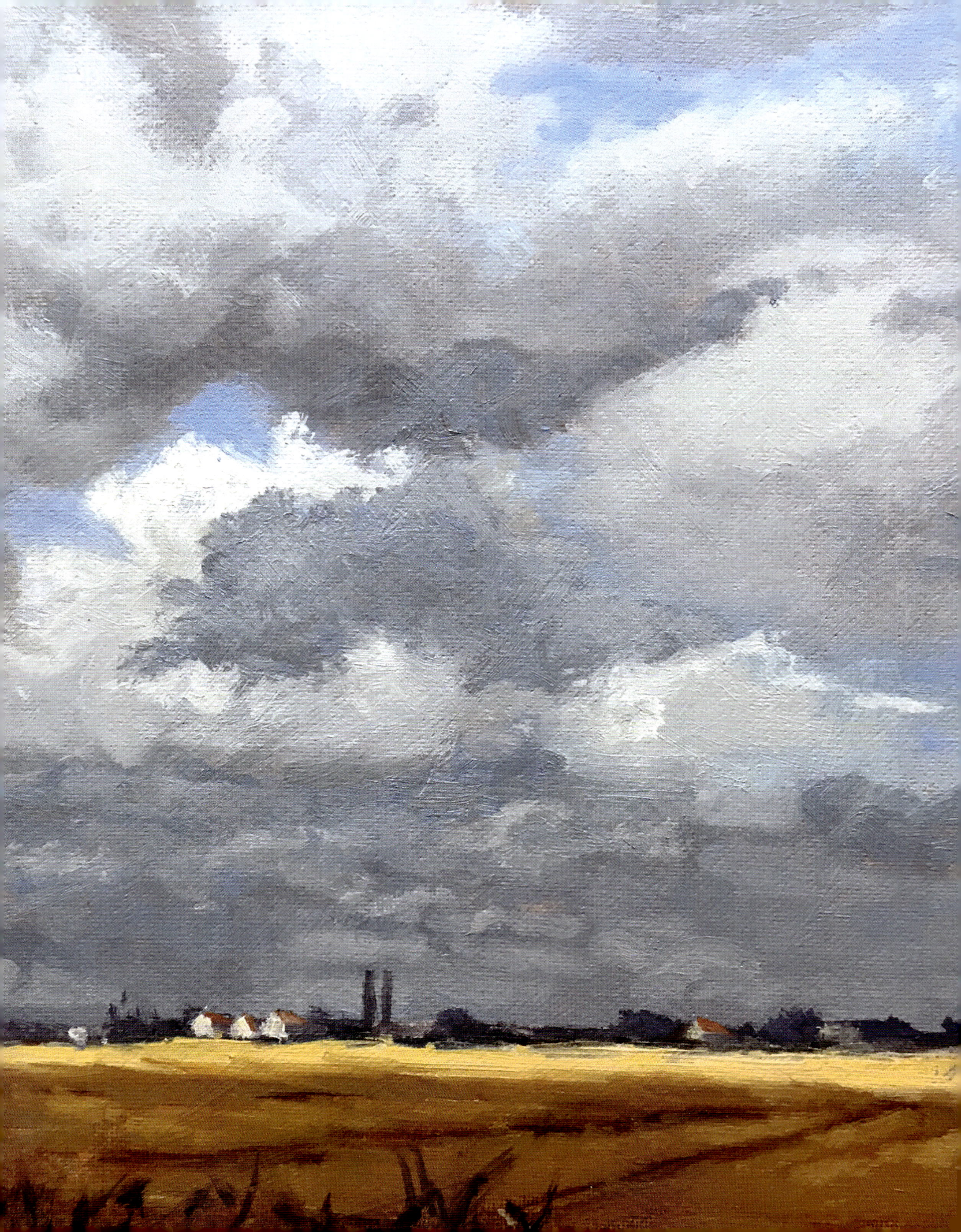

Painting **Clouds and Skies** in Oils

Mo Teeuw

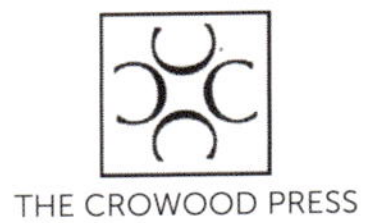

THE CROWOOD PRESS

First published in 2017 by
The Crowood Press Ltd
Ramsbury, Marlborough
Wiltshire SN8 2HR

enquiries@crowood.com
www.crowood.com

This impression 2026

British Library Cataloguing-in-Publication Data
A catalogue record for this book is available from the British Library.

For product safety-related questions contact productsafety@crowood.com

ISBN 978 1 78500 345 5

Frontispiece: *A Skyfull* (detail). Painted on canvas board.

Graphic design and typesetting by Peggy & Co. Design Inc.
Printed and bound in India by Thomson Press India Private Limited

Contents

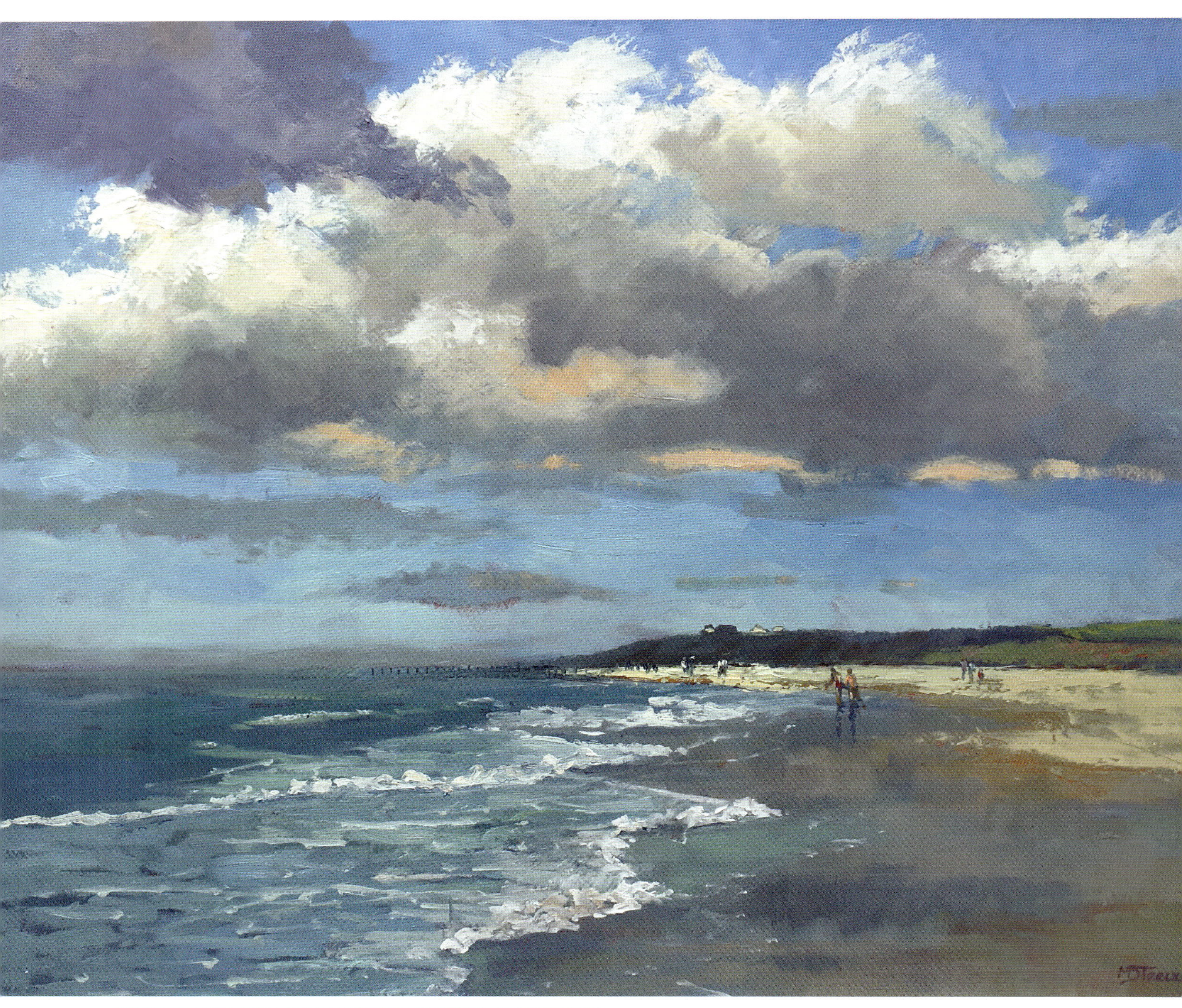

Happisburgh Clouds, 14" × 18". Oil on canvas.
Painted from a *plein air* sketch. The clouds were coming off the land as the tide at Happisburgh receded rapidly. A great day for a windy walk on the beach but not so good for painting.

Foreword

I have admired Mo Teeuw's work, work ethic and teaching methods for many years; she not only produces masterful paintings but also inspires those whom she teaches.

Mo is a professional member of the SAA (The Society for All Artists). She teaches regularly and has helped many members of the SAA, and others, to progress in their painting, especially in painting landscapes in oils *en plein air*.

Mo's style is much in the frame of Constable and she shares his love of skies much inspired by the high skies of East Anglia. She brings several things to help you paint; being self-taught, she approaches painting from her own unique viewpoint and her time as a teacher has given her the gift to communicate her skills. But above all, she works at her art, painting nearly every day, and it is as true for her as for us all: 'the more she practises the better she gets'. Furthermore, she puts herself about, she is a member of several art societies and exhibits at many prestigious exhibitions, and teaches both in England and abroad.

In this book, Mo starts from the beginning and clearly explains how you can create great skies in your paintings. From preparing the ground, to how to create exciting colour graduations. I recommend this book to you and urge you to study her ideas and teachings but above all, follow her and paint every day.

Happy painting!

John Hope-Hawkins
SAA Chairman

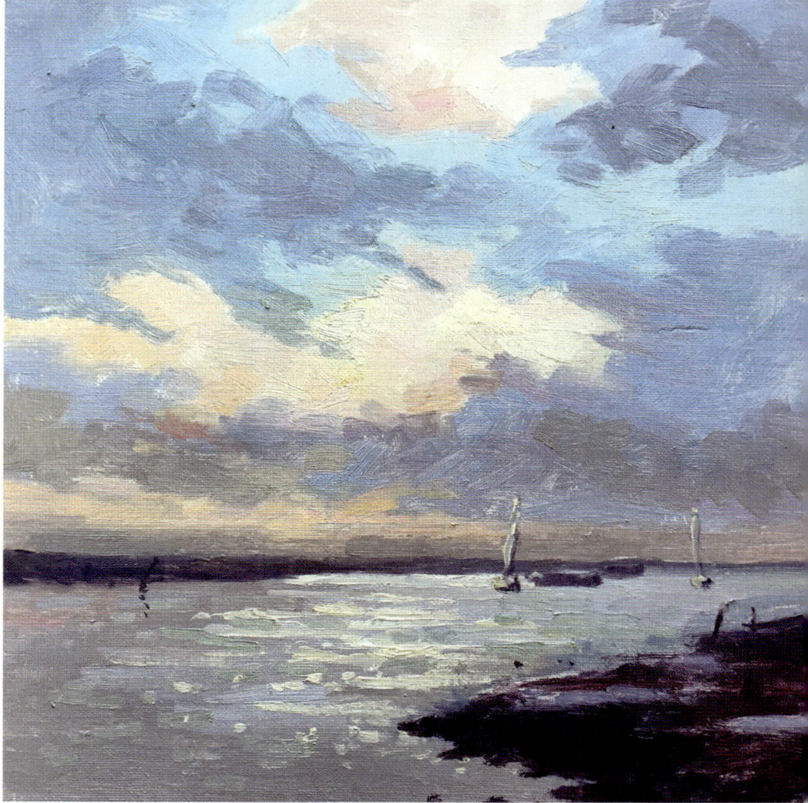

Summer Clouds, Blakeney, 12" × 12". Oil on canvas.

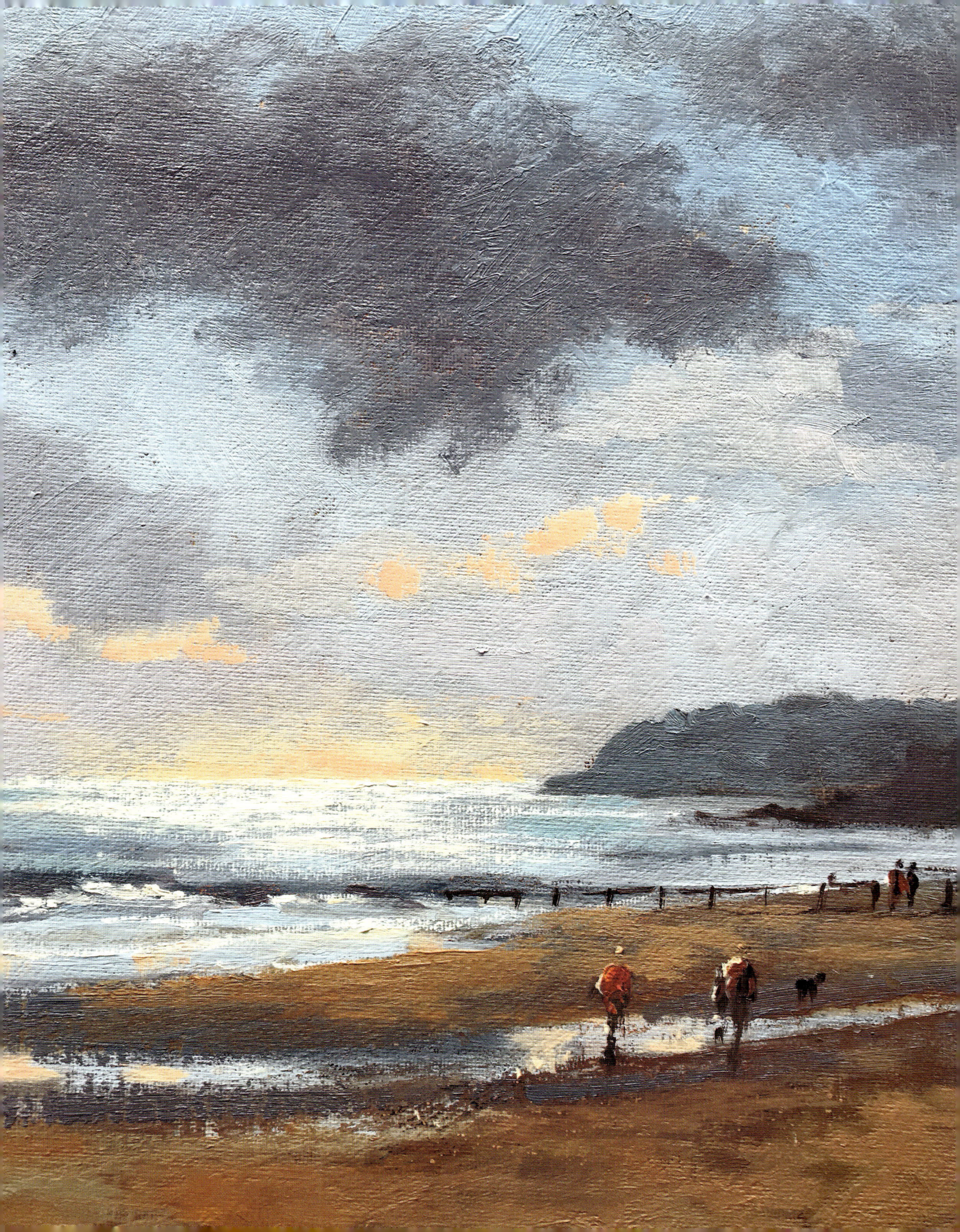

Introduction

From an early age I have always felt the need to paint. I wanted to go to Art College but was persuaded to get a 'proper job' and so I headed off to a teacher training college and ended up teaching art in a secondary school. This, as it turned out, was a blessing as I then went on to run several adult education classes which in turn led me to running residential courses both in the UK and abroad.

Through teaching I have made many good friends and met some amazing artists. I love to teach and pass on my knowledge. Nothing gives me more joy than to see the expression on students' faces when they have that 'Eureka' moment, whether it's a successful painting or the mastering of perspective. I remember one occasion when a student, completely new to painting, came in one day, absolutely bubbling over with enthusiasm. 'Did you see the sky that morning?' and 'It's true what you said, the sky isn't always blue and trees aren't always green and brown.' It was as though they were seeing for the first time. It made me realize how we as artists do see the world differently. This is something we mustn't take for granted.

I learn a lot through my classes too; by giving constructive criticism to groups and individuals, I am analyzing their work and assessing it as to why it does or doesn't work and in doing this, I have been able to recognize faults in my own work.

I live in the fens of Lincolnshire where it is very flat; in fact, just outside my village you can turn in a complete circle and not see any hills. Even the trees are few and far between, making it difficult sometimes to find a focal point.

I have always had a passion for landscape painting and love the big open skies around me so my paintings of Lincolnshire and Norfolk are more skyscapes than landscapes, therefore I was delighted to be asked by The Crowood Press to write this book about painting clouds and skies in oil paint.

By understanding clouds and cloud formations, we can make our paintings more believable. I feel that the sky sets the mood for a painting and I find that if the sky is right, the rest seems to follow.

The step by step demonstrations in this book will hopefully inspire you to have a go, not just to copy my work and style but also to develop your own way and to give your own interpretation of the subject. By following the demonstrations, you will build your confidence and go on to use your own source material. Constant practice and experimentation will help you find your own style, which will happen naturally and continue to evolve.

As mentioned, I have met some wonderfully talented artists on my painting trips in the UK and abroad. I am delighted to be able to have the chance to share with you some of my favourite painters, each artist with their own unique styles and methods of painting. Each artist shows his or her different take on sky painting.

Evening on the Isle of Wight.

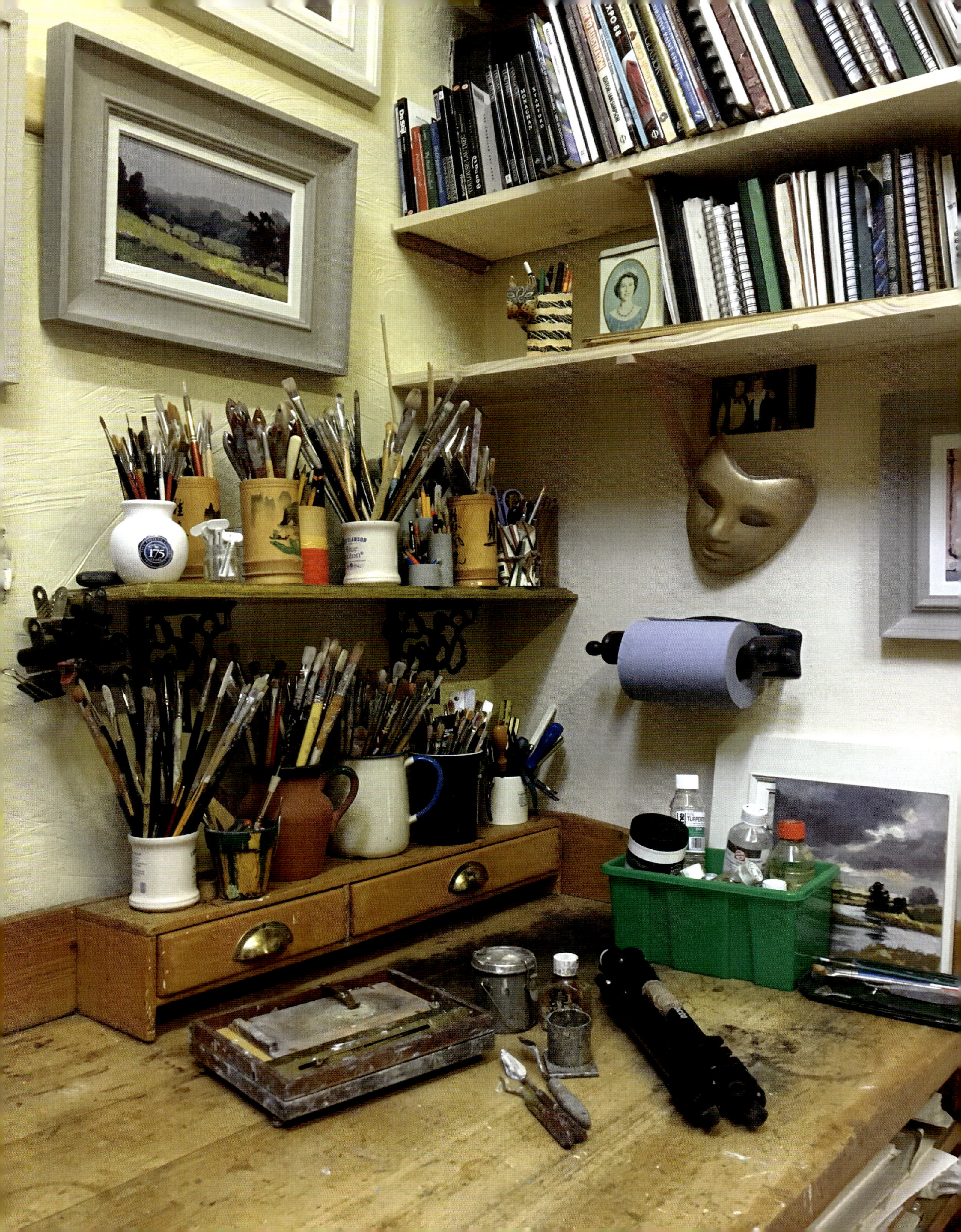

CHAPTER 1

Equipment

Without tubes of paint there would have been no Impressionists.

PIERRE AUGUSTE RENOIR

With so many choices, buying art supplies can feel overwhelming. There are many options when it comes to brushes, painting supports and paints. Having the right equipment is as essential as having the right subject to paint. It is important that you are able to have everything to hand and that you are comfortable. There are vast arrays of easels, paints, brushes, supports, mediums and so on that are out there to tempt us. Finding what works well for you is a matter of personal taste.

BRUSHES

Brushes are a matter of preference. Most artists have a tendency to use bristle or hog hair brushes, preferring the stiffness of the bristle. It is these that are usually associated with painting in oils and acrylics. There are many nylon brushes which, although cheaper and sold as oil painting brushes, tend not to hold the paint as well as the hog hair alternative. Hog hair brushes are often used for painting in oils. They come in four basic shapes: round, filbert, flat and rigger. Some artists like the softer feel of a natural hair brush, an example of which would be mongoose.

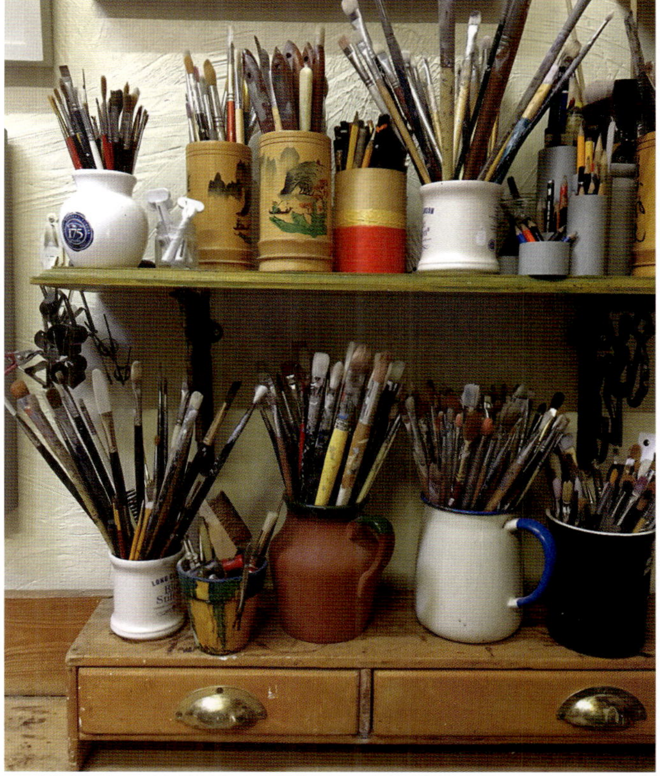

Hog hair brushes come in four basic shapes. Round, filbert, flat and the rigger. It is useful to have a good selection of each. This picture shows brushes collected over the years. As they wear out, use them for underpainting to save wear on your new brushes.

An organized corner of the studio with sketch books and brushes on shelves.

I have found, along with many fellow artists, that Rosemary & Co make very good brushes. They are a UK-based family business that have been making brushes and supplying artists by mail order for thirty years.

A good painter will have difficulty painting with bad brushes.

Flat

Flat brushes will give you sharper edges when you paint, while filberts will create softer, more rounded strokes because of their shape. The flat brush is very useful for applying large areas of paint. They can be bought with long bristles or short (commonly known as a bright). The long bristles will hold more paint and tend to give a softer mark whereas the bright is more likely to lift paint off.

Filbert

The filbert is the same as a flat but has a slightly rounded end, which gives a different kind of brush mark.

Round

Round brushes are very versatile and can be used for making a variety of brush marks and effects. I tend not to use them myself, preferring the flats and filberts but that is purely personal taste.

Rigger

Riggers are great for fine detail such as twigs on a tree or grasses in a foreground. They have long hair and are able to hold a lot of paint. They can also be very useful for signing your paintings.

Rosemary & Co. have a range of synthetic brushes; for oil painting my preference is the Ivory range, they are both inexpensive and durable. They are a cross between the feel of nylon and hog bristle. They have a good spring and perhaps most importantly, no 'spray'; they hold their shape well. They will carry a good load of oil paint unlike pure nylon. Softer, natural hair brushes such as sable come in the same range of shapes as the synthetic and hog hair brushes.

Sable brushes

Sable brushes are useful for painting detail over wet paint but are too soft for painting in large areas in oils; not only that, they are also rather expensive and some can be a bit too floppy. There are other less expensive soft hair brushes. My first choice would be Rosemary & Co's Masters Choice range. It is an interesting hair with distinctive markings and a semi-stiff firmness of stroke, each tip having the softness of velvet. This hair is responsive and firm, yet delicate to touch and is traditionally used with oil and acrylic, ideal for adding highlights and tonal values. It has a very resilient hair, which wears well.

Sizes

You will need a few brushes of different shapes and sizes. My advice is not to go for too many small brushes. It can take a long time to paint the sky with a small brush and not only that, there is also a tendency to fiddle. (Even on a small panel I will often use a size 10 flat.)

A good selection to start with would be:

- No. 2 Flat, filbert and round
- No. 2 Rigger Ivory range Rosemary & Co
- No. 10. Flat and filbert
- No. 6. Flat, filbert and round

Take time to experiment and see what different brush marks each shape will make.

Brush Care

Whichever brushes you do choose, it is essential to look after them well. Use a palette knife to scrape surplus paint from your brush. Always wipe off the surplus paint and rinse them out in turpentine at the end of each session, then give them a good wash with soap, making sure you get paint out from down by the ferrule. Dry them, reshape them and then store them upright in a jar.

EASELS

The radial easel

The radial easel has three legs that spread to give a firm base. It takes up little floor space and can be folded up for easy storage. The advantage of its stability is that it will take a large canvas. The only downside of using this is not having a place to put your palette, brushes and paints.

The box easel

A box easel, on the other hand, is ideal in that you can put the palette on the open drawer, hang brushes from the side in a cut down plastic bottle with a string handle and have the turps pot in front of you. The tubes of paints that you are using can be kept in the tray at the back. Nothing interrupts the creative flow more than having to hunt for that elusive tube of paint. The box easel is useful both in and out of the

If you are already an owner of Pochade but it does not have the tripod fitting, you can purchase this tripod mounting bracket from the SAA, it only costs about £11 and it screws to the underside of your palette or box. It can then be attatched to a camera tripod.

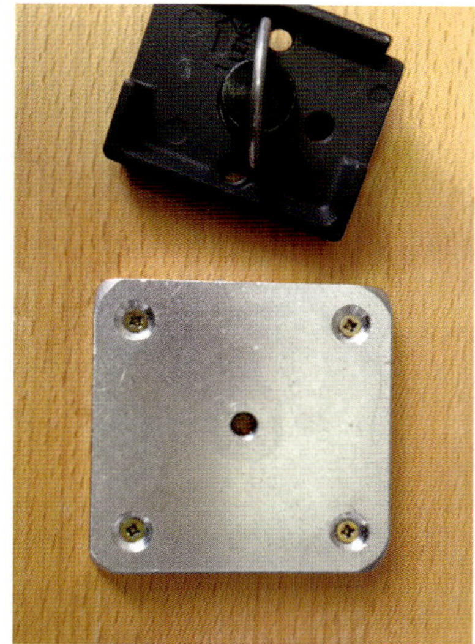

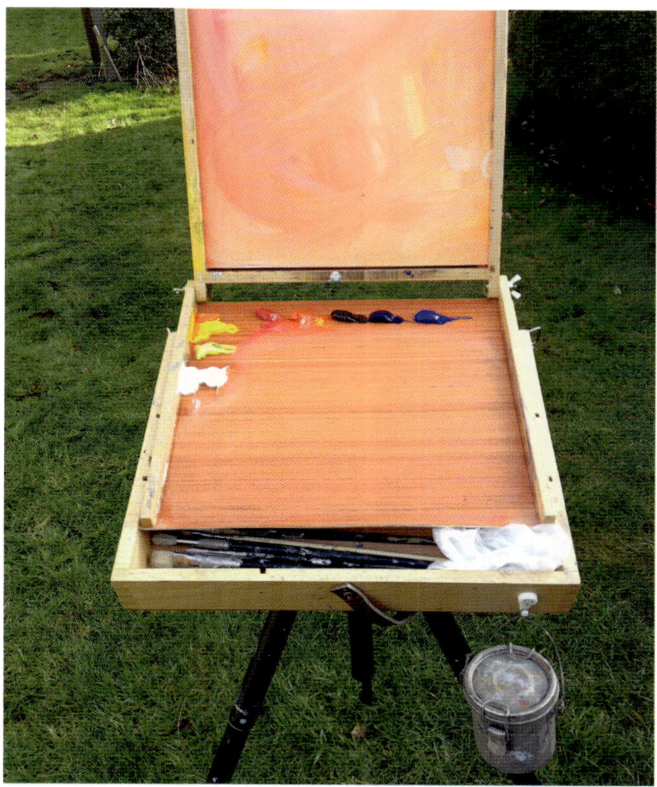

The SAA pochade adapted to the tripod. The plate is screwed to the base. To get an even distribution of weight, it needs to be positioned towards the back. You can replace the mixing palette that had a thumb hole with another piece of plywood the same size to give more mixing space. Note the hook on the front, which neatly holds a container for white spirit or turpentine.

studio. The advantage of using a box easel is that you can pack nearly everything into it that you will need. The disadvantage is that is quite heavy, especially when it contains brushes and paints.

The metal easel

There are a lot of specially designed studio easels, there is no denying how good they are but they can be very costly. You may be lucky enough to buy equipment by keeping a close eye on online auction sites. There can be some amazing bargains to be had.

Pochades

Painting outdoors or *en plein air* has gone through something of a revolution in the past fifteen years or so with the advent of the pochades. Basically, a pochade box is no more than a portable painting box with the facility to hold a canvas but it shouldn't be confused with simple painting boxes, which hold painting supplies and a wooden palette but has no facility for acting as an easel. Pochade boxes are designed to be held in the hand but they will comfortably sit on your lap if you prefer to sit down.

Some have legs built into them but most modern pochade boxes are fitted with tripod mounts, which allow them to be set up onto a tripod. This makes the set up extremely flexible. A lightweight tripod serves very well when travelling abroad whereas a heavy duty one is much more stable and less likely to blow over.

It's a good idea to have a ball head quick release unit, the sort that photographers use to quickly set their camera onto a tripod. These you can buy separately and fix to your palette. The quick release is very useful as it saves a lot of time and fiddling about when setting up.

If you are already an owner of a Pochade but it does not have the tripod fitting, you can purchase a tripod mounting bracket from the SAA, it only costs about £11 and it screws to the underside of your palette or box.

Manufacturers are refining and developing new equipment for outdoor painting all the time, making the practice of taking your studio outside all the more easy for the artist to go out and paint.

The Americans seem to have cornered the market in *plein air* equipment. There are too many to mention but two of the best I have come across are The Strada and the Open Box M.

The Strada easel

This is a strong aluminium box with a self-locking system and keeps everything where you want it. It weighs just over four pounds and it's only one and a half inches thick, therefore it is easy to put in and out of your back pack. These start at around £210.

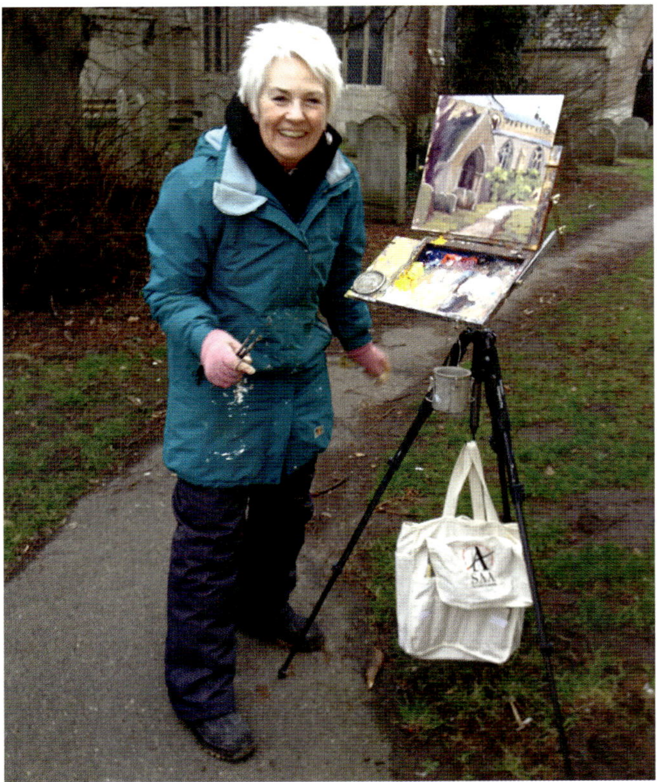

The Open Box M in action facilitates *en plein air* painting. From America, they come in a range of sizes and have a detachable spare palette that clips onto the side.

Open Box M

Another useful bit of kit that again comes from America is the Open Box M. They come in four different sizes and have a detachable spare palette that clips onto the side. The smallest of these is a wooden box, 8" × 10" that will take a five inch panel up to a fifteen inch canvas. It weighs one and a quarter pounds. It requires a tripod to lock on to.

Whichever easel and equipment you decide on when going out to paint, a handy tip is to acquire a shopping trolley with its own seat. This is incredibly convenient. You can strap the easel to the trolley with bungee cords. Canvases, turps, rags and rubbish can be stowed in the shopping bag. Although it is preferable to stand and paint, at the end of a day's painting outside, the seat can come in very handy.

PAINTING SUPPORTS

Although it can be rather time consuming, a lot of artists prefer to make their own panels. Not only is it cheaper but also it means that the artist can achieve the surface that they prefer to paint on.

Mount board

For smaller paintings, mount board is very useful. A good source of mount board is your local friendly picture framer. Have a chat with him or her and ask if you can have the middle bits from the mounts they cut for watercolours. These can be cut to any size but a word of warning: do not go too large, as it is not a very rigid surface. Anything more than twelve inches will bend too much.

The main advantages of using mount board is that not only is it cheap, but it is light, meaning that many panels can be stacked together when travelling. Another great advantage is that while they are inexpensive, you don't feel precious about them, making them very good for quick sketches with the feeling that if it doesn't work out, then it is disposable.

Before painting on the board, it needs to be primed. For this you will need to prepare the panel using gesso.

MDF

MDF can make a more durable and rigid support. It comes in different thicknesses; 3.5mm is a good thickness for smaller panels.

Most hardware stores will cut a full eight foot by four foot sheet to your required sizes. You can then either just apply Gesso as on the mount board or apply fabric or canvas to give a different surface. To do this, you will need good quality professional PVA glue.

First apply a coat back and front to seal the surface, when this has dried give a generous coat all over the front. A stiff brush is best but you could also use a piece of card to spread the glue. Lay the canvas or fabric on top and using either a stiff card or rolling pin, work from the centre towards the edges, ensuring the edges are well stuck down. Turn the board over and trim with a sharp knife; this helps to prevent the fabric lifting. You could turn the fabric over to the back, mitering the corners but if the canvas is stuck down enough, this isn't necessary.

To prepare several small panels, glue canvas onto a large sheet of 3.5mm MDF then, when this has dried, use a T square to mark out the sizes (canvas side up) using a sharp knife and steel blade to cut down onto a cutting mat. This saves an awful lot of time and fiddling about with lots of small panels. If you want larger panels then it is advisable to use a slightly thicker MDF for the same reason as the mount-board, it will be very flexible.

Canvas boards

Many art shops now sell canvas-covered boards in cotton and linen in all shapes and sizes. These are mostly of a reasonable price and more convenient for the busy artist.

Stretched canvas

For working on a larger scale, nothing quite beats the feeling of painting on a good quality canvas. A properly prepared cotton canvas will last a long time and is the most popular surface for oil painting. Canvases can be made from cotton or linen fibres. The advantage of cotton is that it is affordable and is easy to stretch. One of the benefits of using cotton over linen is that cotton can be stretched tighter than linen without straining the wooden support.

Linen is strong and durable. It retains its natural oils which prevent the canvas from becoming brittle over time. Although these can be more expensive, there is a preference among professional artists to use linen canvas. It is known to have a more 'natural' woven finish than cotton – it comes in a variety of textures and weights and is available in both rough and smooth finishes. If you want your painting to last then a linen canvas is a sound investment.

Often, people will turn up at a workshop with a cheap canvas and find that the paint soaks into it very quickly. These canvases are cheap for a reason, they have probably been primed with only one coat of primer or an inferior primer has been used. This is easily remedied by applying two or three more coats of primer. This is the gesso available from most art stores. If the canvas has a heavy surface texture, the gesso will fill in some of the indentations and you will find you have a slightly smoother surface. This can be an advantage, as you won't use as much paint, and it is kinder to your brushes.

Gesso

The purpose of gesso is to protect the support from the paint. It seals the surface and therefore affects the absorbency by preventing the oil from the paint soaking into the surface, which would result in a dull, matte finish.

Gesso dries to a matte, gritty surface that provides a key (surface) for the paint to adhere to. To get a smoother finish, you can sand it. Most ready-made canvases are primed with an acrylic gesso, and are suitable for both oils and acrylics. You can also get canvas primed with traditional gesso for oil paint only.

Gesso is available from most art shops but beware, do not buy a cheap one. The cheaper the gesso you buy, the more watery it tends to be. Consequently, the cheaper alternatives do not give the desired texture to the surface and can be slippery, therefore they do not give a good surface.

A quality gesso can provide a good surface for your canvas or panel but on its own, it does not provide a very deep texture as it is not very thick. You may prefer to have more texture.

Applying the gesso

When preparing your board, it is important to apply one coat to the back of the board to seal against moisture and at least two coats on the painting side.

Use a stiff half inch brush to apply the gesso, varying the length and direction of the marks. If you prefer to paint on a smooth surface, apply several coats of diluted gesso using a wide brush. Work across the surface of the board or canvas and give a light sanding down with a medium grade glass paper in between coats until you have the desired effect.

When the gesso has dried completely, a coloured ground can be applied. The ground is the colour painted over the white surface (there will be more information on grounds in a later chapter).

Texture paste

There are many different texture pastes on the market that can be mixed in with the top coat of gesso. A word of warning here: if the surface is too thick on a flexible surface such as a canvas, there may be a tendency for it to crack.

PAINT

Oil paint is a mixture of three basic ingredients. The pigment, the binder and the thinner.

The **pigment** is the colour, which is suspended in oil.

The **thinner** is usually turpentine or white spirit. This is used to change the viscosity of the paint.

The **binder** is the oil used to bind the pigment. The most common oil used is linseed oil, although other vegetable oil can be used for a variety of reasons. For example, safflower and poppy oils are paler than linseed, allowing for more vibrant whites.

It wasn't until the introduction of the paint tube in 1841 that artists were able to move around more easily with their paints. Artists were able to travel with a greater choice of pre-prepared colours of preserved paint and make quicker colour choices. Back then, pigments were extracted from natural sources such as earth pigment (Sienna, Ochre or Umber), mineral salts (the oxides, zinc and titanium),

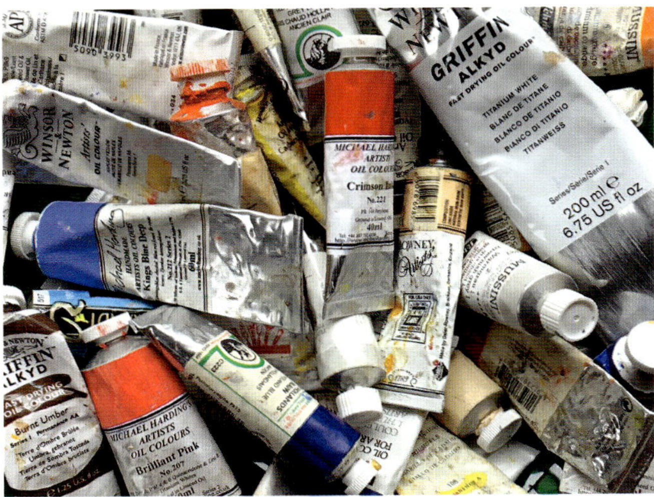

A vast range of paints and colours are now available to the artist. Start with a few tubes and build your collection slowly.

cadmium pigments (red to yellow), cobalt (blue), and pigments of biological origin, plants and animal waste.

With modern technology, there is now a vast range of synthetic pigments that have greatly increased the spectrum of colours available to us. These have been developed and improved in recent years. They are tried and tested for light fastness and in many cases evenness of drying time.

My first experience with oil paints was around the age of nine when I was given a paint by numbers set. A brave step by my parents, as oil paints are notoriously messy in the hands of a child. Nonetheless, I was hooked and the next present was a set of oil paint in tubes. There was very little tuition to be had at that time but I remember avidly watching Nancy Kominsky in the 1970s. Her series on the television, *Paint along with Nancy* ran for four years. She was well known for her colourful, lively palette knife paintings, giving a lively running commentary as she worked and finishing with a painting that the viewer could copy. Things have come a very long way since then. Painting has become such a popular pastime. There is no shortage of information, classes, books, DVDs and courses.

Manufacturers haven't been slow at spotting that trend and to that end, there are many makes of paint and colours available. This can be very confusing to the beginner or even an intermediary painter.

Fast drying oil paint

Winsor and Newton have developed Griffin Alkyd paints that speed up drying time and enable a painting to be built up in layers and glazes more quickly. These paints can also be used in conjunction with your normal oil paints to speed up the drying time.

Water mixable oil paint

Artisan is the brand name of one such paint made by Winsor and Newton that can be diluted with water. It can be mixed and applied using the same techniques as traditional oil-based paint. Instead of using white spirit, paint can be effectively removed from brushes, palettes and rags with ordinary soap and water, thus making it possible to avoid using chemicals such as turpentine, which is ideal for use in an enclosed space, especially schools and art clubs. Turpentine can affect some people's breathing. Unlike the alkyd paint, water-based paint cannot be mixed successfully with normal oil paint.

Student Paints

Nothing is truer than the phrase 'you get what you pay for'; student paints are much more affordable than most paint. The main reason they are less expensive is that the paint has been stretched out with fillers and additives, resulting in less pigmentation. Expensive pigments are replaced by hues, that is to say, an imitation of the pigment.

Artist grade

These paints are made from the purest and highest quality ingredients. Their colours are more vibrant than that of the student grade paint. They are sold in series usually from A to E, A being the cheaper end of the range. These tend to be the earth pigments, which are not as expensive to extract as pigments like Cobalt.

It is advisable to buy the best that you can afford. Sometimes buying the cheaper alternative can be false economy as you will need a lot more paint to tint your mixes. For example, I have a tube of Michael Harding Yellow Ochre paint. If I want to warm up a mix, just a pinprick of paint is enough (in fact, sometimes it is too much).

COLOURS

Every artist or tutor has his or her own preferred colours. This can be confusing if you go to more than one tutor but basically the palette will consist of two each of the three primary colours, one cool and one warm – plus white. These are my recommendations to start you off:

- Ultramarine Blue (warm)
- Cobalt Blue (cool)
- Cadmium Red (warm)
- Permanent Rose (cool)
- Cadmium Yellow (warm)
- Lemon Yellow (cool)
- Titanium White

As this book is primarily about painting skies, I have used a lot of other colours that I have collected through the years. I don't recommend that you rush out and buy them all. Get to know the colours you have first, it is surprising how many colours you can mix from just a few tubes.

If you do feel the need to buy a few more colours then I would add Cerulean, Kings Blue and Blue Black to the above, plus a selection of earth colours:

- Yellow Ochre
- Burnt Umber
- Burnt Sienna

Note, I do not have a green in my selection as I prefer to mix my own but very occasionally I do use Viridian in certain mixes.

PALETTE KNIVES

Owning at least one palette knife is essential. They are invaluable when it comes to cleaning up. The ones with the crank handle have an advantage over the straight ones as it prevents knuckles from getting covered in paint.

A word of warning here, the knives that have been used for a long time can become razor sharp through constant use. Great care has to be taken when using a knife to apply paint to a canvas, one slip and it would slice right through.

Painting with a knife

Many artists choose to complete a whole painting using a palette knife. One such American artist that uses a palette knife to great effect is Mary Bentz Gilkerson.

There is an incredibly large range of different shapes and sizes of palette knives. Some are plastic and others are made from metal and wood. A knife with a metal blade has more spring to it and is more flexible than one with a plastic blade. Both are available in a variety of blade shapes and sizes. Each different shape will create a variety of effects. A lot depends on the effect you are trying to achieve but there is probably a preference for the ones with rounded ends, as they don't make such sharp marks in the paint. A small round one is very useful for painting details as smaller marks can be made. Using a larger knife enables you to apply smooth, relatively flat areas of paint; this can be particularly useful in painting a sky or large areas of water.

It is best to have at least three sizes. A small rounded end, a long blade with a rounded end for painting detail and a medium size for mixing. The long, thin flexible blade of a medium size is ideal for mixing paint on the palette, as you are able to lift just the amount of paint you need to the mixing area.

It is important to wipe the blade in between colours, which saves your paints from getting contaminated with other colours, and you can then thoroughly blend your chosen colours to a nice pool of paint and lift it with the knife to the appropriate place on your palette or straight onto the canvas.

If you've ever iced a cake, you will have an idea of the different textures and marks that you can make when using a painting knife to create an oil painting. Unlike painting with a brush, the palette knife can help you achieve a variety of effects, from broad impasto strokes to refined details. Painting with a palette knife can give very interesting textures but you do need to use a bit more paint. Sometimes it is useful to just apply paint to an area and work it in with a brush.

The way you hold the knife, its angle to the board, the amount of paint on the blade and the direction you pull it through the paint or drag it on the surface, all add to the painterly options and effects available to you.

Another use for a palette knife is to pull the paint out of brushes. To do this, lay the bristles on the palette and gently, using the flat of the knife, squeeze the paint away from the ferrule. This surplus paint can then be scraped together and put at the side of the palette along with previous mixes that have been finished with. At the end of the session, these pools of surplus paint can be mixed together, the result being a lovely neutral grey.

TIP: use the straight edge of the blade for lines such as masts or telegraph poles.

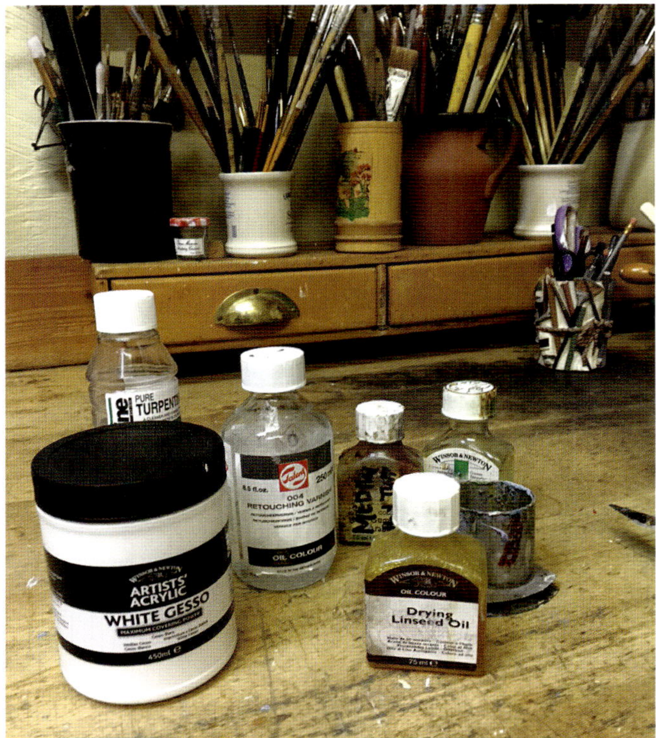

A selection of mediums in the studio. Save small jam jars like the ones from hotels to decant mediums for travelling light. Don't forget to label them.

MEDIUMS

There is a confusing amount of mediums available to the artist working in oils. They have three main purposes.

One is to adapt the consistency of the paint.

Second is to make it more malleable or improve the flow.

Third, is to make it dry faster.

Turpentine

Turpentine is technically a solvent, and one of the more traditional ones that painters use. It is traditionally mixed 50/50 with linseed oil for an excellent medium. In the early stages of a painting, turpentine is useful to thin down paint to apply thin washes and for sketching out the painting.

Genuine turpentine can be bought in small bottles from art stores but you can go to a good hardware store where, although not as refined as the turpentine from the art store, it works out much cheaper. It speeds up the drying time as it dilutes the paint and evaporates. A disadvantage of using too much turpentine in the mixing is that it will dry to a more matte finish.

As turpentine is expensive, it is advisable to buy either a turpentine substitute or white spirit for cleaning your brushes.

ARTIST PROFILE

Mary Bentz Gilkerson

A sense of place, a connectedness to the land is very important to me. Maybe that's part of being Southern. You can be completely immersed in the landscape, here in the deep south, sometimes to the point of being overwhelmed. The atmosphere, the colour and light, take on a physical quality that I'm trying to capture in my paintings.

I don't feel like that ties me to recreating the landscape I've worked in literally. In fact, by the time I'm finished, it may look more like an entirely new, very different landscape. My work is much more about the experience *of place than the reproduction of place. I'm interested in the light, in the way that it reveals atmosphere, weather and passage of time through the play of light and shadow. These can completely transform the natural forms of the environment, creating an entirely different emotional and visual response from the viewer.*

For the last several years, I have been working with places that I consider deeply engaging and mysterious – rural Charleston, Edisto Island, Edisto River, Cowasee Basin, Congaree Swamp and Three Rivers Greenway in the middle of urban Columbia, SC. These are all places that I have a personal connection to, landscapes that I feel like I engage with on a regular basis.

Direct experience is an important part of my approach. When I'm working in an area, I take regular walks, repeating the same path over and over in different weather and different times of the year. I make drawings, sketches and photographs on site that become the source material for my work in the studio. In the process of walking and drawing, something about the essence of the place begins to take over, something that is found in the bare bones of the lines that describe the relationship of earth, sky and water, reflection and light.

When I paint, I'm looking for light: the way it moves across the surface of the landscape, revealing its subtle topography. The process of close observation in painting is one of seeking out subtle differences, like a tracker looking for footprints. The more you observe, the more you see. You begin to see the changes that are different in the light, some minute and some dramatic, much in the way that we see the forms. The same vista will appear completely different depending on the time of day and the weather. I'm fascinated by how those things change, so I'll keep going back to the same spots over and over again. Returning to paint the same part of the landscape means that I become very familiar with it, but I'm still surprised at times by the colours created by the light.

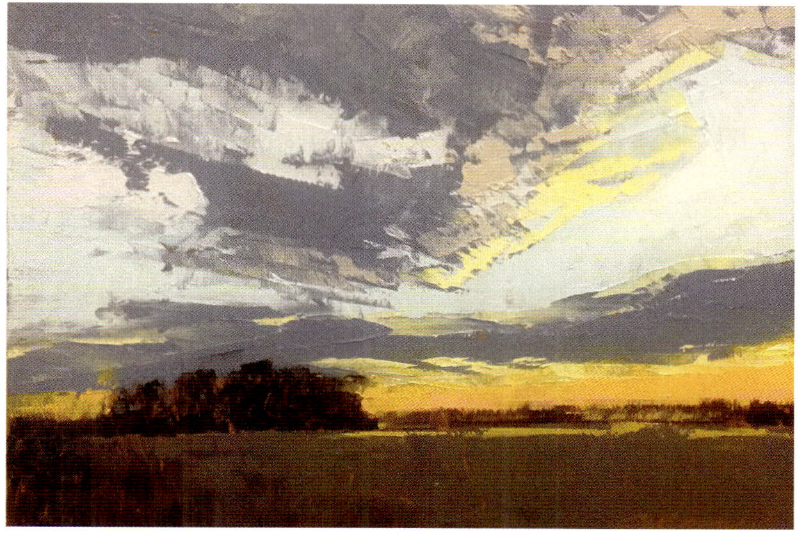

Winter Evening, Mary Bentz Gilkerson. This wonderfully simple but effective painting by Mary is executed with a palette knife. It shows great skill and colour knowledge.

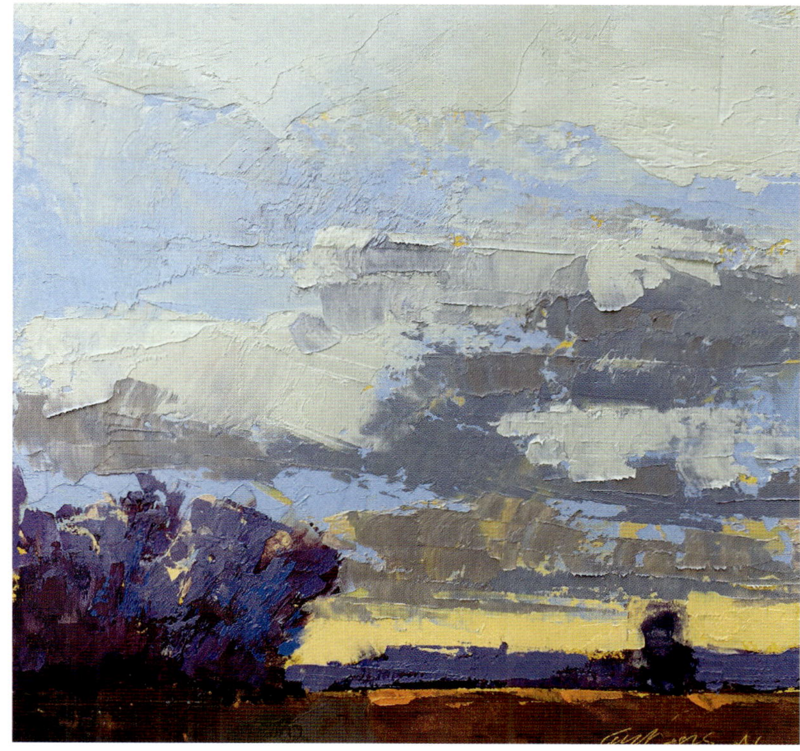

Grey Winter Skies, Mary Bentz Gilkerson. The colours in this painting are so fresh and clean. Mary has chosen blue for the tree colour; it may seem an odd choice but it works so well with other colours in the painting and is the complementary colour for the flash of orange, making it sing out in the painting.

Linseed oil

Linseed oil is a useful, translucent medium; mixed in small amounts in your paint, it improves the gloss and deepens the darks. It also slows down the drying rate of the paint. I like to have a 50/50 mix of linseed and turpentine to dip into as a general painting medium. If you add Damar varnish to the mix in equal portions, it is good for glazes. It does have a tendency to turn yellow over a period of time.

Liquin or Alkyd

Liquin or Alkyd mediums speed up and can halve the drying time of your painting. This is a great advantage if you want to over paint or glaze an area, and it also brings a silky consistency to your paint, giving the surface a glossy finish. You can buy a range of paints that contain the alkyd medium; Alkyd oil paints are well known for their much faster drying properties than regular oil colours, which is very useful for painting holidays.

ARTIST PROFILE

Brian Ryder ROI PPIEA

I paint with shapes placed into a composition, even with skies. I try to catch fleeting views of the landscape I know and love, aiming to catch changing atmospheres normally using close tones to achieve the effect I want. I succeed when the viewer makes the picture ... not me.

– Brian Ryder

Brian paints in most media but over the past few years, has concentrated more and more on his oils. The work is nearly always landscape based, using a distinctive style somewhere between Impressionist and Abstract but invariably trying to capture a 'feeling' in the chosen subject. Brian usually paints in his studio, basing his paintings on his experience of the landscape in all its seasons, but now when on location, he usually paints in pen and wash, being an extension for his love of drawing.

My paintings on location normally end up as illustrative depictions of the subject which I am now not really interested in... I seem to have done all that and continually feel the need to move on. Creating paintings in the studio helps me do just that.

Working method

I have always been fascinated how skies affect the feeling portrayed to the viewer and especially painters of the landscape. I feel many artists, not realizing this, just paint illustrations of

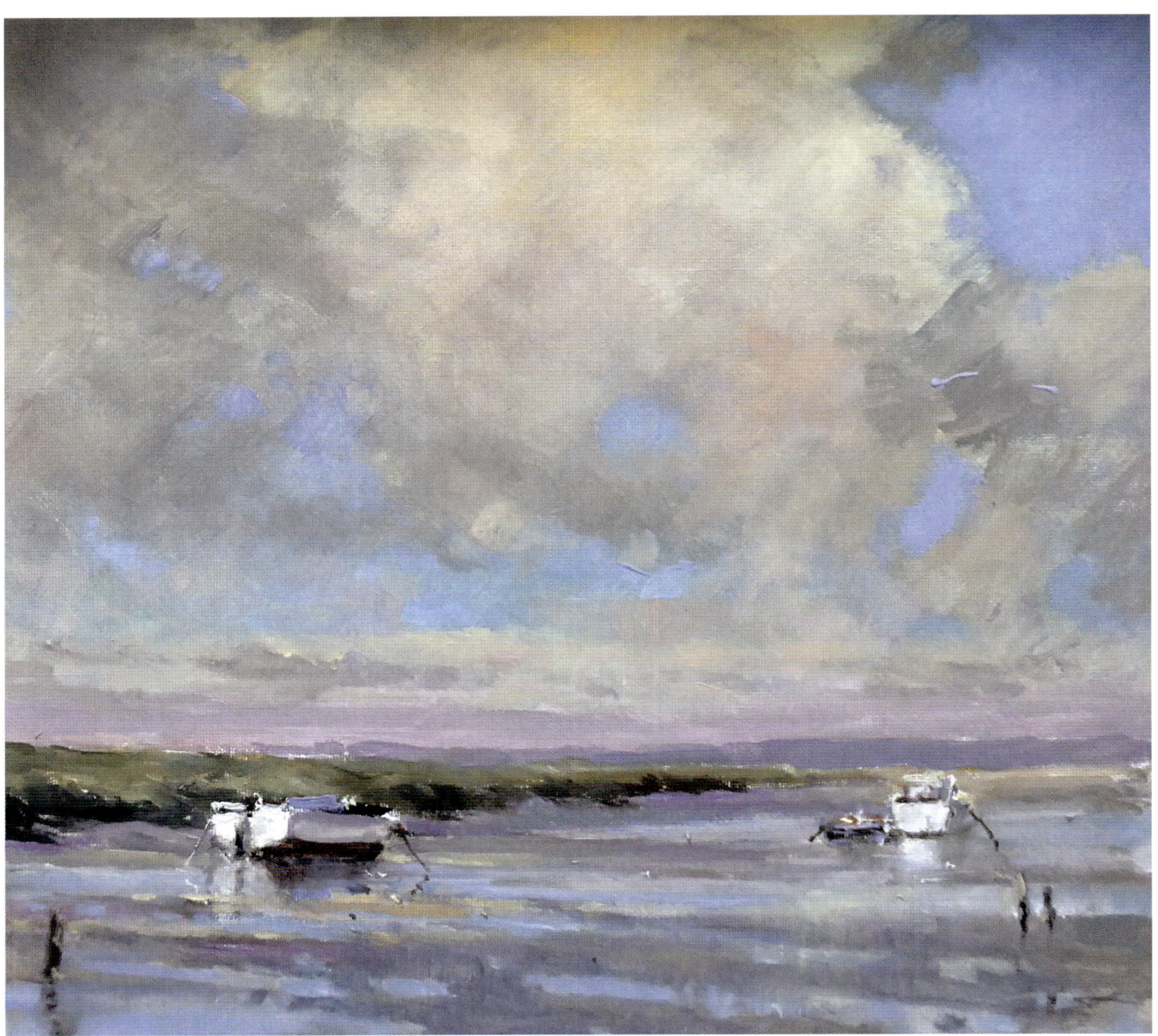

Morston Creek, Brian Ryder ROI PPIEA.

a view in front of them, which on location is normally a fine day. This way of painting gives 'just pictures', however good that illustration may be. In many instances, the artist paints a picture of fluffy summer skies that is pleasing to the viewer but I feel portraying the many variants of the sky above us can produce our feeling of the landscape around us. Painting, after all, is or should be the painter's reaction to life and how it is seen and how it affects us.

I moved to the North Norfolk coast from London to be able to paint the open skies and effect on the landscape. I have, over the past thirty years taught, walked and painted numerous scenes in Norfolk, in Britain and abroad. If I have nothing else, I somehow have the capacity, having spent years on locations, to retain pictures in my head of scenes I see. I now mostly paint in the studio and therefore I only need to compose a painting from sketches on location and add the skies ... from my head ... to paint a picture. I feel this method creates a much better painting, better composed and with feeling.

Sketches on location are normally pencil sketches, pen and wash and sometimes watercolour, leaving oils for studio work, which I now concentrate on.

Brian Ryder's Basic Palette:

- Titanium White
- Ultramarine Blue
- Cerulean Blue
- Raw Sienna
- Yellow Ochre
- Naples Yellow Light
- Cadmium Yellow (Pale)
- Alizarin Crimson
- Light Red
- Burnt Sienna
- Raw Umber

However, over the past few years, I tend to mix my colours less and less as many oil paints from various companies produce some lovely colours and in a way, less mixing, I believe, sometimes give better results. Some soft greys and pinks, for example, are excellent for my skies.

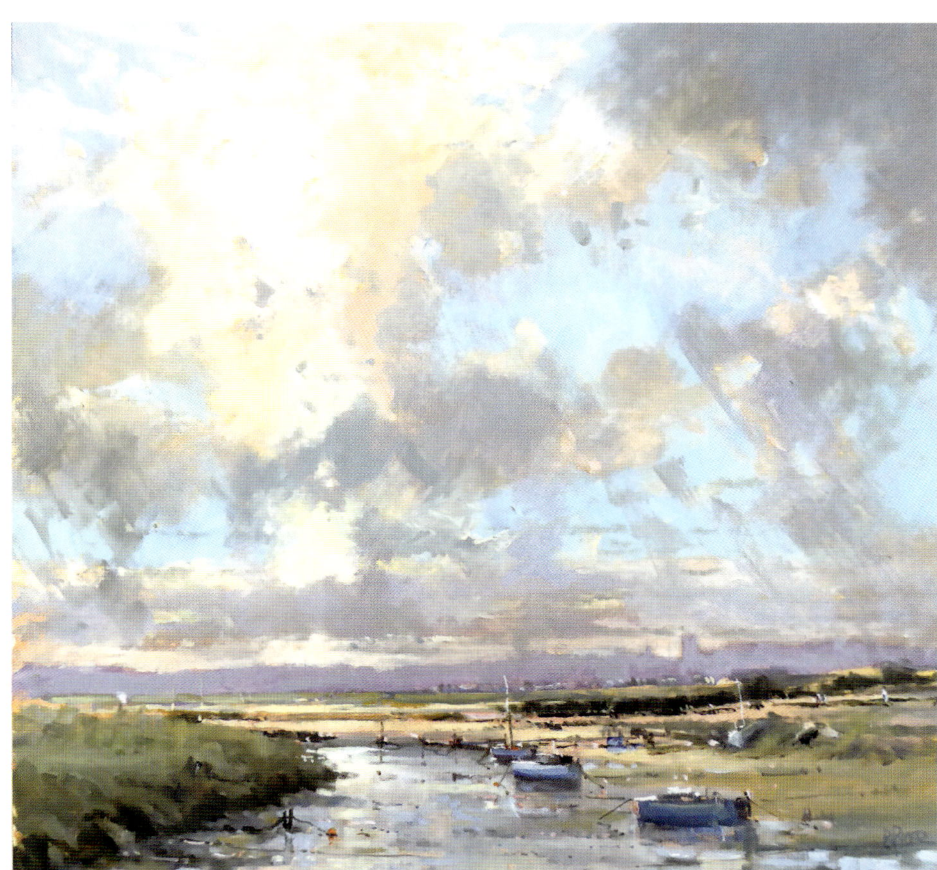

Morston Clouds, Brian Ryder, ROI PPIEA.
Brian has achieved a wonderful range of colours in this sky. He has closely observed all the subtleties and played on them to great advantage. The harmonies of pastel looking colours in this painting are very pleasing.

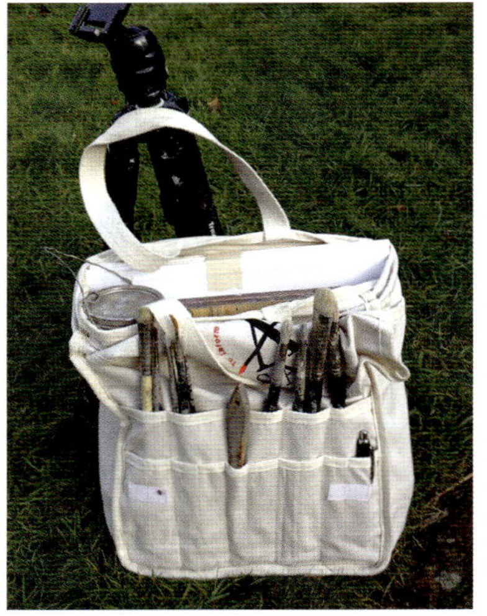

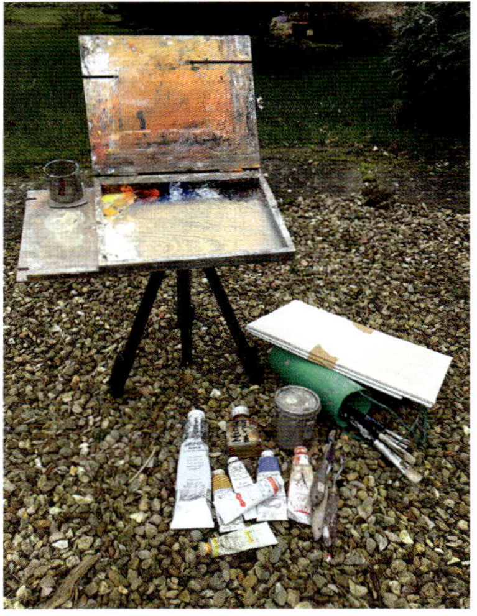

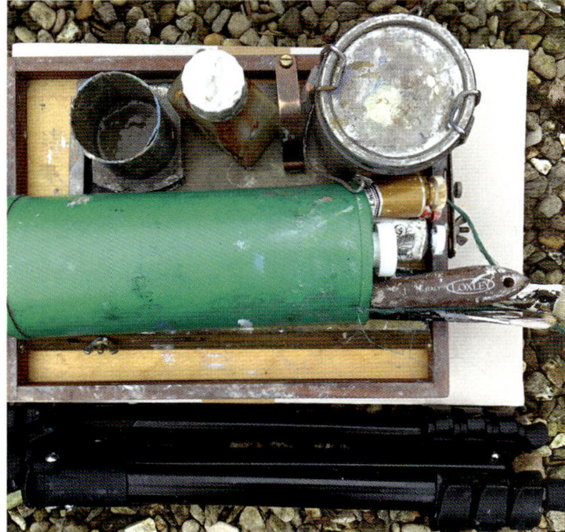

The SAA canvas bag is an ideal size for *plein air* painting. It holds my palette, brushes, turps pot, palette knives, rags and up to six wet canvas boards. I prefer to stand and use a lightweight camera tripod, which my pochade clips on to.

PLEIN AIR

Many people are put off the idea of painting outside because of all the kit they might have to take with them and the handling of wet oil paints. Over the years of painting *en plein air* with other artists, I have picked up numerous tips and have now reduced the essentials down to one small bag.

These are the main colours I use for *plein air* painting:

- Permanent Rose
- Ultramarine Blue
- Lemon Yellow
- Yellow Ochre
- Burnt Umber
- Alkyd Titanium White (it dries fast).

Canvases

I use mainly canvas board and keep to 10–12" and under for two reasons. I can complete a picture quicker and they are easier to transport.

In the studio, I prepare the board by applying a coloured ground (this can be the scrapings off the palette from the day's painting to prevent waste). Four matchsticks are then glued to the back, one on each edge, they stack on top of each other with the matchsticks acting as spacers with a clean one on top (the lid) and they are then taped together to prevent movement and smudges. A thing to note here is to keep the matchsticks to the edge as they may leave a small mark on the edge of the wet painting it touches but this will be under the rebate of the frame. This is very useful for transporting wet paintings, as they can be slotted into a bag with the rest of the painting gear.

For travelling abroad, I take just a couple of boards and tape canvas onto them.

At the end of the day, the canvas is removed from the board and taped to the wall of my accommodation to dry. And the next day's canvases are prepared.

All I have to take home is a neat pile of canvas, which can be dry mounted onto board at home. I use Griffin Alkyd Fast Drying White to ensure all the pictures are dry. If I am aiming to paint more than four paintings, I glue matchsticks to the back of the canvas.

Now you have your kit sorted, the next thing to do is to get out there.

You may not always get it right first time but you will learn a lot from any failures, and there will be many. It's what will keep you painting – knowing that the next one is going to be brilliant!

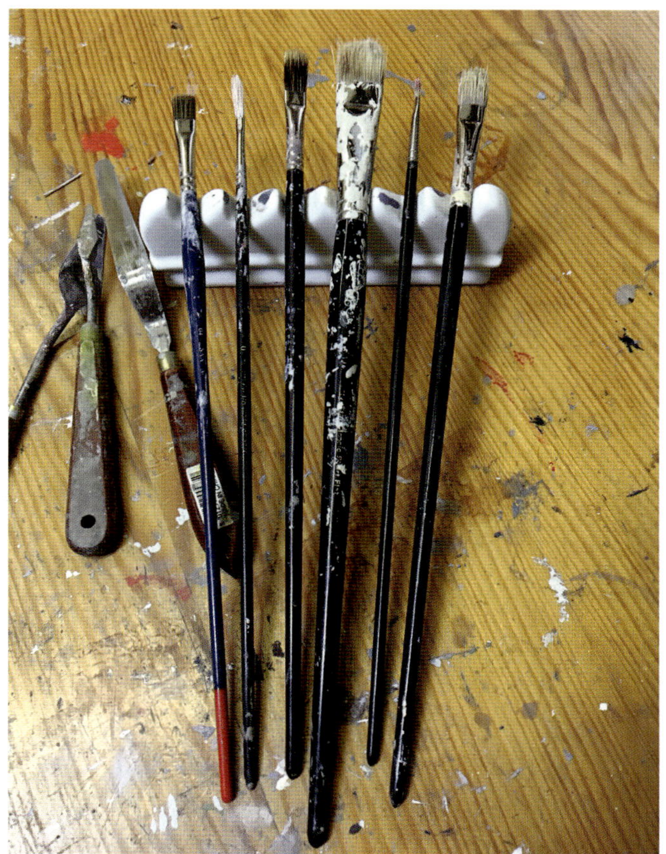

A selection of bristle filberts, flats and a rigger. Rosemary & Co Ivory range are very good quality and value. A cut down plastic bottle with string through it makes a good lightweight brush carrier. Hammer a small hook on the side of your pochade to hang the pot on.

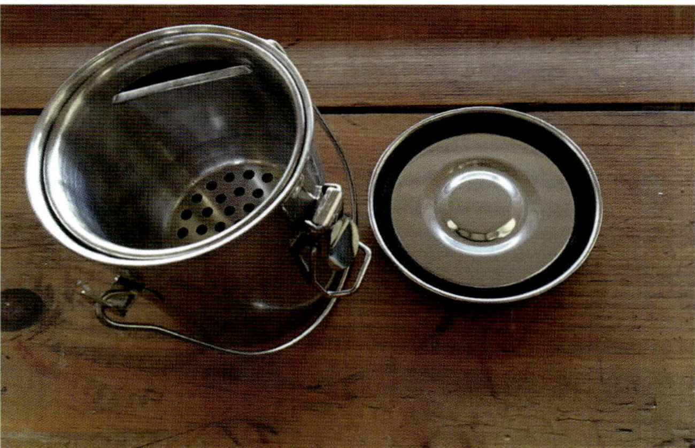

The brush washer is essential. It hangs on the side of my box, has a sieve for the sludge to fall through and seals up tightly.

TOP TIPS FOR PAINTING *EN PLEIN AIR*

Stay warm

My best buy was some skiing trousers. Charity shops are a good place to look, especially after the skiing season. Also fingerless gloves, extra warm socks and a hat are essential. Try standing on a piece of insulation board. That stops the cold creeping up.

Location and subject

Have an idea of what and where you want to paint.

Work small and quickly

Speed will come with experience; working on a smaller scale will enable you to complete a painting in less time. Use larger brushes, don't put in much detail too soon and rely on your observational skills. I hardly ever spend more than an hour and a half on a painting as light and shadows can change so fast.

Onlookers

Avoiding inquisitive members of the public can be a major concern for the not so confident but you must remember that they are mostly genuinely interested and will admire what you are doing.

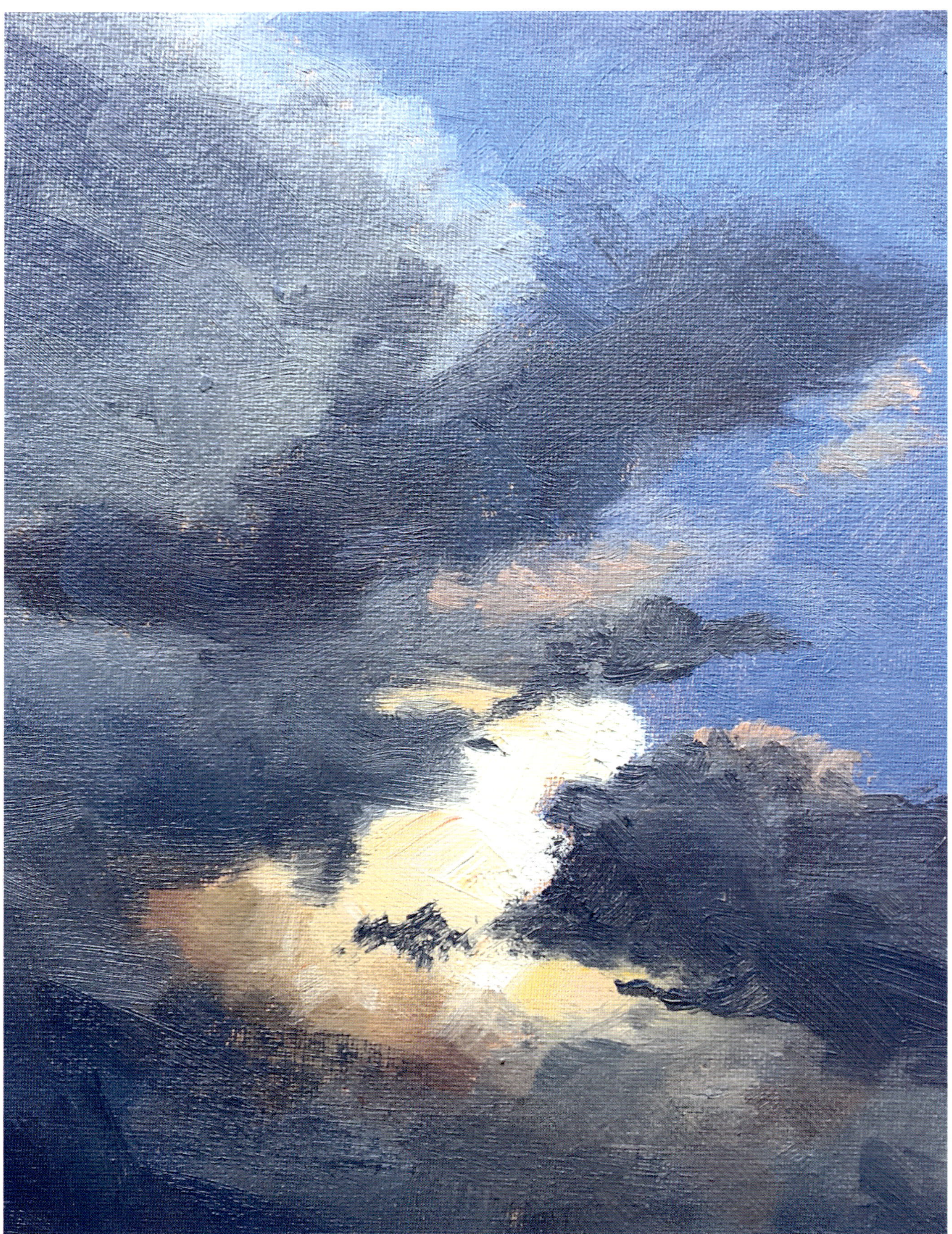

CHAPTER 2

Understanding clouds

Clouds come floating into my life, no longer to carry rain or usher storm, but to add colour to my sunset sky.

RABINDRANATH TAGORE

We are all affected by the weather and it can have a great influence on our mood.

I'm sure we all like to open the curtains in the morning to be greeted by a clear blue sky. It is the promise of a fine day ahead but while it is pleasing to see a clear sky, a painter of landscapes will probably find it more interesting if clouds are present.

For an artist, clouds can add so much more interest and drama to a painting, giving it life and atmosphere. Even in a clear sky, if closely observed, there are many changes of colour.

A cloudy sky is not always an indication that it is going to rain. I'm sure we can all recall as children, long summer days gazing up into a sky of white fluffy clouds, looking for shapes of faces and animals. Unfortunately, a lot of people as they grow up don't give much mind to the beauty that is a cloudy sky.

The sky directly above us tends to be a much deeper blue, getting paler as we look down to the horizon. One of the main reasons the colour changes is pollution in the atmosphere. In other words, the air is purer as it rises.

One of the first but probably the most important part of painting the sky is learning to graduate the colour.

Cloud Study detail.

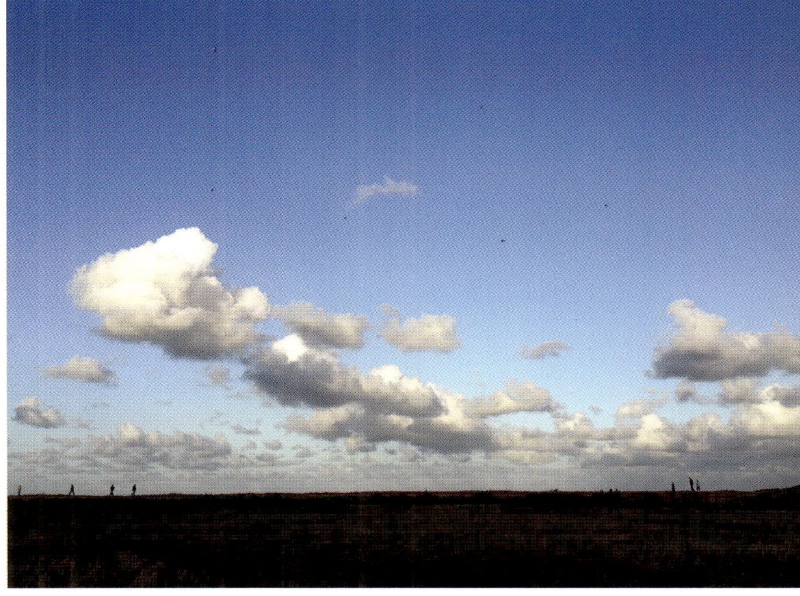

This picture illustrates how much bluer the sky directly above us is, getting paler towards the horizon as we look through more layers of pollution.

Graduation

Graduation is the smooth blending of colours where the shift in colour is hardly discernible. Looking at the photograph above, you cannot see any noticeable line as the colour shifts from dark blue to the pale colour on the horizon. This is a painting skill well worth mastering. There are huge benefits of being able to paint a smooth gradation of colour effectively and efficiently. Graduations are all around us, particularly in

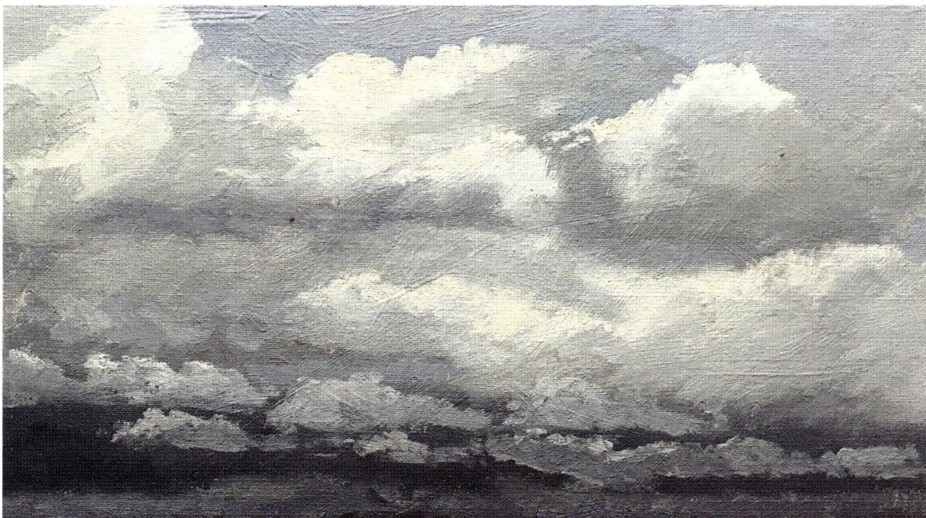

Cumulus clouds: it is useful to make studies of clouds and to learn their behaviour.

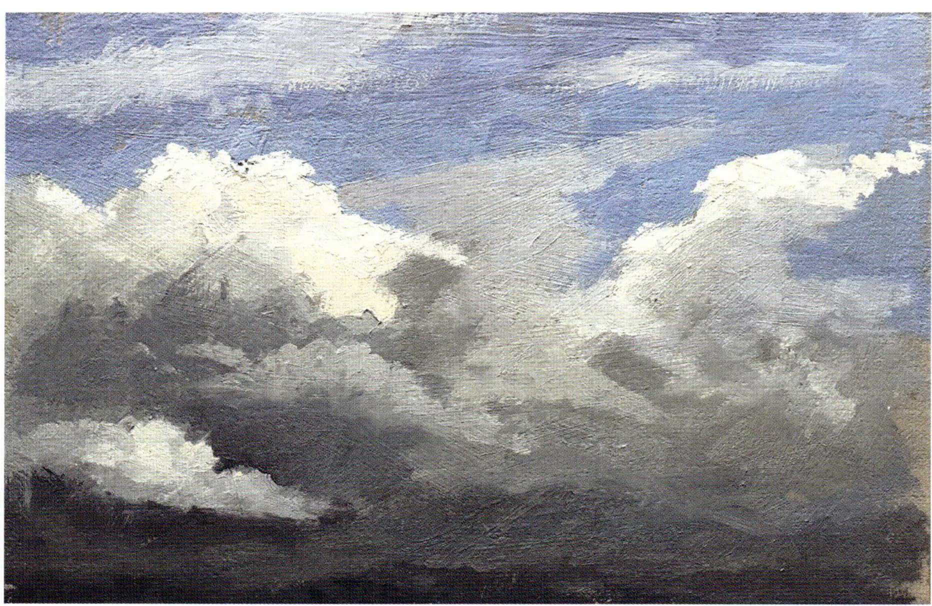

the sky. Really study a sky, think about what time of day it is and notice how it changes towards the evening. Try and analyze the colours you can see. There are many subtle changes in colour (when we look hard enough) caused by changes in the atmosphere.

The air also cools as it rises; air nearest to Earth's surface is much warmer as it is warmed by contact with Earth. This surface heated air expands as it warms and rises And this convection creates turbulence in the air. Even on a very warm day, it can be very chilly up in the mountains or on high hills.

Another thing that happens at higher levels is that there is a drop in pressure. I am sure you are all familiar with the sensation of our ears popping as we climb higher above sea level. As we are ascending and air pressure changes, there is uneven pressure on the inside and outside of our eardrum. Tubes connected to the ear, called the Eustachian tubes, act like a valve, allowing air to be released. This equalizes the pressure, allowing our eardrums to 'pop' back to their original position.

Air pressure is created by molecules of air, which are invisible but still have weight and take up space. The higher you go, the fewer air molecules there are, which means air pressure drops and therefore there is less pressure on your ears. It does also mean there is less oxygen so we need to breathe quicker to take in the oxygen that our body requires.

All of this movement and turbulence has a direct effect on our weather and the clouds that are formed. Our weather mainly occurs in the first layer of Earth's atmosphere, known as the troposphere. The tropospheric atmosphere extends from five to eight kilometres from the ground.

The next main layer of the Earth's atmosphere is the stratosphere. Here, there is a less turbulent atmosphere and it is almost completely clear of clouds and other forms of weather.

The lowest level of the stratosphere contains the ozone layer, which absorbs around ninety-seven per cent of the sun's ultraviolet rays.

'What is a cloud?'

Clouds are made up of tiny droplets of water and ice crystals. All air contains moisture and nearer the ground, it is found in the form of an invisible gas known as water vapour. As the sun heats this water vapour, it rises. The rising vapour then cools and condenses into tiny droplets, which form a cloud.

Their white appearance is caused by wavelengths of light passing through the droplets and scattering to produce white light. Grey clouds are darker because they are denser and therefore, not as much light can pass through them.

There are a lot of influences that gives each cloud its own characteristics. Different clouds form at different heights; their shapes are determined by the amount of water vapour and the temperature at that point.

There are two major shapes of cloud, cumulus and stratus. Probably the most exciting of all the cloud forms is the cumulus.

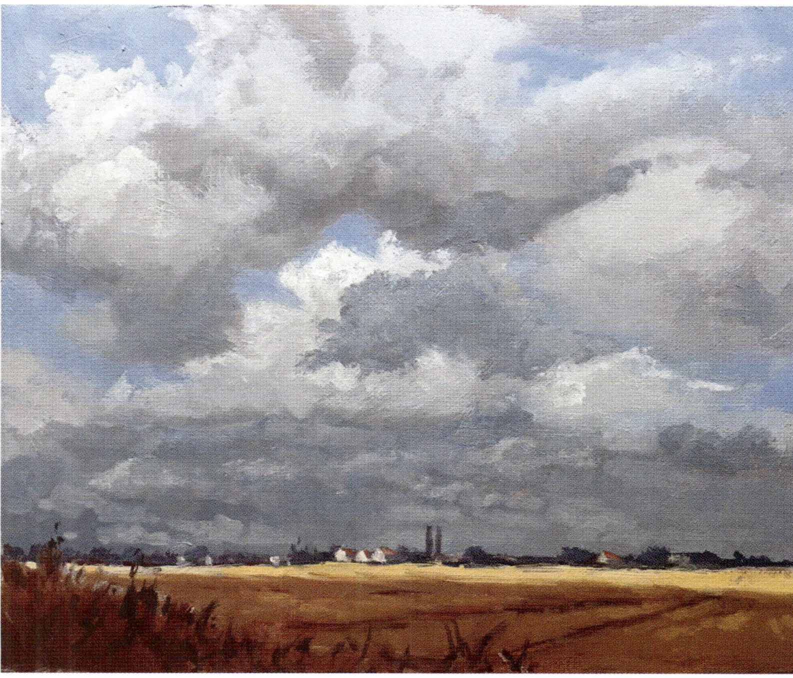

A Skyfull, 10" × 12". Painted on canvas board.
The distant Spalding Power Station and three sunlit houses provide the focal point for this painting. The quickly moving clouds give lots of cloud shadows over the ripe corn. I had to wait for the right moment to put in the streak of sun that lit up the white buildings in the distance. Note how the clouds are banked up and overlap as they come towards you.

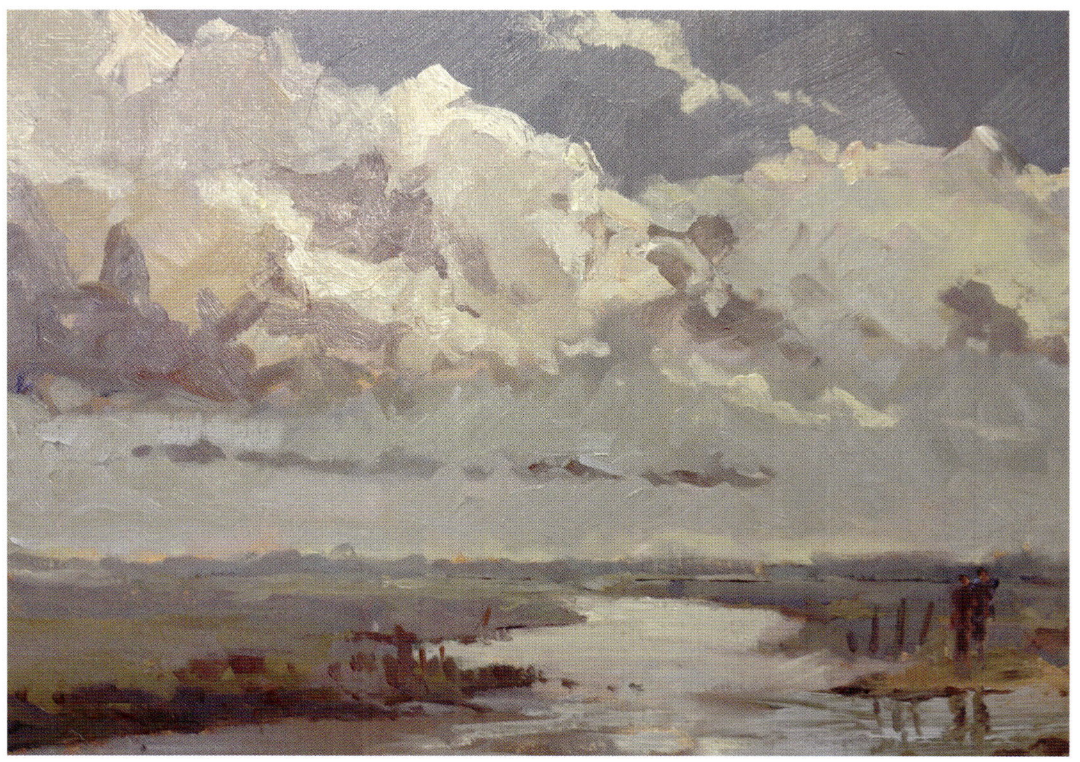

Cumulus at Burnham Overy Staithe
Titanium White
Yellow Ochre
Cadmium Yellow
Burnt Umber
Permanent Rose
Cobalt Blue
14" × 18" Canvas board
Burnt Sienna ground

Painted on location in Norfolk, there was no time for fiddling or blending. The clouds were moving fast so colours were premixed and painted in rapidly with a large brush. The same mixes were used for the water. The shadow colour of the clouds is picked up on the marshes. The two figures and posts add extra interest and scale.

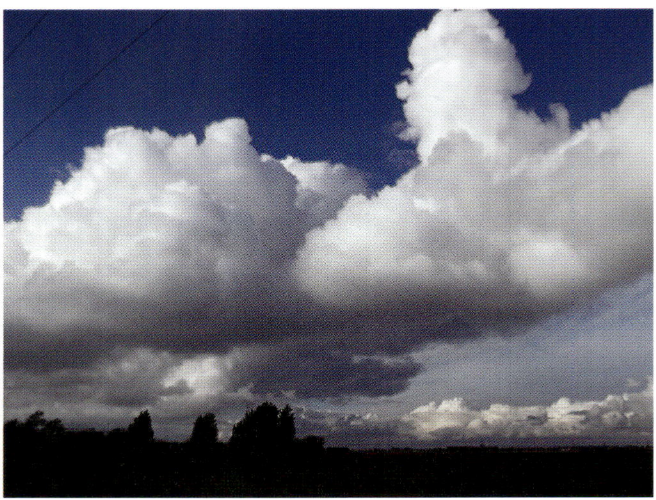

These impressive cumulus clouds dominate the sky in this photograph. Note the dark shadows underneath.

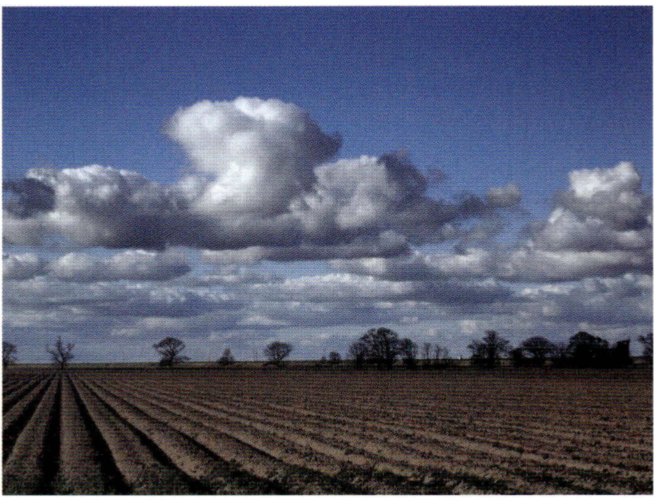

Altocumulus and Cumulus Fractus.
In this picture, the clouds have again formed lines and this time we are looking at them straight on. This gives lines of perspective as we look down the lines. The foreground 'fluffy clouds' are cumulus fractus. They have mostly been broken off from a larger cloud by strong winds.

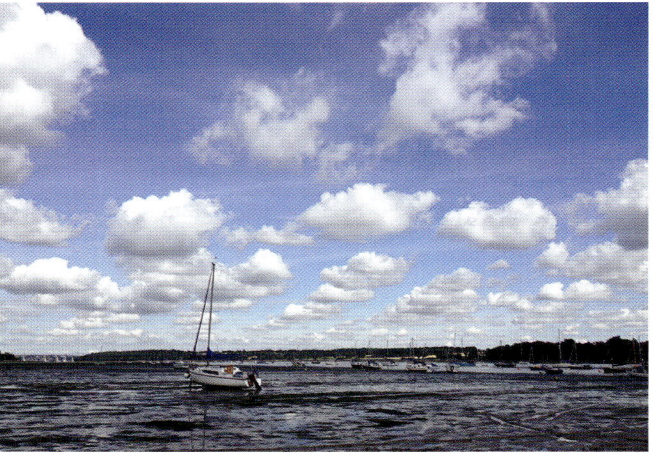

Altocumulus.
These clouds are seen mostly at mid-altitude. Smaller than the larger cumulus, they are globular in shape and often have a flat base. In this picture they have formed in lines and we are looking at them from the side.

Cumulus

Cumulus in Latin means pile or heap, which is a good description of these solid looking clouds that heap and pile up. There are four basic variations of the cumulus cloud. They are cumulus humilis, mediocris, congestus and fractus.

Cumulus humilis clouds look solid, with a slightly flattened shape.

Cumulus mediocris clouds are similar, but expand upwards.

Cumulus congestus clouds are the ones with which we are most familiar due to their cauliflower-like structure that can tower high into the atmosphere.

Cumulus fractus have a much softer, fluffier appearance. These clouds take on different shapes and forms as they rise through the atmosphere.

At a low and mid level, cumulus clouds can be seen as individual clouds, usually with a darker, flat base. They are also known as fair weather clouds as they usually do not threaten any rain. In the mid level, altocumulus can appear as smaller, rounder clouds sometimes set out in parallel lines, one side being darker than the other, helping us to distinguish between them.

To the casual observer, a quick glimpse up at the sky would tend to make you think clouds stay the same but if you were to observe a cloud for a period of ten minutes or so, you will be surprised at the rate that they move across the sky. In fact, the higher clouds can move at the surprisingly fast speed of a hundred miles per hour, their shape changes and in that time can disappear completely. This, of course, poses many problems for a painter working on the spot.

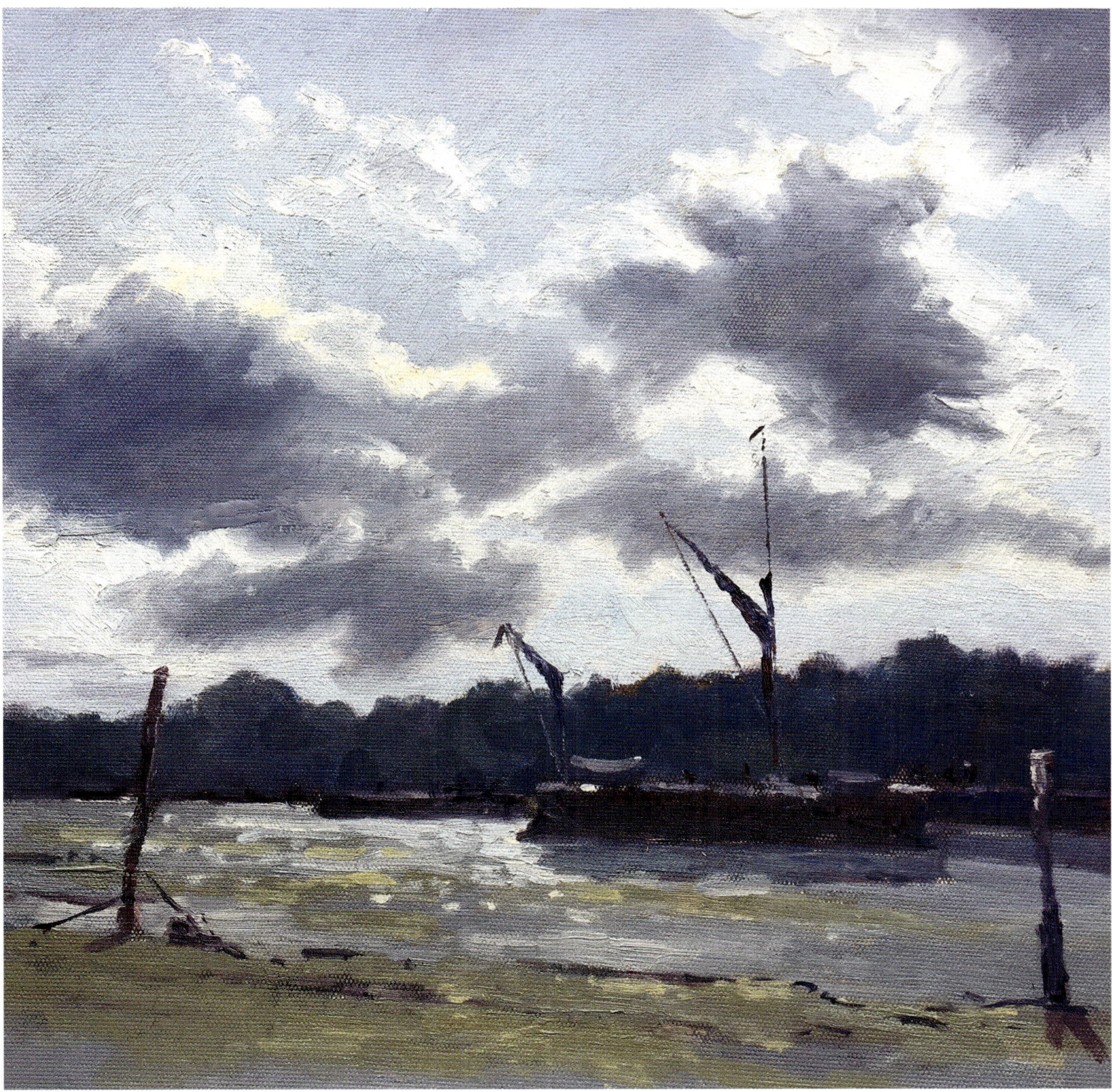

Late Summer, Pin Mill
Titanium White
Michael Harding Warm Light Yellow
Old Holland Blue Grey
Mussini Brownish Grey
Mussini Bluish Grey 2
Ultramarine Blue
Cadmium Red

This was painted over an older painting that had been sanded down. The cloud shapes were painted first using Bluish Grey and Old Holland Blue Grey. The blue of the sky was painted with the Old Holland Blue Grey with a small amount of Brown Grey mixed in; Titanium White was added towards the horizon.

Take care to leave a space between the blue of the sky and the dark of the clouds as you do not want to pick up any of the dark paint, it would mix in with the blue of the sky and muddy it. You want to keep the blue clean. The gap that was left is now painted using Warm Light Yellow and Brownish Grey to tint Titanium White; this is applied quite thickly. Using a small amount on a flat brush, blend the two colours together. Taking the white into the grey and vice versa, you will probably need to use your finger for the softer blending.

The foreground was painted with Bluish Grey and the walkway, Yellow Ochre, was added to make the green darker. Blue Grey was used for the highlights, the lightest area being at the back of the barge to give good counterchange. The lighter green was Blue Grey and Yellow Ochre. The dark side of the barge is Ultramarine and Cadmium Red with the smallest amount of Yellow Ochre to stop it looking purple.

The mast was painted in with the use of a piece of card. Run the card through the dark mix to make sure there isn't too much paint or it will smudge. Carefully apply the card to the painting and give a small downward movement and then lift off. The same method is used for the rigging; make sure the card is the right length. It is useful to have several pieces of card of different lengths available to you.

There was on the day a lot of reflection on the mud but I kept the light areas and a few flicks of light to the centre of the picture and the foreground remains dark to focus attention around the barge.

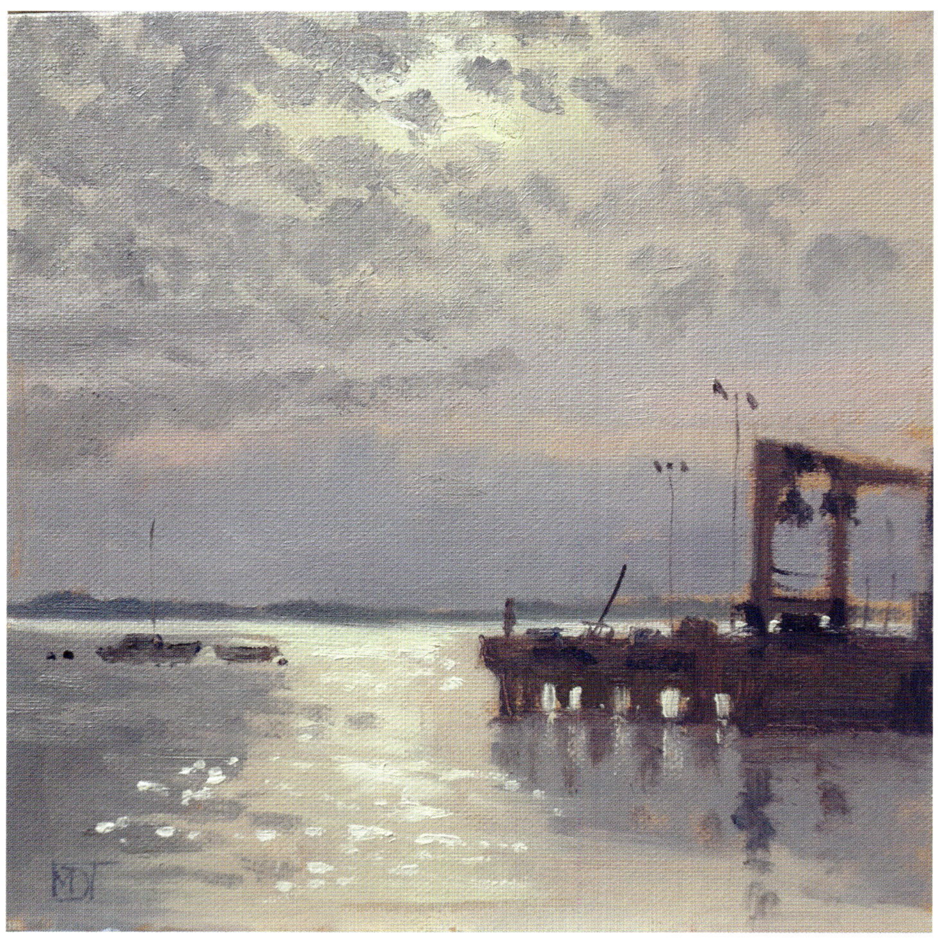

Le Croisic
Cadmium Yellow
Permanent Rose
Ultramarine Blue
Alkyd Titanium White
6" × 6" Canvas board
Thin Burnt Sienna ground

I was painting in Le Croisic, France and the early morning light was wonderful. The cirrocumulus clouds silhouetted against the early morning sky beyond. I used my limited palette. The Burnt Sienna ground flecks through in places. This helps to give warmth to an otherwise pink and blue painting. This painting was completed on the spot in less than an hour, I had to work quickly as, the light was rapidly changing. The grey 'mackerel' clouds were applied last over the hazy sun. A soft brush was used to avoid lifting off the lighter colour. The sparkles of light on the water were also painted with a small sable brush; a small amount of yellow was added to the white for warmth as pure white would have looked too cold.

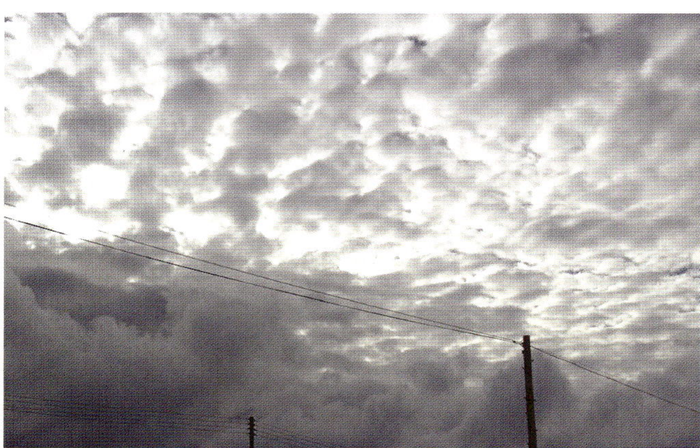

Cirrocumulus clouds form in the higher level from cirrus clouds that are starting to lower and clump together.

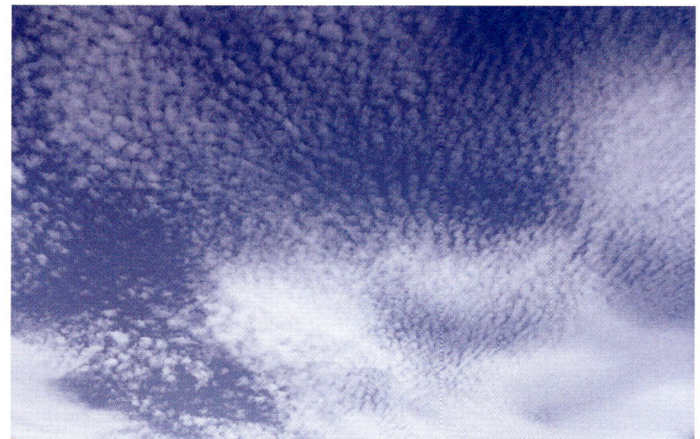

Cirrocumulus have a dappled look and appear as small, individual white rounded clouds in a regular pattern with blue sky showing in between. The rippling appearance gives it the nickname of 'a Mackerel sky' or 'sheep cloud' as it rather resembles a flock of sheep. When you see a sky like this, it is a sure sign that the weather is about to change as it usually precedes a warm weather front. There are many old sayings that sailors used to predict the weather. 'Mackerel sky, not twenty-four hours dry', 'Mares' tails and mackerel scales make lofty ships to carry low sails' and this one that is rather amusing: 'A dappled sky, like a painted woman, soon changes its face'. If given the right conditions, like other clouds, they can build up to become the towering cumulonimbus which we mostly associate with thunderstorms. This can happen at an alarming speed.

Cloud Study 1.
Sometimes it's useful and time well spent doing a few cloud studies. This enables you to experiment with colours and techniques without the worry of spoiling a painting. In this study I used Cobalt Blue, Mussini Bluish Greys 1 & 2, Cadmium Red, Titanium White and Cadmium Yellow. The blue area was painted using Cobalt and a touch of Blue Grey 1. The background cloud was a mixture of Cobalt, Blue Grey 2 and a touch of red. It was lightened at the edges with Blue Grey 1. The lightest area is a mix of white with Yellow and Red added to warm it up and finally the darkest cloud was scumbled over with Blue Grey 2 and Cobalt Blue and Cad Red.

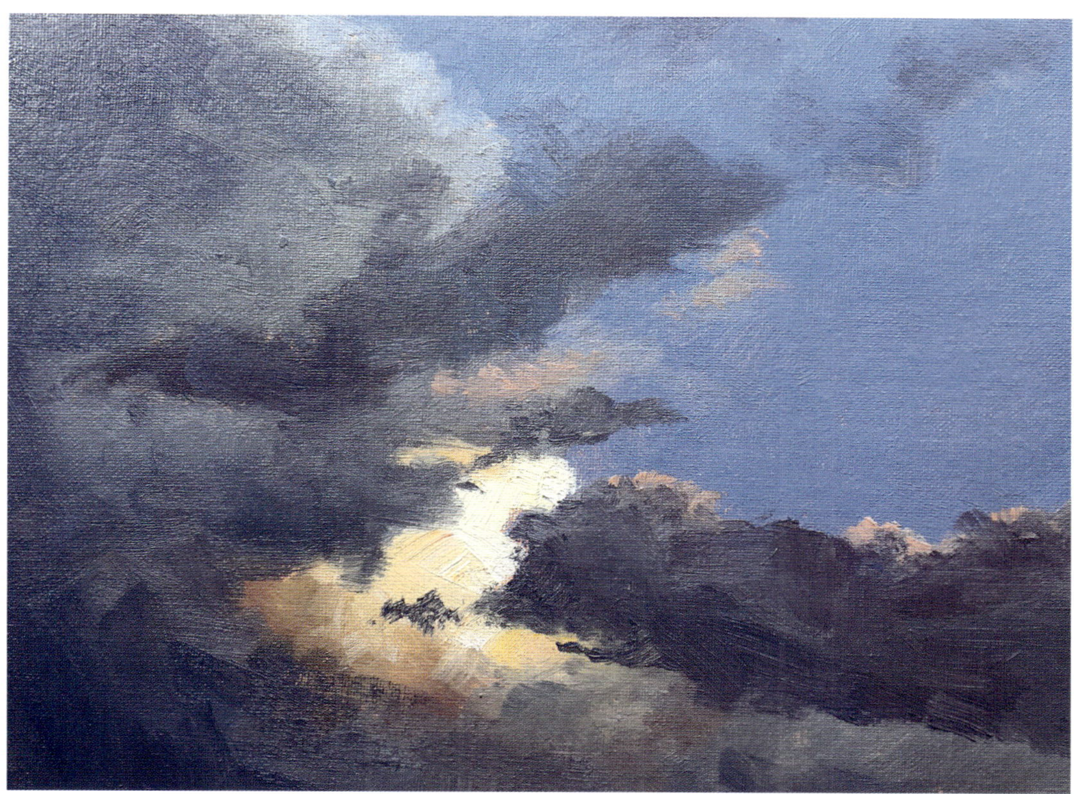

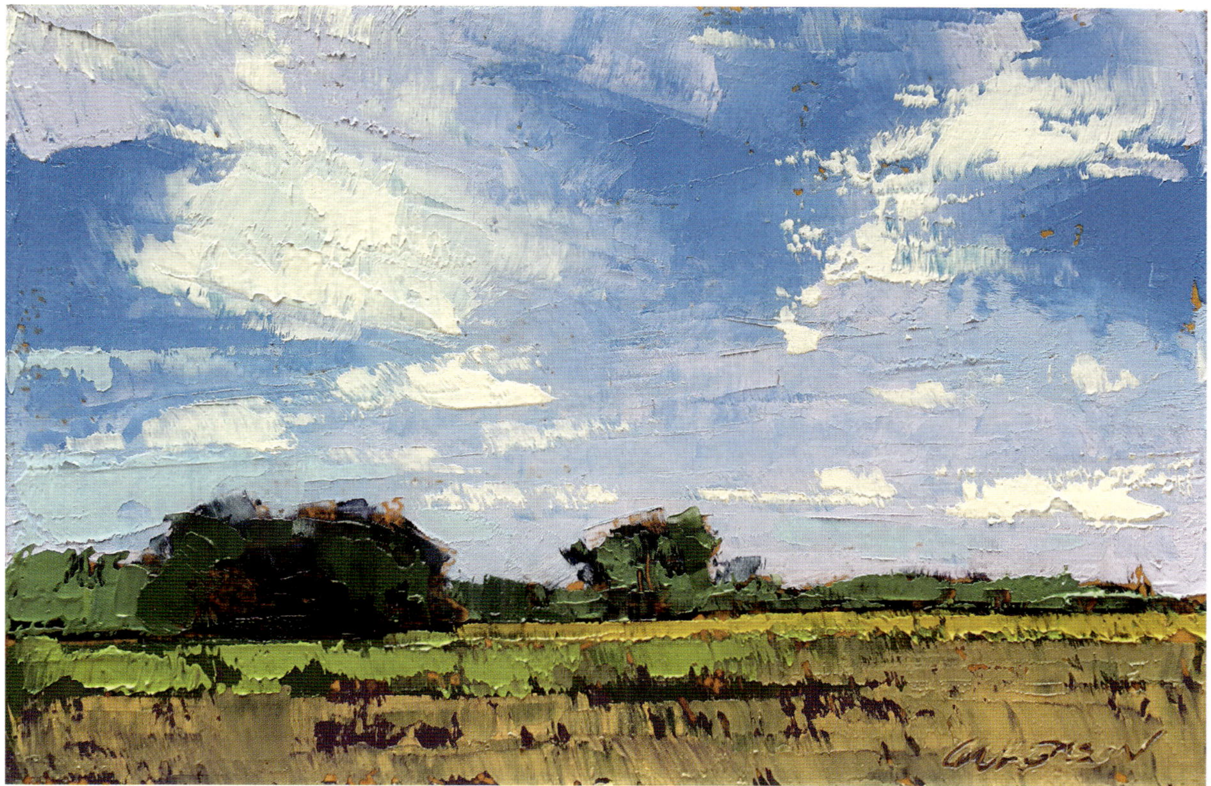

Summer Morning, Mary Bentz Gilkerson.
These summer clouds are captured so well here with the use of a palette knife. Mary gives a good feeling of recession with her excellent handling of the paint.

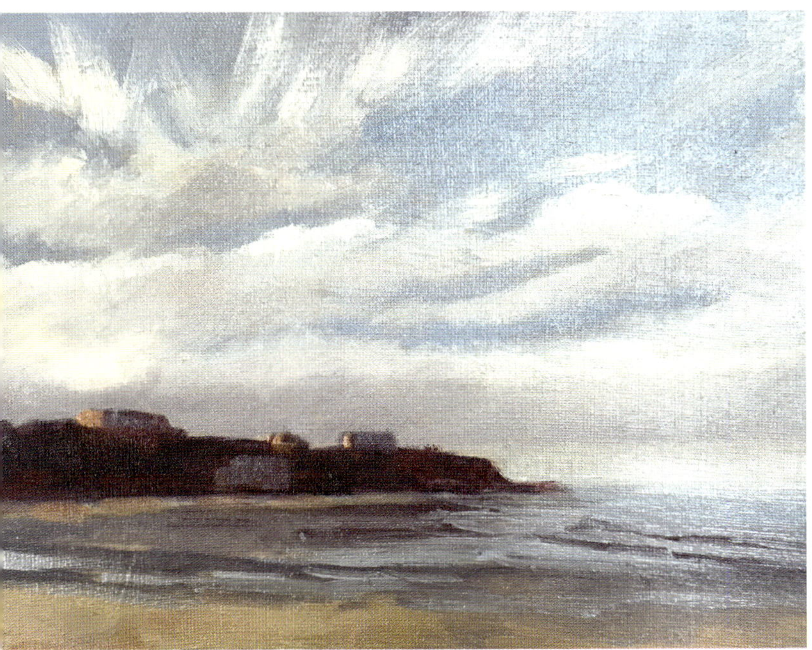

Mares' Tails, Happisburgh, 8" × 10". Linen covered mount board. This beach on the North Norfolk coast is actually pronounced 'Hazeboro'. The wispy 'mares' tails' were blowing towards me and were reflecting in the wet sand. I dipped into my cache of paints and pulled out an old favourite, Unbleached Titanium. This I used for mixing the sand colours and found it to be a good mixer with Kings Blue Deep for the sky colour. Unbleached Titanium was also mixed with white for the clouds, it gives an especially good colour when mixed with Kings Blue and Permanent Rose for the cloud shadows.

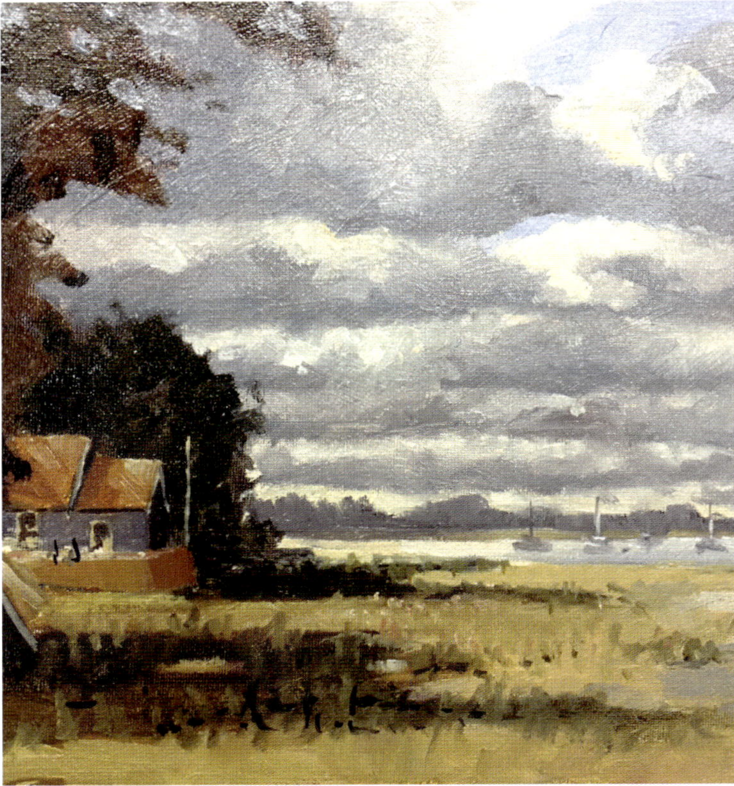

Cloud Streets, Pin Mill, 10" × 10. Canvas board. This was an interesting sky to paint. The altocumulus clouds had formed in lines or 'cloud streets'. The best way to paint these was to start at the horizon, allowing the clouds to overlap each other and become larger as they come forward.

Stratus

Stratus means literally just 'a layer'. At a very low level, stratus clouds form a layer in the form of fog, which can fall as fine rain. There was a fine stratus cloud covering on the day that *Hazy Sun Over Sea* was painted. It gave a lovely milky veil over the sun.

These are the clouds that spread across the sky totally or partially covering it, resembling an even grey blanket or giving us the striated or fibrous clouds that give it a grey/bluish look. Often, when it dissipates we are left with a clear blue sky. These layers can be thin enough to be able to see the sun through them which gives a soft, diffused impression as if looking through frosted glass.

Altostratus

Stratus clouds that form in the mid level are the altostratus.

Nimbostratus (the pre-fix Nimbo means rain)

Nimbostratus are similar to altostratus but are a much denser and greyer layer of cloud blocking out the sun completely, and are almost always associated with continuous light to moderate rain that can often last from several hours to more than a day. This sort of sky is obviously not ideal for the painter as it can add very little interest to the painting as there is not much variations in the light.

In the highest level, where there is less water vapour and it is much colder, cirrostratus cloud is a much thinner layer and is formed of ice crystals. These wispy clouds are blown by strong winds covering the sky in thin, white sheets, often with a fibrous or hair like appearance like feathers. It is these that produce a halo effect around the sun. These clouds are often referred to as 'Mare's Tails'.

Clouds streets

Clouds streets are parallel lines of clouds, usually cumulus that form in the lower atmosphere usually three kilometres from the ground. They are fairly evenly spaced and can extend as far as the eye can see. There have been photographs taken from space that show over a hundred of these parallel rolls that can also extend for over a hundred kilometres.

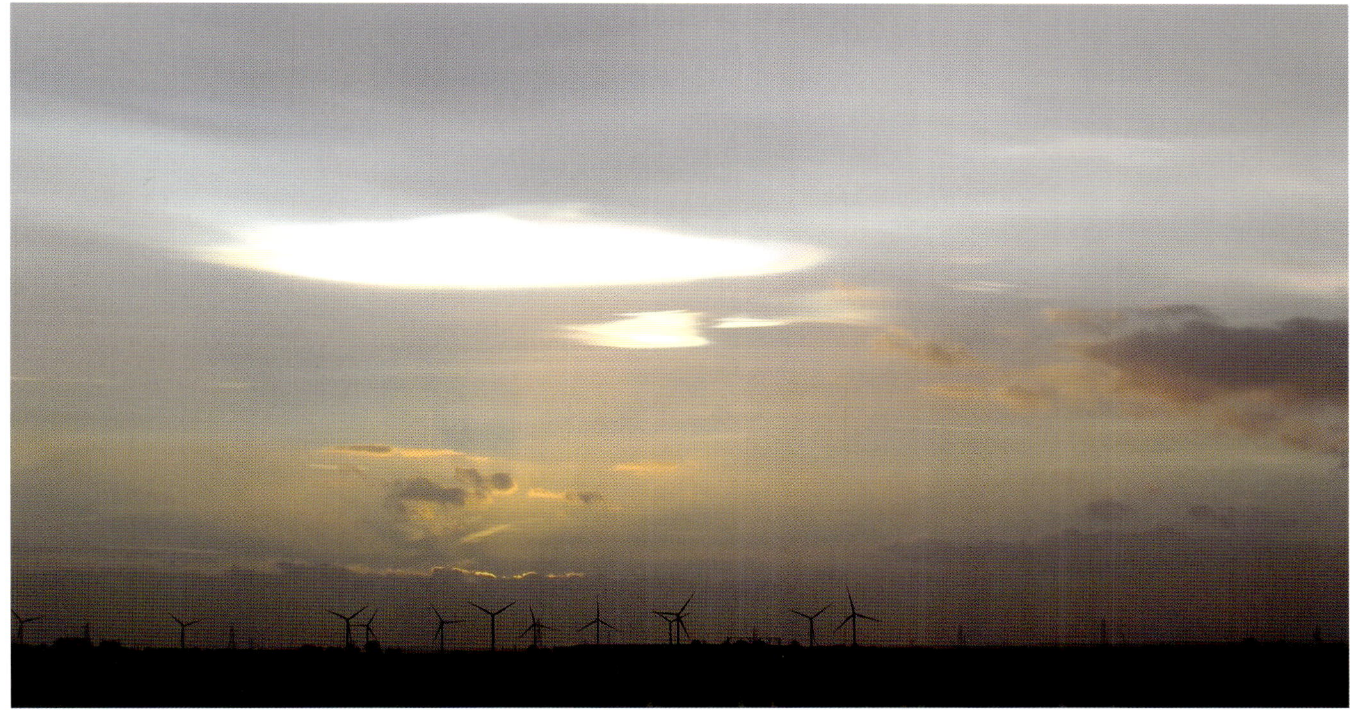

Nacreous Clouds, Lincoln. 2016.
In February 2016, I was delighted to witness this phenomenon as I was driving to Lincoln. The sun was going down which is the best time to see these clouds. As the other clouds got darker, this nacreous cloud continued to glow in the sky even after the sun had set. This is when they look the most dramatic because they are seen against the dark sky, and although the sun had dropped below the horizon, the light from the sun was still on these clouds which, due to the height, are full of ice crystals. Social media was buzzing as people were looking up and seeing these clouds, the best views of which were further north.

Although they are normally straight as they follow the wind's direction, they sometimes curve as the wind changes. Their formation is rather complicated.

Cloud Streets usually occur in a sky that has light cloud covering when the wind direction is constant. Warm, turbulent air rises until it meets a more stable layer of air at a different temperature, and this causes the air to sink down and create the rolls of cloud. We are often not aware of the fact there are clouds in this formation. If the wind is blowing from the side and we look out across the landscape, we can see straight lines of clouds as we look across the bottom of a sea of parallel lines. It is only when we look up that we see the blue space or non Street Clouds above us. When the wind is blowing from behind us, we can look down these amazing straight lines of cloud. Although we know they are parallel, they look to be disappearing into the distance because of perspective.

Nacreous Clouds

These clouds are formed in the lower stratosphere ten to fifteen miles high where clouds rarely form because of the dry atmosphere. Requiring temperatures of -78°C, they are mostly seen in the Polar Regions in winter. The water droplets that form the clouds are much smaller than the droplets forming the more common cloud, causing the light to scatter in a different way, giving the clouds their distinctive pearlescent glow which has earned them the nickname 'mother of pearl' clouds. It is extremely rare for them to be seen over the UK and only happens when the cold air from the Polar Regions is displaced, creating the very cold conditions required for these clouds to form.

Sunrays (crepuscular rays)

As the sun sets, it is common to see rays or beams radiating from the sun or holes in the clouds. These rays can be going up, down or both. The rays, which can be seen as either beams of light or dark shadows in the atmosphere, are in fact parallel. We only see them as converging because they are so far away. We get the same perspective effect when looking at a long parallel road.

The next time you see sunrays, if you turn around you may be lucky enough to spot anti-crepuscular rays; they are fainter and subtler than crepuscular rays. They are usually visible at sunrise or sunset. Like crepuscular rays, they are parallel shafts of sunlight from holes in the clouds and their convergent impression is a perspective effect.

ARTIST PROFILE

David Simons

David Simons is a self-taught artist with a superb control of paint and a unique style. I love his use of thick impasto focal points, seemingly achieved in one masterful stroke. David brings his signature style to life with his dramatic, captivating oil paintings and his landscapes of Arizona and the Southwest.

Oil painting for me is a meditative experience – essential to my well-being, and a necessary part of my life. Painting brings me great joy, and, I hope, uplifts the hearts of those who view my work. I like to explore the subtle ways that light affects the subject. I also enjoy colour, but the value of relationships in a scene are what interest me most. I also like to emphasize the abstract nature of what surrounds us.

I work with oils on board and canvas. I approach a painting by studying the value of patterns that I see. I work from dark to light. I usually touch in and identify the larger shapes and values and then go into the smaller shapes within them. I try to do suggestive brushwork, suggesting things rather than copying. I work with loose brushwork, always keeping the darks thin and thickening up for the mid-tones and highlights. I remind myself 'a painting should transcend the subject' which for me means that it's not the subject that's important but the way it is painted and described.

You should see in a painting how the artist felt about what he was looking at and seeing in his subject.

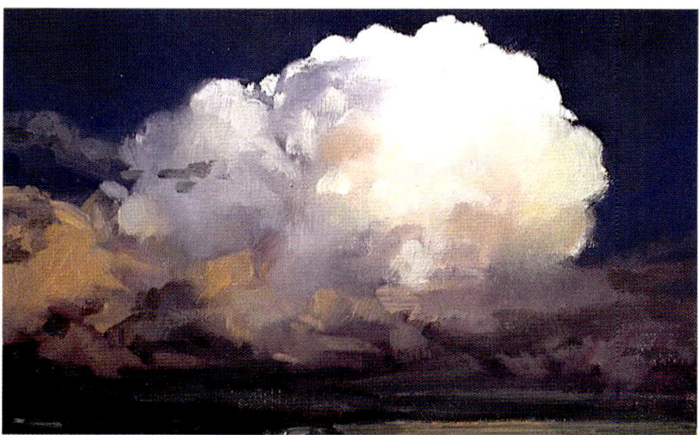

Dramatic Sky 2, David Simons.
The drama of this sky is made all the more dramatic by the strong contrast and the complementary orange and blue colours. Note how your eye is automatically drawn to the point of strongest contrast. It is at this point too that there are harder edges. The rest of the clouds have blended edges, which do not hold our attention as much.

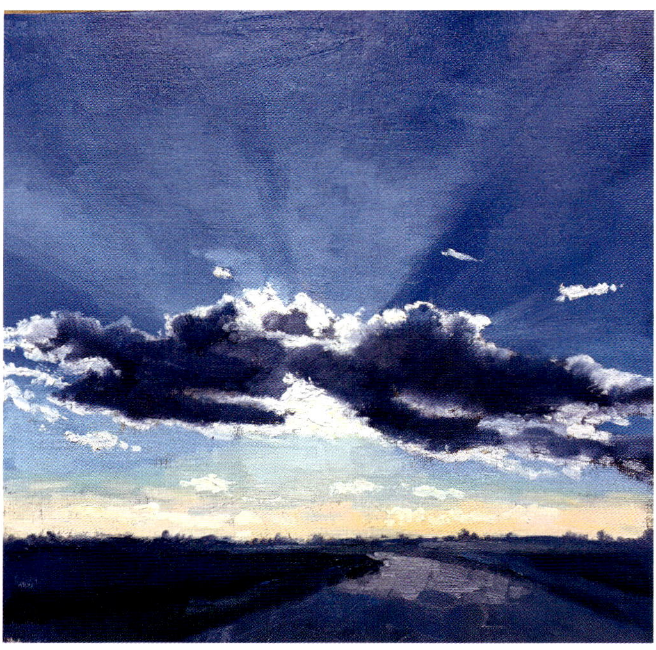

Sun Rays.
This was one of those skies that you couldn't stop looking at. It changed all the time and with my camera, I was able to catch it at its best. To make this painting work, a really dark colour was needed for the sky. Old Holland Blue was chosen for its deep rich colour. The cloud cast shadows, making the sun's rays radiate out into the sky in a fan like a pattern. The dark foreground helps to balance the dark in the main cloud and gives a strong contrast to the warm light on the horizon.

COLOURS AND LIGHT

The sun is our main natural source of light and the light we get from it is something we probably take for granted and possibly give little thought to what it actually is.

Light is a kind of energy known as electromagnetic radiation (EM) and there are other forms of EM radiation such as x-rays and microwaves that are invisible but light is one we can see with the human eye.

Light travels fast and straight in the form of waves. These waves have various lengths and the human eye sees each different wavelength as a different colour. When we see all the wavelengths mixed together, they produce white light. This is the reason clouds look white, it is all the wavelengths mixing together as they bounce off the water droplets.

When light is shone through a prism, it fractures the wavelengths and we are able to see all the colours of the spectrum. These are the same colours and in the same order as the colours we see in a rainbow: red, orange, yellow, green, blue

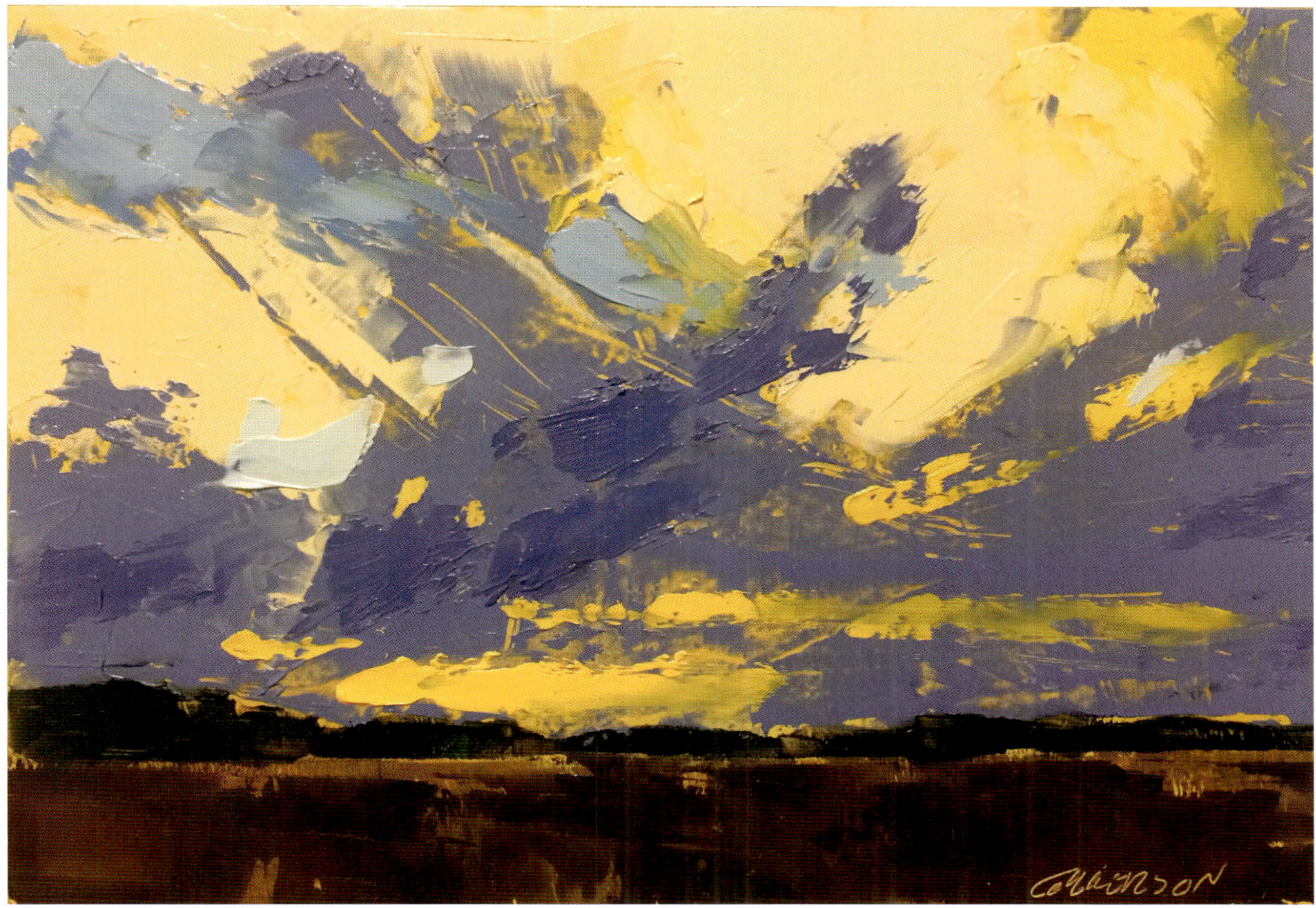

Fall, Sunset, Mary Bentz Gilkerson.
This painting works so well with the strong yellows and purply-blue clouds. There is plenty of movement in the sky in contrast to the silhouetted landscape. By using the palette knife, Mary is able to layer up the clouds without disturbing the first layers.

and violet. When a rain shower has just passed overhead and the sun comes out and shines on the raindrops, the raindrops act like a prism and refract the light; we then see the colours of the spectrum creating the rainbow effect.

As the light leaves the sun, it travels in straight lines through empty space but as it nears Earth, dust particles, water droplets and molecules in the atmosphere cause the different wavelengths to scatter by changing their direction as they hit and bounce off. The size of the particles determines how the light waves get scattered. The blue/violet light waves are more readily scattered by small particles, which are in the upper atmosphere, and explains why we see the sky as blue. The red end of the spectrum is scattered the least. This is why that as the sun sets, the longer, red waves have to travel through more atmosphere so by the time we see it through, wavelengths are scattered, leaving only the pink, orange and red colours for us to see.

The more particles in the atmosphere, the more dramatic a sunset can be. Clouds look amazing as they reflect the light from the sun and since the earth is round, the clouds change colour at different times according to their height. The lowest clouds turn red first but as the sun sinks lower, the high clouds gradually turn red. If you were to travel to somewhere like the Arctic where the sky is clearer and there is a dryer atmosphere, you will notice that the sky stays blue as the sun sets as a glowing bright orange ball.

STEP BY STEP DEMONSTRATION

Cloud Reflections, Cromer

Paints and materials

- Kings Blue Deep
- Ultramarine
- Cadmium Red
- Blue Grey
- Warm Light Yellow
- Blue Black
- Yellow Ochre
- Titanium White
- 10" × 12" canvas board

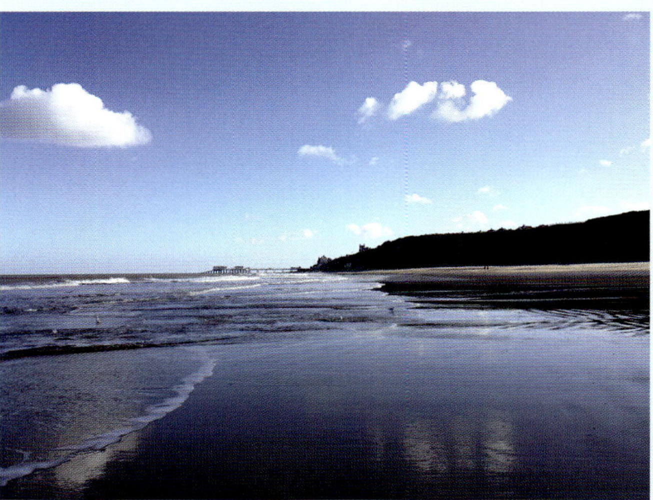

East Runton beach in Norfolk shelves only slightly so that when the tide goes out, it seems to recede very quickly. This means that the exposed sand is wet for longer, giving wonderful reflections of the sky and clouds. This demonstration shows just that but with the addition of a few extra clouds for interest.

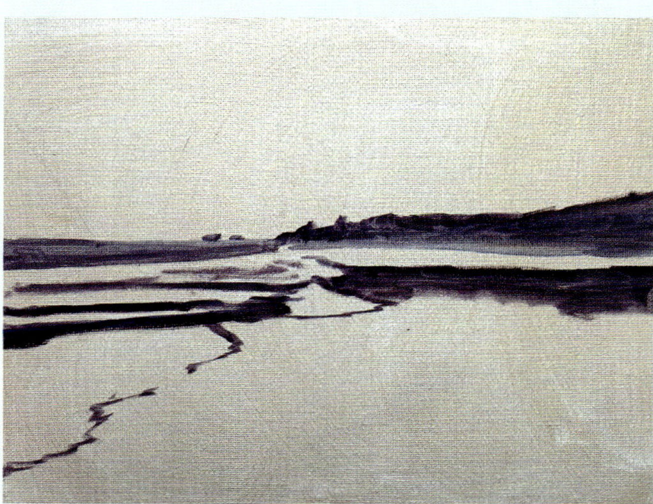

Step 1. Working on a light grey ground, draw out the composition with Ultramarine and Cadmium Red diluted with turpentine. Block in the dark areas of the cliff and cliff reflection.

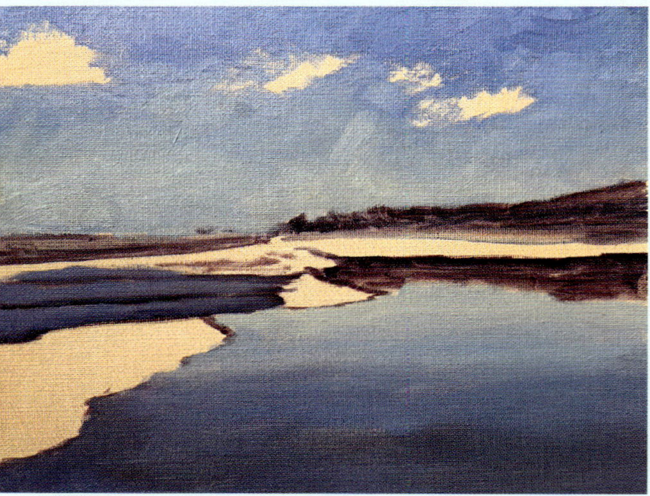

Step 2. Kings Blue Deep is a wonderful rich and versatile colour that could be used, and many do use it on its own for sky colour. I tend to temper it with another colour; in this case Blue Grey was used.

Start at the top, working your way across the canvas and gradually lighten with Blue Grey and Warm Light Yellow down to the horizon.

Working from the cliff shadows on the beach, work the same colours in the reverse towards the foreground. The area at the front of the picture needs to be darker so add a little Blue Black.

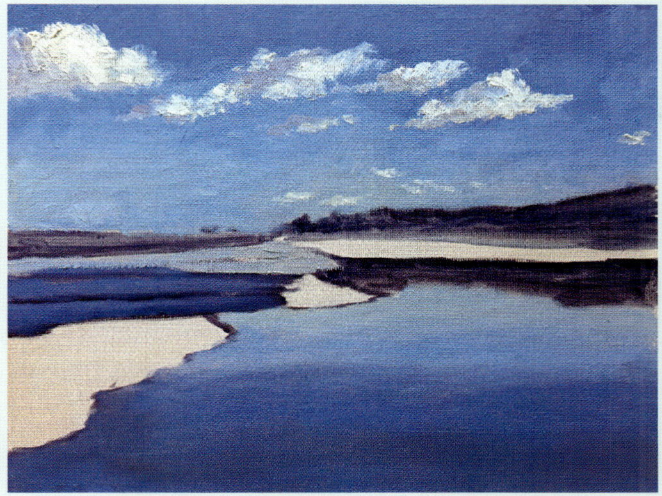

Step 3. Paint the clouds using Warm Light Yellow and white. The cloud shadow is the same colour as the clouds but with the addition of Kings Blue and Cadmium Red. Use some of the same cloud shadow mix for the light area of the sea.

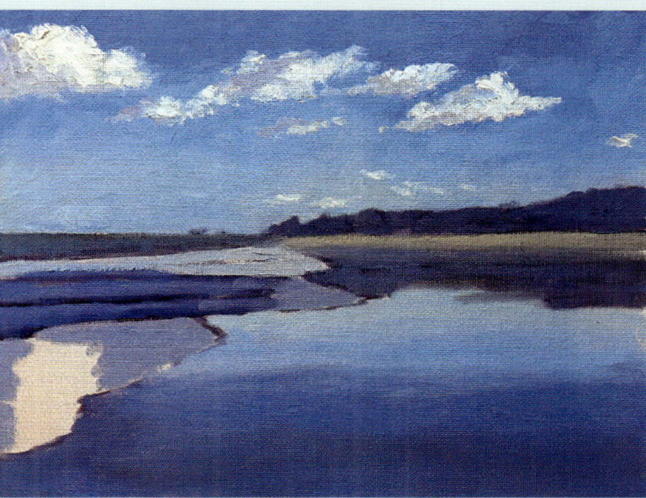

Step 4. The distant sea at the horizon is painted with Kings Blue, Cadmium Red and a touch of Yellow Ochre. Use the same mix with more blue and the smallest amount of Blue Black added for the shadowed cliffs and its reflection on the wet beach. The sand in front of the cliff is a mixture of Yellow Ochre and Warm Light Yellow. To avoid hard lines in the distance, the sand is blended into the cliff reflection. An area in the foreground has been left to add a cloud reflection.

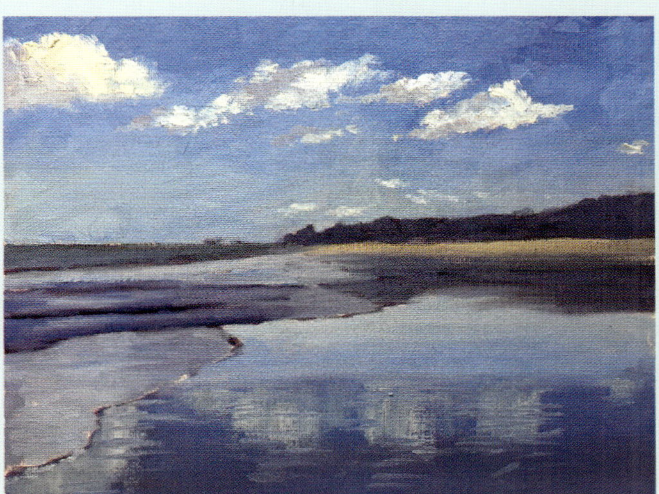

Step 5. For the cloud reflection, use Warm Light Yellow and with a flat brush, pull the colour downwards with light downward strokes. Next, using the tip of the flat brush, make horizontal marks, pulling the light paint into the dark and vice versa; this breaks up the reflections and gives the illusion of the flat surface of the wet sand. Using the same method, make light horizontal strokes through the rest of the water and blend. Leave some of the original dark under drawing as this will help to make a contrast against the white of the surf.

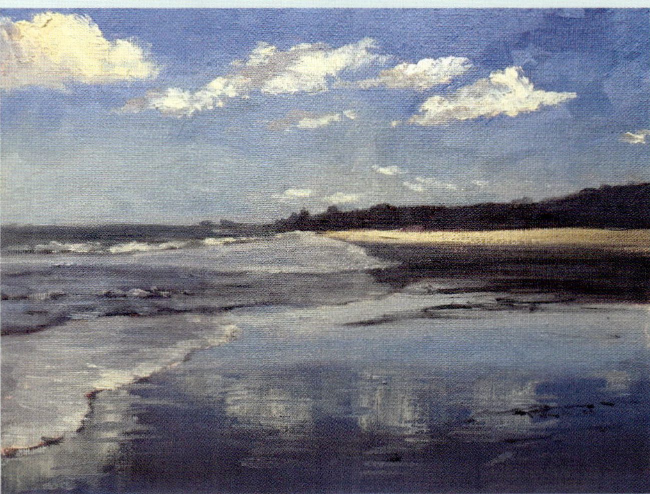

Step 6. Add the surf using Warm Light Yellow and white. Ensure that the tone of the surf is not lighter than the clouds as this would distract the eye and make the picture too jumpy.

Warm Light Yellow is added to the beach at the edge of the cliff in the centre of the painting to make a strong contrast to draw the eye in.

The distant pier of Cromer is indicated with a rigger; do not try to put in too much detail as the pier is so far off in the distance and all detail will be lost.

Finally flick a few dark marks in the foreground using the colour that was used for the cliffs and a rigger.

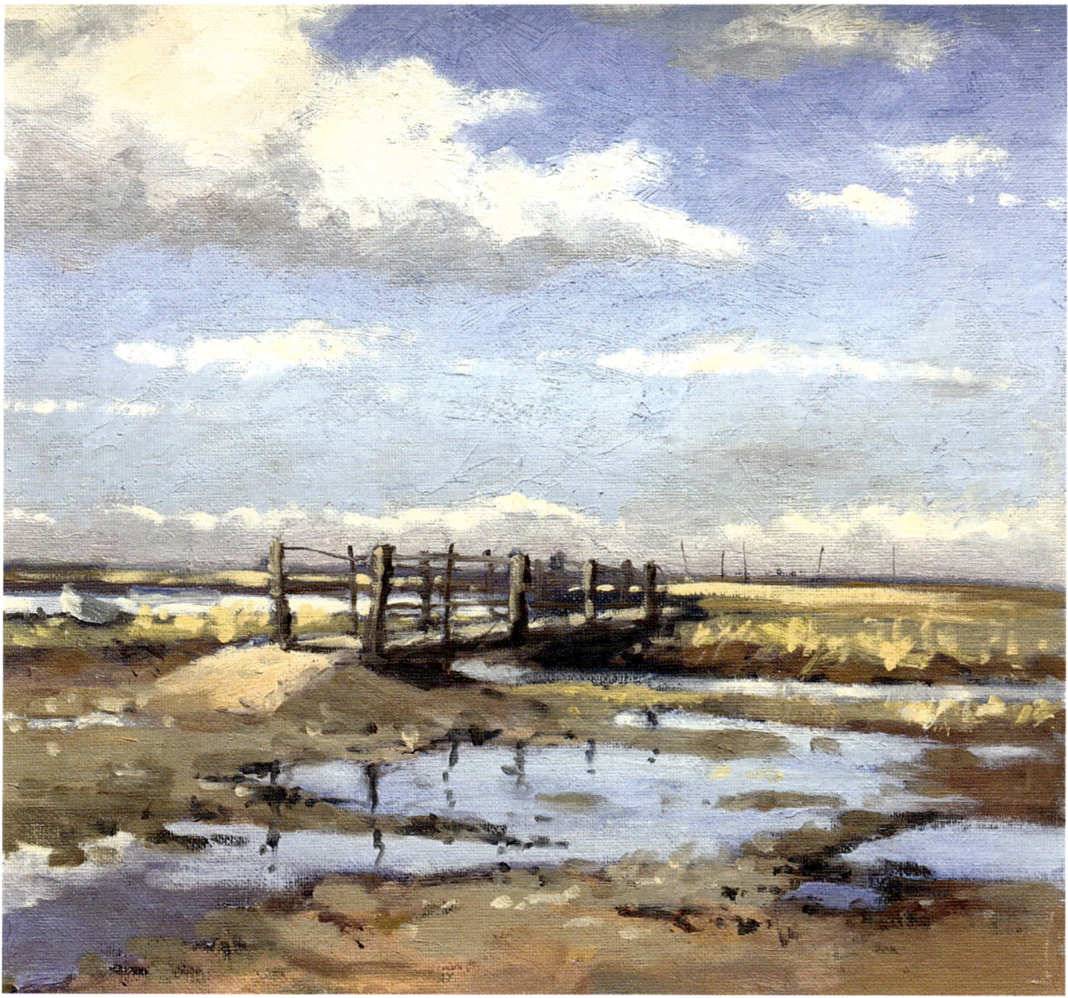

After the Spring Tide, Blakeney.
The clouds were moving very quickly this particular day. I had to study them for a while before deciding on the best formation for my composition. When the decision was made, they were put in quickly and then left alone. Blakeney is very prone to flooding, especially on a spring tide. This was the case here, leaving large puddles, which reflected the deep blue of the sky.

The clouds building up on the horizon help to give a feeling of distance to the painting.

Shadows

It is wonderful to observe a child when they first discover they have a shadow. They either try to jump on it or run away from it. What is a shadow? This may sound rather obvious but it is something we may not have considered before. The reason we have shadows on a sunny day is that the light wavelengths from the sun travelling in straight lines cannot pass through a solid object. This blocking of the light creates a shadow in the shape of the obstruction.

As with objects on the ground, clouds also have shadows. Cumulus clouds can create wonderful cloud shaped shadows and patterns that move slowly across the landscape on a sunny day as they drift along in the breeze. These can be used to the painter's advantage as they give a pleasing connection between sky and land.

Cloud shadows can also be used to break up an area in a painting to give added interest. A dark foreground can make a great lead into a landscape painting and it provides the dark required to create a strong contrast for a burst of sunlight.

A sky with a lot of broken cloud can create a patchwork of small darker areas on the ground, giving interest, whereas larger clouds can cover a larger area. Like any shadow, the size of the shadow changes with the size of the cloud. A mostly overcast sky with a small break in the cloud can add that splash of light that can give a picture more drama. The heavier the cloud, the more dense the shadow is.

Some of the most dramatic and spectacular cloud shadows are the ones cast from one part of the sky to another.

Direction of light

When starting a painting, one of the most important elements is establishing the direction of light. The sun will cast light not only on the ground but also on the clouds. If a cloud is lit on one side by the sun, the shadow will be on the side furthest from the sun. The same goes for objects on the ground. This is something to be aware of when painting. It would look wrong to have light on one side of the clouds and light on the other side of solid objects. It's obvious when you

Hazy Sun over Sea.
There was a hazy low level of cloud over the sun, which gives this view a soft subtle glow, which is reflected in the water. Second levels of clouds, which are darker, drift across the sun to help give a bit more contrast and depth to the picture. The dark colour from the clouds is picked up in the ripples on the water.

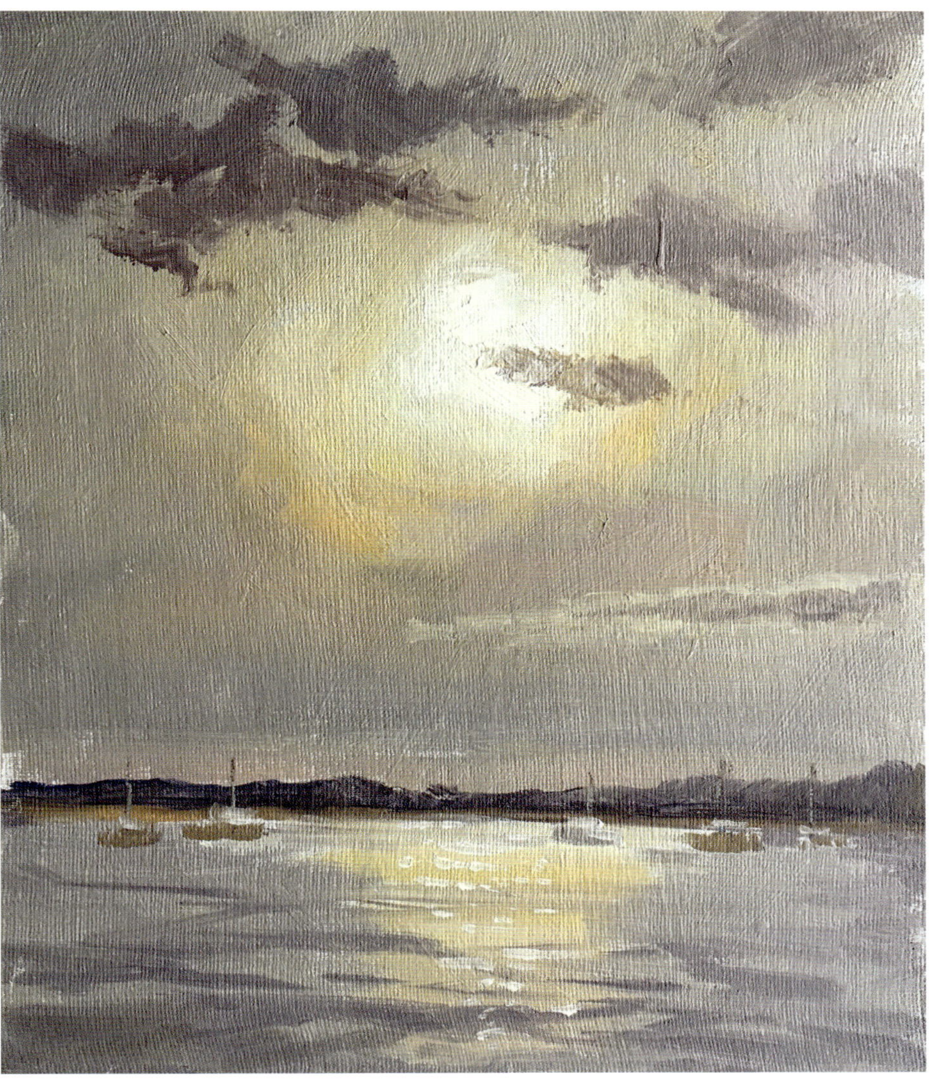

think about it but I have seen many a painting that has been spoilt by this lack of observation.

Another trap an artist could easily fall into is not putting all the shadows in at the same time. I have seen paintings that have been started in the morning and finished in the afternoon. A cast shadow from a telegraph pole has gone from left to right and in the evening, the shadow from a tree has gone from right to left. The best solution for this problem is to establish which direction the sun is travelling and decide at which point the shadows will best work in your painting. The position of the shadows will often be best at the start of the painting, this is because you were drawn to the subject by the way the shadows fell and lit up different shapes.

It is possible to drive past a place daily and not think it worthy of a painting and then one day, the light will fall just right and it's as if you had never seen that place before. Even on a sunny day there will be dark clouds and light clouds in the sky. Clouds can appear to look dark for various reasons. One such reason is because they fall into shadows cast by other clouds. A large cumulus cloud lit from behind will cast a large shadow on clouds in between itself and the sun. A cloud lit from behind can also appear dark if it is dense enough. How grey the shading on cloud looks will vary according to the brightness of the sky behind it.

Colour in shadows

The brighter the light is, the darker the shadows will look. Don't be fooled into using black. The longer you look, the more your eyes will adjust and the more colours you will see. Shadows are affected by the colours around them. There will be reflected local colour and light. If you look hard enough for long enough, you should see colours in a shadow from cool to warm, giving the potential for some exciting painting.

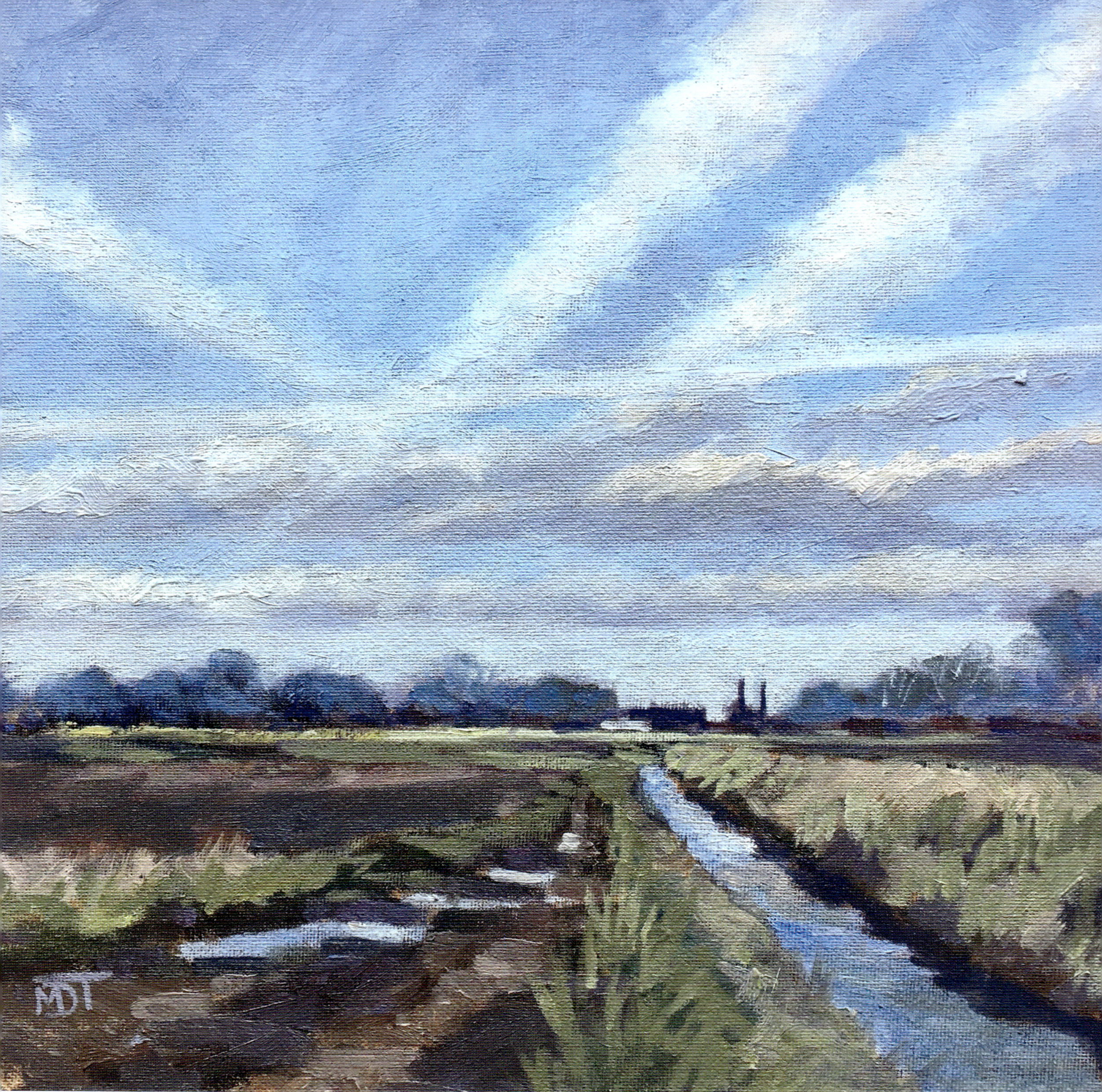

Vapour trails – or contrails as they are also known as – are now officially recognized in the World Cloud Atlas as clouds.

Vapour Trails
Titanium White
Yellow Ochre
Burnt Sienna
Cobalt Blue
Cadmium Red
Burnt Umber
10" × 10" gessoed board
Burnt Sienna ground

There are a lot of strong lines of perspective in this painting. Most of the focus is on the far end of the dyke as this is where we have the strongest contrast of tone. The rest of the lines in the field also lead us to this point. The clouds were mainly going from left to right but the diagonal vapour trails break this pattern and lead into the picture. Note that even the vapour trails have their own perspective, wider at the front and tapering away into the distance. In areas of heavy air traffic, it may be necessary to be selective about which vapour trails you use. If you try to put them all in, the resultant picture could end up a bit confusing and fussy.

Note the steep perspective, the foreground of the track and the dyke take up the whole width of the painting but by just over a third of the way up, they have converged. Emphasize perspective to give a greater feeling of distance.

CHAPTER 3

Perspective

From abstract to pure realism, not all paintings will be to our taste but one thing they will mostly have in common is a good composition. Composition is mostly instinctive. We are all able to recognize a well-composed picture. It will have a good balance and feel to it as well as being pleasing to the eye. Almost without being aware, we are drawn into the picture and the eye is led around the painting to the focal point.

The essence of composition is the plan, placement or arrangement of elements in a work to make up the whole.

A basic, calm, landscape composition would be based mainly on horizontals and verticals. The horizontals would be the horizon and clouds and the verticals being trees, buildings and telegraph poles. The danger with having strong horizontals will be that the eye is prevented from being led into the picture. The introduction of diagonal lines will make a more interesting and vital painting. This can be done by the introduction of winding roads, hills and the clouds horizontal in the sky. The painting *Vapour Trails* has strong diagonal lines, leading us into the picture to a focal point.

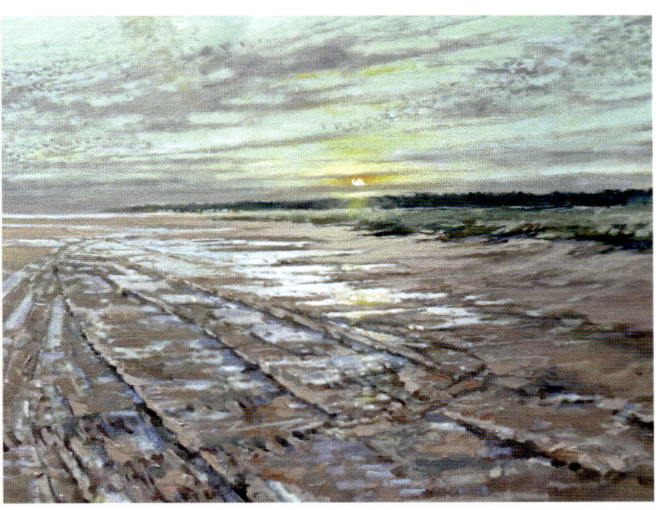

Low Tide, Holkam Beach, Brian Ryder ROI PPIEA.
Puddles left in the tyre tracks on the beach lead us nicely into this painting. The water reflects the sky colours and the subtle reflection of the sun helps tie the whole painting together.

Perspective

When we talk about perspective, we often think back to the early days of art lessons in school, learning about vanishing points and lines of telegraph poles disappearing into the distance. It is a subject that a lot of people struggle to understand. There are two forms of perspective, linear and aerial.

Linear Perspective

Linear perspective is the technique used to represent three-dimensional objects on a flat 2D surface such as your canvas. A simple example of this is a cube.

When putting figures into a picture, bear in mind their eye level. Visualize them next to the house and think of them going through the door. Wherever the figure is in the picture, then the head will remain at that level (assuming that the landscape is flat). If the figure is near to you then the feet will be in the foreground and the head will still remain at eye level.

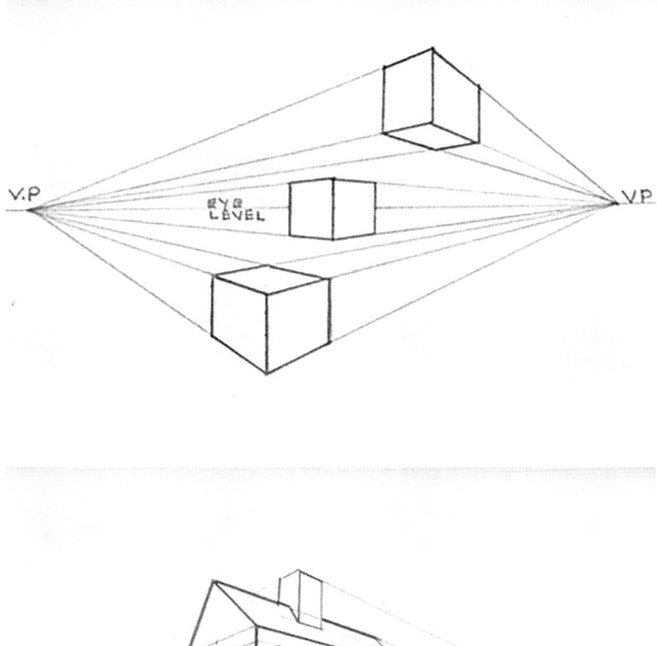

If a cube is above us, the sides will slope downwards to the eye level (or horizon) and we will be able to see the underside. When a cube is below, then the lines slope upwards to the eye level and we are able to see the top of the object and when a cube is straight in front, then the lines above us slope down and the lines below slope upwards and we are unable to see either the top or bottom of the cube.

These simple rules also apply when drawing buildings. The thing to remember is that, the higher the building or chimney, the steeper the perspective.

Aerial Perspective

Aerial perspective is the name given to the effect of distance. The atmosphere changes our view of colour and objects as they recede into the distance. Mastering the simple rules and applying them to our painting will give the work more depth. For example, if we are painting a landscape with no obvious straight lines then we have to consider what elements we can use to convey the feeling of depth and recession in our painting. If you were to stand on the top of a hill and look out over a vast landscape, you will notice how the details in the distance become hazy and less defined as it gets further away. The same with a mountain range, which will appear hazier, bluer and lighter the further away it gets. This optical effect is due to particles in the atmosphere. The same can also be said of the sky; as the clouds recede they are less sharp. The clouds in the distance should therefore be painted in the same manner as the distant hills. To paint them with thick impasto brushstrokes would bring them back into the foreground.

Aerial perspective is not only easier to learn than linear but it is a very useful tool for the landscape painter. There are four key rules to bear in mind:

- Objects look smaller the further they are away from the viewer
- Details become less evident the further they are away
- Strength of tones become much weaker as they get further away from the viewer
- Colours look weaker and begin to fade the further away they are.

If all these elements are borne in mind then you are well on your way to conveying the illusion of depth and distance in your painting. Even as objects on the ground recede in size as they get nearer to the horizon, so do the clouds. Perspective plays a big role in drawing skies and the same rules also apply. Don't think you can just draw distant clouds as smaller versions of clouds that are close to you, though. Consider tones, hues and detail.

As the clouds change in size, they also appear to change in shape as in the painting *Melissa at Pin Mill*. Notice how the clouds nearer to the horizon are flatter and narrower than the ones in the foreground. This is an example of aerial perspective.

To convey the feeling of distance, overlapping, the clouds will help to give a feeling of space and distance. Layering and overlapping is more effective when there is a difference in tone and texture between the two overlapping objects.

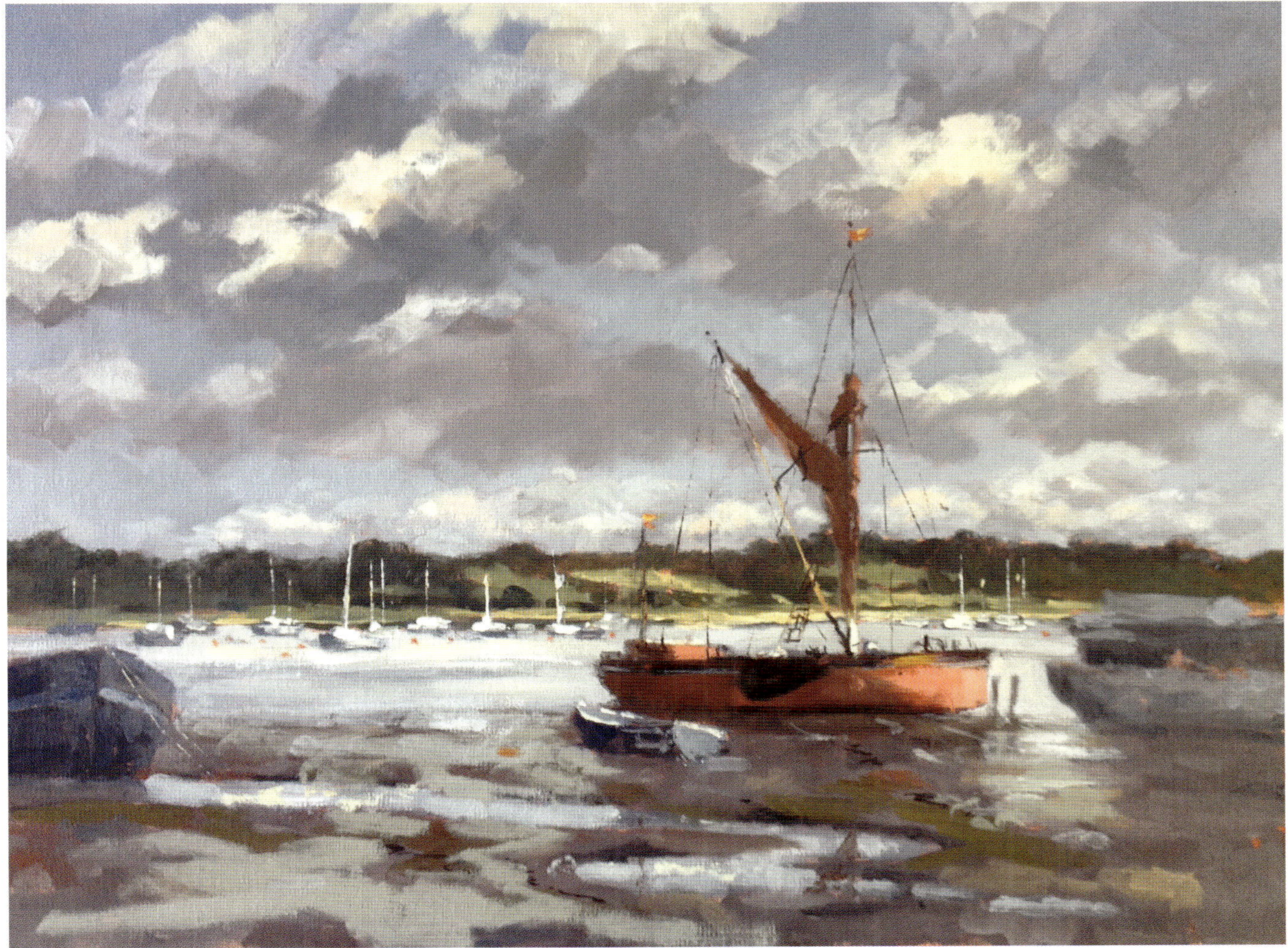

Melissa at Pin Mill
Cobalt Blue
Magenta
Cadmium Red
Yellow Ochre
Cadmium Yellow
Alkyd Titanium White
8" × 10" Gesso primed MDF
Warm ground

Pin Mill, Chelmondeston, is a favourite place to paint for many artists. There is always something to catch the eye. This little *plein air* study was done on a very windy day. The clouds were moving so quickly I had to really study them well and try to portray them from the image in my head. The nearest clouds appeared big and fluffy and as they receded, they gave the illusion of becoming flatter and smaller. This was because the clouds overlapped each other as they came forwards, revealing less of the distant clouds.

The sun kept disappearing too but when it appeared, it cast wonderful cloud shadows and patches of light illuminating the distant hills. The introduction of the red of the old Thames barge helps to give warmth to what would have been a rather dull painting. So that the red isn't isolated, I have added touches to the barge on the left and the addition of floats in the water help to carry the red through.

This helps to separate the objects from one another. You will achieve this by reducing the tones as the clouds recede into the distance.

Occasionally, when there are fewer clouds in the sky, they do not overlap; if they were all of the same size and shape then they would appear to be all on the same plane so by decreasing them in size, shape and tone, you will again give the illusion of distance.

TIP: when painting a picture that has a lot of distance in it, try to introduce a point of interest such as an object or strong shadow. This will help to enhance a sense of depth and lead the viewer into the painting.

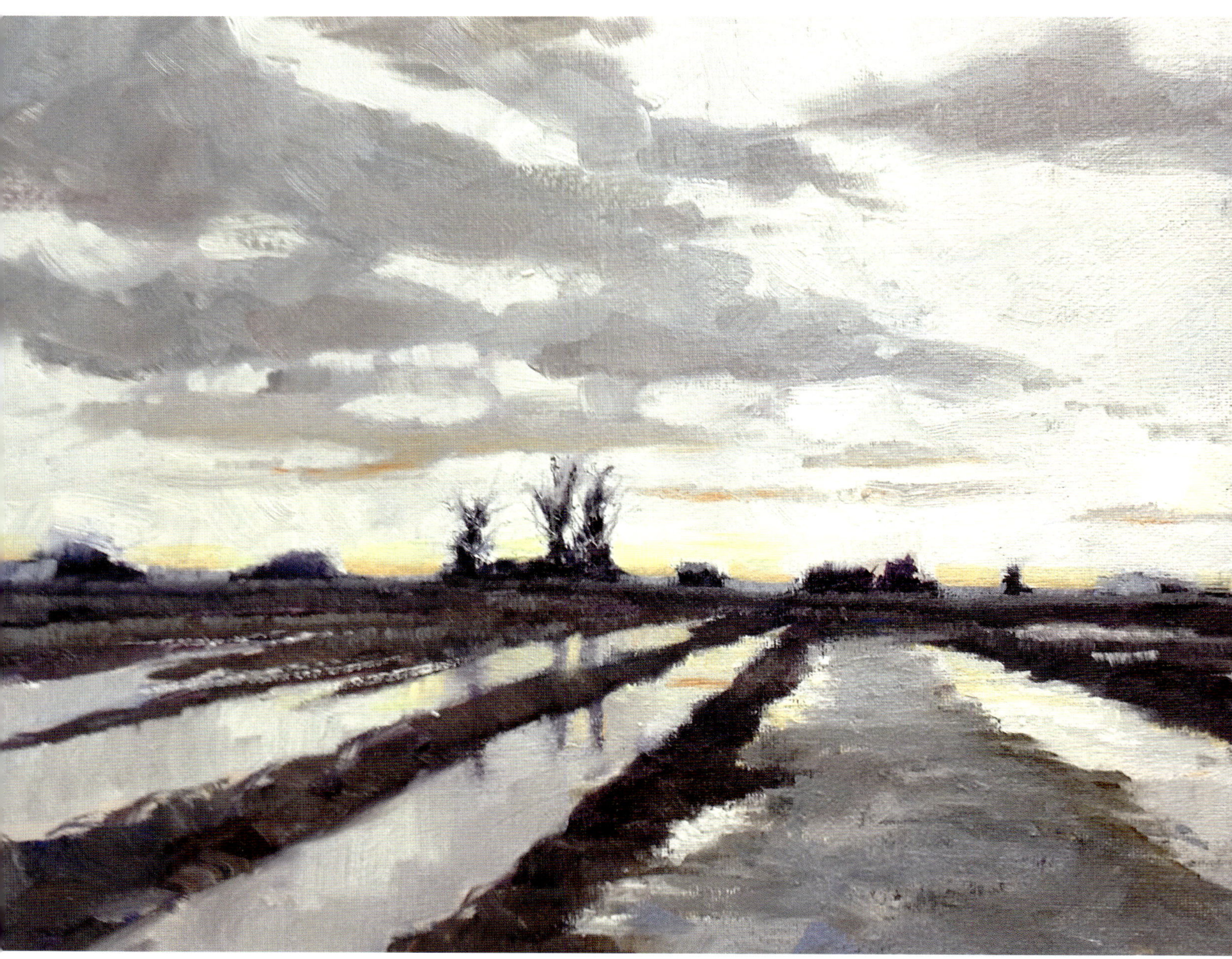

Flooded Fens
Titanium White
Burnt Umber
Kings Blue Deep
Lemon Yellow
Permanent Rose
10" × 12" oil on canvas board

I like the simple colours of this painting. There had been excessive amounts of rain over a period of a week. All the dykes were full and the fields were flooded. The sky was still heavy with rain but there was a glow on the horizon. The edges of the dyke and furrows in the field provide a strong perspective. The dyke, the trees and bushes were blocked in first with Burnt Umber and a touch of Permanent Rose. Next, the lighter part of the sky and water were painted from a mix of Burnt Umber, Titanium White and a touch of Kings Blue Deep. Lemon Yellow and Titanium White were added near the horizon and in the puddles. The road and clouds were of the same mix of Burnt Umber, Kings Blue Deep and Permanent Rose. Lemon Yellow was added in the lower clouds. The whole painting was completed in one session in about one and a half hours.

ARTIST PROFILE

Peter Barker

The painting Brancaster Staithe *depicts a view of Burnham Overy Staithe in north Norfolk, a harbour that has been painted thousands of times by artists over the years. The real 'hook' for me for this painting was the intense sunlight bouncing off the shallow water.*

To make a painting like this 'sing', you have to make sure the register of the sky is right against the reflection on the water. By squinting, I could see that the brightest part of the painting would be that reflected sunlight, so after scrubbing in the main elements with diluted (with white spirit) Alkyd oil paint on the toned board, I placed a band of pure Titanium White where the sunlight reflection would be – it being the lightest pigment the painter has in his arsenal, so everything else in the painting would be a tone down from that, so placing the lightest light early on is always prudent.

So, that placed, I then attacked the sky. With skies, I used just three primary colours plus white – Cadmium Yellow Light, Permanent Rose and Cobalt Blue – from which I can mix any colour and tone required. I use Permanent Rose instead of a more crimson red because it gives me the option of making the most vivid violet when needs be in a painting, and if I ever need a really bright red, I can just mix some yellow with it.

I like to work over a whole painting, rather than concentrating on one part, especially the sky. If you paint the sky in isolation, honing it to perfection, it may indeed seem perfect, until you place the adjoining skyline of trees or whatever, and then the sky can appear totally wrong in tone or colour. So, the key is to keep it all moving, then minor changes can be made, rather than having to repaint a whole passage.

So, for this painting, using a no. 5 long flat bristle brush, I placed broad brushstrokes of varying mixes of warm and cool greys, and the band of blue sky near the top with the adjacent light clouds. Before it was all completed, I placed in the distant headland and made any adjustments to the sky before continuing with the boats and foreground, then dragged in thick impasto strokes of Titanium White with a palette knife over the water to really make the sunlight reflection 'pop'.

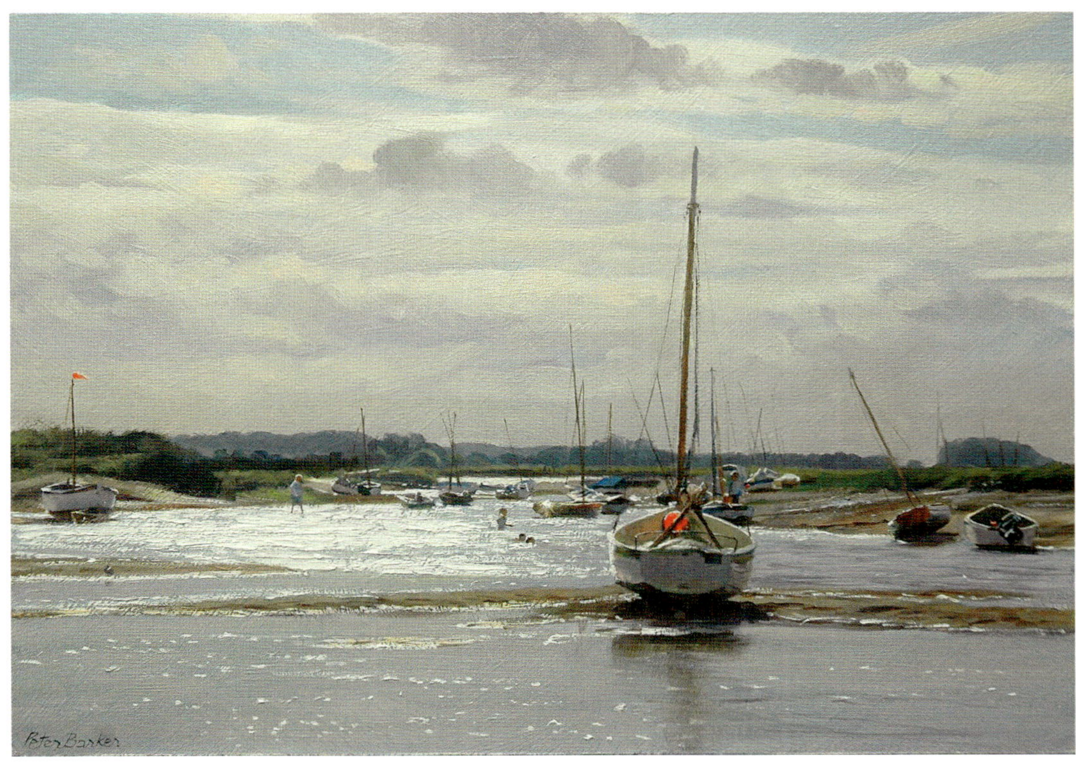

Brancaster Staithe,
Peter Barker.

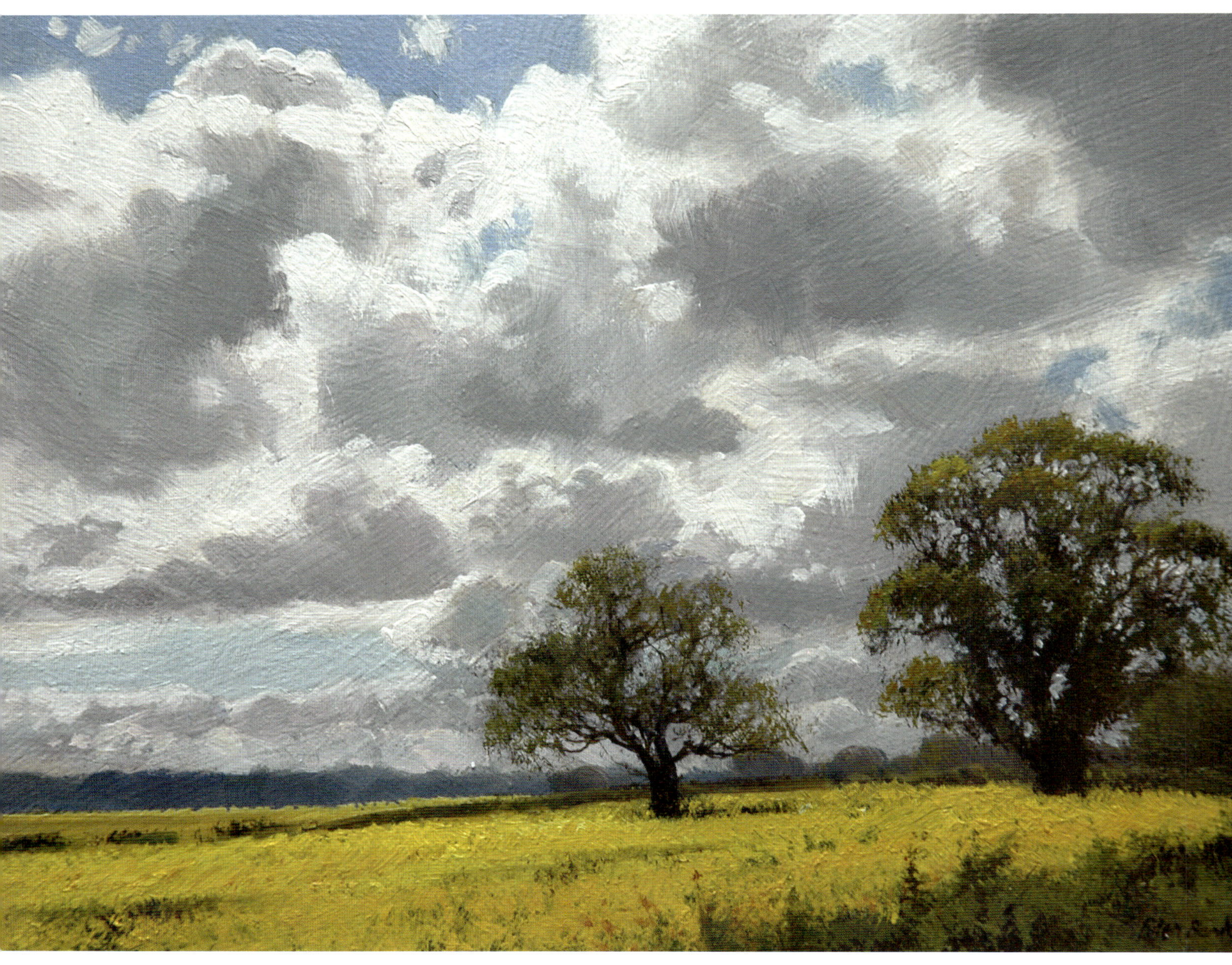

Rape Field, Peter Barker.
This painting of a wonderful summer's day shows how the mass of clouds in the sky recede into the distance, overlapping as they come towards us.

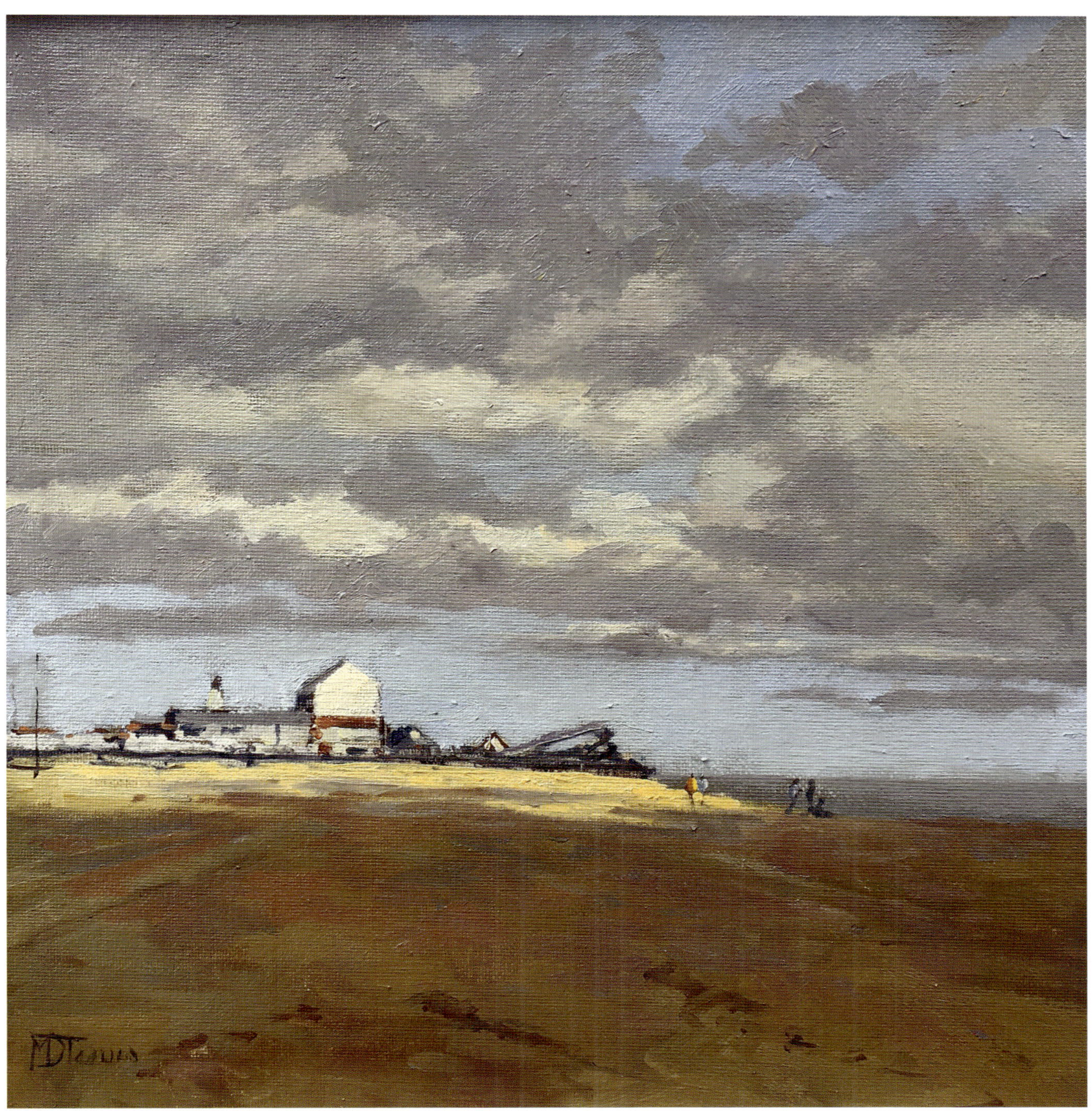

Great Yarmouth.
Titanium White
Cadmium Yellow
Cadmium Red
Ultramarine Blue
12′ × 12" gessoed board
Yellow Ochre ground

This simple composition draws the eye straight into the picture to the details of the pier at Great Yarmouth. The cloud shadows on the near beach have lines of perspective to help emphasize distance. The strong sunlit areas of the beach and the buildings on the pier provide the tonal contrast, which places it in the centres of attention. Strong, solid cloud shapes add interest and recession in the sky and balance the heavier tones of the foreground.

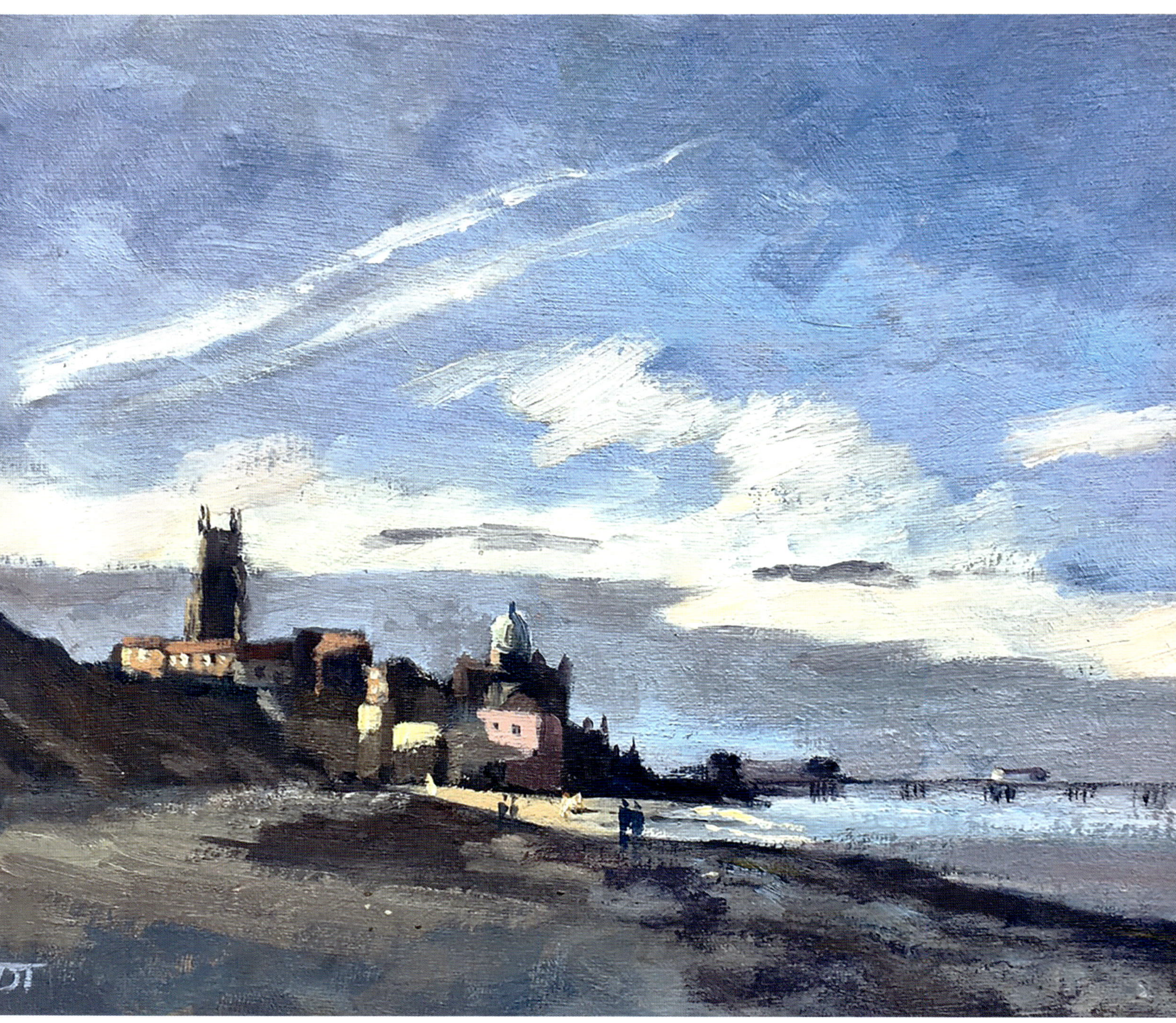

Cromer, 10″ × 12″ on muslin covered board. Being winter, the sun was low in the sky, catching the side of the buildings and creating a wonderful shaft of light across the beach in the distance.

The positioning of the clouds helps us to compose a painting. We can also use vapour trails from passing aircraft. Sometime these vapour trails are mistaken for clouds as they spread out across the sky. Different air temperatures and wind conditions can make them look very cloud like and we can use them to our advantage. An example of this can be seen in the painting *Fenscape*.

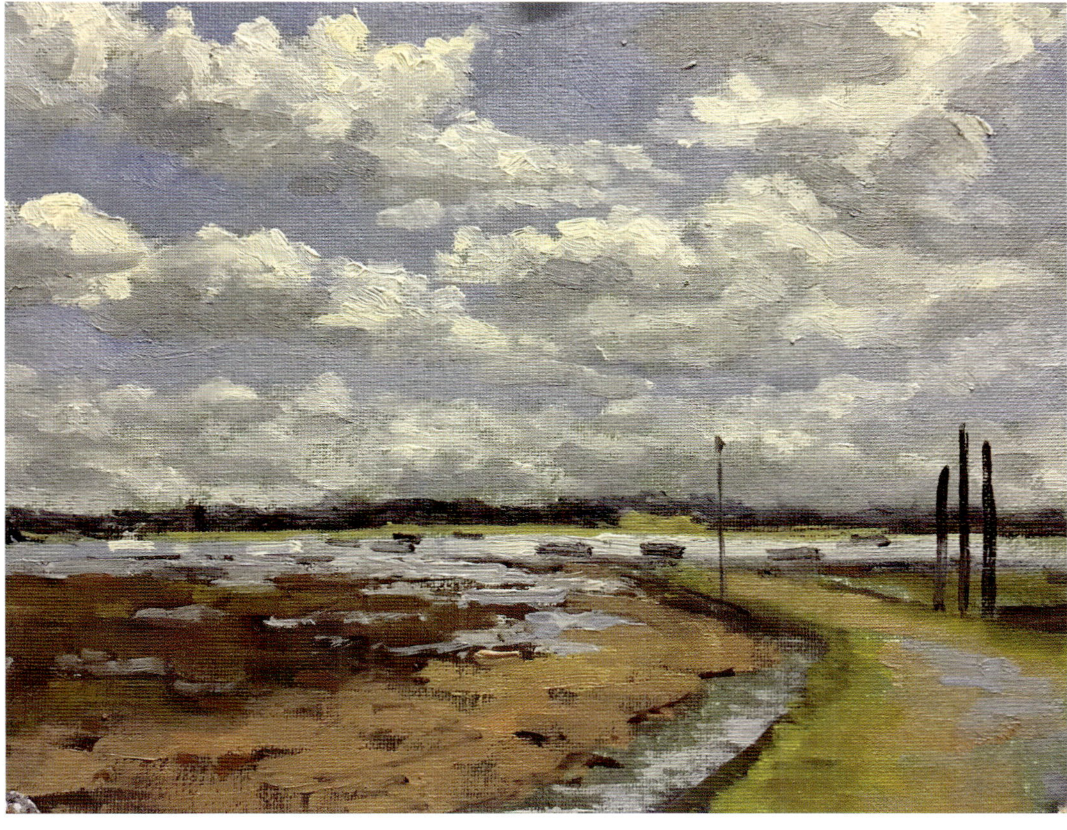

Perspective, Pin Mill.
There are some very steep lines of perspective in this painting. Notice how wide the curved path that leads us into the picture is at the front and how quickly it tapers out as it reaches the water's edge. The same applies to the clouds. They are much wider in the front and narrower as they taper away from the viewer.

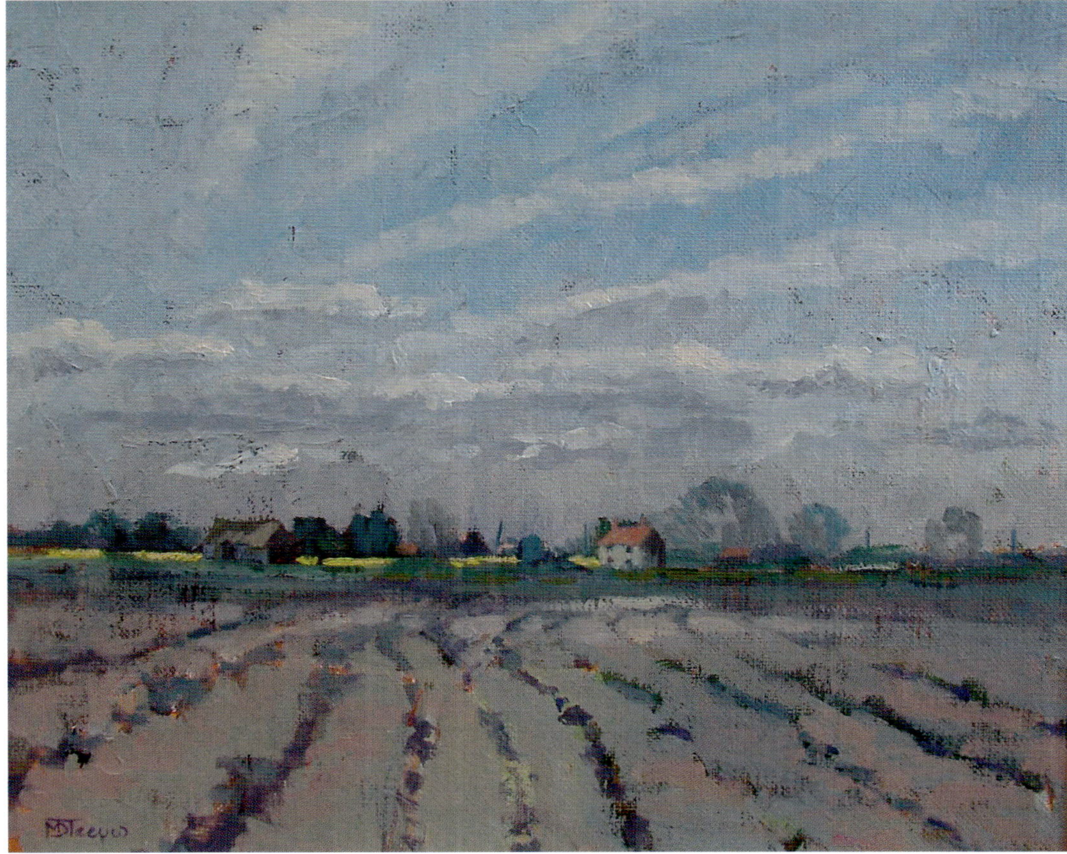

Fenscape.
There were clouds and vapour trails in this painting and I selected the best of both to help me compose a pleasing arrangement in the sky.

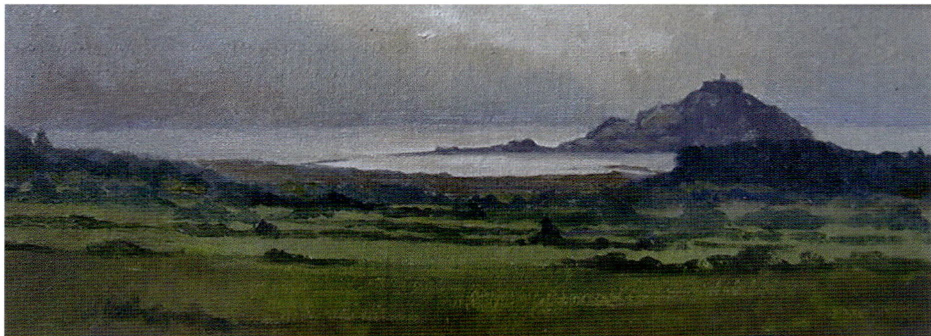

St Michael's Mount.
This long, thin canvas was the perfect proportion for the painting of St Michael's Mount.

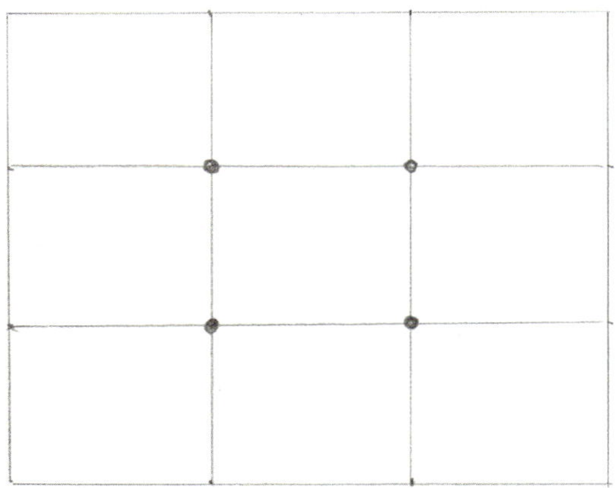

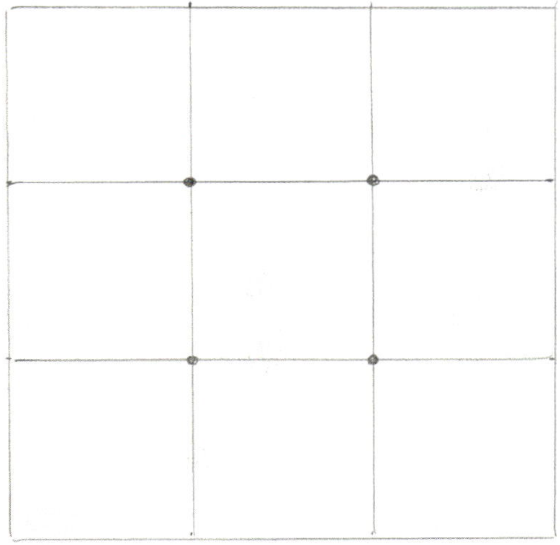

The rule of thirds is in fact more of a guide to artists rather than a strict rule. It is a guide as to the positioning of important elements of the painting. The divided canvas gives us a grid with four intersections. It is suggested that the centre of interest would be best placed at one of these points.

Proportions of your canvas

A main consideration when composing a painting is the proportions and orientation of your board or canvas. Should it be square or rectangular, portrait or landscape? It is a good idea to have a few stock sizes to choose from. The main advantage of having canvases that are stock size is that you can usually find frames that are off the shelf, enabling you to swap paintings around.

Different formats tend to evoke different atmospheres. It is thought that a horizontal format is more calming and restful than a vertical format, which might be more dramatic.

Dividing up the canvas

Another consideration is how will you divide it up? We have to determine the main viewpoint, and this will depend on whether the horizon is high or low. The main thing to remember is that a high horizon will give you more foreground whereas a low horizon will give you more sky.

Golden Mean

There is a mathematical formula, which occurs naturally in nature. It has many names but is mostly referred to as the Golden Mean or Golden Ratio. It is often taught to art students as an aid to the perfect composition. It is a method of dividing up the canvas into set proportions. We know that by doing this, the composition will appeal more to the human eye, but why, we are not quite sure. It is quite a complex formula for which there is a lot of information available on the Internet. For our purposes we will look at the rule of thirds.

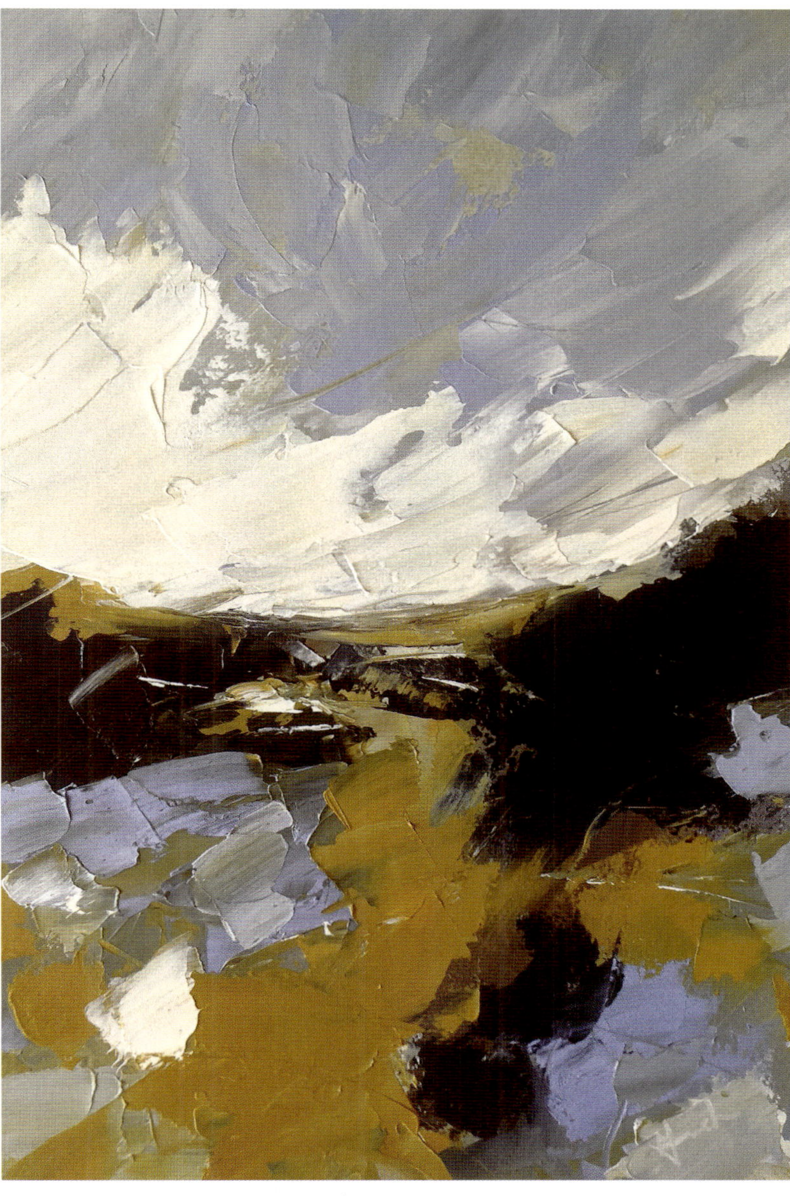

Looking North, Mari French.
Mari has used a tall portrait canvas for this painting, *Looking North*. She has also given us a very good example of how the rules are there to be broken. Although it is generally not a good idea to put a horizon in the middle of a painting, Mari has done just that. Why it works here is that it is not a straight line. There is also a strong diagonal movement in the brushstrokes, which give the feeling of movement. The colours in the foreground have been echoed in the sky, tying the painting together.

Rule of Thirds

The rule of thirds is not to be confused with the Golden Ratio, it is a much simpler formula to understand and follow. It can be used to divide up any shape of canvas whereas the Golden Ratio rules are based on a rectangular shape of set proportions.

Most of the paintings in this book will have a horizon placed at either a third or two thirds of the canvas with the focal point a third of a way in. This is something that a majority of artists will do subconsciously as we know that it works compositionally.

TIP: avoid putting the horizon in the centre of the picture. It will make the painting more interesting if the proportions of sky to landscape are unequal.

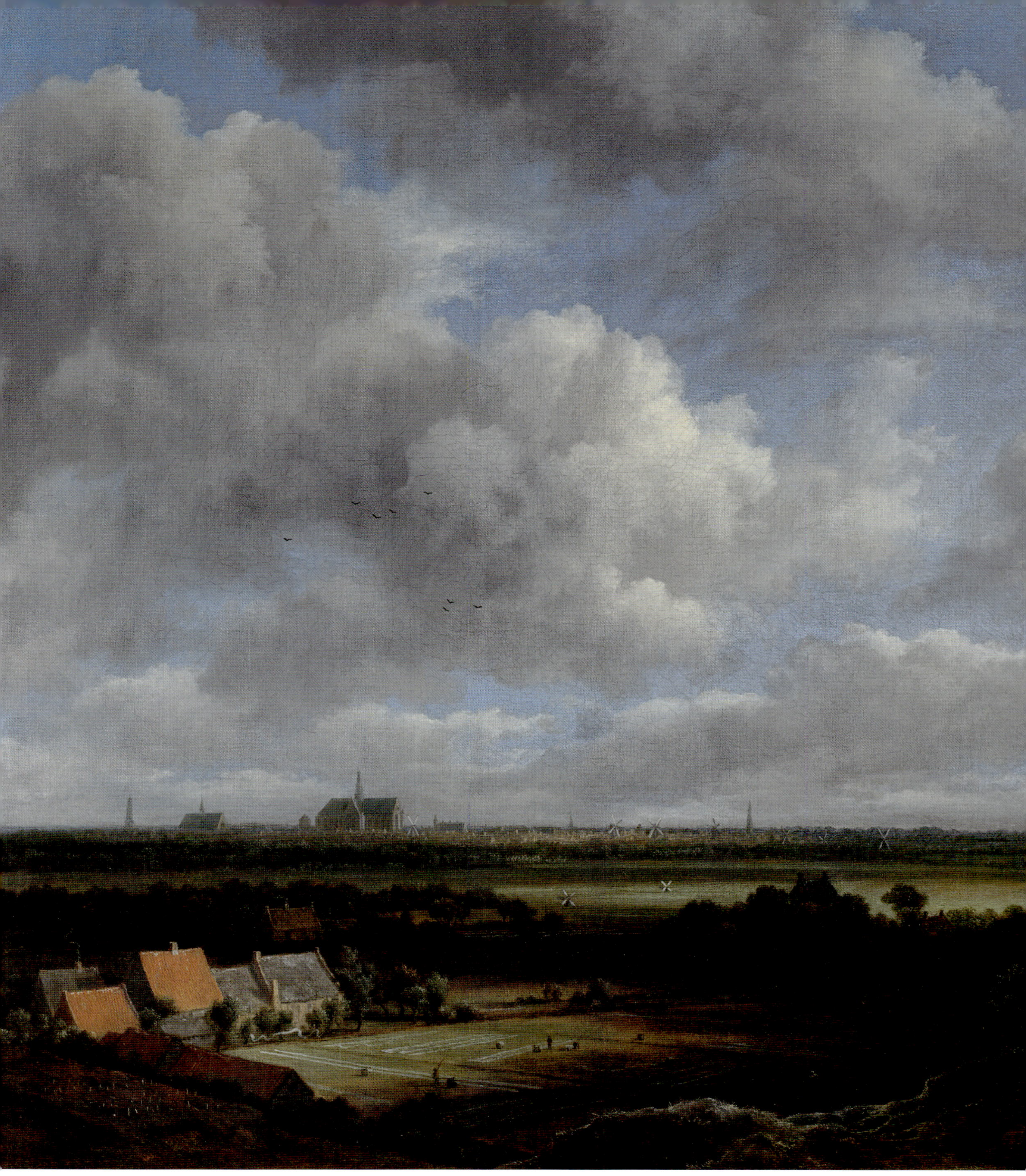

View of Haarlem from the Northwest, with Bleaching Fields in the Foreground, Jacob Isaack van Ruisdael, Rijksmuseum, Amsterdam.

This impressive painting is not as big as you might imagine, it measures 17" × 15". Ruisdael shows great observational skills in the details of the sky.

Ruisdael was born in Haarlem in 1628. He is recognized as one of the most prominent and influential landscape painters of the Dutch Golden Age. It is thought that he had lessons from his father but his uncle, Salomon Ruysdael, was also a well-known painter and no doubt had an influence. It is known that, although Ruisdael was a doctor, he travelled a lot for inspiration and made sketches and drawings to take back home.

CHAPTER 4

Painting the landscape

From all the subjects that an artist can choose to paint, landscape must surely be the most popular. There is such diversity from green pastoral landscapes, to rolling hills and rugged mountains.

Up until about the early to mid sixteenth century, landscape painting was only secondary to the main subject, which could be human or animal. For example, the rich and titled liked to be painted with their land or estate behind them. Horses and cattle were popular subjects as were genre paintings, in other words, scenes from everyday life such as peasants working in the field.

Landscape painting in its own right was not taken more seriously until the seventeenth century when artists such as Rubens, Ruisdael, Gainsborough and Poussin, to name a few, painted landscapes as settings for religious themes. Throughout the eighteenth century, attitudes towards landscape painting continued to change and by the nineteenth century, it was considered one of the most popular genres by artists and collectors. Some people would argue that some of the greatest landscapes ever painted were done throughout the nineteenth century.

One important movement in the development of landscape painting that had in turn been influenced by the Dutch tradition of painting came from France. Theodore Rousseau was the organizer and leader of a group known as The Barbizon School. This group of artists, which included Camille Corot, concentrated on *plein air* painting. By painting directly from nature, unlike previous artists that had just made a few sketches and then taken them back to the studio to paint from these and imagination, the Barbizon artists were concentrating on observing fine details and the changing light and colour of the seasons in order to capture naturalism.

Two of the better-known English artists of the nineteenth century were John Constable and J. M. W. Turner. Turner was a controversial artist at that time but is now regarded as one of the finest landscape artists, as is Constable who painted in a more traditional style but was not recognized as a great painter in his time. In fact, he was more popular in France than England. He studied the paintings of Gainsborough, Claude Lorrain, Rubens and Ruisdael but he was not happy with copying the work of others; he is quoted as saying:

For the last two years I have been running after pictures, and seeking the truth at second hand... I have not endeavoured to represent nature with the same elevation of mind with which I set out, but have rather tried to make my performances look like the work of other men... There is room enough for a natural painter. The great vice of the present day is bravura, an attempt to do something beyond the truth.

At the same time that Turner and Constable were working in England, John Crome and John Sell Cotman founded the Norwich School of Painters in 1803. Here was a group of artists that liked to paint outdoors and would paint rural and coastal scenes around the county of Norfolk.

Later in the century, in 1884, the Newlyn School was founded. Reminiscent of the Barbizon School where artists

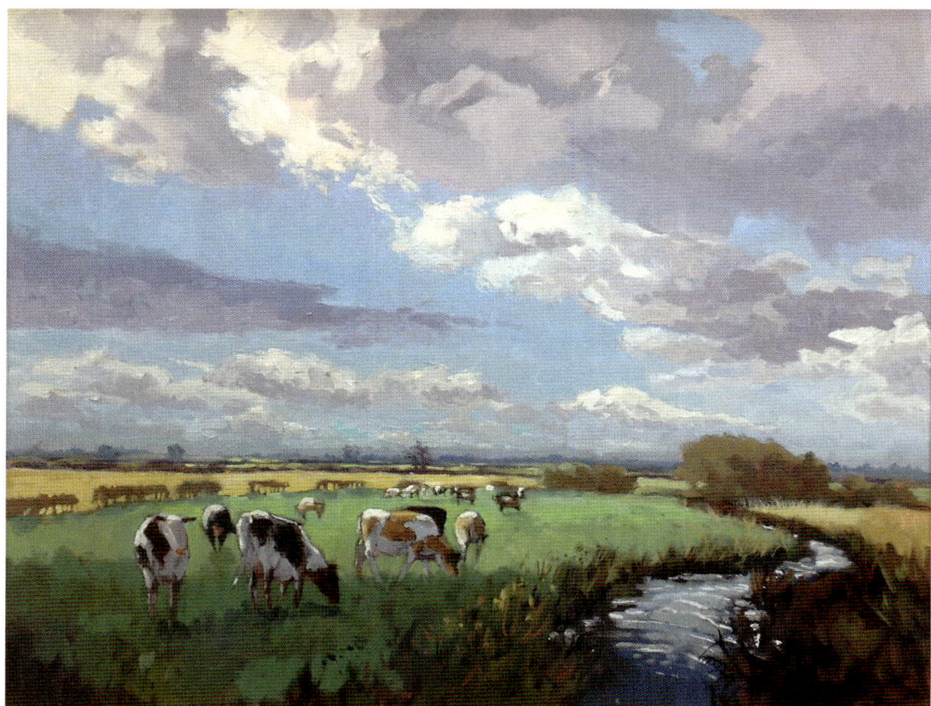

Summer Meadow
Titanium White
Yellow Ochre
Burnt Umber
Permanent Rose
Ultramarine Blue
Stretched linen canvas
Yellow Ochre ground

This large studio painting is made up from sketches and photographs. I had a photograph of the sky that I wanted to paint on a large scale but I needed the foreground to go with it. Not an easy task because the light had to be in the right place. If you look at the clouds in the picture, you can see that the sun is shining from the left which means that the foreground had to reflect this. It would have looked rather odd if the cows had been lit from the right. Cloud shadow at the front has a twofold purpose. Firstly, it adds weight to the foreground and secondly, it serves to give a contrast to the light of the sky reflecting in the water. This painting is a good example of perspective in the sky. The clouds at the front are much larger and decrease in size towards the horizon.

wanted to paint the light, this was a group of artists based and working in Cornwall, of which the best known is probably Stanhope Forbes. This colony of artists specialized in landscape, rural and fishing scenes.

In France, another group known as the Impressionists had emerged. This group probably had the greatest influence on artists of today. The name itself came from the title of one of Monet's paintings *Impression, Soleil Levant*, which translated means *Impression, Sunrise*. This group that was based in Paris was facing criticism from the more traditional artists in France. Their style was quite different to anything else that had been painted before; breaking the rules of traditional painting, their free brush strokes replaced lines and contours. Their short strokes of thick paint captured the essence of the subject rather than concentrating on detail. Colours were applied side by side, giving stronger, brighter colours that were mixed optically by the viewer. They rarely used black, preferring to mix their greys with complimentary colours, giving a much livelier effect. The Impressionists often painted outside, as they liked to pay close attention to natural light. Shadows were painted blue from the reflection of the sky. This gave such a feeling of freshness not seen before in landscape paintings. They found that by using pure, unmixed colour, they could capture the transient light of the sun.

By this time too there was a wide range of synthetic colours available commercially and the Impressionists took full advantage of them. Colours such as Cobalt Blue, Viridian, Cadmium Yellow, Ultramarine and Cerulean added a lot more vibrancy to the artist's palette. Following on from this came Post Impressionism, although this phase didn't last for long. This was a phase of modern art when artists tried to reach beyond the limiting imitative style of the Impressionists by distorting and emphasizing form for dramatic effect. Artists in this movement included Claude Monet, Paul Cezanne and George Seurat.

We are lucky to have so much information and access to pictures over time. Although movements have come and gone, and although some may have been ridiculed at the time, we are able to see the great leaps artists have made and to learn from them.

All these different styles have had – and still do have – a great influence on today's artists.

ARTIST PROFILE

John Stillman

John was born in Carshalton, Surrey, in 1968. He is a member of the Wapping Group of Artists. He is completely self-taught and has been drawing and painting ever since he can remember. John has worked as an illustrator for books and as a graphic artist in advertising in London. He now paints full time as a professional artist. The many subjects John paints are landscapes and scenes of Surrey through to marine subjects concentrating on light and atmosphere.

For Evening on the Solent, *I started by mixing a warm base colour using Titanium White, Cadmium Yellow and Burnt Sienna with some Gel Medium mixed in to advance the drying time. I then mixed some Cobalt Blue and Alizarin Crimson into the top left of the sky, keeping the paint mix very wet to allow it to all blend together. Then I added a wash of Lemon Yellow Hue and a touch of Cerulean Blue into the top right of the painting, you can see the two base colours at the top of the painting as well as the tone of the board showing through. By using a cloth to 'wipe out' the wet paint, I could create the shafts of light coming down from between the clouds. Where the sun was shining through the clouds, I kept the areas dark in tone as I knew as soon as I applied the highlights to this area, the 'counterchange' of the dark cloud against the sunlight behind would give me the effect I was looking for. Then a thick mix of Lemon Yellow Hue and Titanium White was used to define the sunlight behind the clouds. I added some Cadmium Orange to the paint mix and indicated the distant orange clouds as well as painting the orange horizon in. The tanker and factory were all painted in back at the studio. By painting the tanker in the foreground within the shadowed area, I made this a good example of 'counterchange' with the dark tanker against the light of the horizon. With the tanker and the factory added, the scene had distance to it. By having both these elements in the picture, it also gave a sense of scale to the size of the sky.*

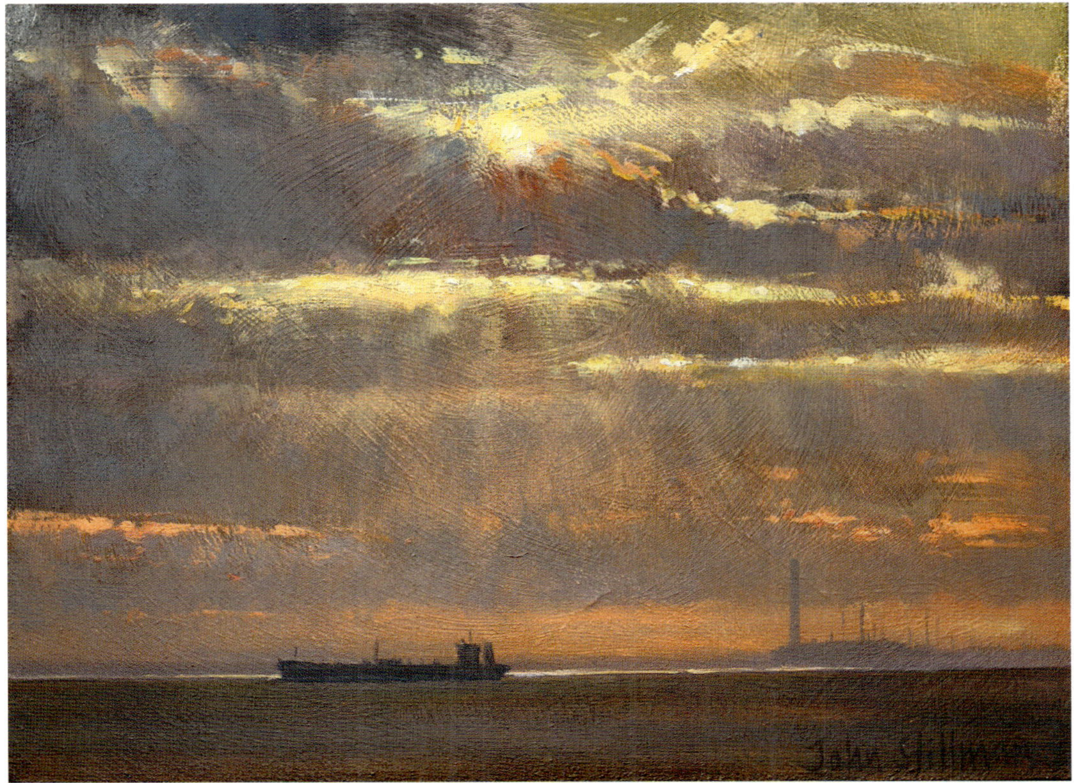

Evening on the Solent, John Stillman. 6" × 8". Oil on board.

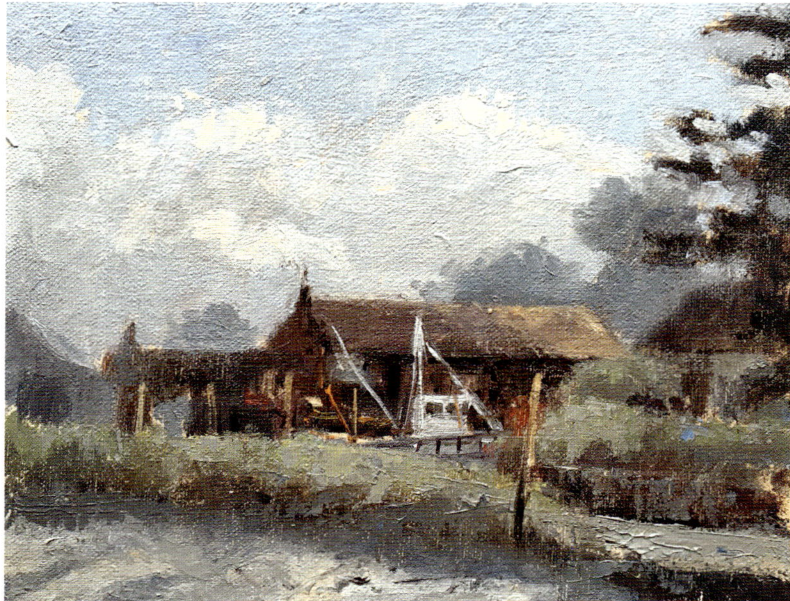

Brancaster Staithe, Summer
Titanium White
Yellow Ochre
Burnt Sienna
Ultramarine Blue
8" × 10" Linen on card
Burnt Sienna ground

The afternoon clouds are slightly understated in this picture as the focus is on the fishermen's huts but they still play an important part in creating the atmosphere of the day. The very limited palette creates a good harmony in the painting.

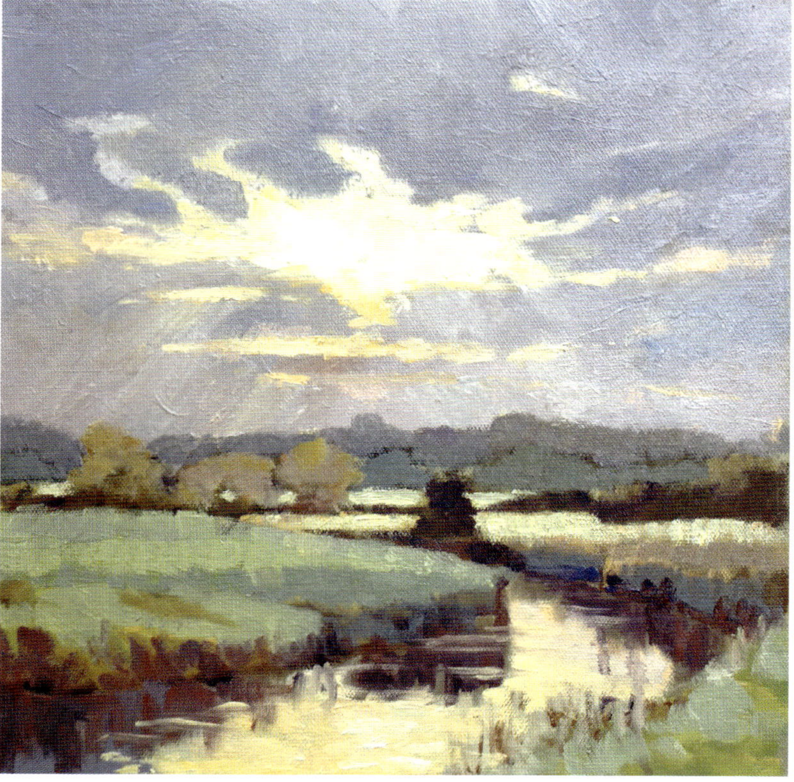

Afternoon Sun Reflections, Cley, 12" × 12". Canvas board.
The reflection of the sun in the water perfectly balances the light in the sky whilst the river leads us into the picture. The dark tree just off centre serves as a contrast against the sunlit fields behind it, making it a focal point. The greens have been played down so as not to be too bright and to harmonise with the other colours in the painting.

It is fascinating to walk around an art gallery and to see the world through another artist's eyes. The style and interpretation can vary so much from one artist to another. As landscape artists, we have to battle with all the challenges that nature throws at us, like the changing light, and blustery skies. Each element brings its own problems and challenges.

PAINTING THE SKY

Painting Techniques

Probably one of the most important elements in painting a landscape will be the sky.

The sky will establish the mood and atmosphere of the whole painting.

One of the most common mistakes beginners make when painting the sky is not placing the paint onto the canvas, but spreading it almost as if they were painting the cupboard.

There are several disadvantages in this approach, one is that the sky looks very smooth and uninteresting but also, it may not match the foreground where perhaps a different approach has been used. By using different brush marks to paint foreground and by adding fine details, it can result in the painting looking as if it is in two halves. Another disadvantage of over spreading your paint is that it results in the paint being applied too thinly. Correctly loading the brush with the right amount of paint is very important.

Try to make sure you mix enough paint; a common problem is not mixing enough. Unless you are really familiar and experienced with your colours, it could be hard to replicate the original colour. If you do start to run out then mix more, don't try to scrape around, trying to spread it out.

How we hold our brushes makes a difference to the way the paint is applied. If you hold your brush too close to the ferrule (the metal part) you will not have the fluidity that you have by being able to use your whole arm as when you hold your brush at the end. Over blending, applying too much pressure, angle of the brush are also common errors.

An overcast sky will mean a landscape devoid of strong shadows; this does not mean that the painting will be uninteresting as shown in Peter Barker's painting *January Fog*.

Grounds

Before starting a painting, whether it is a landscape or a still life, you will need to prepare your canvas or board by giving it a 'ground'.

So what is a ground? A ground is simply the flat colour that has been applied to the canvas.

You may wish to experiment with different coloured grounds.

Why apply a ground?

All pre-stretched canvases are primed with white gesso, giving us a white ground that is ready to paint on. In oil painting, white is our highlight colour, the lightest colour we put on last to give our painting that pop.

If we start by painting on a white surface, it is difficult to judge our tones as, even a light colour will look darker on white. We generally start a painting with thinner paint and it would take several layers to prevent the white shining through which could lead to possible wrong colour choices. The answer is to lose the white by applying a flat layer of

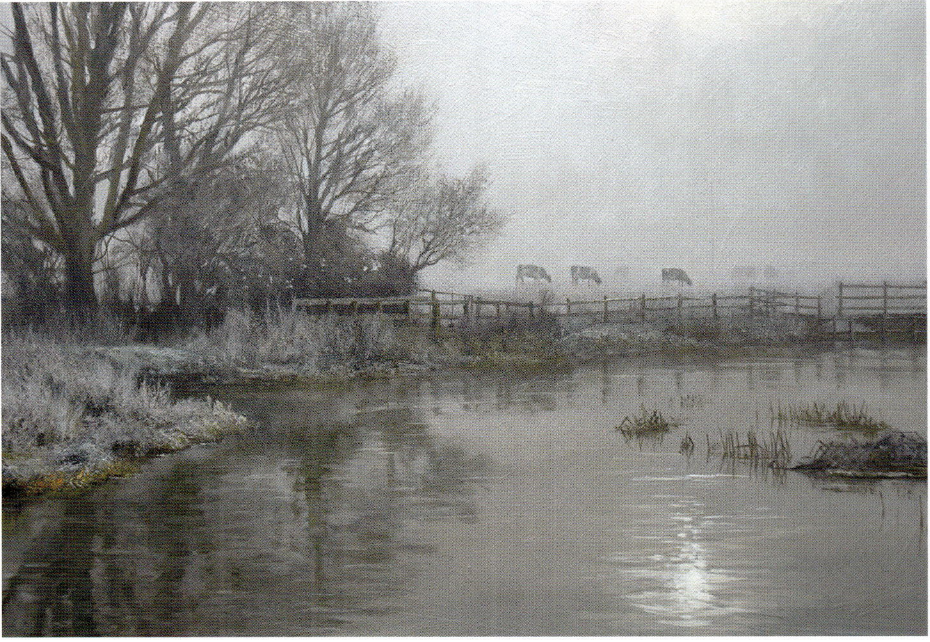

January Fog, Peter Barker.
This painting is a fine example of how you do not always need to have a bright sunny day to paint a picture. With subtle tones and contrasts, Peter has created a very harmonious painting. The sun, which is just out of sight in the sky, is reflected in the water, giving a lovely highlight in the painting.

paint, our ground, over the white canvas. This base colour must be allowed to dry fully before you start to paint. The new colour will help us to better see the true colour and tone of our paint, as it is not competing against the glaring white.

What colour ground to choose?

A complimentary colour can work well as it can give a perceived intensity and saturation to your colours. For example, a green field would look brighter and more intense with a red background. This is an extreme example, most artists stick to a neutral ground colour for all their paintings, regardless of their subject or the colours they are using.

For sky and landscape paintings, good colours to use would be earth tones and Ochres. When flecks of colour are allowed to show through the finished painting, it helps to give a unity to the whole painting.

In the painting *Morston Church*, you can see how the Burnt Sienna ground shows through and helps to unify the painting.

Graduating colours

Having prepared our canvas and let it dry we now need to practice one of, if not the most important aspects of painting the sky – graduating colours. This means blending colour smoothly so that the transition point between colours is not evident. We saw in Chapter 2 how the sky above is a much darker blue and gets paler towards the horizon. This is true of most skies, whatever the time of day, and by mastering the effect in our painting, we are able to paint a more convincing sky.

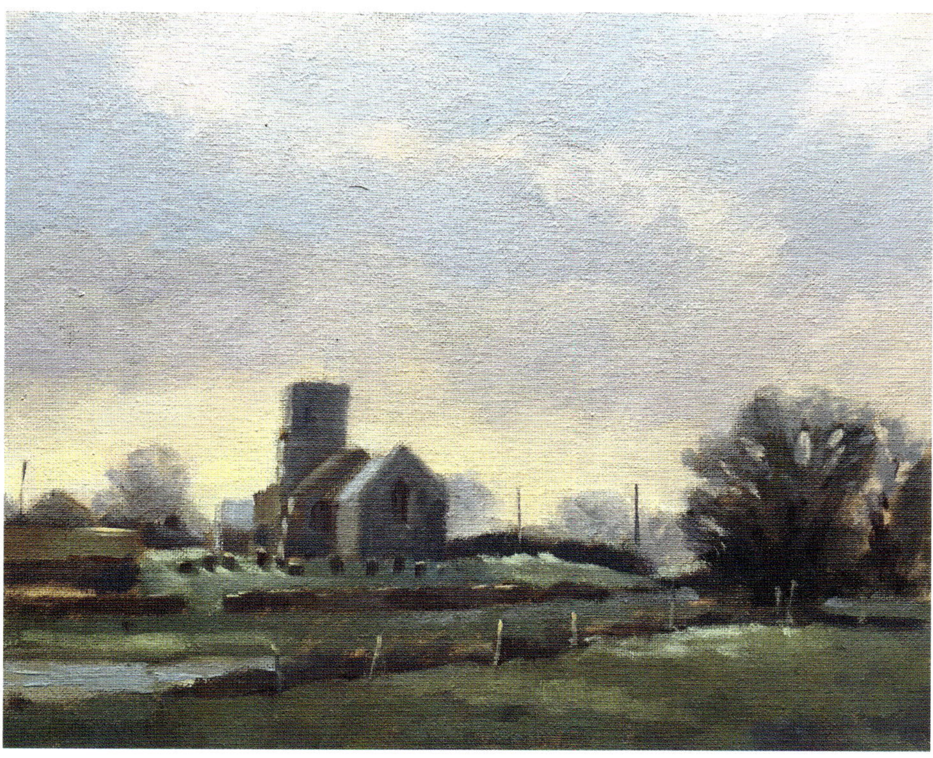

Morston Church
Titanium White
Cadmium Yellow
Burnt Umber
Permanent Rose
Kings Blue Light
10" × 12" Gessoed canvas board
Burnt Sienna ground

Not quite a sunset but the end of a very cold day painting at Morston in Norfolk. The sun was sinking fast, giving some lovely soft pinks in the sky. The church and the trees are dark as they are *contre-jour*, which basically means 'against the light'.

This subject makes for a good composition. The horizon is a third of the way down, reducing the foreground and making it more about the sky. The church is off centre and the shape of the church is balanced by the tree on the right, which, in turn, acts as a stop for the eye, preventing it going out of the picture. The diagonal line of cloud in the sky mirrors the diagonal line of the road, leading us around the picture. The telegraph poles register dark against the light sky and the fence posts are registering light against the darker green of the roadside, acting as punctuation marks, breaking up the straight lines.

The warm Burnt Sienna ground showing through serves to give a unity and warmth to the greens.

Of course, not all gradations are a perfectly smooth change. However, if you can master the skill of this valuable exercise, you will be able to adapt it to the subject in front of you.

There are many different blues that you can use for the sky, most will need slightly modifying and not used straight from the tube, as they could prove to be too vivid.

Blending from dark to light in one colour is comparatively easy. The tricky part is introducing other colours. To move through three or four shades and hues smoothly can be slightly more complex. If you want to apply pure white, you will need to clean your brush thoroughly, *before* you add any paint to your brush. Any remaining colour in your brush will taint your white.

There can be a lot of yellow in some skies, adding it to blue can be tricky, as we all know that yellow and blue make green. Here is where working from blue through red to yellow will help. Selecting the right yellow is not always easy. Lemon Yellow, for example, will very quickly become green if anywhere near blue. Yellow Ochre is subtler and is often used with blue in small amounts to alter the hue.

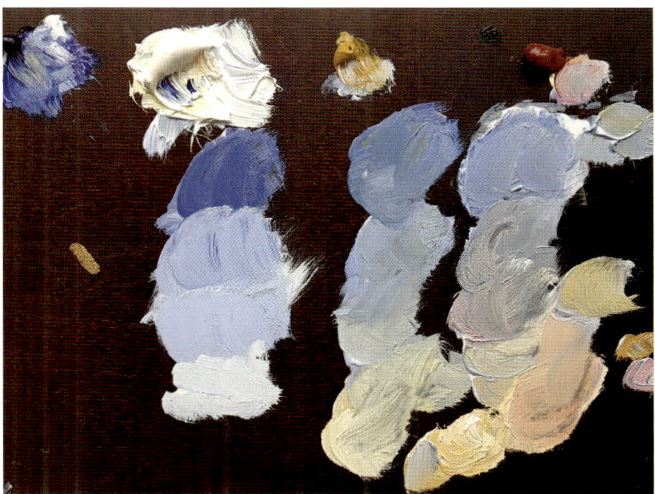

An exercise well worth practising is to prepare a piece of scrap card or board with gesso. Start at the top with a darker colour and gradually work down the board, gradually introducing white until you have a very pale version of your starting colour at the bottom. This is a technique that is very useful to practise when painting skies. If there is a strong light on the horizon, you will find it useful to create good contrasts between the light tone of the sky and the darker tone of your horizon features.

Grad 1. In this exercise I have chosen Ultramarine. Start by taking a little white paint and add the blue gradually until you can add the tone you require. If the paint has a strong pigment, you will very quickly overstep the tone you need. By starting with white you will use less paint. Starting with neat blue means you would be using a lot of white to obtain the right tone as Ultramarine is a strong colour. Ifa particularly dark sky is desired, you could try starting with the blue.

Grad 2. Try this exercise on differing sizes of board. Gradations over varying sizes will test your skill.

Experiment by using different blues and seeing which colours you can use to change the hue. Yellow Ochre, Cadmium Red and Umber are useful colours to add to blue.

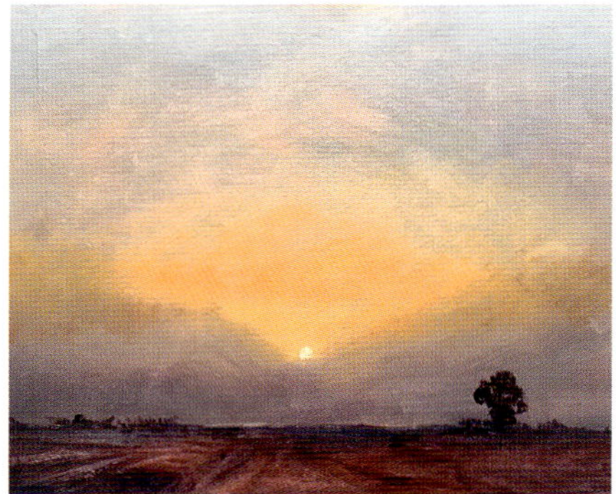

Sun Rise – Graduated Colours.
This is an example of a graduated sky using several colours. The sun was rising up through the atmospheric layers that had turned a wonderful purple colour. The top of the painting shows a much clearer sky with the gradual introduction of warm pinks and yellows.

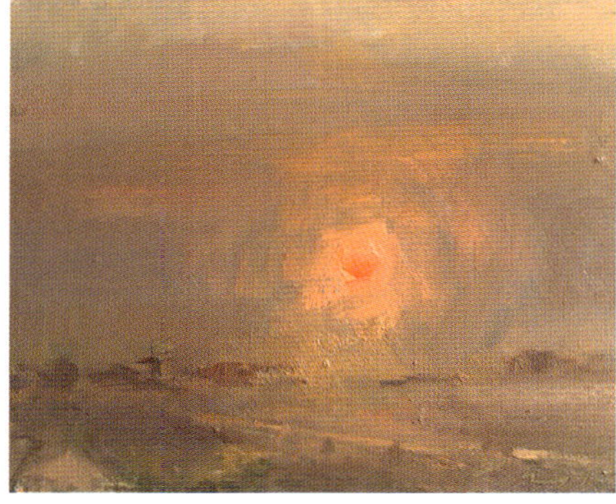

Fog in the Morning, Red Sun, Roos Schuring.
Another example of graduating colours is in this painting by Roos. The colours blend seamlessly together but are then overpainted with subtle orange hues, which carry the colour of the sun through the painting.

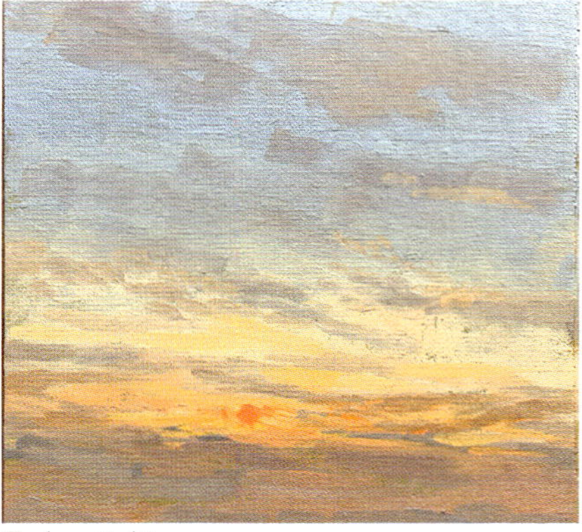

Dark on Light.
This is another example of how tones can look altered on a different background. The clouds at the top of the painting are the same colour as was used for the dark clouds at the bottom. The colours used for this were:
Old Holland Grey Blue
Flesh Tint
Cadmium Orange
Warm Light Yellow
Brilliant Pink.

Often when we look at the sky, we perceive grey clouds as being different tones of grey. The cloud at the top of the sky where the sky behind is darker will look lighter than the cloud at the lower level where the sky behind is lighter. If you look at them through a colour isolator (a piece of paper with a small hole will do) you will see that they are often the same tone.

Grey on Blue 1.
In this exercise, the background sky was painted first. The clouds were then painted over the graduated colour using just Greyish Blue 2 with no mixing.

You can see that the cloud at the top of the sky does not stand out against the darker colour behind it as well as the cloud at eye level. In the second diagram, colour that was mixed for the lighter area of sky is now used to define the shape of the clouds.

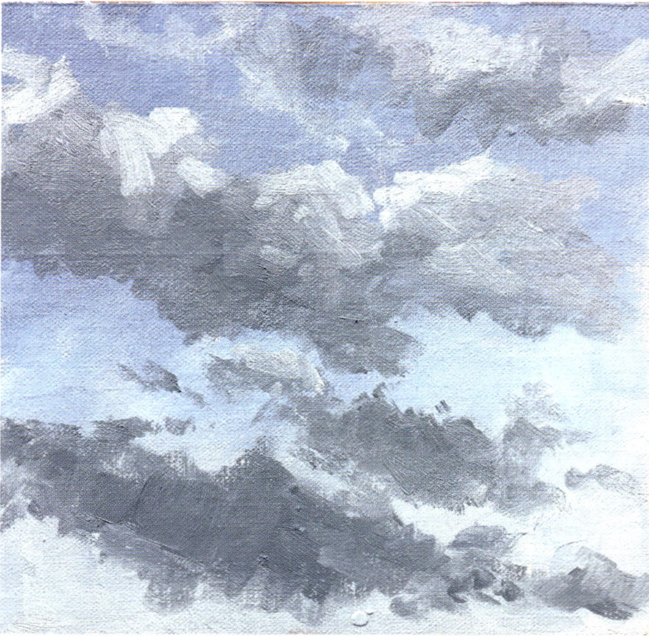

Grey on Blue 2.

ARTIST PROFILE

Louise Balaam

My way of working is to draw/make studies outside, and then paint in the studio. I draw using a range of media – watercolour, gouache, oil sticks, oil pastels, graphite, ink, charcoal and so on. I'm aiming to capture the aspects of the landscape which I find interesting and exciting – the quality of the light, the tonal pattern of the clouds, the colour relationships between the land and sky – and I'll usually do a range of studies using different media. I prefer painting in the studio, not plein air, *because I like to allow imagination and memory to come into play in the making of the painting. I don't work directly from my drawings, as I find there is a tendency to copy, and then all spontaneity and excitement is lost. The making of the drawings is critically important, however, because the experience of sitting and drawing in the landscape gives me a real feeling for the characteristics of that particular place, and that will (hopefully!) find its way into the final painting. I use oil paint (because I love the depth of colour it gives), using a 50/50 linseed oil/turps mixture as a medium, and try to paint intuitively and gesturally. Generally my paintings are made* alla prima, *in one shot, which I feel is important to keep a sense of freshness and liveliness over the whole surface. I'm trying to create some equivalent for my feelings about the landscape, one which hopefully will evoke a response in those looking at the painting.*

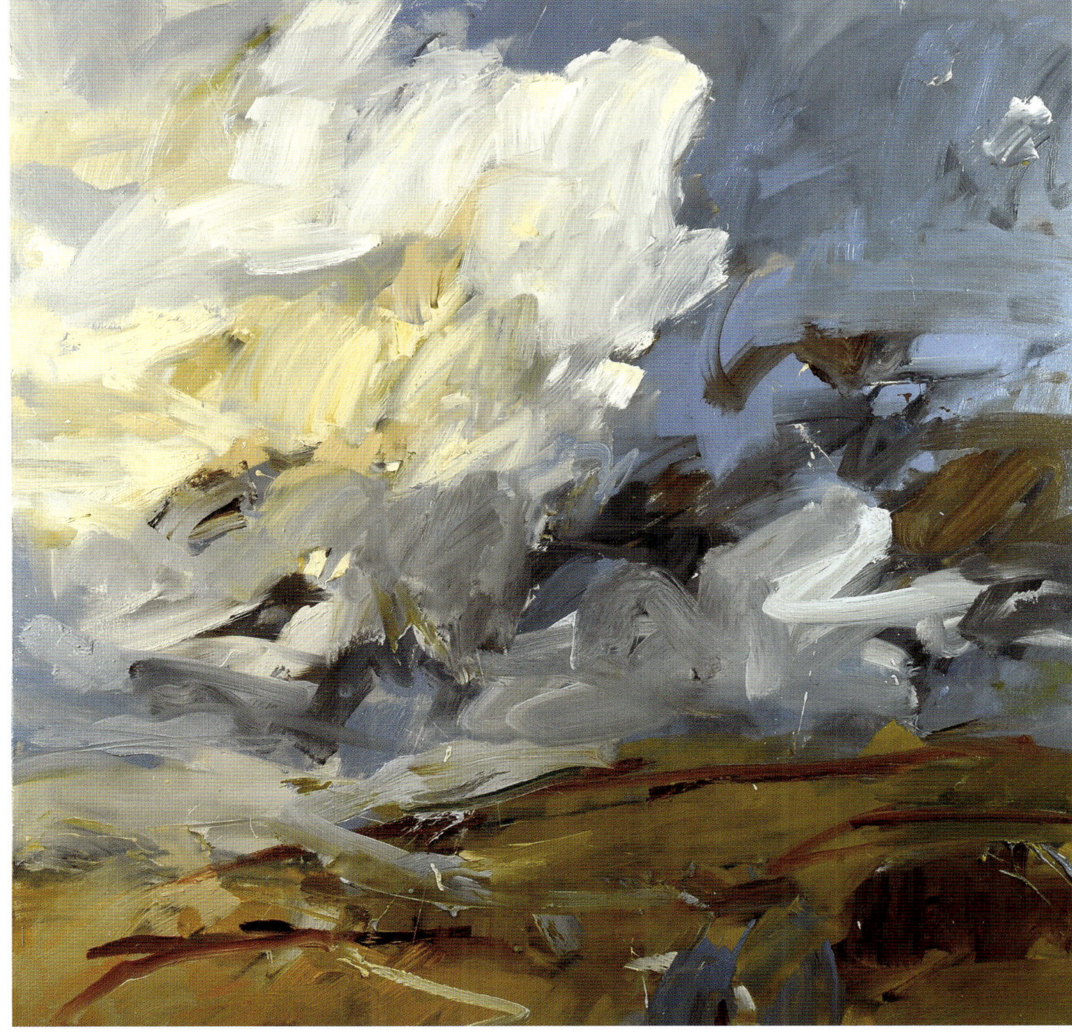

Turf Underfoot, Huge Sky, Louise Balaam. The emphasis here is on the sky. In this wonderfully loose painting, Louise has used the same colours throughout the painting to unify the composition. The 'pop' here are the light-coloured, loose brush strokes against the darkest area of sky. (Photo: John Caruana)

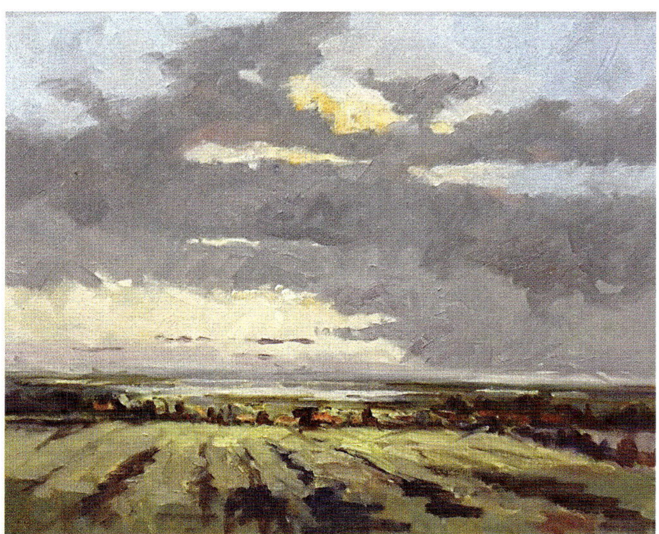

Brancaster Common
Titanium White
Yellow Ochre
Cadmium Yellow
Burnt Sienna
Cadmium Red
Cobalt Blue
Ultramarine Blue
14" × 18" canvas board
Burnt Sienna ground

At the end of a day painting with friends, we drove up to Brancaster Common. The light was flat and the clouds were heavy. As we were deciding what to do next, the sun broke through and lit up the landscape. There was no further discussion, never have I seen easels put up so quickly.

This painting was painted back in the studio from two studies made on the day at Brancaster Common. I set myself a time limit for this painting as I wanted to keep the freshness and urgency that one has when painting on the spot. I worked quickly, trying to recreate the feeling and excitement of the moment.

The darks were laid in first with French Ultramarine/Burnt Sienna. I had a sketch of the cloud formation, which I put in first with Cobalt Blue/Cadmium Red and Titanium White. I varied this mix to portray deeper shadows and to give form to the clouds. The sky colour was painted in between the clouds. This enabled me to paint into the cloud shapes to give more varied edges.

As the sky lightened towards the horizon, Cadmium Yellow/Yellow Ochre/ Titanium White were added to the mix and on the horizon. Just above the sea level there was a pinkish glow, which I put in using a paler version of the clouds.

The greens in the picture were mainly made up with Cadmium Blue/ Yellow Ochre and Cobalt Blue/Cadmium Yellow. Note how thin bands of green and strips of water on the marshes suggest to the eye a feeling of space and distance.

To give the suggestion of cloud shadows, the foreground was kept dark, as were the rooftops on each side of the picture. The dark lines in the field give a good feeling of perspective to lead us into the picture and to the sun-lit area where Cadmium Yellow was added to Burnt Sienna for the rooftops. The cloud shadows over the marshes add interest.

In the middle distance, some houses were left in shadow and towards the centre, they were illuminated by the sun.

Selecting the subject

It is important when reaching our painting location that we look for the best viewpoints. Often, there are so many potential subjects that it is hard to focus on any one. A few minutes walking around, familiarizing ourselves with the environment will pay dividends. You never know what may be just around the corner. Look for less obvious subjects. Maybe the corner of a field or garden would make a good composition, better than the wider panorama. By moving around, you will see your subject from different angles and see the different ways the perspective changes.

On a cloudy day, sometimes it is worth just observing the scene for a while to take in the shifting light. The painting *Brancaster Common* is one such occasion where this paid off.

Using a viewfinder

Until you have gained a bit of experience in painting outside it is advisable, however beautiful a vast panorama may look, not to go for the bigger picture. Painting the whole scene in front of you is technically challenging, as you have to consider so many different elements such as recession of colours, impression of depth and distance whilst still creating a focal point. So it is advisable to look for the smaller subject by cropping with the viewfinder.

Finding our subject and homing in on it is when the use of a viewfinder comes into its own. The viewfinder will help you focus on a particular part of the scene, enabling you to decide on the best format and composition at the same time it will isolate it from the rest of the scene, giving you less distraction. Look for a focal point or points of interest.

Hold the viewfinder in front of you and move it backwards and forwards, also move to the left and to the right. By holding the viewfinder closer, you will see more of the subject in front of you and by moving it away you will reduce and crop the amount you see.

Consider also turning the viewfinder on its side to give a portrait format, this can give some very pleasing results.

Try to find a subject that pleases you or excites you, and ask yourself, what is it about the subject that has attracted you, is it the play of light, the colours, the composition or maybe a combination of all three? Really squint at your subject, this will help you to see the values. Really look hard at the scene in

Tip: have a selection of shapes and sizes of viewfinder handy. Sometimes a square format can work very well. Make sure the format of your viewfinder matches the shape of your canvas or board.

Moulton After the Rain. There are a lot of strong tonal contrasts in this painting. The ridges in the field provide a good foil for the cloud reflections. Another example of good use of tonal contrast is the painting by John Stillman of the Millennium Bridge. Here, the contrast is not as strong but is equally effective, drawing us in to the boat in the centre.

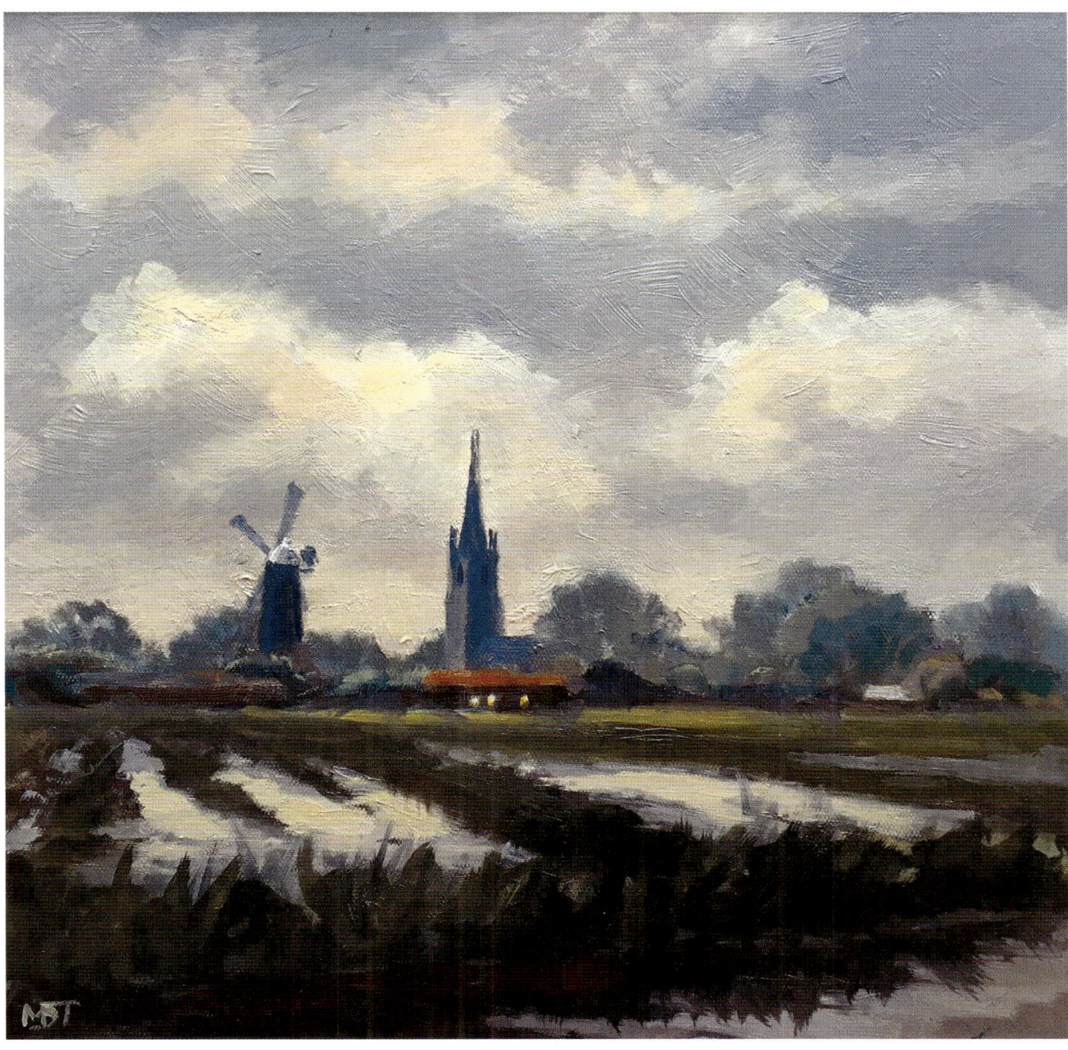

front of you – looking at your subject is as important as looking at your painting. The more you look, the more you will see.

Tonal value

Tonal value and contrasts are extremely important in a painting. Tones are simply the light and dark areas of a painting and the strongest contrasts appear where the darkest tones are adjacent to the lightest tones. The stronger the difference in tones, the greater the contrast and therefore the greater the impact.

It takes a good deal of practice to judge tonal values and a lot of practice to apply them. Always consider which is the darkest point and the lightest point and judge your tones in between. One surface will always be lighter or darker next to another.

Remember that bright light will cast deep shadows but when the weather is overcast then the tones will be a lot closer in value.

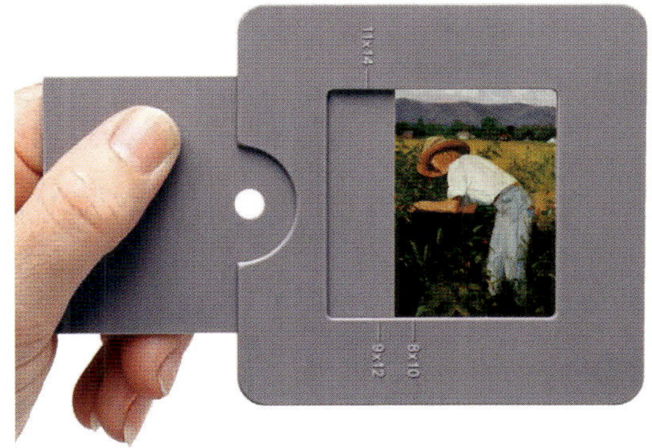

This viewfinder from the SAA is one of many available on the market. The slider can be moved in and out to match the proportions of your canvas. This one also has a small hole, which is very useful to look through to isolate a colour. It is not always easy to judge a colour or even a tone when it is next to other colours.

ARTIST PROFILE

John Stillman

I am very proud to be a member of the Wapping Group of Artists and this picture was painted on one of our Wednesday meetings along the Thames. I painted this using my 8″ × 10″ pochade box and as the lid of the box allows me to carry three 8″ × 10″ panels, I always have a selection of pre-prepared coloured panels to choose from. It is good to have a selection with you as it does save some time when applying a base colour. One other important aid I carry with me is a viewfinder called a View Catcher to help me select and frame my subject. It will save you time in selecting your subject and open your eyes to all sorts of potential paintings.

On this occasion, the base colour of the panel was the background blue you can see in the sky, which was a mix of Cobalt Blue and Titanium White. I then mixed a 'warm grey' to indicate the darker clouds. I used my finger to soften the edges of the clouds, making sure I cleaned the paint from my finger with a clean piece of cloth so that the blending did not transfer any unnecessary paint to the painting. It is good practice to do this when a base colour is already applied to the board as you can control the soft and sharp edges of the clouds against the background colour. In applying paint like this on a dry base colour, it allows you to achieve a 'broken brush' stroke effect to the edges of the clouds and lets the base colour show through, which all adds to the shape and depth of the clouds. I then took a no. 4 rigger to add the highlights of the clouds and the light effect on the water. Try not to get too carried away when using a rigger to apply your highlights as you do not want to overwork the highlighted areas – keep it simple! Again I used my finger to soften some of the highlights so the clouds did not look too hard edged. It's good to have a balance of soft and hard edges when painting clouds because the more you do this, the more experienced you will become at knowing when to leave certain areas alone. The next stage of the painting was to indicate the bridges and foreshore. As the sky was still wet, I simply indicated the main pillar of the Millennium Bridge and made two marks either side of the painting as to the height of the walkway across the Thames. To draw the straight lines of the bridges, I used the edge of an 8″ × 10″ panel to draw a straight line with a no. 4 rigger brush to indicate the distant bridge and the wooden breakers in the foreground. The boat, figures and any additional highlights were all added back at the studio the next day.

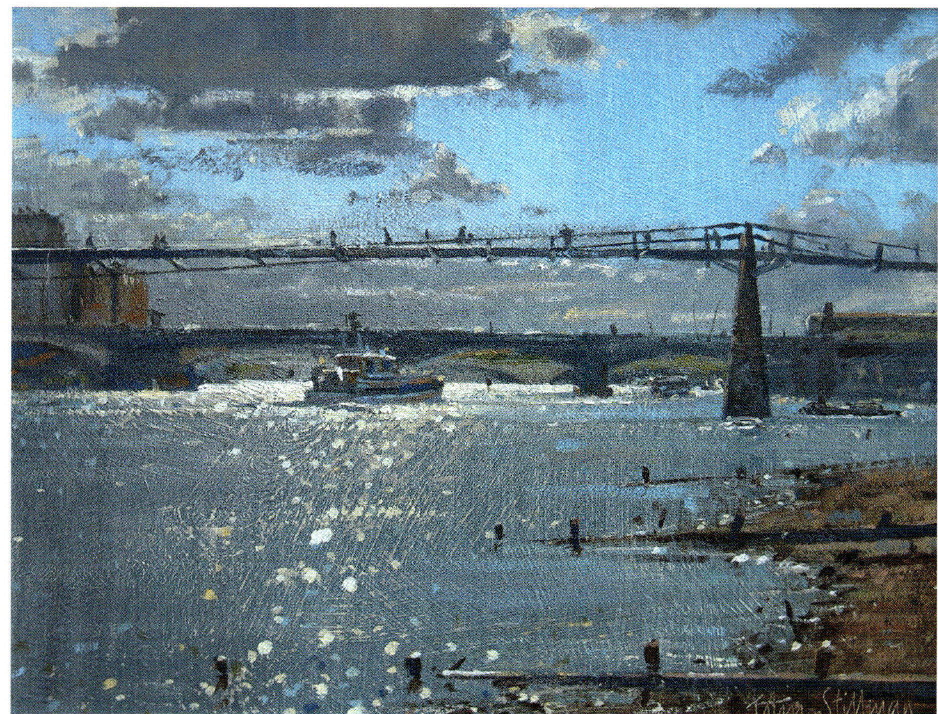

The Millennium Bridge, London, John Stillman. 8" × 10". Oil on board.

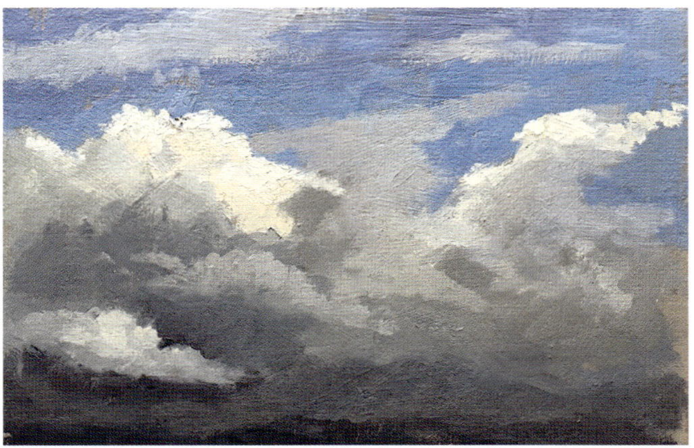

Storm Coming.
This cloud study shows various layers in the clouds. The background has light clouds in the upper level whilst in the mid level, cumulus clouds are building up for a storm. There are a lot of subtle colour and tonal changes in this painting.

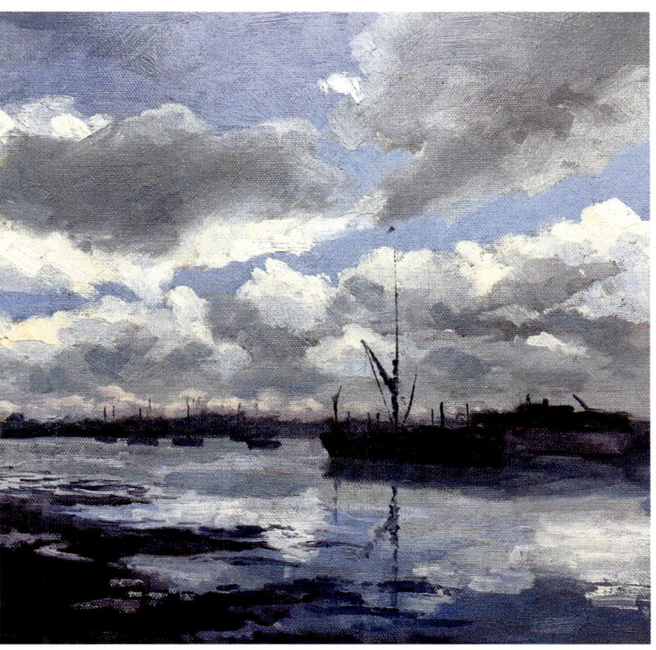

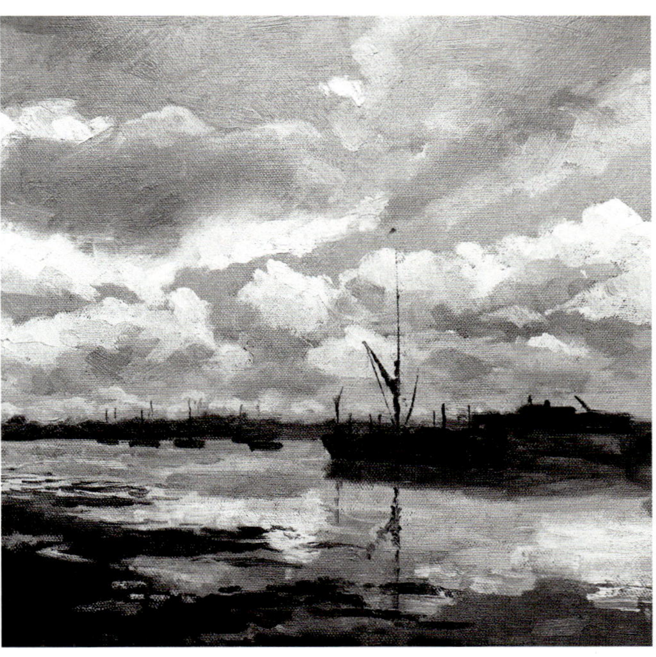

By converting a painting to grey scale as in the painting of Pin Mill, it is easy to see the different tones in a painting. A painting that does not have these tonal differences would have no contrasts in it.

Tone

We're comfortable with the idea that there are different 'intensities' of grey, from very dark (almost black) to very pale indeed. In fact, we have all seen photos in newspapers that are completely in shades of grey. So, how do the photos or paintings done in grey shades (or monochrome) manage to give a convincing feel of depth and form? The answer is in the use of different tones. Tone is vitally important in painting; this can be well illustrated when a photograph of the painting is reproduced in black and white. A subject with no tonal contrast will lose a lot of detail and impact. All too often a beginner will adjust the colour rather than the tone, resulting in a flat looking painting. The best way to resolve the problem of seeing colour in tones is to squint through your eyes. Squinting makes it easier to simplify large areas and see which fall into light, half tones and shadows.

A good test to see if your painting has good tonal values is easy to do on a computer. Firstly scan the picture and create two copies of it. Then, using photo editing software, convert one copy into a greyscale version and compare the full colour version and greyscale side by side. If you find that definition is lost in the greyscale version then chances are that the tonal values are not correct.

Using only one colour, if tone is used correctly, may produce a successful painting.

Most subjects can be brought down to three main tones: the light tones, the mid tones and the dark tones.

The focal point of the painting is the point where you should aim to create the greatest tonal contrast, as this will draw the eye to it. In *End of the Day, Morston*, our eye is taken to the standing figure as it is the lightest point against the dark of the landing stage poles.

Waiting for Customers is the same subject as before but this shows what a different palette can make to a painting. The eye is still drawn to the figure in yellow but in this painting, we have the impression of a warmer, sunnier day with the sky being painted in hues of yellow and pink.

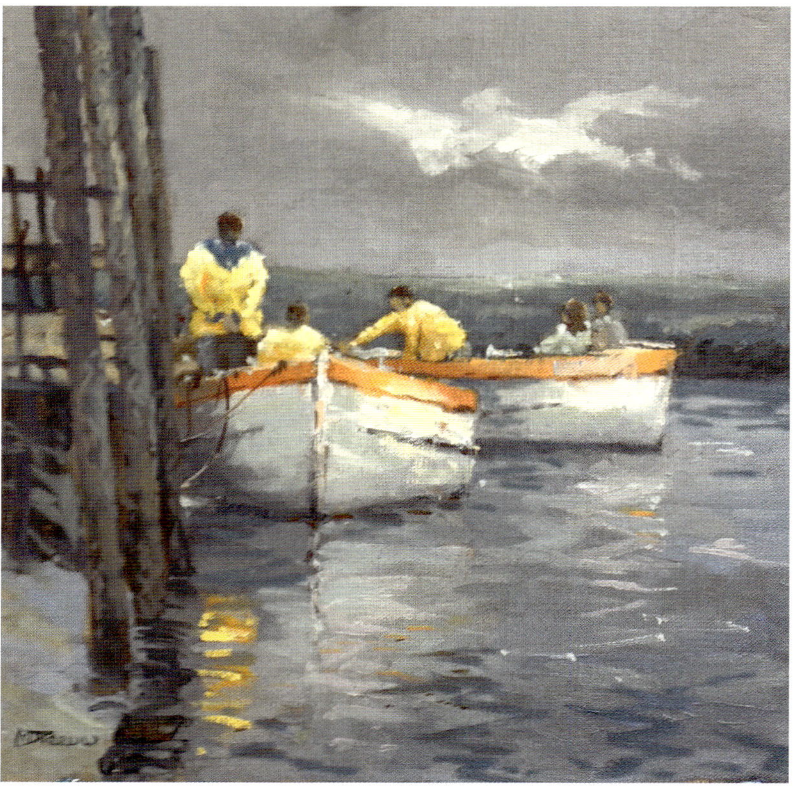

End of the Day, Morston
Warm White
Cadmium Yellow
Burnt Umber
Cadmium Orange
Cadmium Red
Cobalt Blue
12" × 12" Canvas board
Burnt Sienna ground

Even on a grey day, when the tide is up, there are trips to see the sea lions out at Blakeney Point from Morston Quay. There is a harmony of greys in this painting punctuated by the bright yellow of the boatmen's coats and white of the boats. The light in the sky, where there is a break in the clouds, echoes the light colour of the boats. This is further reflected in the water pulling the painting together. The strong, dark verticals of the landing stage posts are offset by the brightness of the yellow coats. It was important to keep the post outlines soft as too hard an edge would have made them stand out in the painting.

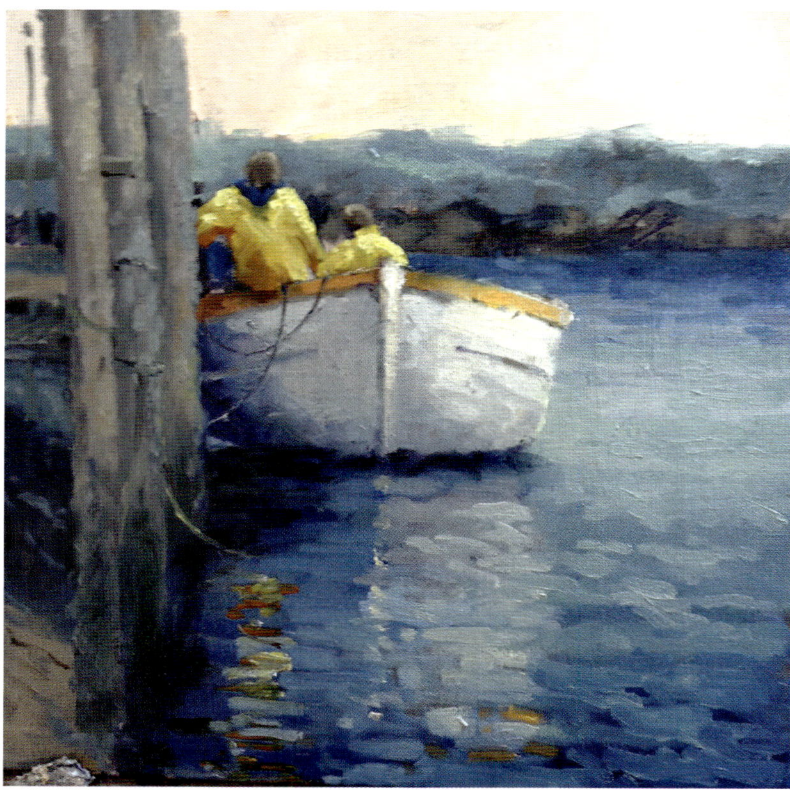

Waiting for Customers
Titanium White
Cadmium Yellow
Ultramarine Blue
Cadmium Red
10" × 10" Canvas board
Yellow Ochre ground

This was painted from a photo reference that I took on the same day that I painted 'at the end of the day'. The first painting echoed the greyness of the day and I wanted to try out a different palette. To do this, I converted the photograph into a black and white image on the computer so I would not be influenced by the colours that I saw.

To set the atmosphere of the picture, I painted the sky using Titanium White/Cadmium Yellow/Cadmium Red. The marsh was painted next with Ultramarine Blue/Cadmium Yellow/Titanium White. I wanted the water to be blue as a complimentary colour to the yellow of the boatman's coat. The dark blue was laid in first and then successive layers getting lighter with more yellow and white were added. The reflections were put in after I had painted the boat and the figures. It was important to do it this way as I had to be sure that the reflections were going to be in the right place, in other words, directly underneath to mirror the light areas. The ropes were put in last with a rigger. Note how the rope registers light against the dark area and dark against the light area of the boat.

Sketch for painting of *Salthouse, Norfolk*.
Making an initial sketch is very useful in sorting out the tones for a painting. By reducing the drawing to three main tones, it is easier to get an overview of the subject without getting too tied up in detail.

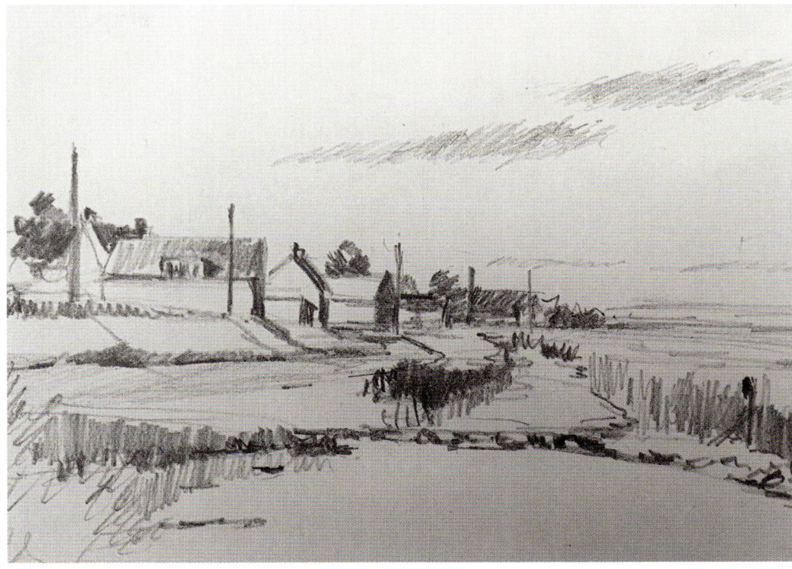

Salthouse, Norfolk
Titanium White
Cadmium Yellow
Burnt Umber
Permanent Rose
Cerulean Blue
Ultramarine Blue
10" × 14" Canvas board
Ultramarine Blue/Cadmium Red diluted ground

I worked up this loose painting from a sketch of Salthouse in Norfolk. It is a very simple composition. The weight of the building on the left takes the eye, which is then led into the picture by the sweep of the water.

The horizon was deliberately kept very low, as I wanted the painting to be about the sky. The dark of the buildings were painted with a thin wash of Ultramarine Blue/Permanent Rose/Burnt Umber. This was allowed to run down the blue/grey ground. The darker clouds at the top were indicated with Ultramarine Blue/Permanent Rose/Cadmium Yellow and Titanium White. The blue areas are Cerulean Blue/Titanium White built up in layers, the subsequent layers having more Titanium White and a little Cadmium Yellow. The green areas are Cerulean Blue/Cadmium Yellow/Titanium White dashed in quickly with loose strokes. The lightest clouds were put in with the use of a palette knife, which was also used for the highlights in the water.

A lot of the under painting was left exposed as the colour worked so well with the painting and I liked to see where the paint had run.

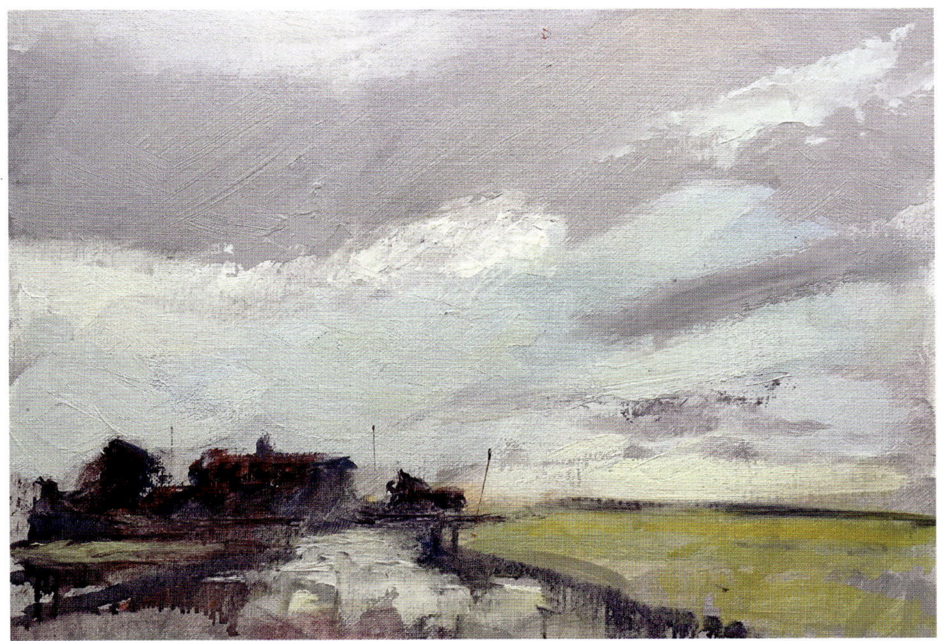

A painting will not look convincing, however many colours are used if the tones are incorrect. This goes to show that tonal value is more important than colour to the design and success of a painting. Tone is used to create a focal point within a painting or drawing. The human eye is immediately drawn to a light element against a dark element. This creates the focal point of interest.

To create the illusion of depth, gradations of value are also used. Areas of light and dark give a three-dimensional illusion of form to subject matter. There's a lot of confusion about tone when using colour. Just changing a colour does not change the tone unless it is a darker colour. Tonal contrast is easier to understand when we are using a dark pencil and a white piece of paper.

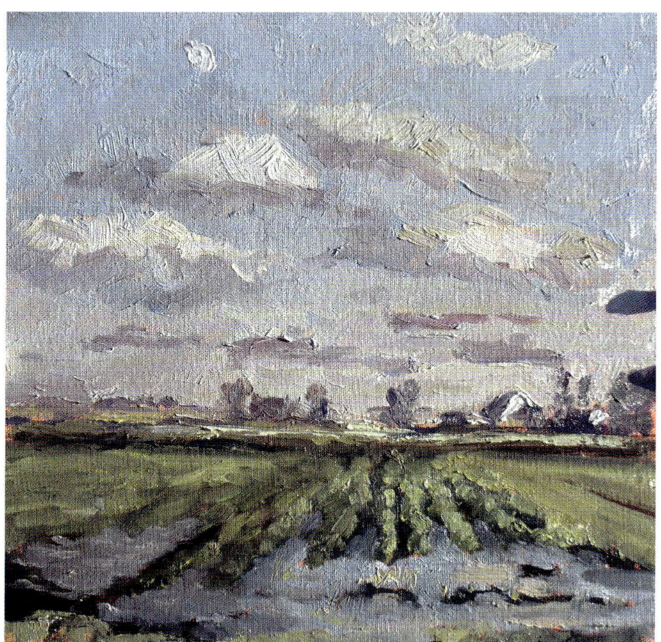

Flooded Cabbage Field
Titanium White
Yellow Ochre
Cadmium Yellow
Burnt Umber
Permanent Rose
Cobalt Blue
10" × 10"
Burnt Sienna ground

A low horizon was chosen for this painting; the weight is in the foreground, leading us in towards the sky. This was a crisp, windy day in the Fens. The small, individual clouds were moving quickly across the sky. The full moon was showing up against the blue of the sky.

The clouds, being lit by the sun, had warm shadows on the underside. Cobalt Blue/Permanent Rose/Titanium White/Cadmium Yellow made a good mix for the cast shadows in the clouds, the distant clouds and the trees on the horizon. The fact that the same colours have been used in the foreground and flooded field, and the greens have been mixed in the same colours as the sky, (in different quantities) make for a harmonious painting.

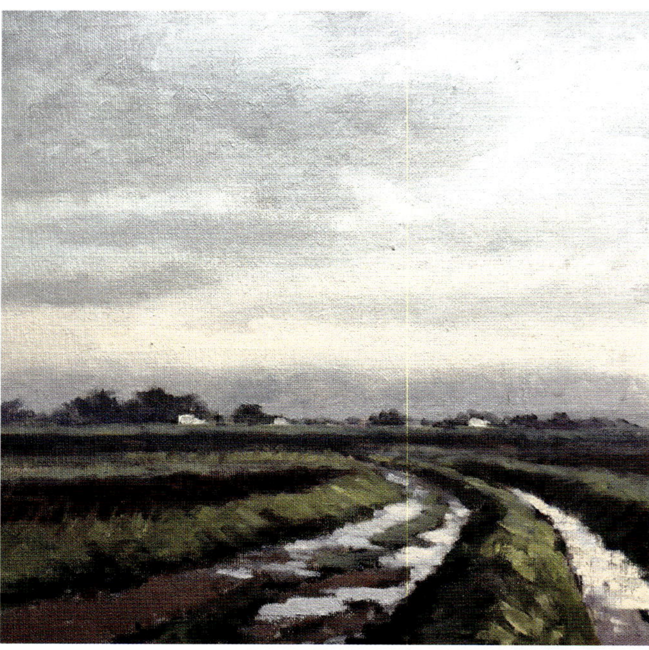

Flooded Road and Dyke, 12" × 12". Canvas board.
Even on a rainy day it is good to get out and paint. The rain had fallen heavily overnight, leaving a lot of water standing on this little back road into the village.

There is little to focus on in this part of the Fens, no hills or mountains or leafy glades. Even so, the water in the dyke, the puddles on the road and the sweep of the verge make for a pleasing composition. All the elements lead us into the picture. The stormy sky is reflected in the water in the dyke and on the road. There are a lot of small lanes in the Fens, many with grass down the centre. Most have dykes running alongside for drainage of the fields. This combination makes a good composition, especially with the addition of a curve in the road.

This picture is a good example of how to make a painting out of virtually nothing. Mussini Brownish Grey 1 and Mussini Blue Grey 2 are mixed for the dark cloud in the top left corner. The same mix with the addition of more Brownish Grey and Warm Light Yellow are used for the sky colour. About halfway down, add a touch of Cadmium Red for warmth. Continue almost to the horizon, adding more Warm Light Yellow and then use the original mix for the clouds on the horizon. The same mix is used for the horizontal clouds halfway down the sky. Once all the clouds are applied, blend the hard edges into the wet paint, using your finger or the tip of a brush to soften them. Use the lightest mixes for the sky reflections in the puddles. The distant trees and landscape are a combination of Ultramarine, Cadmium Red, Cadmium Yellow and Titanium White.

Tip: the use of a Claude Glass can help to simplify things for us. This is simply a black mirror, which when used to look at a scene, reduces and simplifies the colours and tonal range. Traditionally they were slightly convex in shape. It is possible to make your own by spraying the back of a piece of glass with black paint. I would advise putting tape around the edges.

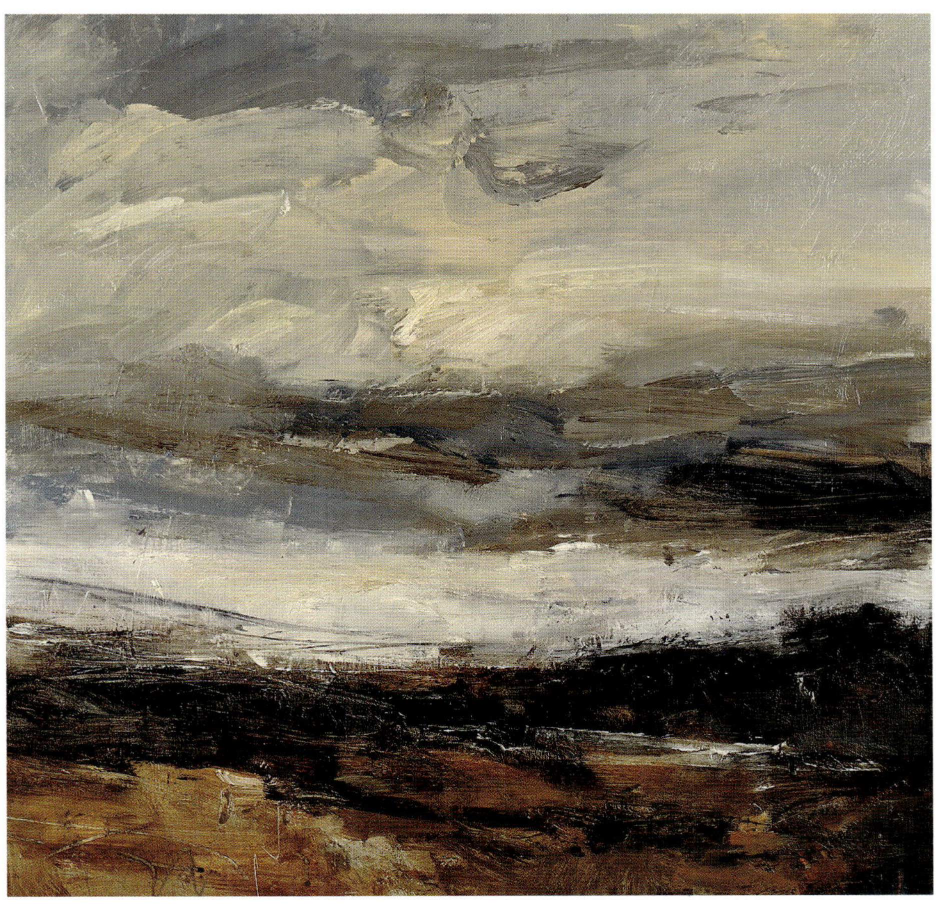

Near Dozmary pool, Louise Balaam. The lower third of this painting has strong tones contrasting with the lighter tones just under midway, which leads us up to the sky area. The overall effect is a pleasing balance of tones and colour. (Photo: John Caruana)

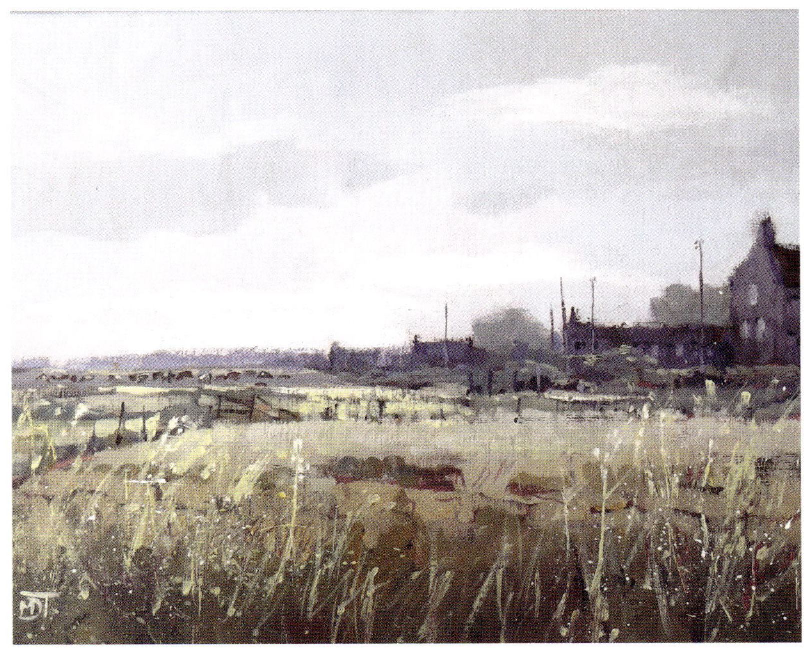

Salthouse
Lemon Yellow
Yellow Ochre
Burnt Sienna
Burnt Umber
Ultramarine Blue
Cadmium Red
14" × 18" Gessoed board
Burnt Sienna ground

This studio painting was painted in two sessions.

The sky is a subtle mix of warm greys. I started with white and added very little Ultramarine Blue and Burnt Umber. Working from the top of the canvas, more white was added towards the horizon where the smallest amount of Cadmium Red was introduced for warmth. The distant trees are a darker mix of colours used at the top of the sky, and the buildings again are the same mix but stronger. This helps with the impression of recession. The darker greens were mixed with Yellow Ochre and Ultramarine Blue.

I left this painting to dry for a day and went back to it. First the sky, then the clouds which were light against dark and dark against light. I used the same mix for the dark clouds against the light as I had used it in the upper part of the painting and the lighter horizon colour for the light clouds. The colour change is quite subtle so even though it was painted onto dry paint, the edges don't stand out too much. The light green distant fields are Lemon Yellow and white, as are the foreground reeds that were flicked in with a rigger.

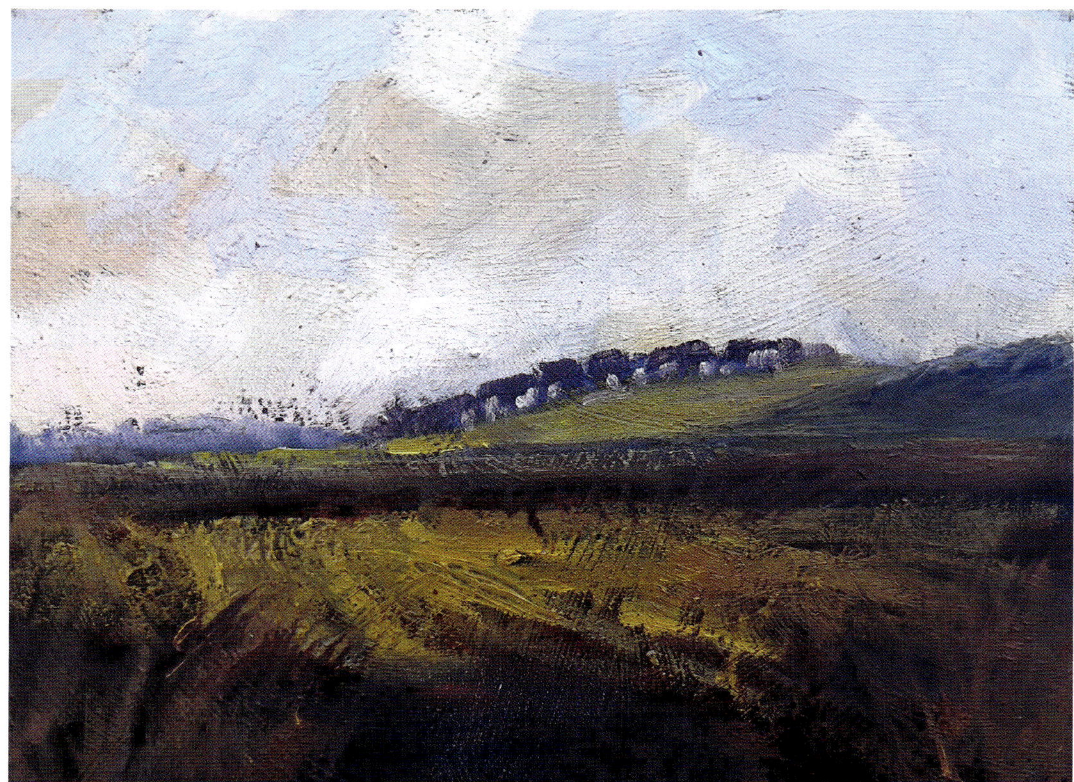

Norfolk Pines
Ultramarine Blue
Cadmium Red
Cadmium Yellow
Burnt Umber
Titanium White
10" × 12" Textured MDF
Dark blue/brown ground

The texture of the board in this little picture did most of the work. By dragging paint over the surface, I was able to get broken lines and soft edges. This works particularly well with the sky. I liked the warmth of the pink in the clouds. This colour was mixed with the red and yellow and tempered by the blue. The very dark background acts as an underpainting, giving depth to the picture.

Alternative palettes

It is good practice to keep to a set palette of colours until you are comfortable with them and can confidently and instinctively mix the colours you want. When you are completely familiar with the colours you use, you will know what the limitations are and therefore will have an idea of the new colour you would like to buy. For example, the yellow on your palette may not be quite bright enough. Just by introducing one more colour, you extend your range of mixes extensively. It is not advisable to buy too many new colours at once but to learn what each new colour can achieve for you.

The list of recommended basic colours are what most artists tend to use with sight variations but there are a lot of alternatives that are fun to try.

The Zorn palette

The Zorn palette is named after internationally successful artist Anders Zorn (1860–1920). He is well known for using a palette of only four colours:

- Yellow Ochre
- Cadmium Red
- Black
- White.

There has been a lot of debate as to which black Zorn used but it is believed to be Ivory Black, which is the colour I used for the painting *Zorn Palette Demo*. Ivory Black works well as a blue but possibly even better is Winsor & Newton's Blue Black. Blue Black is a colour I recently discovered and use a lot in my sky paintings now.

It is possible that the red may have been Vermillion; you could try this as an alternative. The white I used was Titanium White but back in Anders Zorn's time it is more than likely to have been Lead White.

It might at first strike you as an odd selection but the main three colours are just the earthy equivalents of the three primary colours, black being the blue.

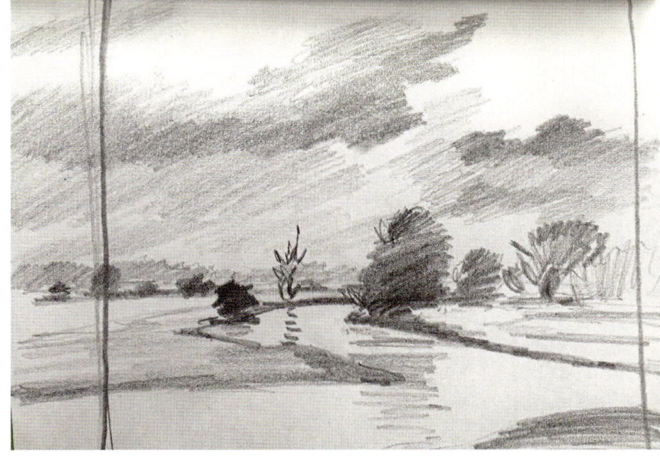

Cropped sketch, Dedham.
This painting was done working from a photograph taken in Dedham, Suffolk. Having drawn the sketch, I decided that it would be a better composition if it were cropped to a square.

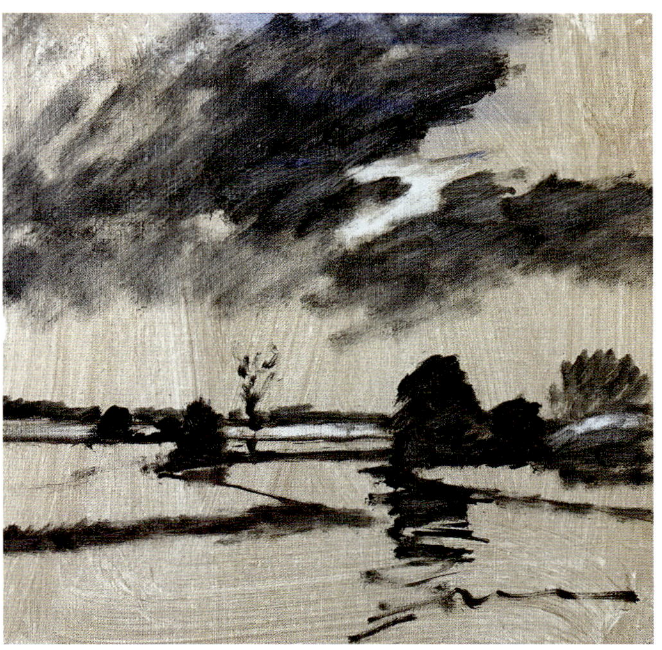

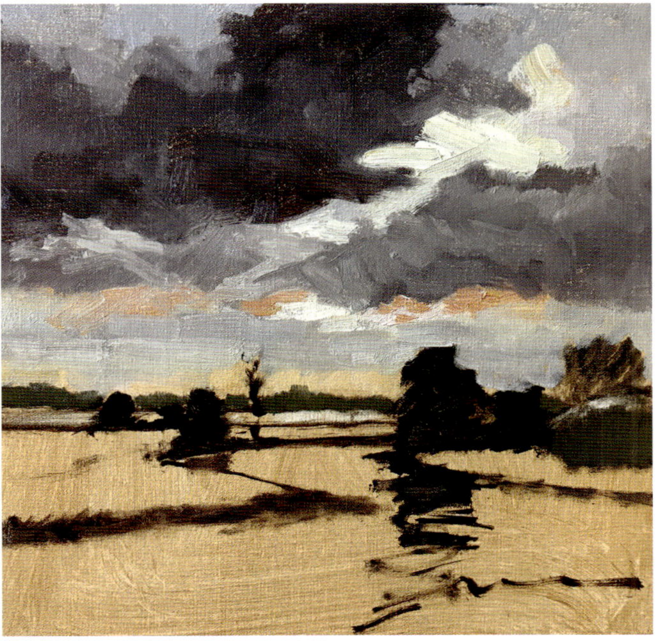

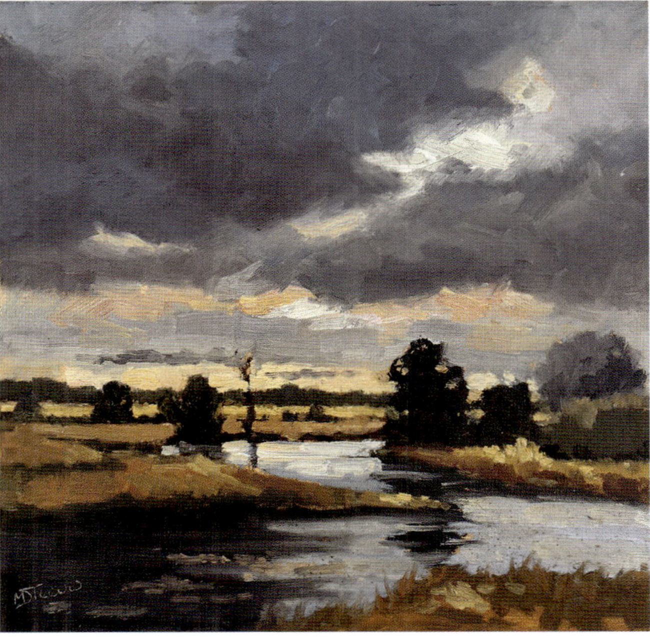

First sketch in the main lines with black and red diluted with turps. Mix the dark cloud colour starting with white and adding black until you have the tone you want. Make sure you mix plenty and then split it, add a little red to one part and then a touch of yellow to another, and some with both. This will give a variety of hues within the cloud.

For the blue sky area, start with white and add a little black. It may not look blue on your palette but on the canvas next to the other colours, it will; you may even want to add some yellow to take the colour down a bit.

Make sure your brush is clean when you mix the light colour near the horizon with white, yellow and a touch of red. The colour here needs to be fresh.

The distant trees are a mix of white, black and yellow; they need to be dark enough to register against the sky but not too dark that they jump forward. In front of these, the distant fields are white with a small amount of yellow. It is very important to make sure there is no trace of white in your brush when you mix the colour for the dark trees. Even a trace left in the brush will make your colour 'milky'. Paint in the reflections at the same time. The water should reflect the sky colours; paint this around your reflections. The meadow area is yellow with varying amounts of black and, in some places, red is added.

STEP BY STEP DEMONSTRATION

Soft Clouds

Paints and materials

- Michael Harding Warm White
- Old Holland Blue Grey
- Naples Yellow
- Kings Blue Deep
- Permanent Rose

Step 1. Start with Michael Harding Warm White and add Old Holland Blue Grey and a touch of Naples Yellow. As you progress down the board, gradually add more white and yellow, decreasing the amount of blue. At the halfway mark, add the slightest amount of Permanent Rose to the yellow. Just above the horizon, the colour deepens; this is a mix of the Permanent Rose and Naples Yellow with Blue Grey introduced back into the mix.

Step 2. The snow is the same colour as the top half of the sky, the distant trees and marks to break up the distance are Kings Blue with Permanent Rose and Yellow Ochre.

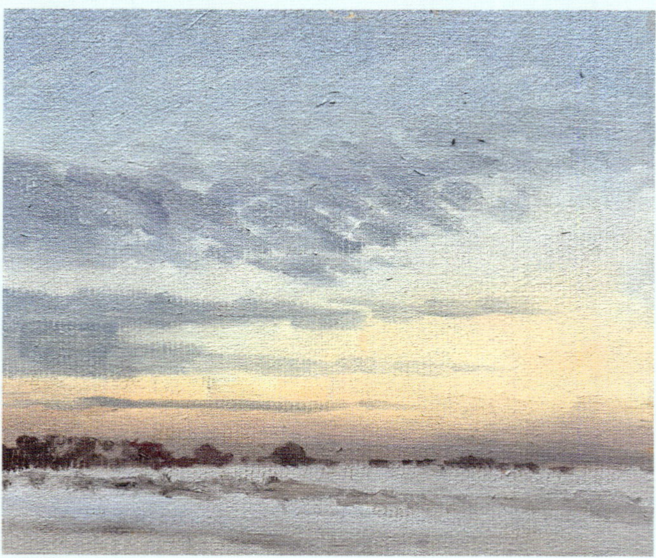

Step 3. Using a soft brush, the clouds are painted over the wet paint and the edges are blended. A bristle brush would have resulted in removing paint rather than laying it on. The mix for the clouds is just a darker version of the sky. Be mindful to keep the edges soft.

STEP BY STEP DEMONSTRATION

Pink Sky

Paints and materials

- Michael Harding Warm White
- Old Holland Blue Grey
- Naples Yellow
- Michael Harding Brilliant Pink

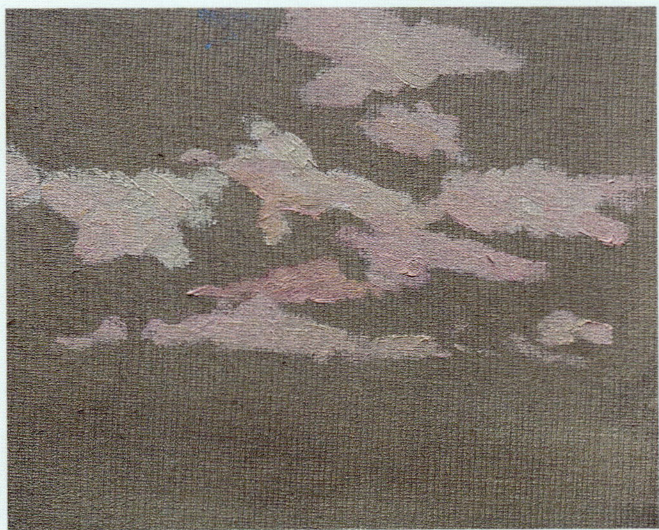

Step 1. This is one of those 'wow, look at that sky' moments. The painting was worked from a photo taken in Portugal. Working on Burnt Umber ground, I started by plotting out the pink clouds.

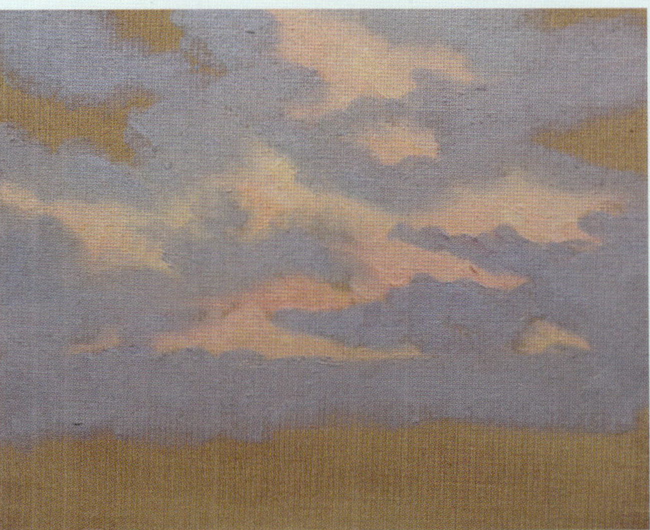

Step 2. The thin grey clouds were put on next with Blue Grey, Brilliant Pink and a touch of Naples Yellow. On the left, you can see where the clouds have been blended and on the right, the ones that have not been blended. To pull the two colours together and soften the edges, I used a bristle brush.

Old Holland Blue Grey and white are used for the colour of the sky in between the clouds. On the right, you can still see how the paint was applied before blending.

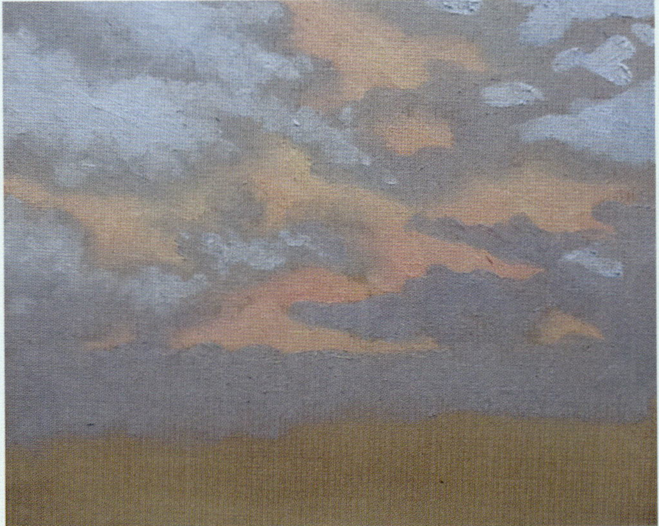

Step 3. Finally, the highlights are put on the pink clouds with Brilliant Pink and Warm White, as well as a touch of Naples Yellow. The horizon is lightened to pick out the shapes of the trees. Not wanting to draw attention to the foreground, it is put in with a few loose brush marks using the same colours as the sky.

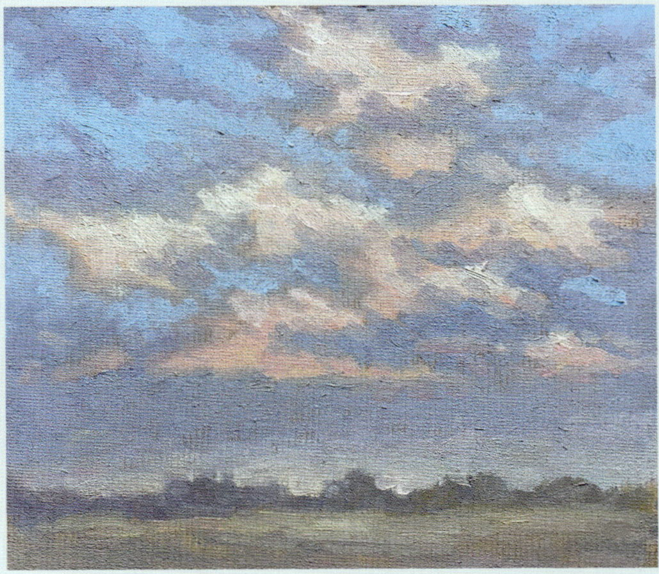

Demo: Pink Sky

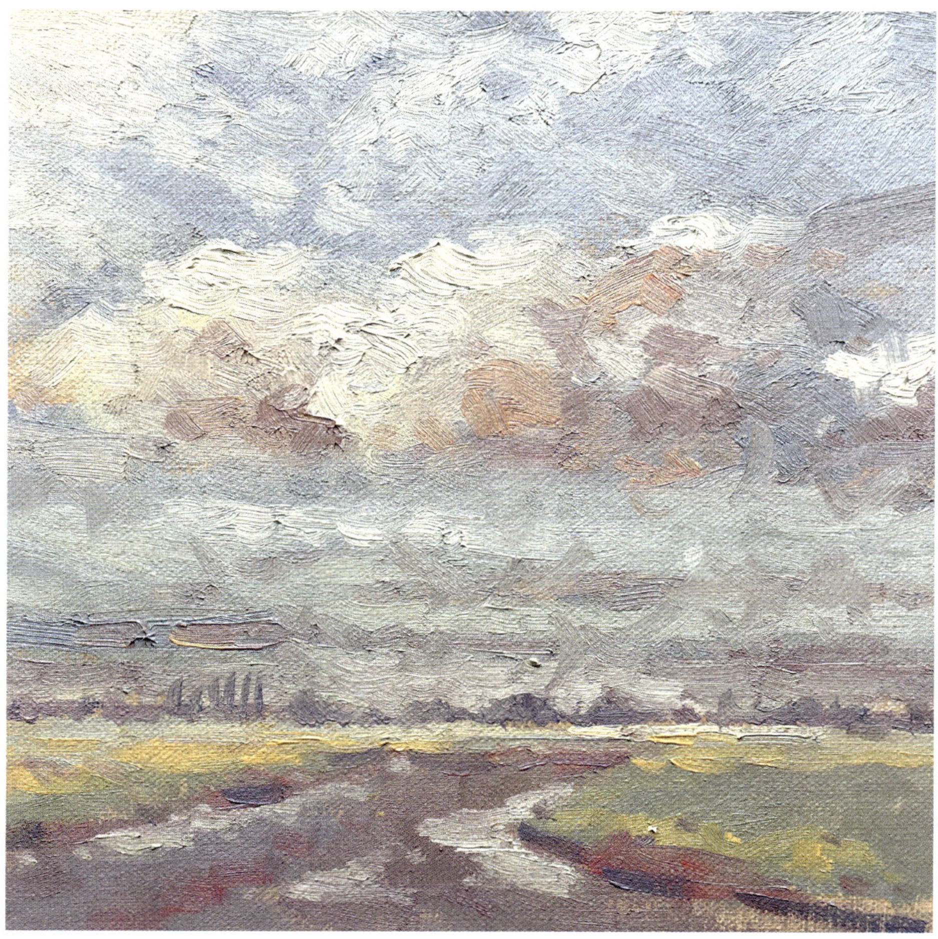

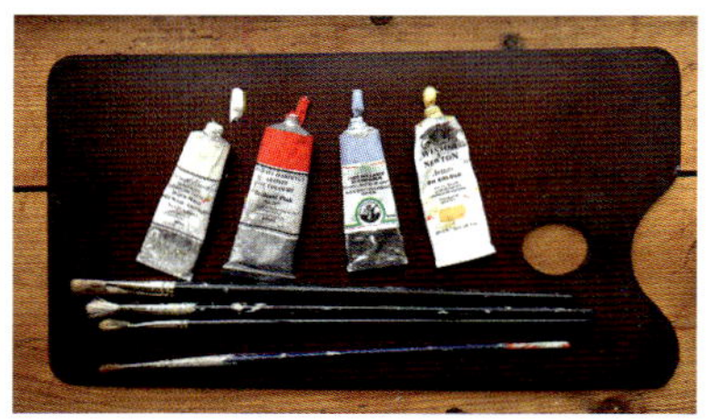

Pale Palette:
Daffodils at Moulton
Brilliant Pink
Blue Grey
Naples Yellow
Warm White

This is quite a challenge as there is no dark colour. The darkest colour you can mix is the equivalent to the darkest colour on your palette. Nonetheless, I like the harmony that these four colours create.

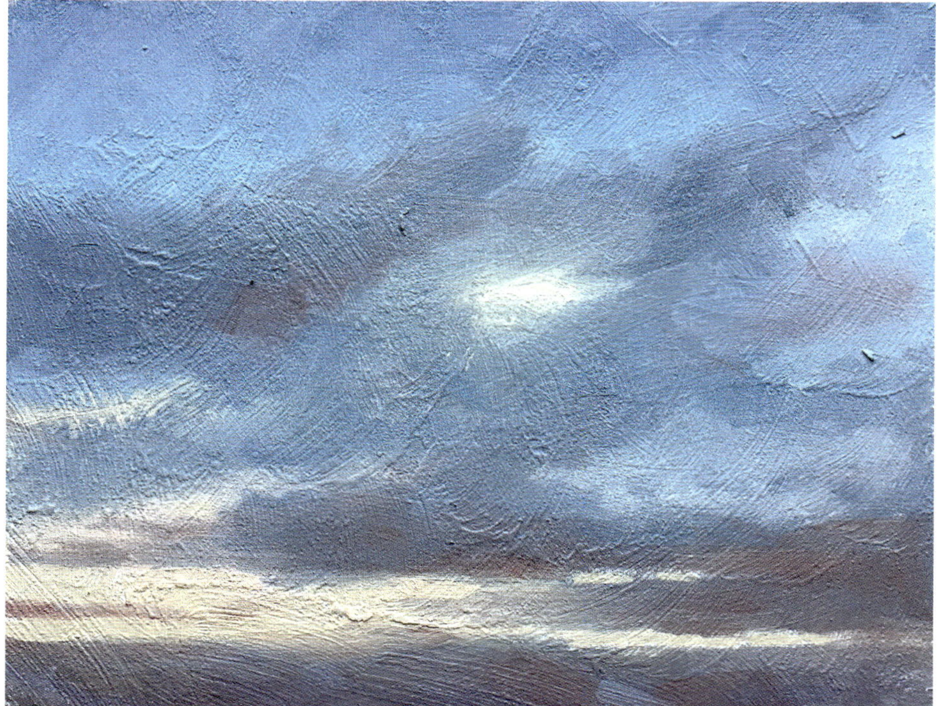

Sky Study
Blue Black
Flesh Tint
Naples Yellow
Permanent Rose
Titanium White

This is an unusual palette of colours, which produced some very pleasing effects. The Naples Yellow works very well with Flesh Tint for the warm glow in the sky and the Blue Black makes a pleasing blue colour when mixed with white and a touch of Naples Yellow.

Another sky study using a limited palette of:
Warm Light Yellow
Old Holland Blue Grey
Mussini Bluish Grey 2
Flesh Tint

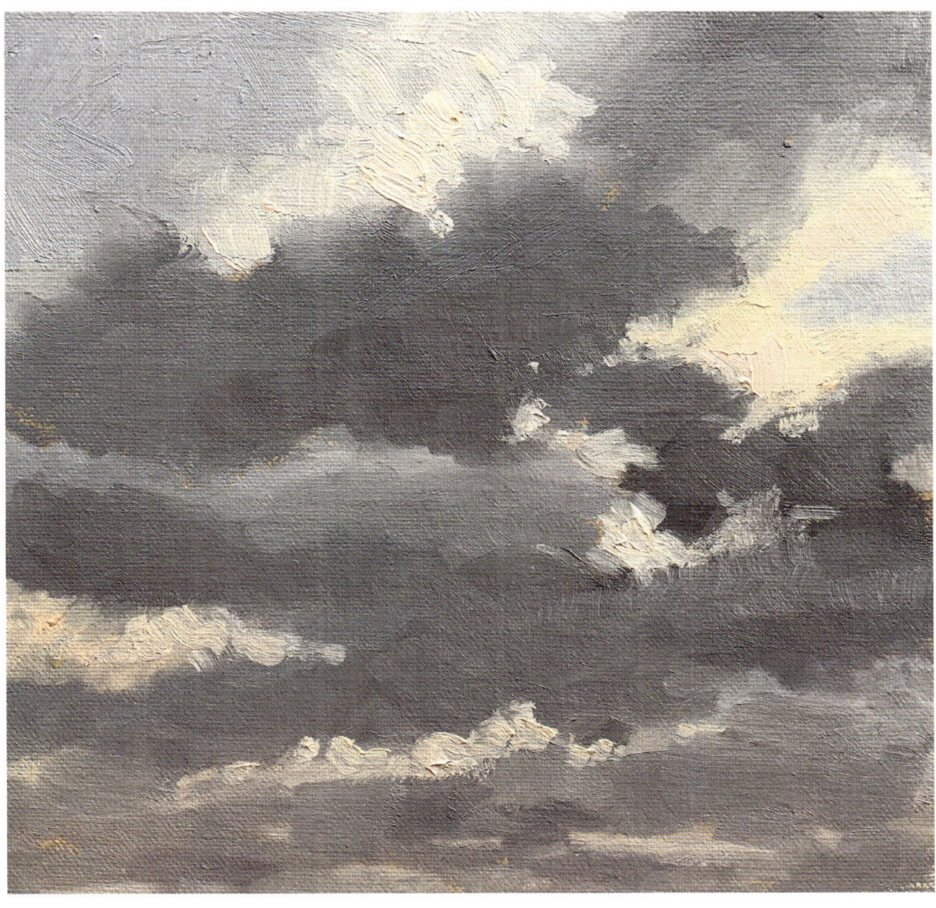

Grey Day, Norfolk Broads.
This was painted on location in Norfolk. I kept to a time limit to prevent overworking the picture. It was a very grey day so selecting my palette was easy. I used a selection of greys made by Mussini, along with Naples Yellow, Warm White and Ultramarine.

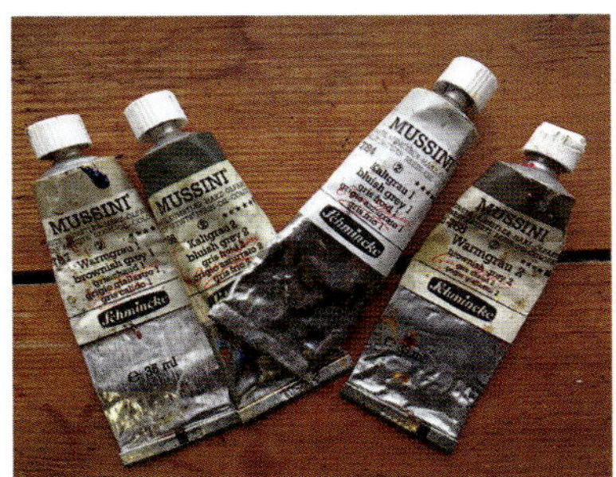

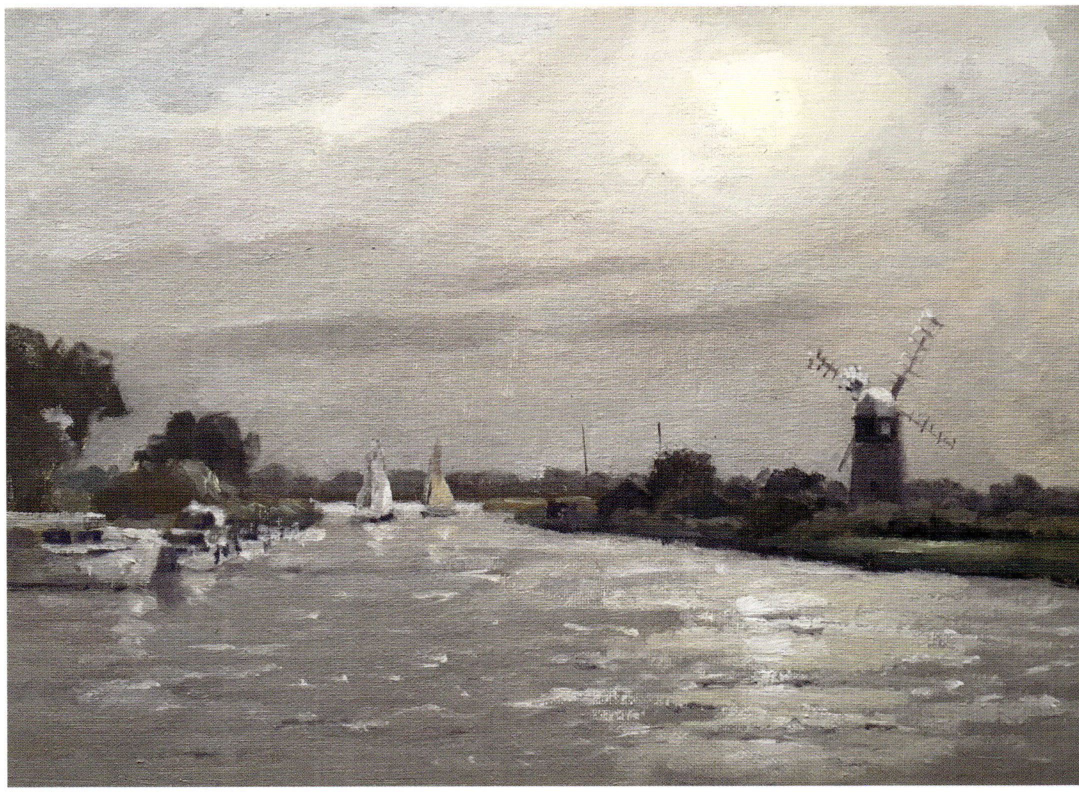

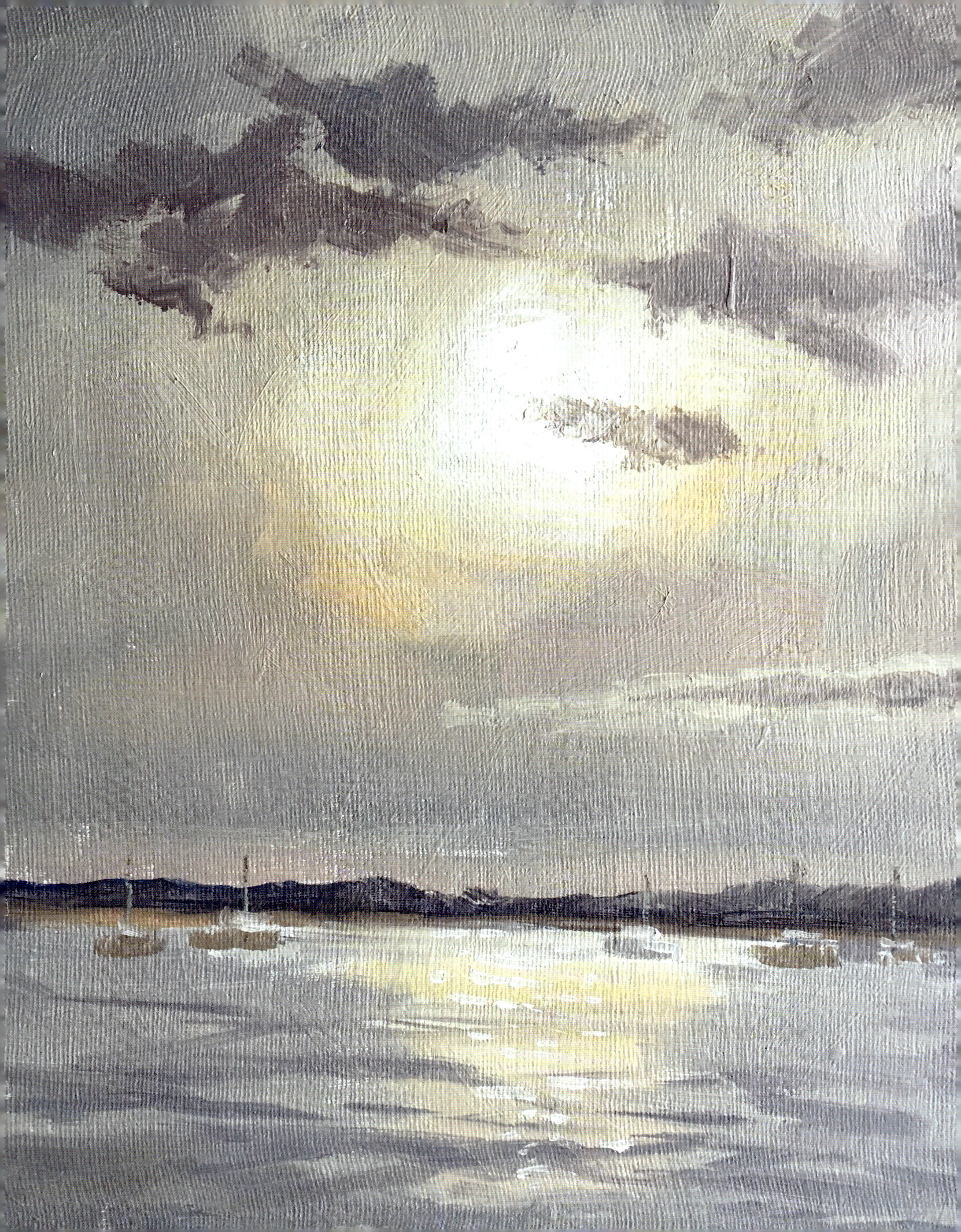

CHAPTER 5

Sky and sea

The sea, once it casts its spell, holds one in its net of wonder forever.

JACQUES YVES COUSTEAU

Winter or summer, fair weather or foul, the ocean and vast stretches of water are a continuous draw and challenge to the artist. The perpetual movement of the sea as well as the sky is probably more of a challenge to paint than a pastoral landscape. It is possible to achieve amazing colours in sea paintings as we can really play on the reflected light from the sky to the sea. I always try to make sure in my landscapes that there is some element of the sky colour in the land and some colour from the landscape in the sky. Painting water makes this all the more easy. Of course, a limited palette helps to keep a painting harmonious. By using the same colours throughout we are echoing colours in the sky.

Brian's painting *Moon Over Holkham* picks out colours from the sea and plays on them in the sky.

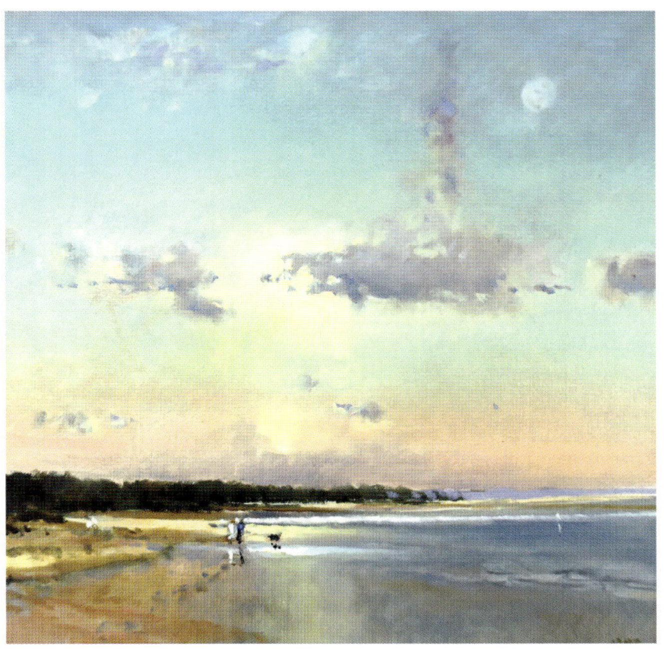

Moon Over Holkham, Brian Ryder ROI PPIEA.
This square format painting works well for this subject. The horizon is just below a third of the canvas, focusing our attention on the sky. The dark headland provides a good contrast and break between beach and sky.

Hazy Sun over Sea, 10" × 8" on muslin-covered board. There can be some wonderful effects when the sun is shielded by fine clouds. This picture is one such example. To keep the colours clean, I started with the hazy sun and worked outwards, using a limited palette of greys. The same colours were used in the sea. The clouds drifting across the sun were painted last with a darker mix of the sky colour. Note how the clouds in front of the sun are not as dark. I felt the contrast would have been too strong.

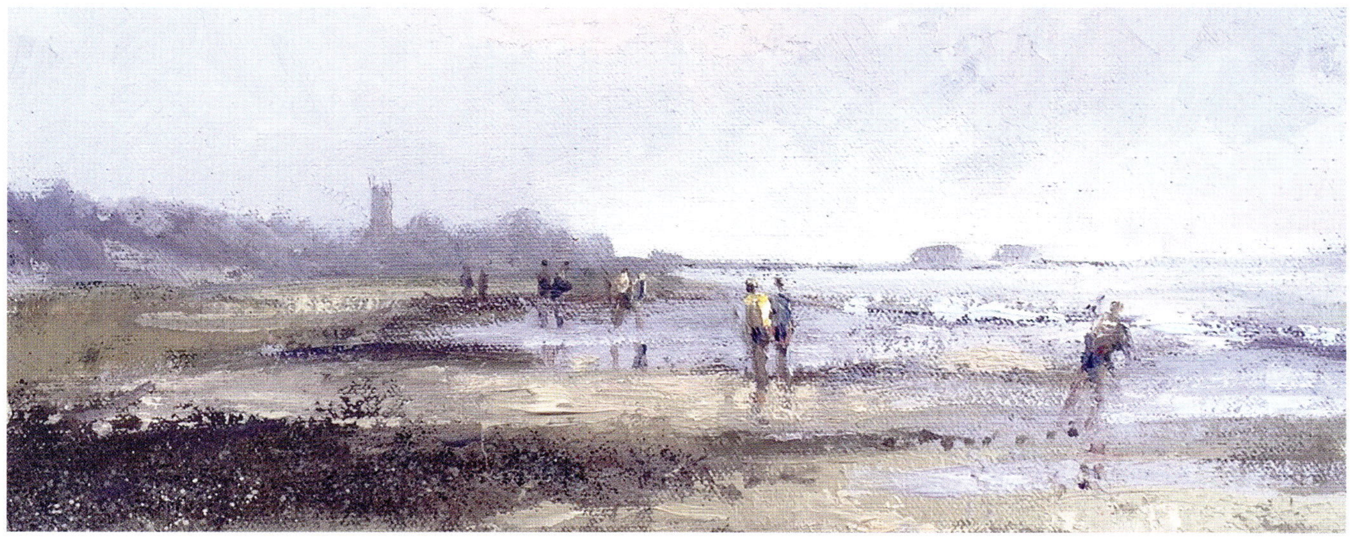

Cromer Beach.
This is predominantly a 'blue' painting broken with the yellow of the sand, which is picked up in the sky. The figures give interest and aerial perspective to the painting. The sea on the right side of the painting is at the halfway point in the canvas but slopes up as we take in the outline of Cromer town, thus avoiding the effect of the painting being dissected in half.

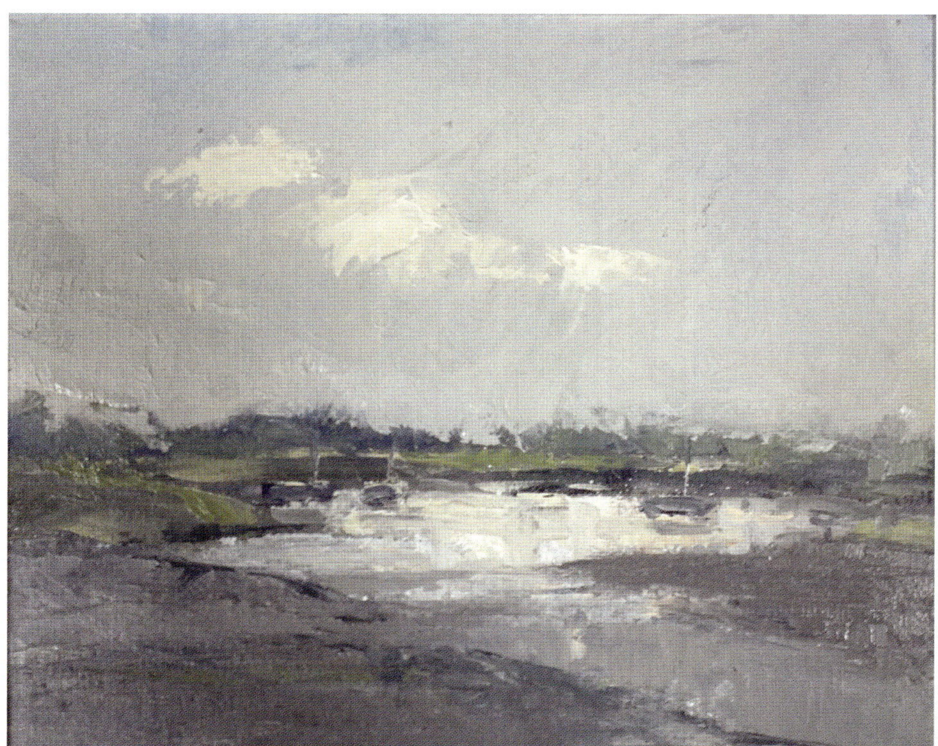

Winter Light
Warm White
Cadmium Yellow
Cadmium Red
Ultramarine Blue
Titanium White
10" × 12" Gessoed board
Blue/grey ground

The limited palette here makes for a harmonious painting. The darks of the foreground were painted in with Ultramarine Blue/Cadmium Red, using a large flat bristle brush. The sky next with Ultramarine Blue/Titanium White. Subsequent layers were applied with a palette knife and dragged down over the trees to give a broken outline. The touches of green, mixed with Ultramarine Blue/Cadmium Yellow/Titanium White, are the only colours, added to give the painting a lift in an otherwise grey painting.

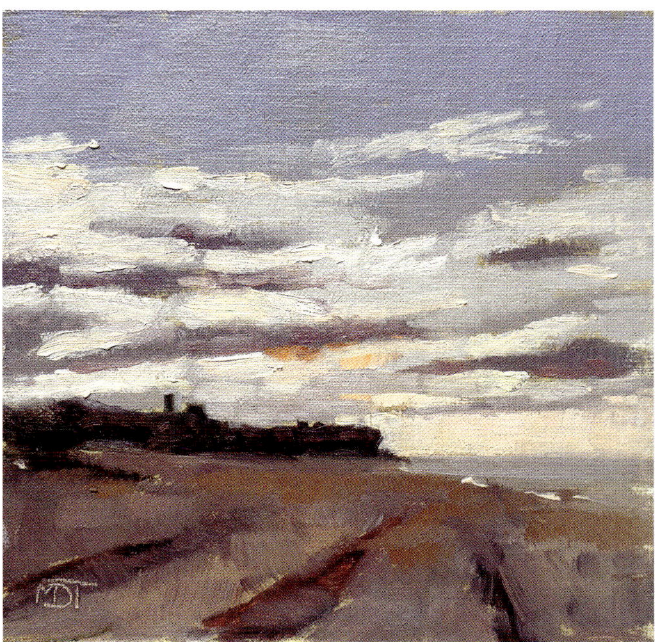

Hunstanton Clouds
Titanium White
Yellow Ochre
Burnt Sienna
Cadmium Red
Ultramarine Blue
6" × 6" Linen on board
Yellow Ochre ground

This half hour cloud study was painted on location. The shape of Hunstanton cliff with its distinctive lighthouse on top was sketched in with a thin mix of Ultramarine Blue/Burnt Sienna.

The diagonal shapes of the clouds suggest movement. These were put in next with Ultramarine Blue/Cadmium Red and a touch of Yellow Ochre. The blue of the sky is Ultramarine Blue/Titanium White. The clouds are applied with a loaded brush of Titanium White warmed with Yellow Ochre.

As this painting was about the sky, I didn't want to make much of the beach so this was kept very simple with broad thin strokes of Yellow Ochre/Burnt Sienna and touches of Ultramarine Blue.

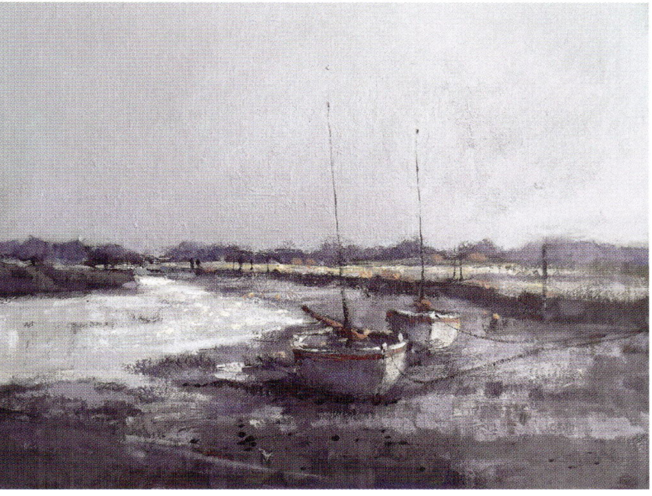

Morston, Low Tide.
The sky in this painting is kept very simple because the foreground is quite busy. I kept to a grey-blue palette of colours. The next painting, *Moored at Morston*, was painted at the same place on a different day. A muted palette was used for this painting. The boats were in fact bright white in colour but by playing that down, it has kept coherence within the painting. The foreground was kept simpler and clouds were employed to balance the composition.

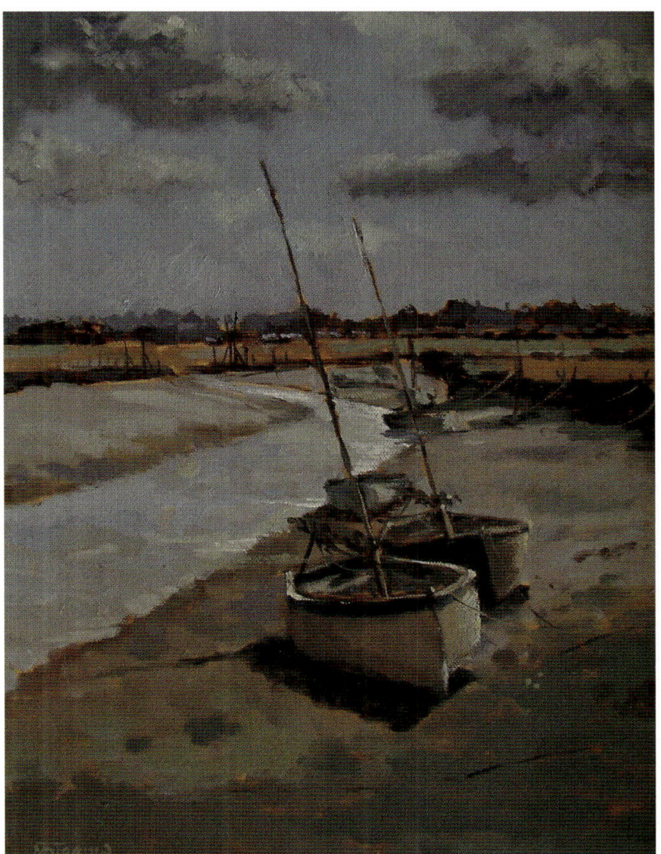

Moored at Morston.

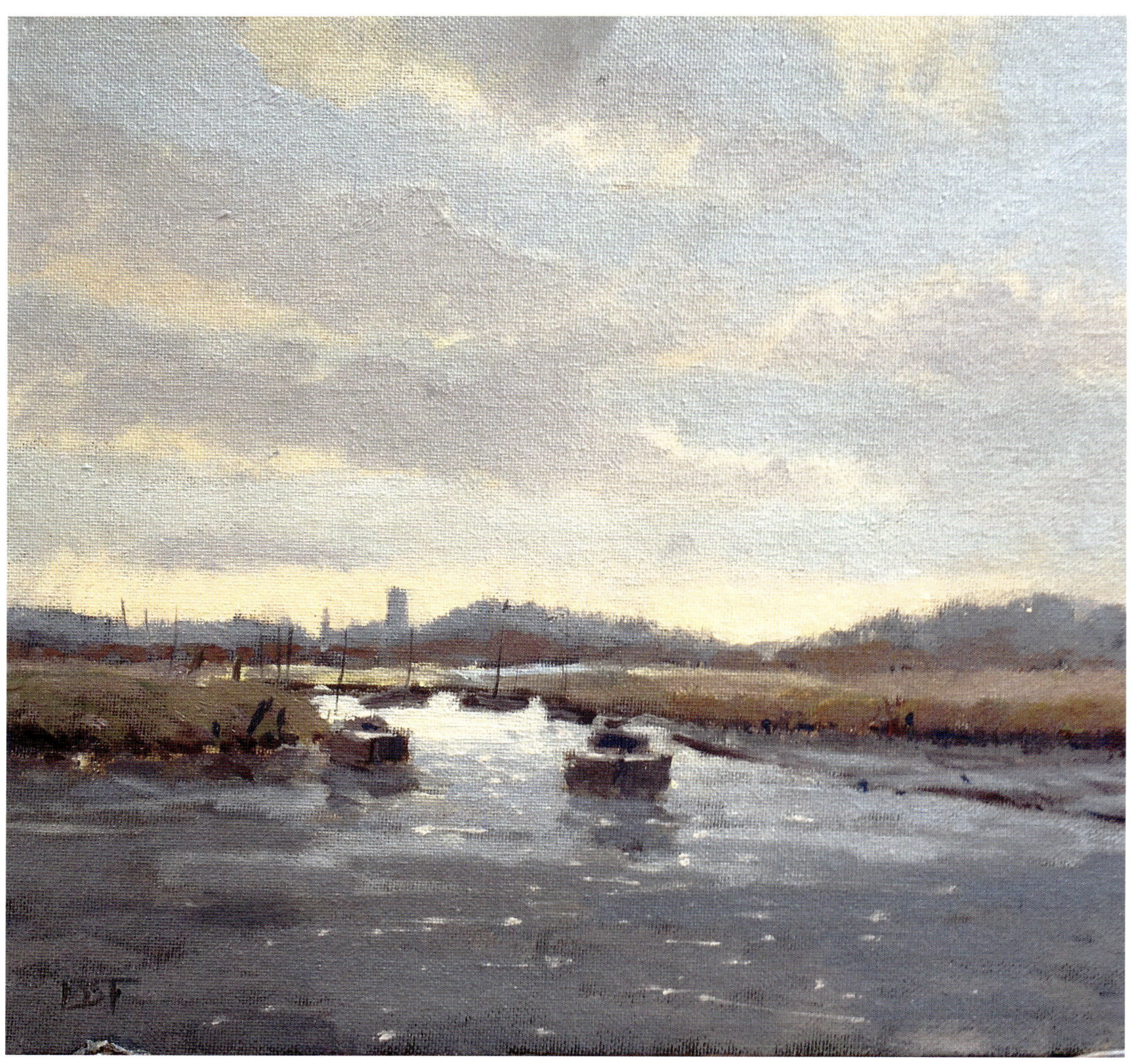

Early Morning, Morston, 10" × 10". Canvas board.
On this day, I arrived early to run a workshop at Morston, Norfolk. I went to do a recce and found the tide was in so I quickly got my paints out and painted this. The early morning, I find, is one of the best times to paint at this location as the sun rises from behind the church at Cley.

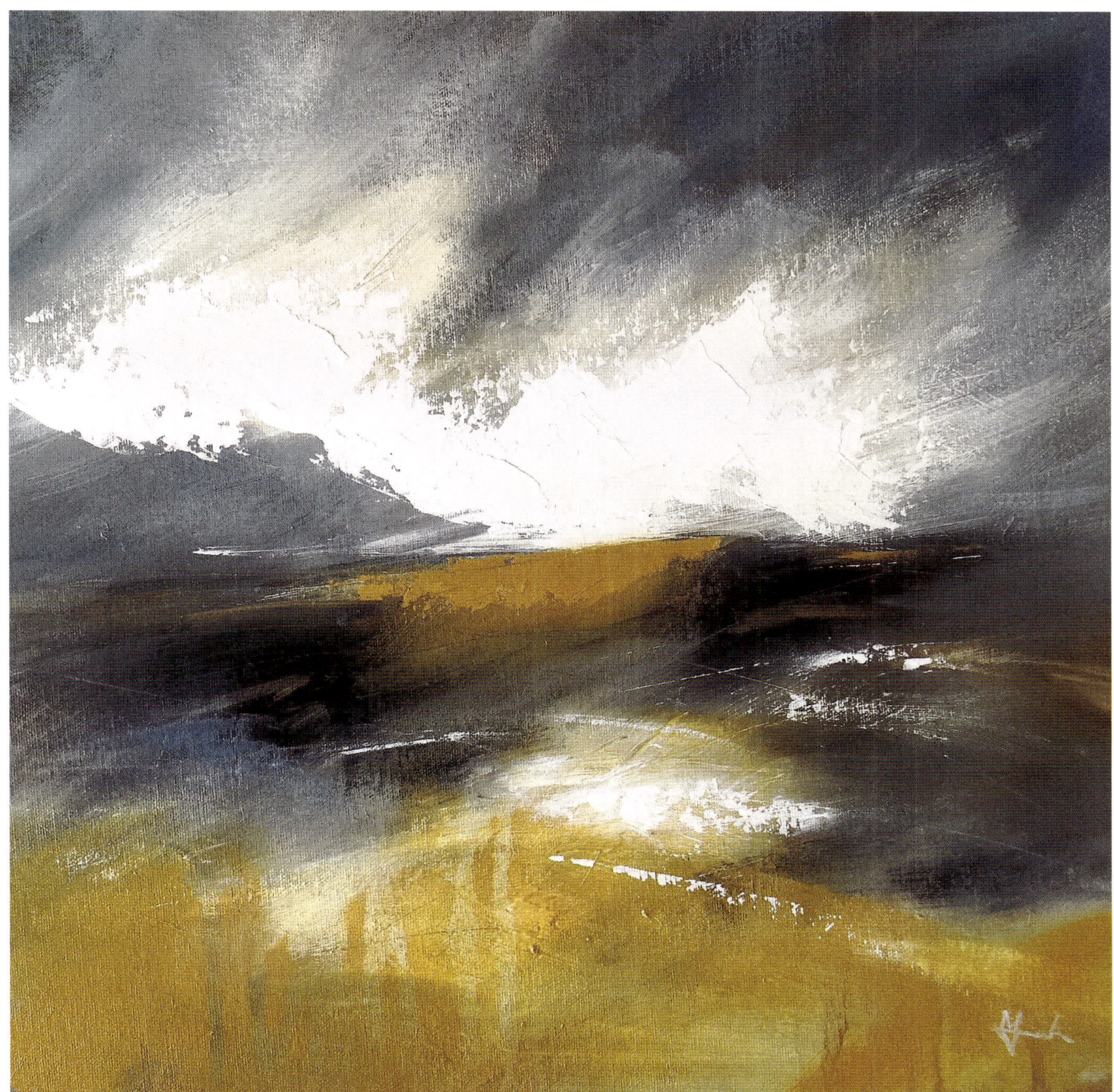

Headland, October, Mari French.
Although quite abstract in its form, we are left in no doubt what we are looking at. The sweeping clouds make a perfect foil for the distant headland. The ochre colour is suggestive of the beach and the white linear marks indicate the presence of the tide coming in. A very expressive and skilful painting.

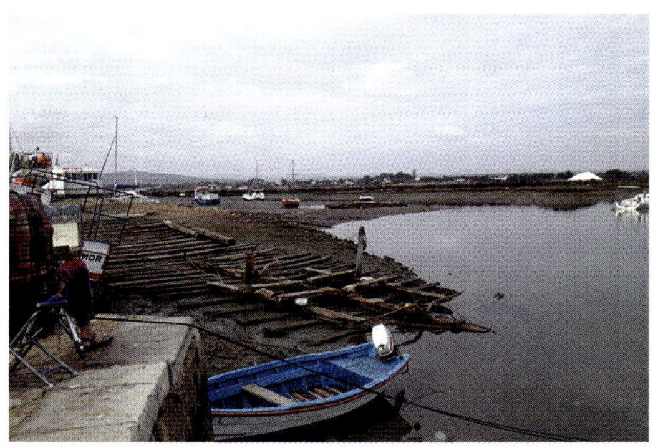

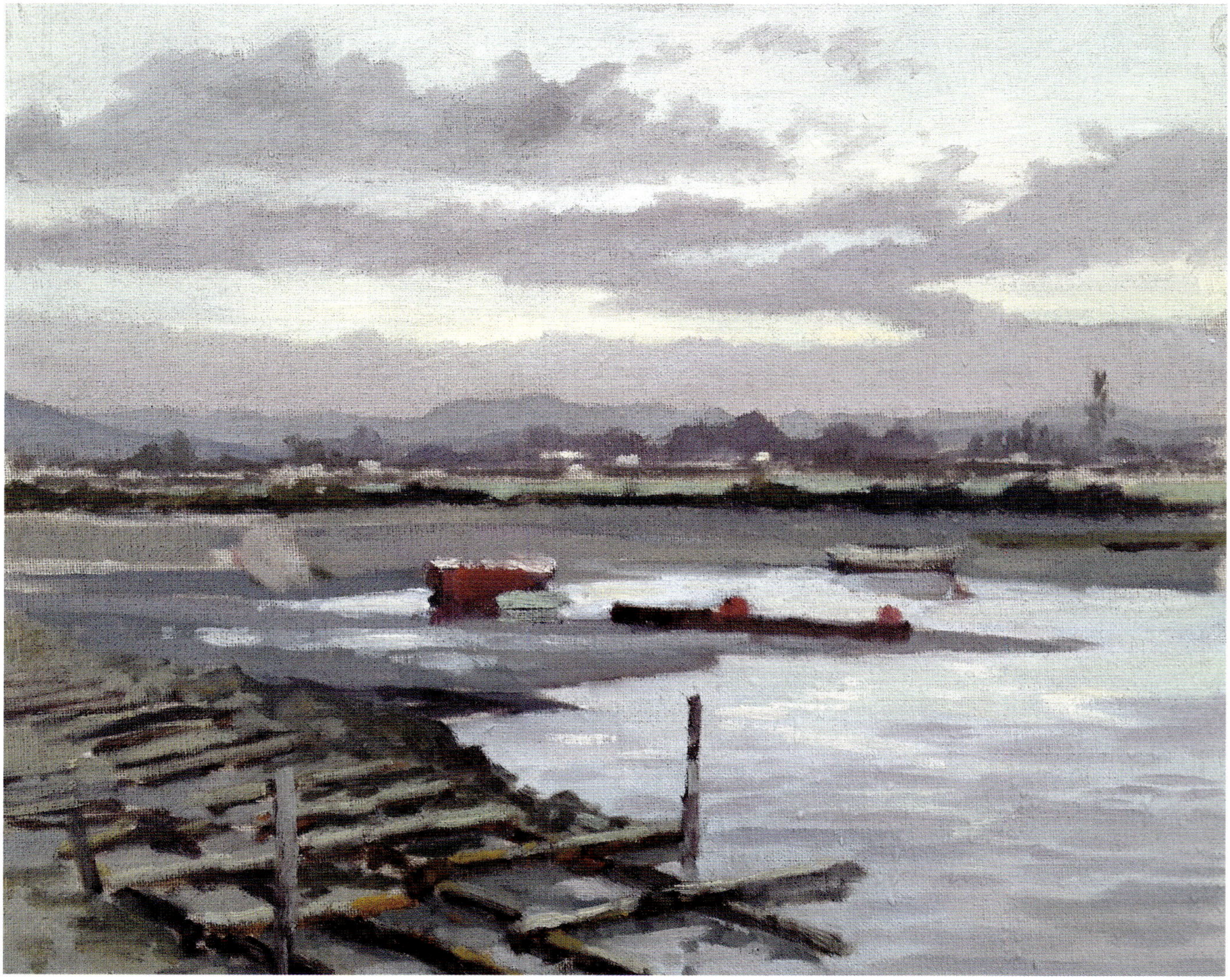

Fuseta 2
Titanium Alkyd White
Cadmium Yellow
Burnt Sienna
Cadmium Red
Ultramarine Blue
10" × 12" Linen on board
Burnt Sienna ground

The painting above was painted on location in Fuseta, Portugal. The photograph shows the wider picture from which the final subject was selected with the use of a viewfinder. The foreground, blue boat and jetty were left out so as to focus more on the slipway and the middle distant boats. The photo was taken before the painting was started and I could see that the tide was coming in. The decision had to be made about when to put in the water line. I decided to wait until the boats had some reflections but didn't want to wait too long or I would have lost the complex lines of the slipway.

The cloud colours have been used extensively in the distant hills and in the water's ripples, helping to tie the painting together.

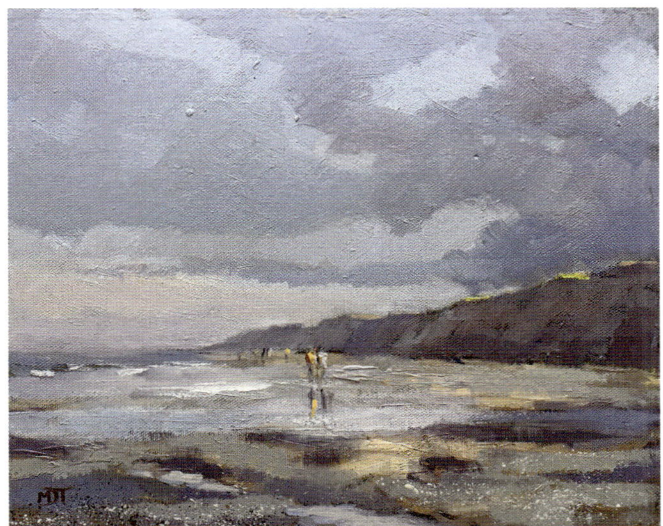

West Runton Clouds and Cliff
French Ultramarine
Burnt Umber
Cadmium Red
Yellow Ochre
Titanium White
10" × 12" canvas board
Yellow Ochre ground

The Yellow Ochre ground in this painting provides instant warmth and harmony. The clouds were moving very quickly in this early morning painting. The sky graduated from a warm mix of Ultramarine, red, white and a pinprick of yellow. More white was added towards the horizon where more red was added to the original colour to create the haziness on the horizon. The clouds were painted into the wet sky, the shadow was painted first, then a few swift strokes to capture the feeling of movement of white warmed with red and a touch of Yellow Ochre. The cliff shape adds an interesting contrast whilst leading the eye into the picture towards the distant Cromer Pier. The foreground pebbles help add depth to the painting. Burnt Umber and Ultramarine was put down for the dark shadows and highlights added afterwards.

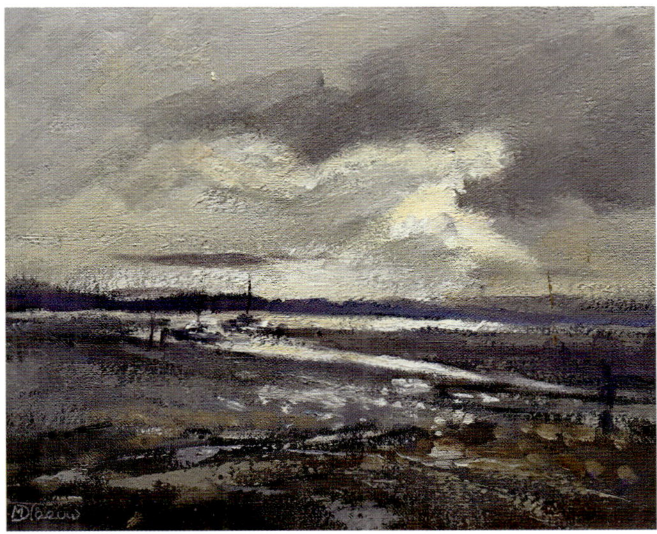

Stormy Sky, Brancaster
Warm White
Cadmium Yellow
Burnt Umber
Cadmium Red
Prussian Blue
10" × 12" gessoed canvas board
Ultramarine Blue ground

This painting packs a punch, as it is a picture of contrasts and a limited palette. The blue ground was used to full effect by leaving areas untouched. In the foreground here is an 'S' sweep into the painting, created firstly by the marks in the mud and then by the water left in the channel as the tide goes out. The post on the right acts as a stop for the eye.

Prussian Blue is a strong colour and needs some careful handling if it is not to take over a painting. Here, I used it in the sky for the clouds mixed with Cadmium Red/Warm White. The foreground, mixed with Burnt Umber and Prussian Blue, makes for some lovely darks. This painting was built up over several layers, working from dark to light and wet over wet. The final highlights are Cadmium Yellow/Warm White.

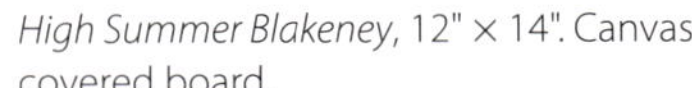

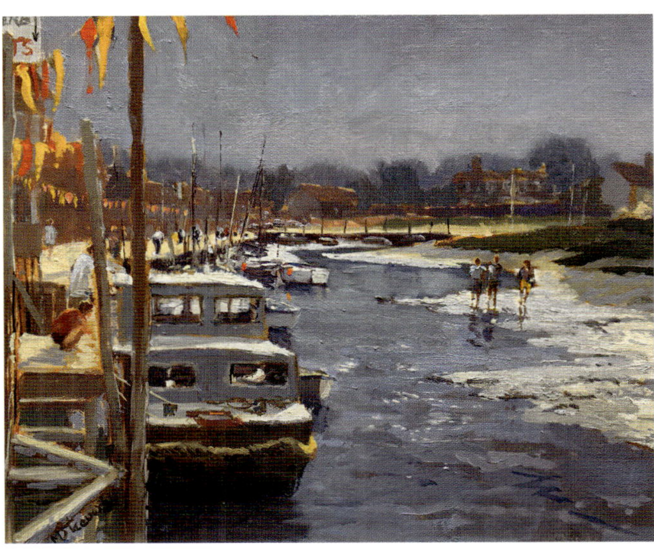

High Summer Blakeney, 12" × 14". Canvas covered board.
Warm sunny day paintings do not necessarily have to have a bright blue sky as we see in *High Summer Blakeney*. The sky has been kept tonally dark to give a contrast to the sunlight that filters through the hazy heat. We are given the impression of heat because of the figures in the water. The light shining on the wet muddy estuary and bouncing off the top of the boats discloses the presence of the sun.

An expedition to Katwijk

One March, I was fortunate enough to have the opportunity to paint at Katwijk in Holland with Roos Schuring. The weather was freezing and there were strong winds. Not deterred, we returned to the same spot on the beach for four consecutive days, painting on average three or four paintings per day. The changing tide, figures, horses and most of all the varying skies, presented different subject matter each day.

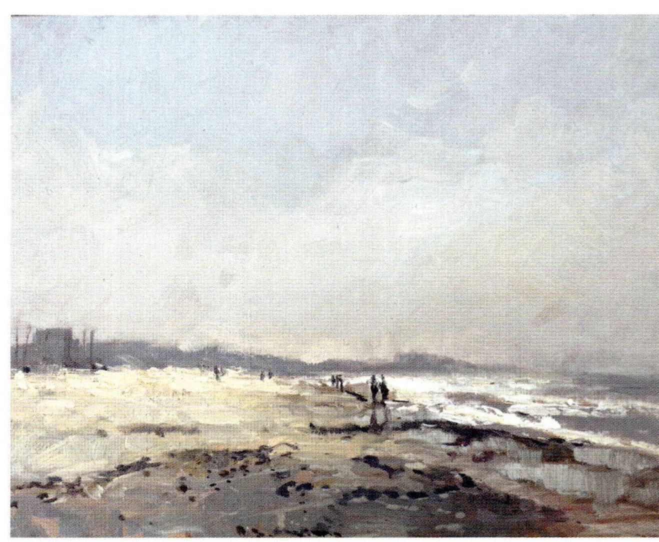

Katwijk 1
Ultramarine Blue
Cadmium Red
Yellow Ochre
Cadmium Yellow
Titanium White
10" × 12" Gessoed board
Yellow Ochre/Cadmium Red ground

I kept the colours cool in this painting but the warm ground shows through to give a contrast. The cool grey in the foreground was mixed using Ultramarine Blue, Cadmium Red, Titanium White and a small amount of Yellow Ochre to kill the purple. There were very subtle colour shifts in the sky. I started at the top with French Ultramarine, Cadmium Red and Titanium White. The clouds are a mix of Titanium White, Yellow Ochre with Cadmium Red added towards the horizon. I was careful to keep the lightest part of the sky central and the clouds to the right slightly darker. That and the shoreline ensure the eye is drawn in to the picture. The sand was mainly yellow and Titanium White with small amounts of Cadmium Red and Ultramarine Blue to prevent it from being too yellow. The middle distant figures and the dark marks representing stone and debris in the foreground provide contrast to the waves which were a mix of Titanium White and Yellow Ochre.

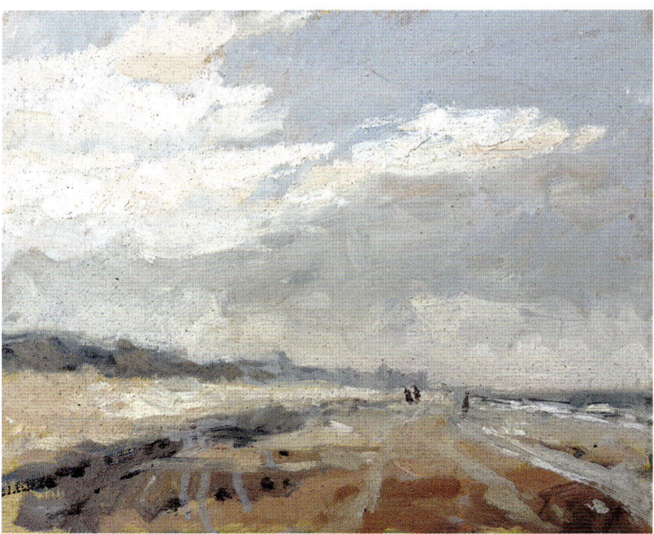

Katwijk 2
Kings Blue Light
Titanium White
Yellow Ochre
Burnt Sienna
10" × 12" Gessoed board
Yellow Ochre ground

This is another painting from the series from my trip to Holland. I started the under painting with rapid strokes of paint that had been diluted with white spirit. Firstly I blocked in the dark of the dunes and the beach detritus. The sky was a brighter blue on this day so I chose to use Kings Blue Light. This was lightened with Titanium White and the smallest amount of Yellow Ochre. The fast moving clouds were put in quickly using Titanium White that had been warmed with Yellow Ochre. I was careful to keep the edges soft and to help with the feeling of movement. Moving on to the dunes, I used a mix of Yellow Ochre and Burnt Sienna, leaving a lot of the under painting showing to indicate depth and undulation. Again, I was careful to keep the edges soft. The sand on the beach area was painted in several layers working from dark to light with Yellow Ochre toned down with Kings Blue Light and for the last layers, more Titanium White. The figures were dotted in last to give interest and scale. I painted them at a slight angle to suggest movement as they walked into the wind. Note how the heads of the figures are in line with the horizon. This is because although they are at a distance from me, their eye level would still be the same as the beach was flat. If you look carefully at the painting, you will see sand all over it that was blown up from the beach.

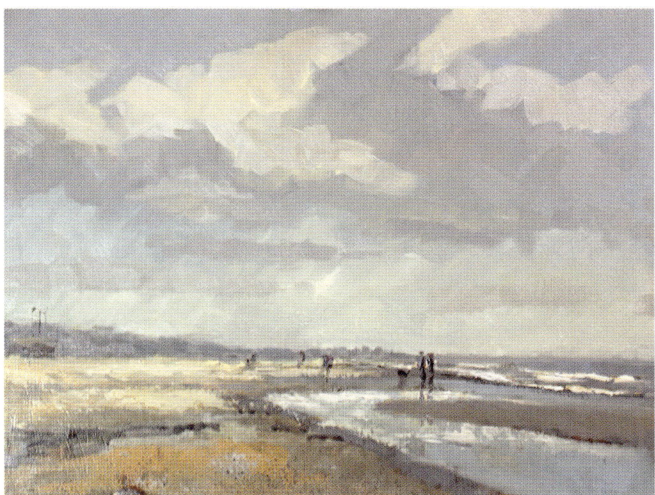

Katwijk 3
Kings Blue Deep
Cobalt Blue
Yellow Ochre
Cadmium Yellow Deep
Cadmium Red
Titanium White
10" × 12" Gessoed board
Yellow Ochre ground

This was another windy day on the beach in Holland. On this particular day, I moved further down the beach towards the sea. The tide was going out, leaving interesting reflections and sand banks, and the sky had a lot more colour in it. I used both Cobalt Blue and Kings Blue Light for the first layer and built it up with more of the blue mixed with Cadmium Red and touches of Yellow Ochre before painting in the clouds. I kept the cloud colour warm using Cadmium Yellow Deep and Cadmium Red. All the colours used in the sky are reflected in the sea and the wet beach. The dark sand colour was achieved with Cobalt Blue and Cadmium Red added to Cadmium Yellow; this was my first layer, which I built up, working from dark to light. The highlights on the beach are Cadmium Yellow and Titanium White. For a bit more warmth in the foreground, I lightly brushed over some Cadmium Yellow. There were more figures on the beach today; I used them to advantage. The taller couple and their dog gave subtle reflections in the wet, foreground sand, whereas the distant, smaller figures gave depth and interest leading into the picture. The waves and the water inlet on the right create an S shape and a strong diagonal line, taking the viewer into the picture. The suggestion of a shingle at the front was flicked in first with a very dilute mix of white spirit and Burnt Umber. and for contrast, a second mix of warm white and white spirit. To do this, you can either use an old toothbrush or the end of a bristle brush. A word of warning, though: do practise first and mask off the area you want clean by laying torn kitchen roll over it. A fair bit of the ground colour helped to add a unity to the picture.

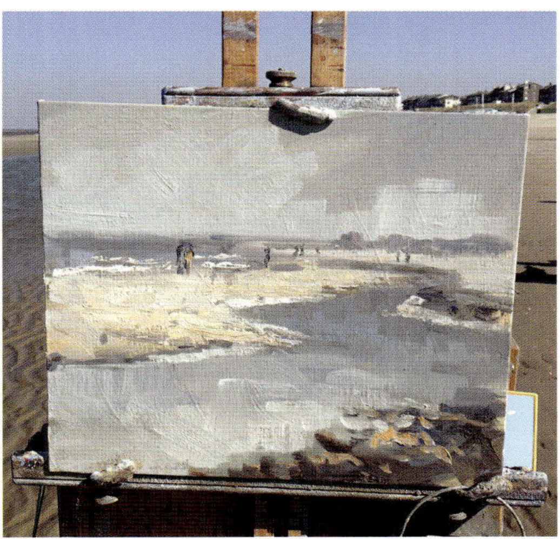

Katwijk 4
Titanium White
Cadmium Yellow
Burnt Umber
Cobalt Blue
Cadmium Red
10" × 12" Gessoed board
Yellow Ochre ground

The tide was on its way out, very rapidly leaving sand banks, which created interesting shapes. The sky was clear blue and not very remarkable so choosing a high horizon was the best option for me here. I also decided to keep to the muted palette I'd been using for the last couple of days as I was really getting to grips with mixing the colours that I wanted, and liked the overall effect. The bottom right hand corner adds weight to the composition. Note how the water in the foreground registers light against the stones whereas the middle distant water registers dark against the lighter sand bank. These contrasts all help to attract attention to a painting. Imagine how flat it would look if the water and the sand were the same tone and colour. Likewise, the water on the horizon is painted dark to add emphasis to the lighter sky.

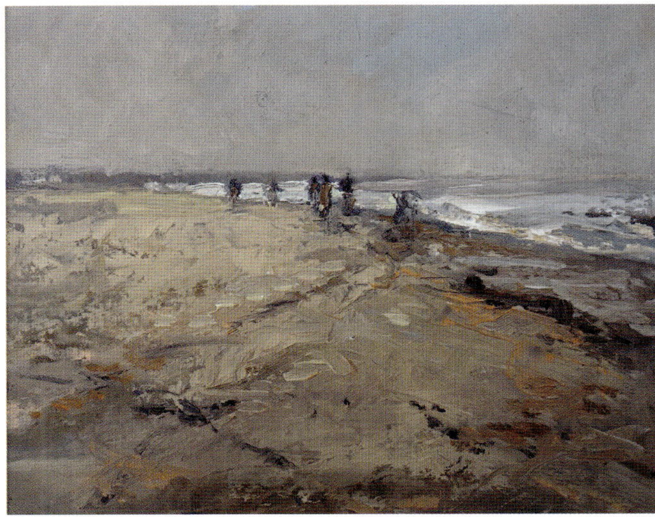

Katwijk 5
The same palette as in the previous ones in the series, this time with less sky and more beach. The same colours were used in the sky and sand.

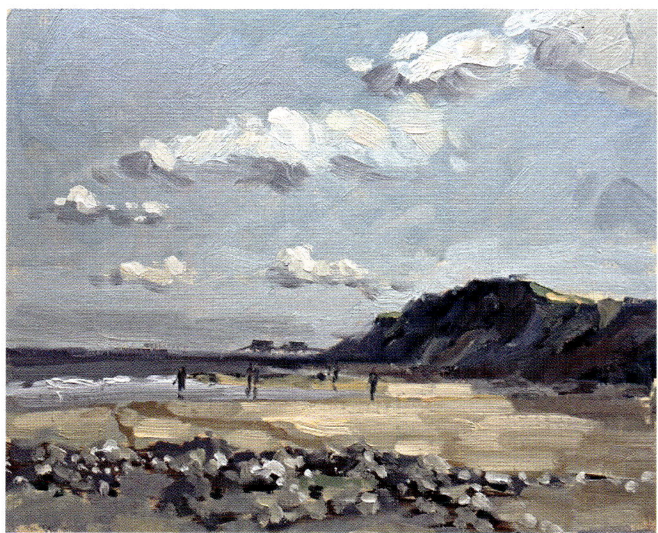

Summer Clouds, West Runton.
This *plein air* study was painted in an hour to keep a fresh, airy feel to it.

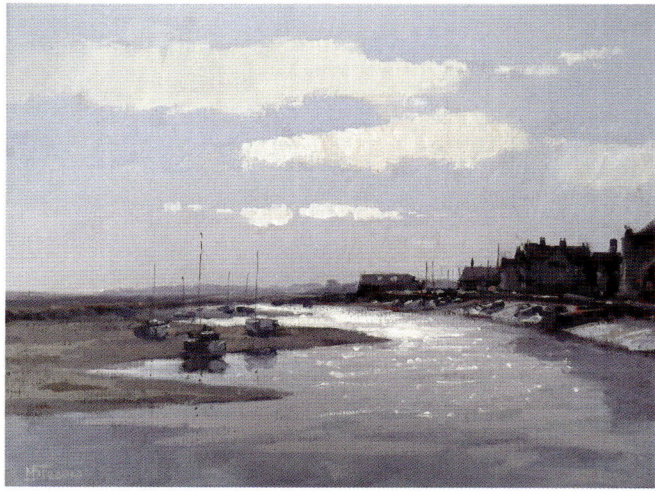

Wells-Next-the-Sea
Kings Blue Light
Burnt Sienna
Cadmium Red
Warm White
14" × 18" Gessoed board
Burnt Sienna ground

The simplicity of the sky echoing the shape of the sand bank helps to make this composition work. With a busy foreground, a simple sky is sometimes all that is needed. The limited palette also helps to hold the painting together. Kings Blue Light is a wonderful colour but I usually knock it back a bit by adding a touch of Cadmium Red and/or Burnt Sienna. Painted from the top of the board, leaving the bulk of the area for the main clouds, more Cadmium Red and Warm White were added towards the horizon. The main clouds of Warm White and touch of Burnt Sienna were allowed to mix with the blue sky and the lower cloud was painted on with a softer brush so as not to disturb the paint underneath. The water reflects the sky colours. Lastly, the sparkle on the water was flicked in with Warm White using a rigger.

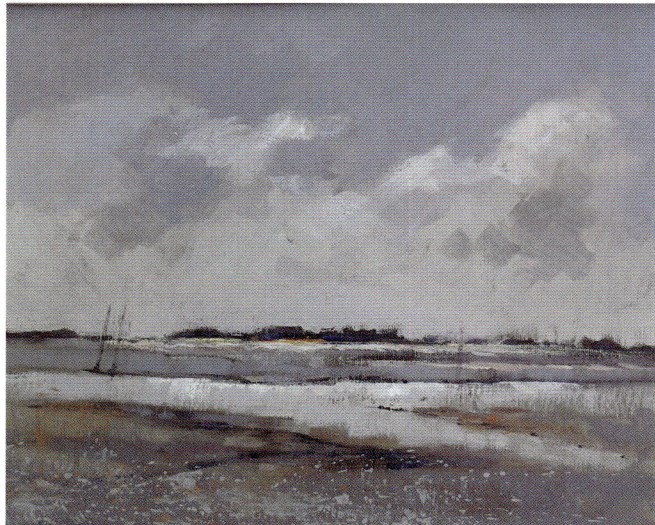

Wells, Low Tide
Kings Blue Light
Ultramarine Blue
Cadmium Yellow Deep
Cadmium Red
Titanium White
14" × 18" Stretched cotton canvas
Yellow Ochre ground

The low horizon emphasizes the vast sky. The clouds were building up and coming forwards. There was a warm light just above the horizon giving a good strong contrast to the distant trees. The trees were kept loose and on the blue side, and the strong yellow in front serves to lift the painting. The water was dragged over the nearly dry mid ground, giving soft edges. Echoes of the Cadmium Yellow were added to the foreground. Reflected clouds in the water add highlights and help to give interest. The final touch was to dilute some white with turpentine and flick some suggestions of stones into the foreground.

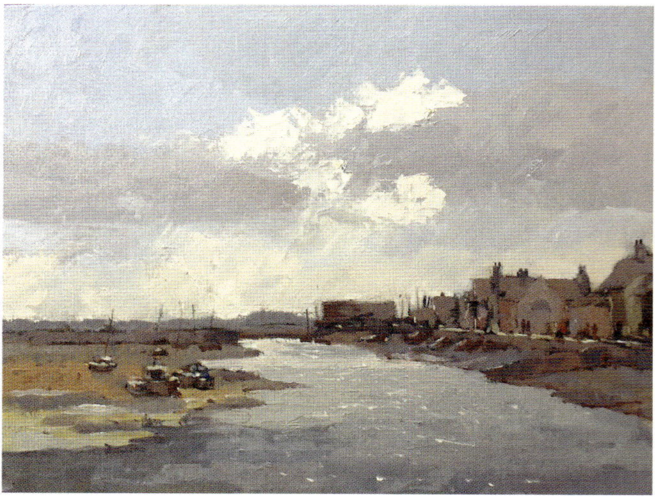

Summer, Wells.
This is the same subject as Wells-Next-the-Sea, but with warmer colours. Note how the sandy bank in the first picture registers dark against the sea in the foreground whilst in the second picture, we have a different register enabling the effect of light on the sand.

STEP BY STEP DEMONSTRATION

Towards Hunstanton

This is a particularly good composition. The beach with its lines of seaweed and detritus leads us to the cliffs which act as a focal point. The grassy dunes and the pine trees also lead into the picture. Figures give scale and more interest.

Paint

- Alkyd Titanium White
- Cadmium Yellow
- French Ultramarine
- Permanent Rose
- Palette knife to mix pools of paint
- Canvas board 14" × 18"

Brushes

- No. 4 Round
- No. 6 Filbert
- No. 6 Flat
- No. 10 Flat
- SAA Acrylic brushes

I am working on a toned canvas using just three colours plus Alkyd White. This has a few advantages: first, it keeps the weight down when travelling; second, you get to know your colours and mixes really well; third, it creates a harmony within the painting and fourthly, the Alkyd White dries very quickly and the picture can be touch dry the next day – also good when travelling.

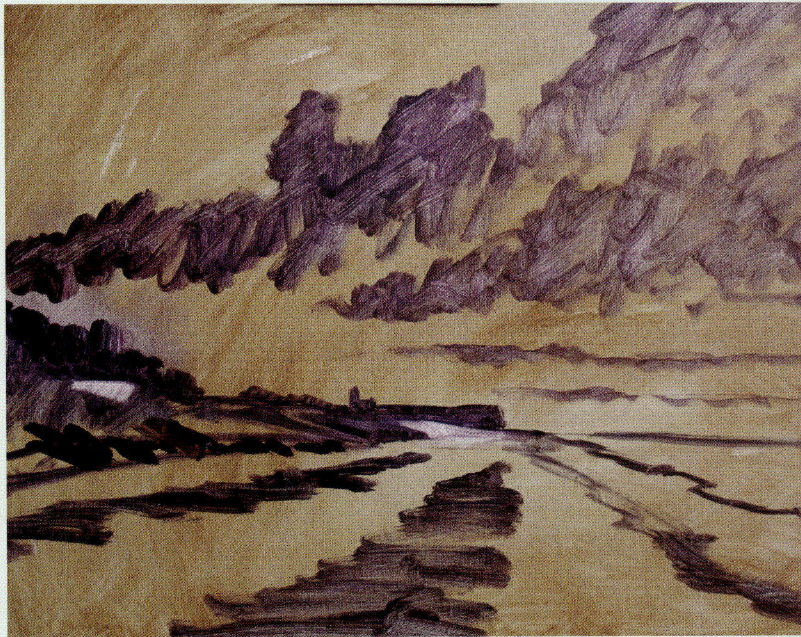

Step 1. I mixed a dark using Ultramarine Blue, Permanent Rose and a touch of Cadmium Yellow. This was diluted with turpentine to make a thin wash. With this, I blocked in the composition and the cloud formation.

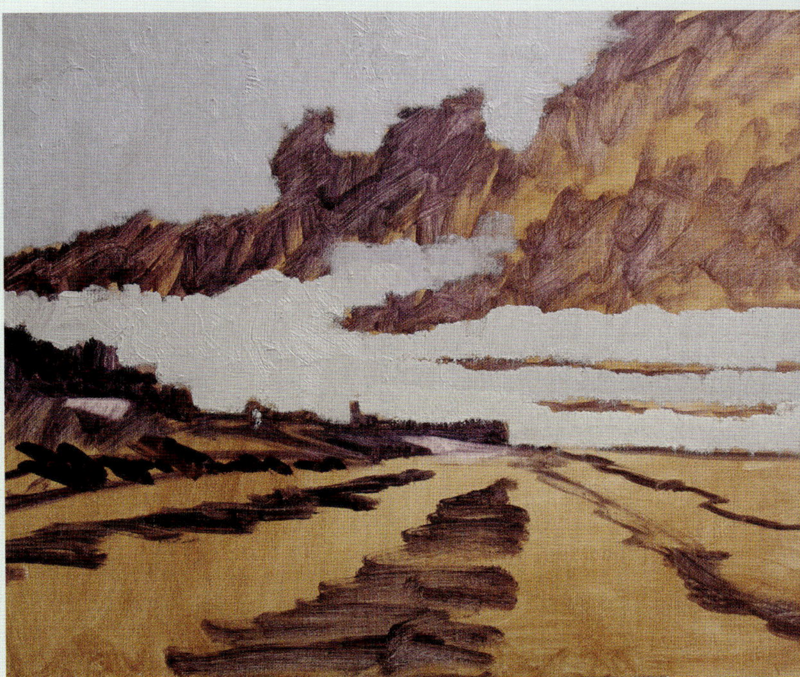

Step 2. The sky colour was mixed starting with a large amount of white, gradually adding the French Ultramarine until I achieved the tone I wanted, then I added a pinprick at a time of Cadmium Yellow. This softens the blue and gives a more natural looking colour. I added more white and yellow as I got towards the horizon. I applied the paint with my large brush, not spreading it too thinly. Note: Cadmium Yellow is a strong pigment and you can very quickly end up with green.

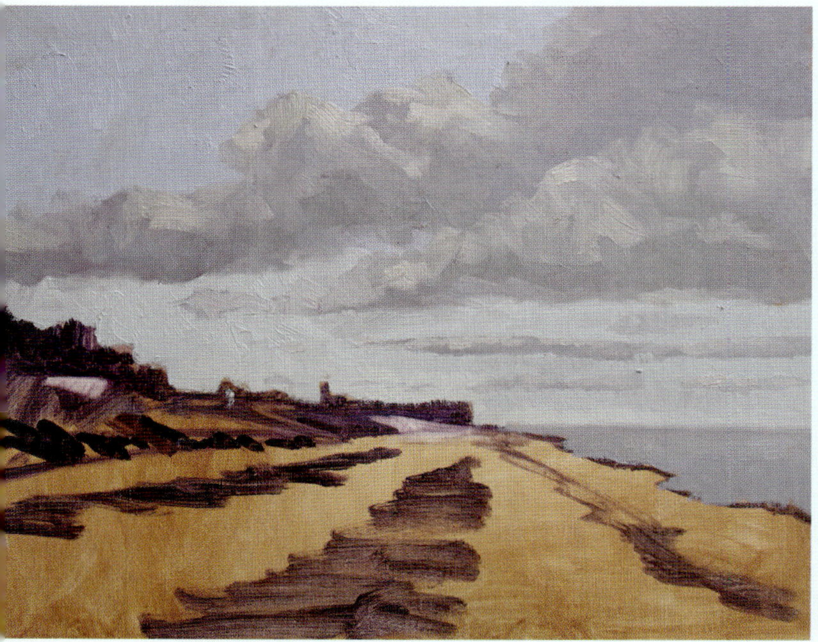

Step 3. The clouds are predominantly French Ultramarine and Permanent Rose with a touch of Cadmium Yellow and White. I made a couple of pools varying the tones. Using a large brush, I applied the paint in broad, loose strokes and avoided over blending. The highlights on the clouds are white with the smallest amount of Cadmium Yellow and Permanent Rose with a touch of French Ultramarine to knock back the brightness. The sea was put in next, using some of the colour left from the sky.

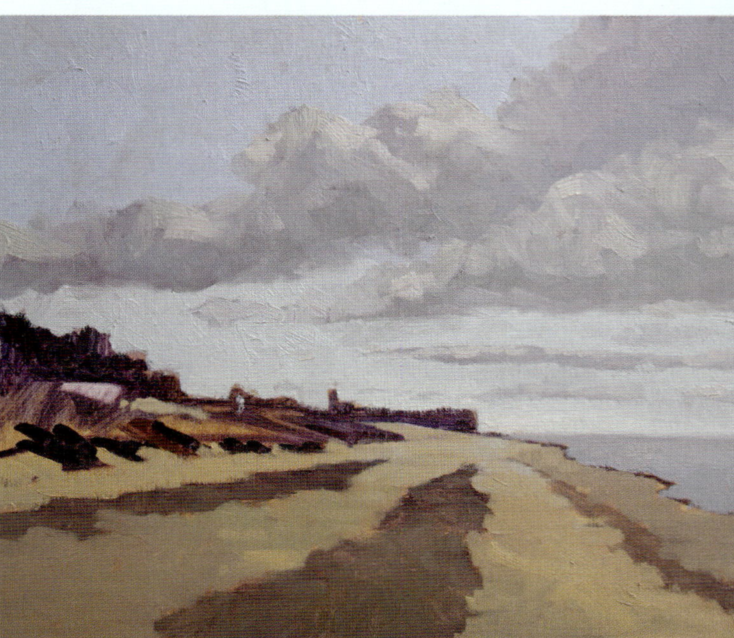

Step 4. The sand is a mix of Cadmium Yellow and Permanent Rose with a little French Ultramarine added. I worked dark to light in order to scumble (drag a dry mix of paint lightly over the surface) with a lighter mix. I applied the paint in a loose, lively manner and lightened the sand as it recedes into the picture. The area of detritus washed up on the tide line gives a wonderful perspective leading into the painting. This was painted using some of the cloud shadow colour.

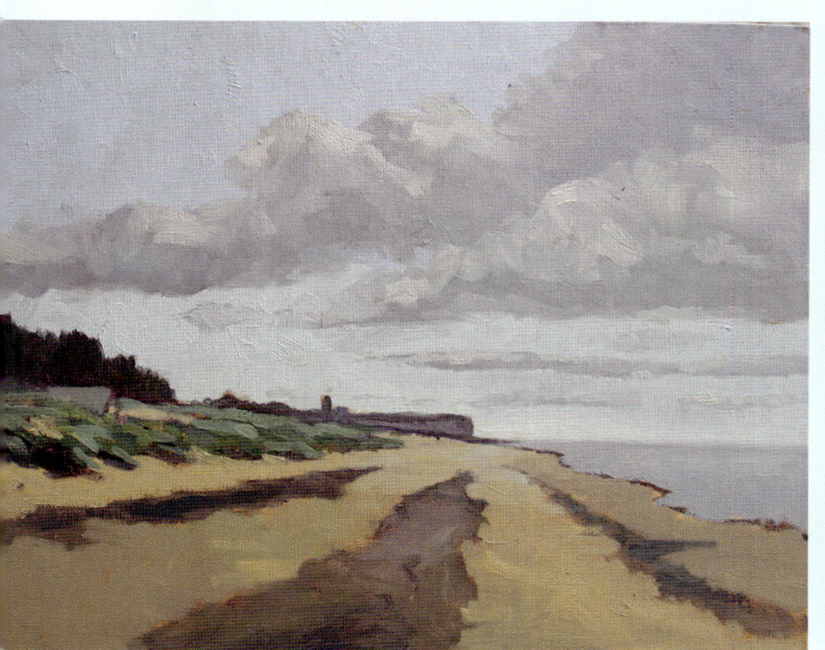

Step 5. Using mostly French Ultramarine and Permanent Rose with a touch of yellow, I added colour to the tree line, avoiding hard edges. Next I gave the distant cliff a bit more definition and started to give form to the sand dunes using a filbert hog brush. For the grass on the dunes, I mixed French Ultramarine and Cadmium Yellow and a hint of Permanent Rose. More blue and white towards the distance, letting some of the dark under painting show through. This gives the feeling of depth.

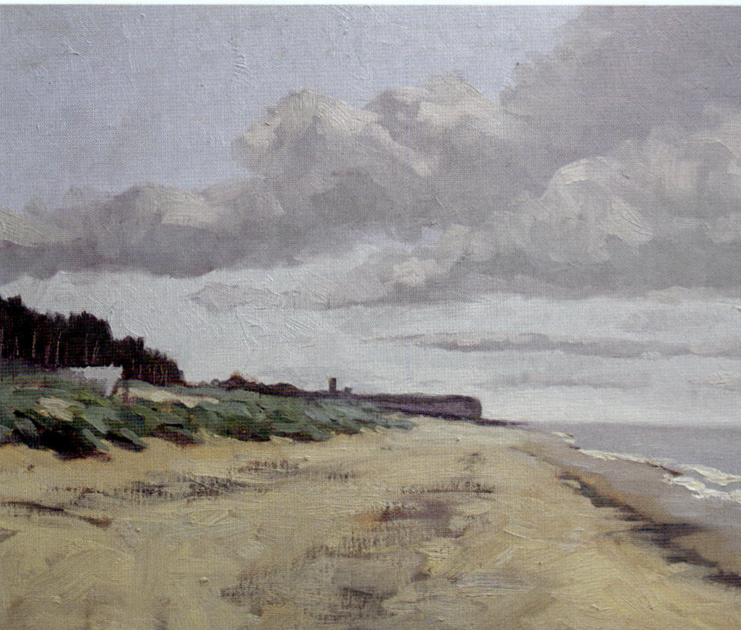

Step 6. Waves were put in using white with a dash of Cadmium Yellow and the wet sand was sky colour dragged into the sand. I lightened the original sand colour and with a large hog brush, I lightly dragged it across the darker colour.

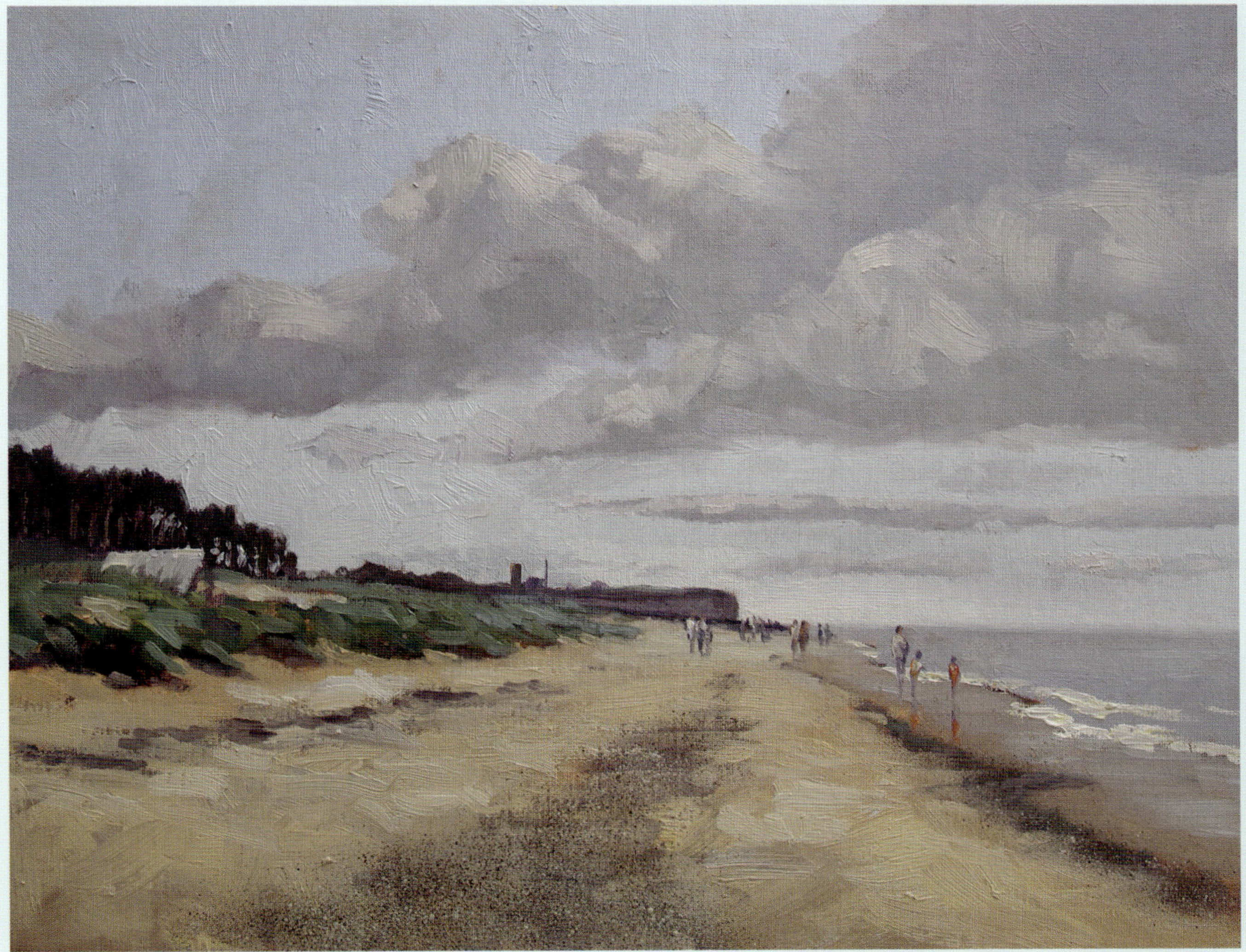

Step 7. Finally, a few highlights on the sand dunes and beach hut. Using my no. 4 round brush, the figures were added for scale and interest. The texture added to the foreground was done using my first-diluted dark. I flicked paint using my finger and a bristle brush. Then I repeated with a light sand mix diluted.

(Practise splattering on a spare piece of board first. If the mix is too wet then your splatter marks will be too big. When you decide the mix is right, cover areas to be kept clean with torn kitchen roll to protect the painting.)

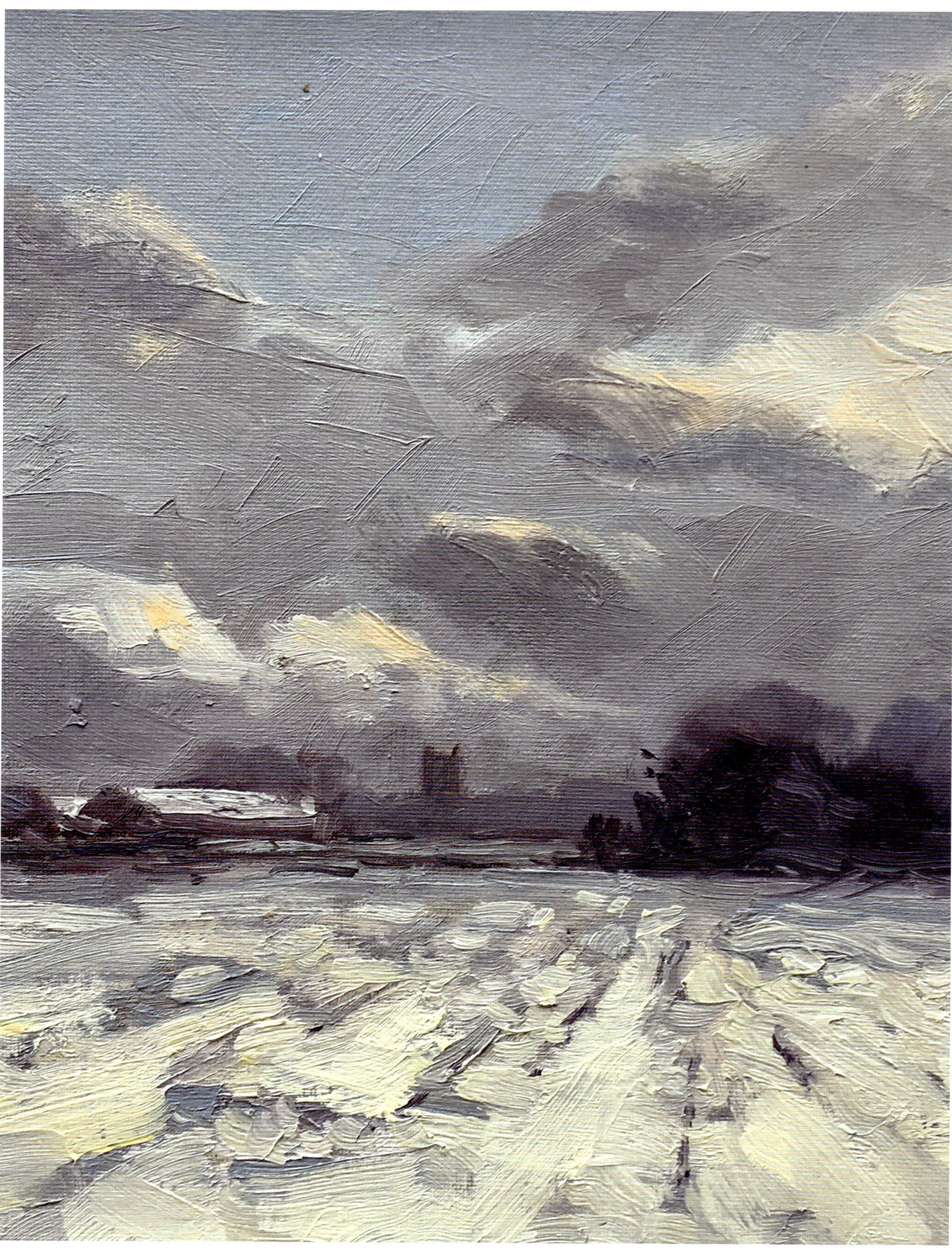

CHAPTER 6

Sky and snow

Snow is a favourite subject of many artists. It presents its own challenges. As shadows and light reflect in different ways, different colours may need to be employed.

In the UK we do not get many opportunities to paint snow as it is a bit of a rarity so when we do get the chance, you will find the *plein air* artists out in force, making the most of it.

In Holland, one such dedicated artist is Roos Schuring. When the snow falls, she has been known to drive many miles to reach it and she will be out regularly in the snow, often just before dawn, making the most of the opportunity.

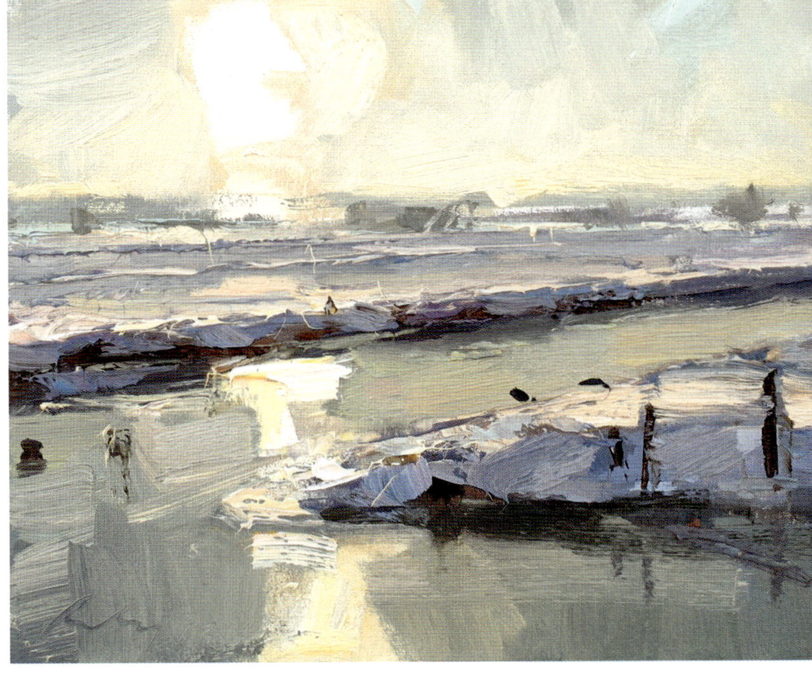

Landscape Winter Sun Reflected in Ice and Snow, Roos Schuring.
A simple subject and a limited palette are brought to life by the thick, broad, impasto brush marks. Imagine that this was painted with a small brush and blended – it would not have the same effect at all. Roos's handling of the brush and paint shows great confidence and her own unique style.

Whaplode Across Snowy Fields, 12" × 12" on canvas board.
When painting snow for the first time, a common mistake is to reach for the white paint. If you look at this painting, you will see that there is no white at all. In fact, the snow is pale grey/blue. Even when illuminated by the sun, it is rarely pure white, there will be subtle shades of pinks, blues and yellows reflected from the sky. Colour in this painting comes from the sky as the sun has dipped below the horizon, leaving the church in silhouette.

STEP BY STEP DEMONSTRATION

Hazy Sun and Snow

Paints and materials

- Warm White
- Yellow Ochre
- Ultramarine Blue
- Blue Grey
- Brownish Grey
- Magenta
- 8" × 10" linen board

Not every painting is a success. Painting over failed or old paintings not only is economical but the prepainted board or canvas often provides a surface that is good to paint on. This demonstration is painted over an older painting that has been sanded down to remove any obvious brush marks and to give a key to the gesso. Two coats of gesso were applied, the second being tinted with Pale Umber.

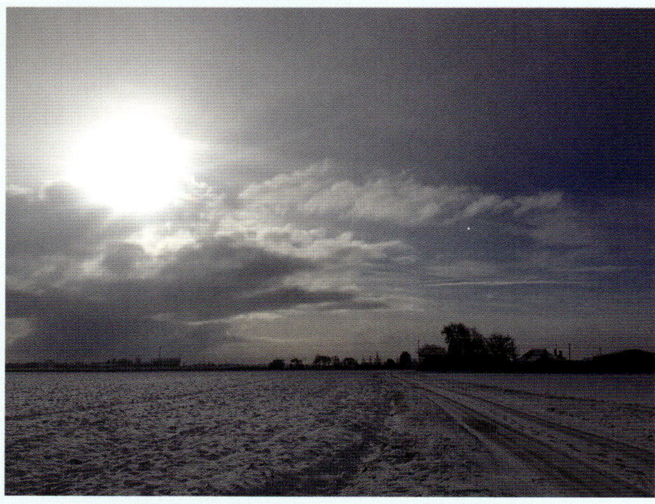

Hazy Sun and Snow.

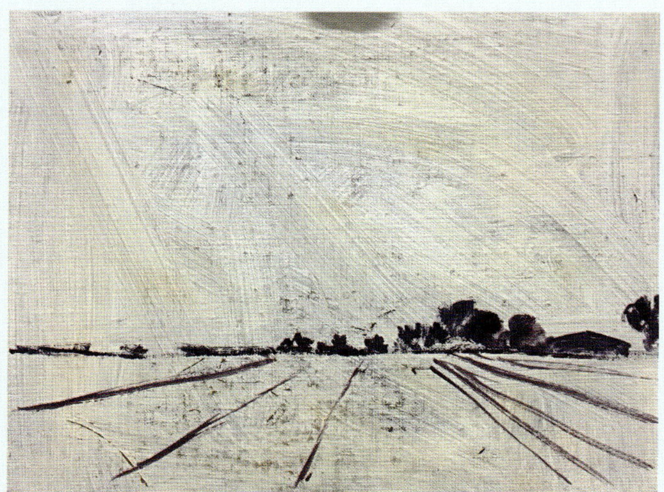

Step 1. Using a rigger, the trees and the building are indicated with a mix of Ultramarine, Magenta and a touch of Yellow Ochre. The lines of the field are also put in at this stage, giving a guide to the lines of perspective.

As it is predominantly a sky painting, the horizon is kept to a third. If the horizon were higher, there would have been a lot more foreground which would have unbalanced the composition and detracted from the sky.

The building on the right is moved in and another tree put to its right to balance the composition.

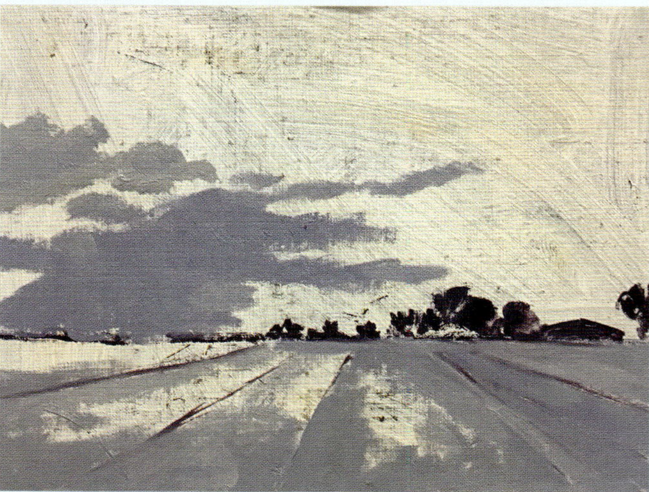

Step 2. Mix a few pools of grey using Blue Grey, Ultramarine and Brownish Grey.

The darkest clouds are painted thinly with a mixture of turpentine, Blue Grey, Ultramarine and Brownish Grey.

The dark areas in the field are put in at the same time using a combination of the prepared mixes.

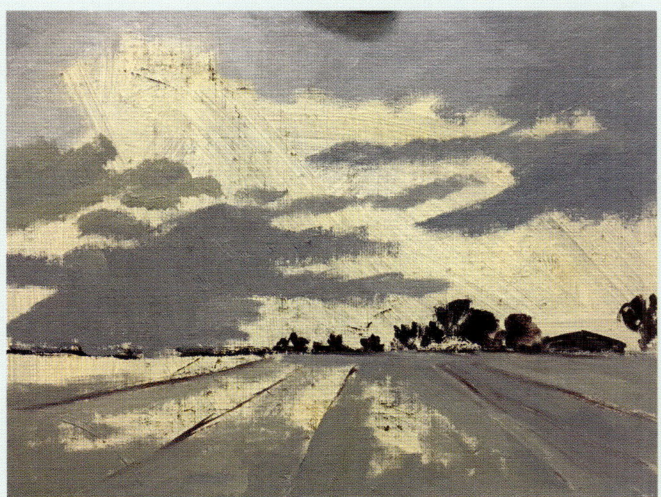

Step 3. The sky is a mix of Ultramarine and Blue Grey. A darker colour is applied in the top right corner with white and Brownish Grey added towards the left hand side. The areas for lighter clouds and sun are left untouched.

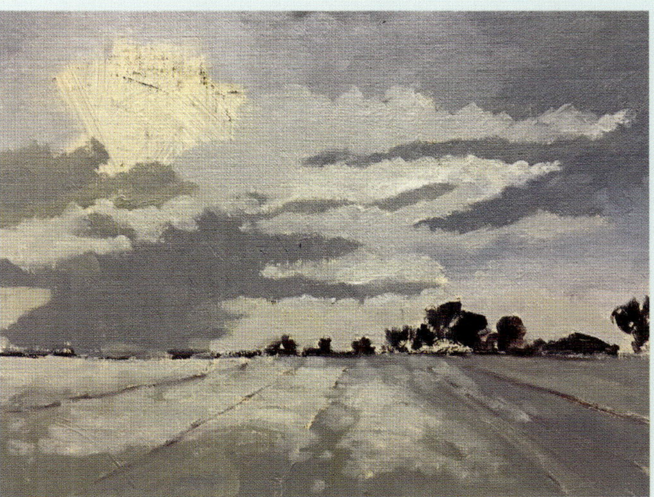

Step 4. Paint the lighter areas of the sky in between the clouds using a flat brush.

At this stage there is no blending. The lighter colour is also used on the fields. Yellow Ochre, Magenta and Warm White are added to Brownish Grey nearer to the horizon.

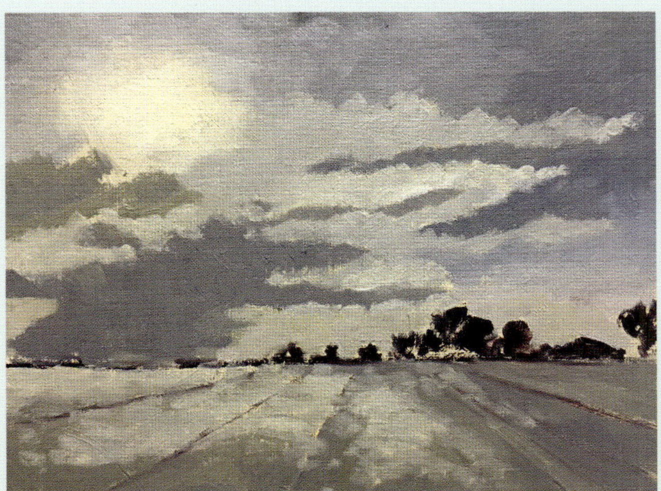

Step 5. The lightest area of sun is painted with Warm White and Yellow Ochre.

A big tip here is to start from the centre of the light area and blend towards the blue. By doing this, you will not be in danger of losing the fresh, clean colour of the centrer by picking up the surrounding, darker colour.

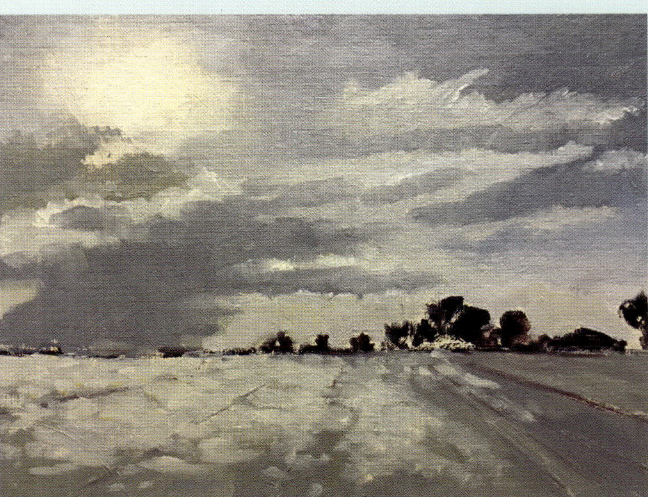

Step 6. Using a soft brush, start to blend the colours more to soften the edges of the clouds. Use two brushes: one with the light colour on and one with the darker colour on and switch between light and dark as appropriate.

Some of the dark cloud colour has been used to re-indicate the perspective lines in the field.

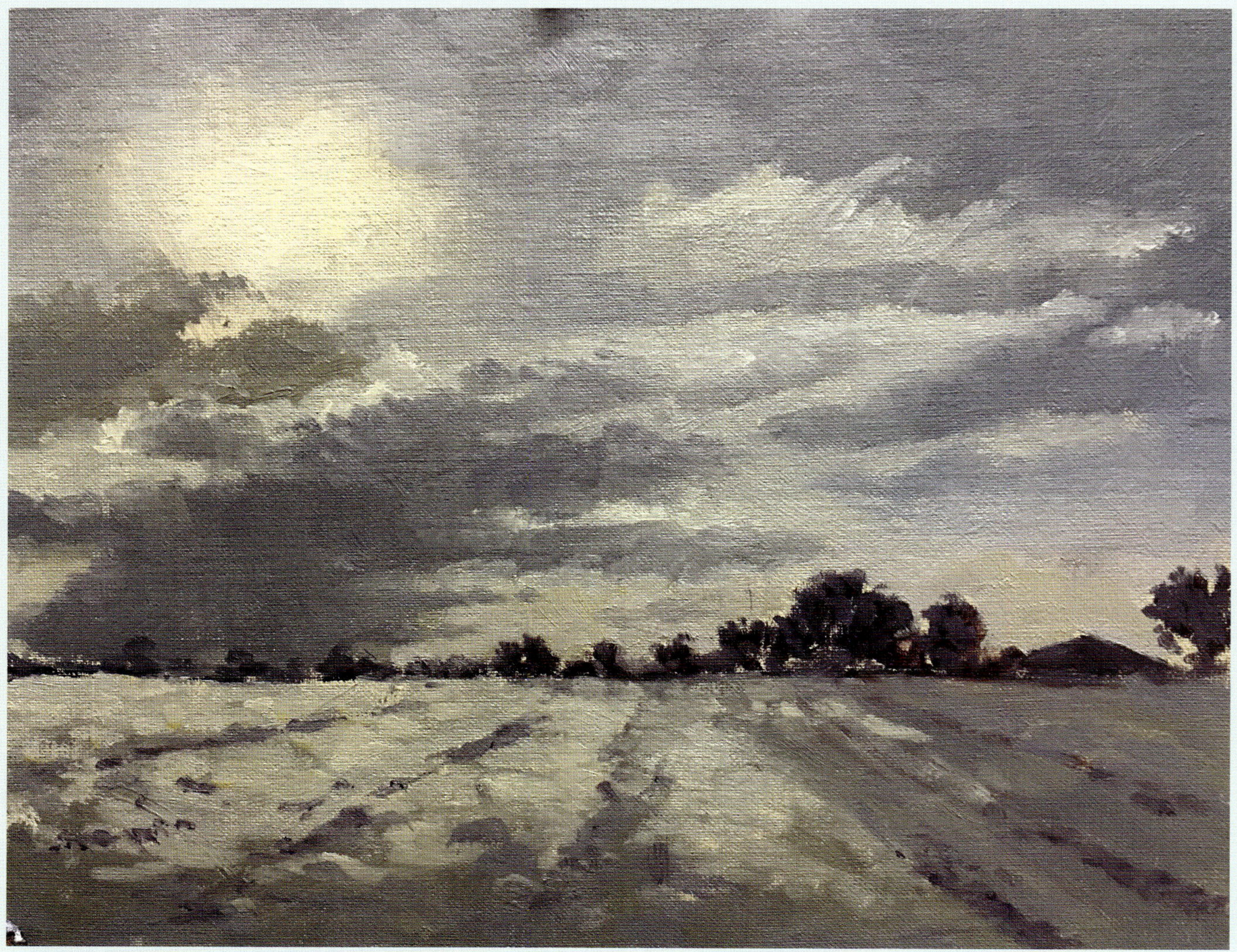

Step 7. The trees are the last to be painted. Until now they have been painted round carefully, and some may have lost their shape. To reinstate them and make them merge into the picture more, a mix of Ultramarine, Magenta and Yellow Ochre are painted over the initial colour.

Take care to leave some of the original dark colour showing as this helps to give depth.

Using a rigger, use some of the same colour to make some darker marks in the foreground to give some detail and added contrast.

Sun and Snow
Warm White
Cadmium Yellow
Cadmium Red
Ultramarine Blue
Titanium White
10" × 10" Gessoed board
Yellow Ochre ground

Sometimes the quick, spontaneous paintings are my favourite. This painting took about an hour to complete on location. It is a simple subject at first glance but there is a lot going on. The upper clouds took on a warm colour as the sun sank further. There was a glow on the snowy field, reflecting colour from the sky and the dark shifting clouds made interesting shapes in the sky. There was no particular focal point in the landscape to focus on. The interest really just comes from the contrasts in the sky. I kept the painting loose by using a no. 8 flat brush and working quickly with the limited palette. The last of the paint was applied thickly and I avoided any temptation to fiddle.

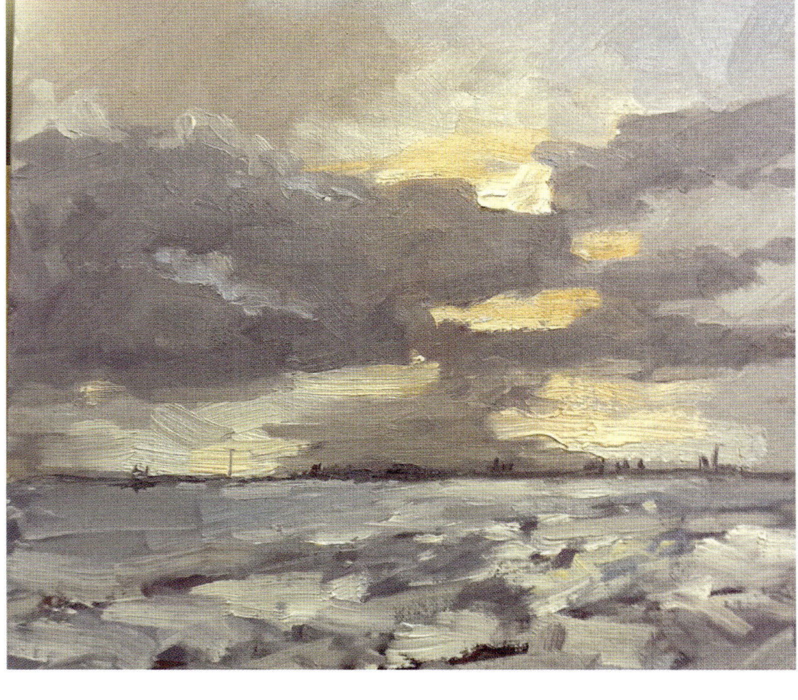

Frost and Fog
Cobalt Blue
Permanent Rose
Yellow Ochre
Warm White
8" × 10" Gessoed card
Burnt Umber ground

Another frosty morning. This time the sun had burnt off the hazy clouds above, showing a lovely cool blue sky. There was a low fog, which created a soft outline to the distant trees.

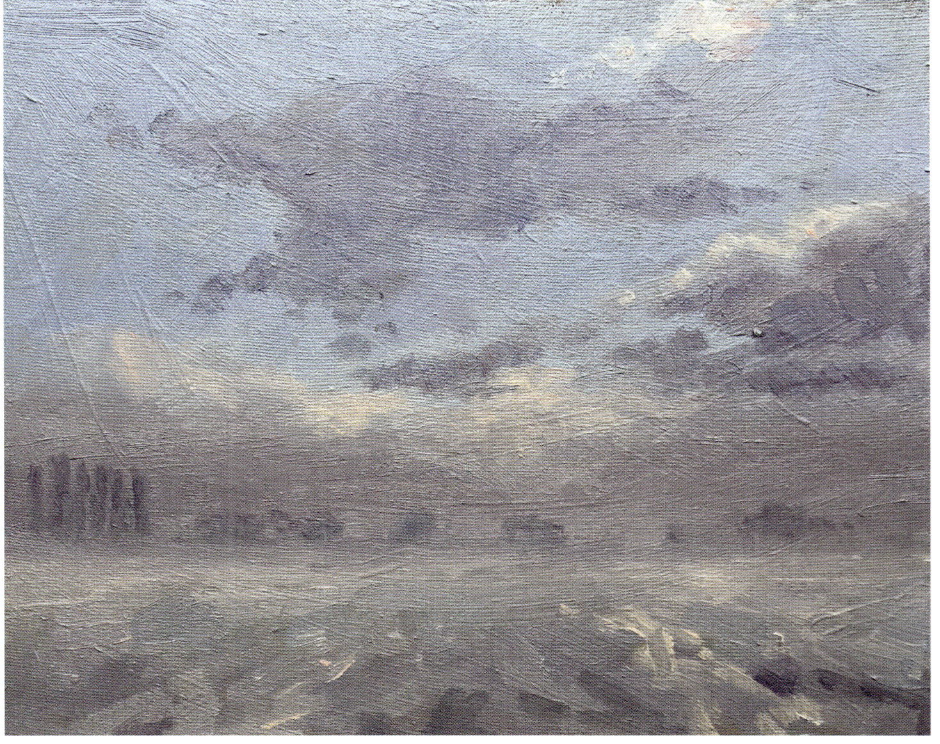

Frost

A good frost can have almost the same effect on the landscape as can snow. The same colours need to be employed, the main difference is that you don't have quite the depth of white as with snow and it tends to disappear a lot quicker.

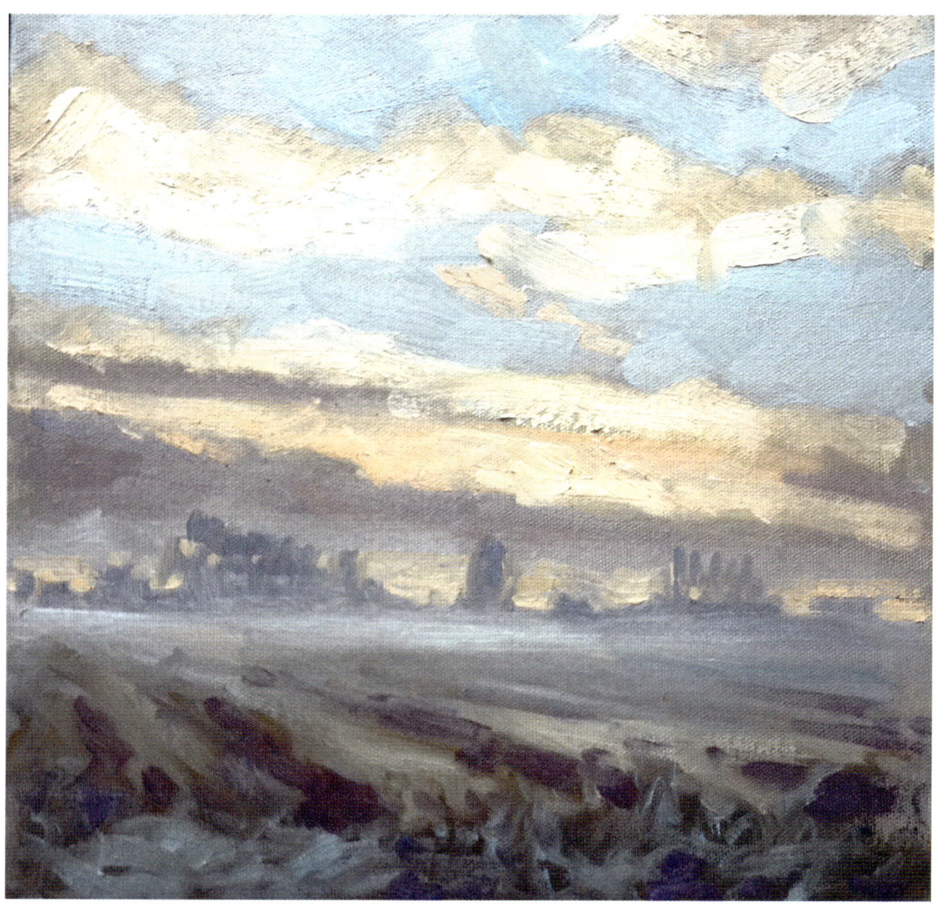

Misty Start
Titanium White
Yellow Ochre
Permanent Rose
Cobalt Blue
Burnt Umber
10" × 10" Gessoed card
Burnt Sienna ground

In this half hour study, I wanted to catch the early morning sunrise across the fields. There was a mist rising and the grass in the foreground was covered in a hoar frost, which adds for interest.

After deciding on the horizon level, the distant trees were indicated with Cobalt Blue/Permanent Rose and a little Yellow Ochre. Next, the dark clouds were put in with Permanent Rose/Cobalt Blue/Yellow Ochre, followed by the Yellow Ochre/Titanium White clouds and the Cobalt Blue sky. White was gradually added to the Cobalt Blue/Burnt Umber colour of the earth in the foreground as it travelled into the misty distance. By now the sky had lightened somewhat. I had to decide if I was going to leave my first colour or 'chase the light'. Having stood back and assessed the painting, I decided it would look better lighter so more Titanium White was added to the first Cobalt Blue mix. Also, more light was added to the underside of the clouds. Finally, Titanium White /Cobalt Blue was diluted with white spirit and, keeping the edges soft, was dragged lightly across the distance with a soft brush. The same mix was used for the grass at the front of the picture.

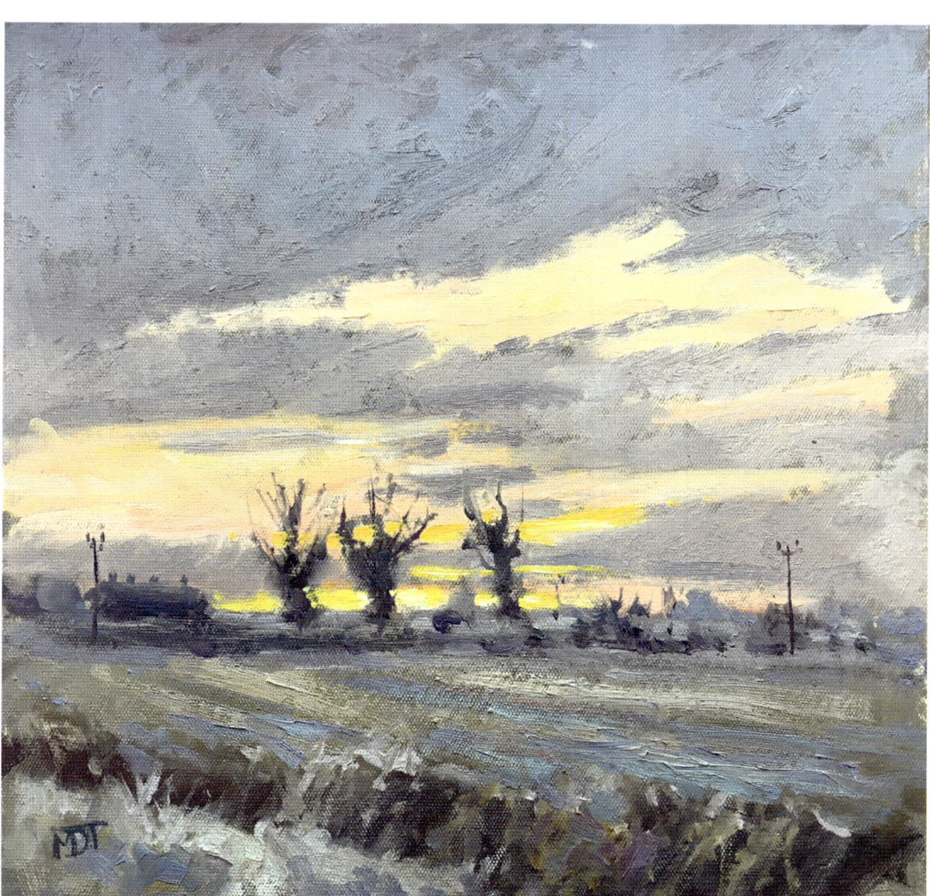

Frosty Sunrise
This was another early start. I set up and painted this at 7 a.m. one winter. It took about forty-five minutes to capture this sunrise. As I packed up, the sky turned the most wonderful red, going to show that timing is all-important when painting the sunrise.

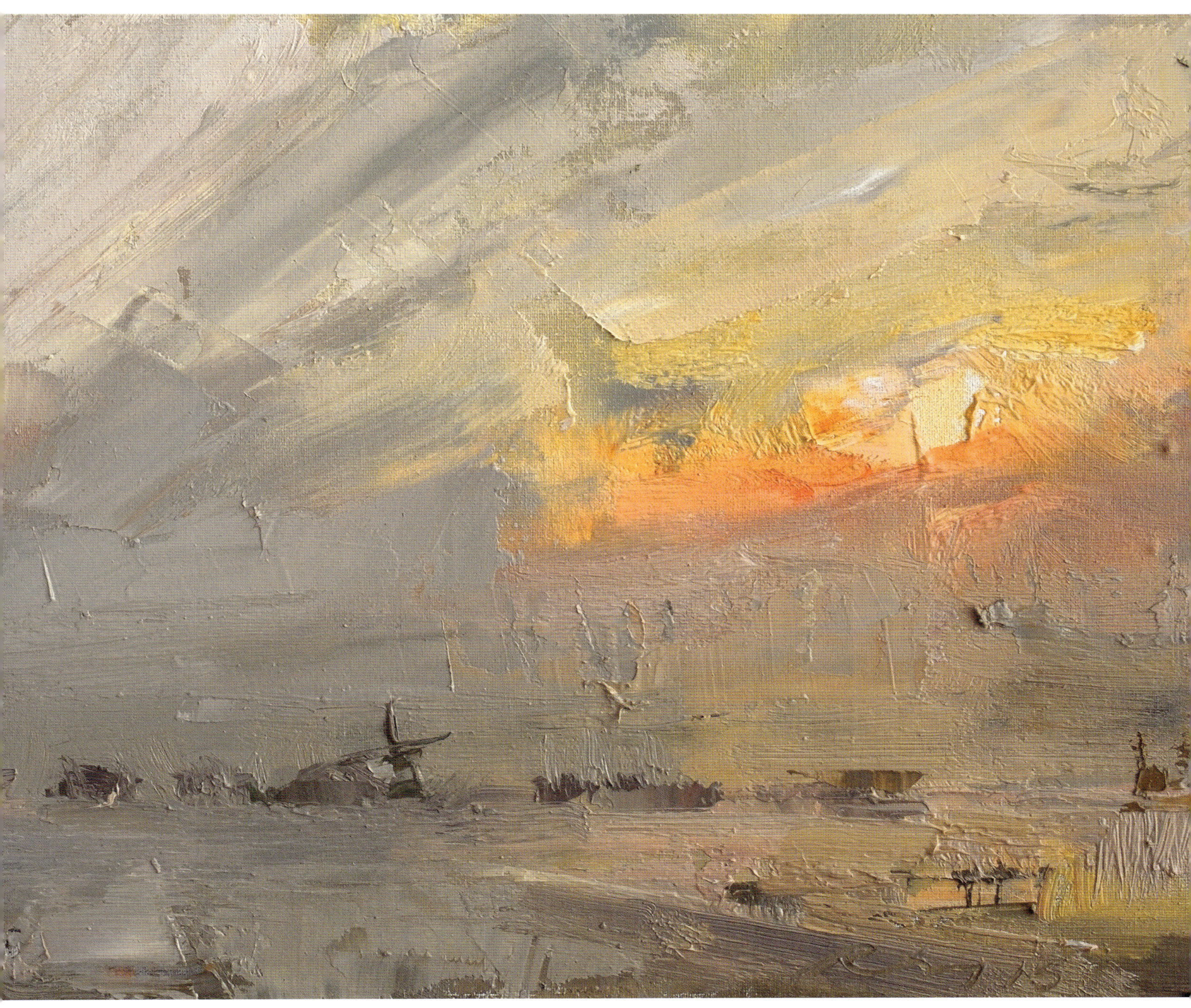

Misty Morning, Sunrise, Roos Schuring
At first glance, there is very little in this painting but there is indeed a lot happening. The windmill and the trees on the low horizon punctuate the misty haze. The same colours are used throughout the painting, both in the sky and on the land. Our eyes are drawn to the glow of the sun breaking through the haze and the glow of it is carried on down and softly reflected in the snow. Note how the sun is not a perfect orb, the broken shape works much better with the impasto marks.

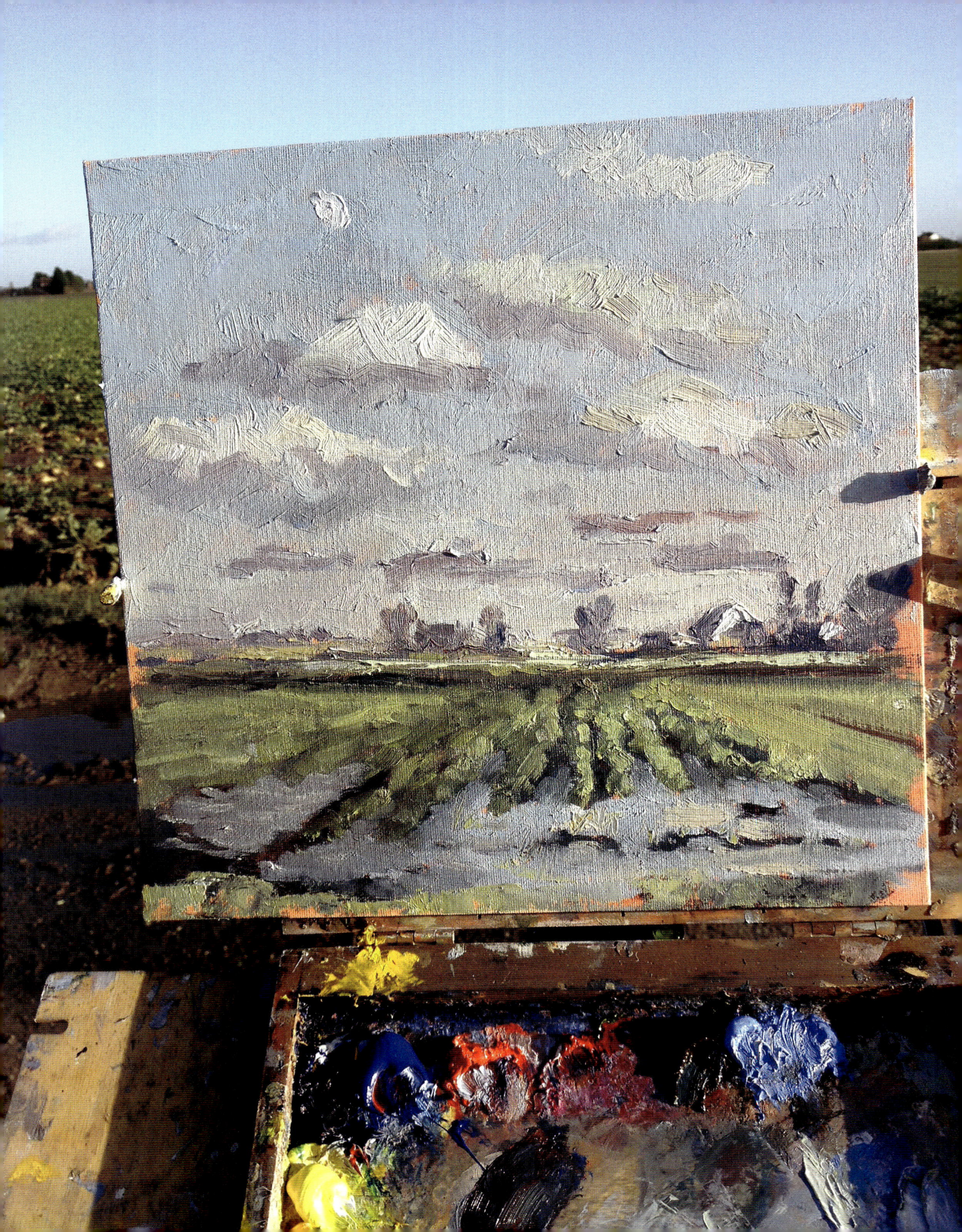

CHAPTER 7

Plein air vs studio

There are pros and cons for both *plein air* painting and studio work. Some artists prefer to paint out of doors in all weather whereas others rarely venture beyond the confines of their studio. Ultimately it really doesn't matter where or how a painting is created; what really matters is the end result. Does it have quality and does it express the feeling and meaning that the artist intended?

PLEIN AIR

Painting *plein air* means different things to different artists. One thing all *plein air* artists would agree on is that the experience of the landscape is essential to their own work. It makes each piece more memorable. There is also usually a story to tell, be it visiting wildlife, the weather or the public.

Some artists aim to complete a work in one session, while other artists will start work in the field, and add the finishing details in the studio and others just use their sketches as reference for larger works in the studio.

Plein Air Flooded Field, 12" × 12". Canvas board.
This was painted just after heavy rain while water still sat on the fields. It provided a good opportunity to reflect the colours of the sky. The clouds were moving quickly so close observation was of the essence as they had completely disappeared by the time I had finished the painting an hour later.

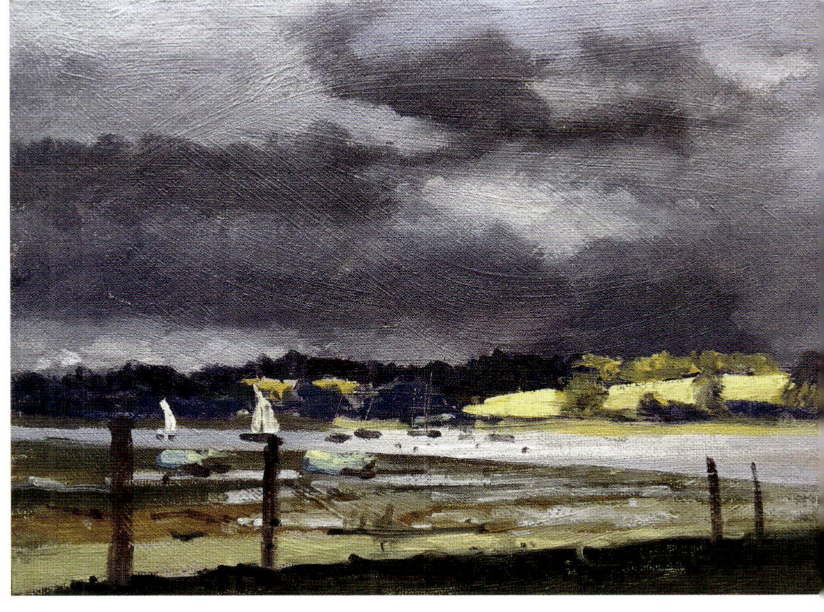

Dramatic Sky, Pin Mill
Titanium White
Lemon Yellow
Burnt Umber
Cadmium Red
Ultramarine Blue
8" × 10" Canvas board

This little picture was painted in between showers at Pin Mill. It was a flat, dull landscape until the sun popped out from behind the clouds, illuminating the distant rape field for a few minutes. I quickly grabbed the Lemon Yellow and dashed it in. The effect of putting in the yellow had totally transformed the painting. Had I not seen that strong contrast with my own eyes, I don't think I would have had the courage to put the yellow in quite as strong as it was.

'Being there' is one of the great advantages of *plein air* painting.

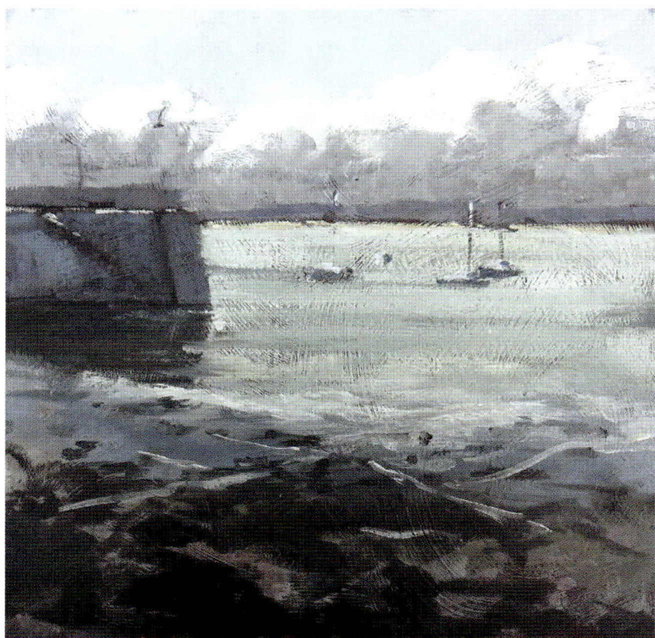

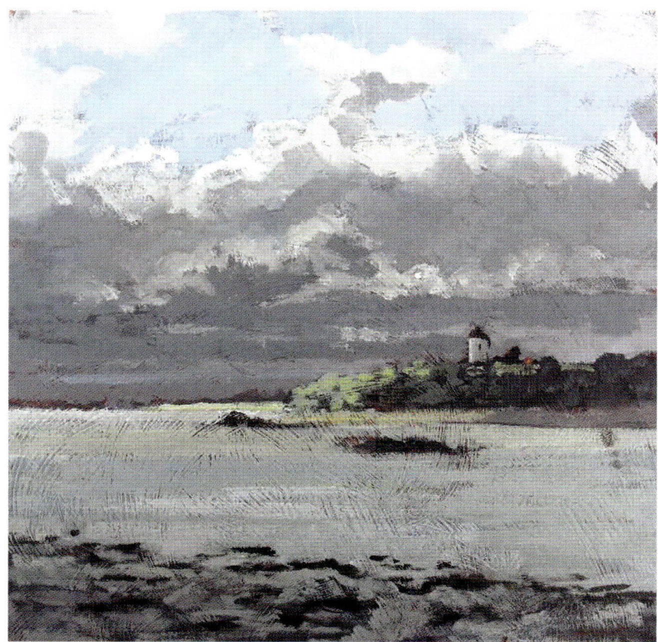

Concale
Cobalt Blue
Cadmium Yellow
Cadmium Red
Burnt Umber
Titanium White
6"x 6" Mount board, primed with gesso
Burnt Sienna ground

These two paintings at Concale, France, were painted on the same day at the same location.

In the first picture, there is a high horizon line, making the sky less important. The harbour and boats provide the interest. The strength of the rocks in the foreground provides weight and depth. As the painting progressed, the clouds on the horizon were building up rapidly so I turned to the right for a second painting. This time a low horizon makes the painting more about the clouds. I placed less emphasis on the foreground rocks this time. There was a strange light on the water as it reflected the sky and in both cases, it gave a good foil to the sky.

A common misconception about *plein air* painting is that some people view it as a style of painting. Granted, there is a certain style associated with it as most paintings are completed in a relatively short space of time, resulting in a looser style. There is also a belief that when painting outside, you have to work quickly and apply lots of paint. This is a skill that will develop through experience over time; don't try to rush to this stage, it will come with experience. Meanwhile, be thoughtful, take it slowly, observe closely and build layers up gradually.

Working wet into wet can also be a challenge and the most common trap people fall into is overworking the paint, resulting in muddy colours. Working from thin paint to thick paint will help to minimize this danger. Don't apply thick paint until you are sure you will not need to revisit that part of the painting again.

Tip: if you do need to apply a stroke or two over wet paint then use a soft brush.

Painting outside

It can be quite daunting to venture out on your own for the first time. For a start, there are so many elements to consider such as what equipment to take and where to go. We can easily talk ourselves out of painting outside by persuading ourselves that it is more difficult than it actually is, whereas the truth is that it just needs a bit of thought and careful planning.

What to take

Knowing what equipment to take is half the battle. In years gone by, artists would haul large heavy easels, canvases and paints out into the field, either to paint a finished painting or to make preparatory sketches. We are very fortunate today that art material manufacturers have addressed the situation by making more compact, sturdy and lighter field equipment. It is worth investing in a lightweight, compact easel if you intend doing a lot of outdoor painting but equally important is a good sturdy studio easel, for larger studio paintings.

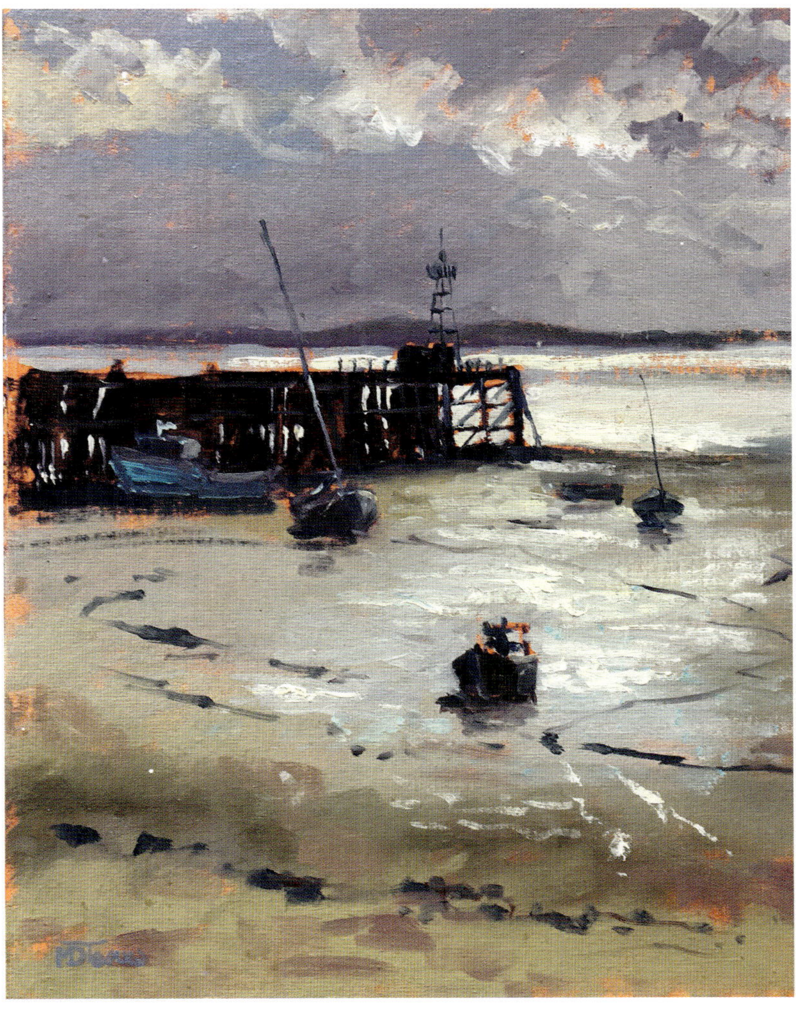

Concale, Low Tide
Titanium White
Yellow Ochre
Burnt Umber
Cadmium Red
Cobalt Blue
8" × 8" Canvas board
Red Ground

The red ground comes through as a good contrast in this quick study. The main focus of this painting is the pier, or jetty. The eye is drawn to this, as it is where the strongest contrasts occur. The clouds are reflected in the wet mud, giving juxtaposition to the stranded boat. A rigger is used to flick in the final light and dark marks in the foreground to break up the surface and help the eye travel around the painting.

Finding a place to paint

First you must decide on your intentions. Do you aim to complete a painting or just make on the spot studies? When faced with the wider landscape, there is so much to look at and to choose from that we have to make certain decisions.

A painting is often more about what we leave out than what we put in. Before setting out on a painting trip outside, try to have an idea of what you would achieve and where you would like to go. Many wasted hours can be spent driving around trying to find the ideal spot to paint. You must remember that just because a scene is beautiful, it does not mean that it will translate well into a painting; what really matters is how you respond to the subject.

Some people are put off by the idea of looking and feeling conspicuous when painting out. If this is how you feel, it might be an idea to find a quiet spot away from the general public. Even then you are bound to have someone come along and ask if they can have a look. You have to remember that if they have asked to see your painting, it is because they are genuinely interested and are usually very encouraging.

If you really don't want people to approach you, try to position yourself against a wall or object that will prevent people coming up and looking over your shoulder. Earphones, whether connected or not, will put people off trying to talk to you. Also, avoid eye contact; if you keep your head down and look busy, people will be discouraged from interrupting. If all this fails, just smile politely and say, 'Sorry, I can't talk right now as I only have a short time to get this done.'

Many artists have a favourite location that they return to time after time. The subject will never be the same as the weather and seasons change and there will always be something new to capture.

When painting in Concale with the Wapping group of artists, my picture, *Concale, Low Tide*, is a painting done from a position that I was continually drawn to. Each time I went back, the changes in light and weather were always different.

There is undeniably a freshness and immediacy in work

Tip: take a friend along. Try to find a painting buddy. Painting out with a friend can be a very companionable way to spend the day. You don't have to stand side by side and paint the same subject. One important point to make here is that once you have found your painting spot, agree before you start to paint on how long you will be there for. If your companion were a slow worker, it would be very frustrating to have finished your painting only to find they have only just sketched theirs out.

that has been executed outside. Nothing can quite compare to being in the actual landscape that you are painting. You can often feel the energy that the artist has put into the painting. You get a sense of place and can react to it. The atmosphere, feeling and light are something that the camera couldn't possibly capture.

I would encourage all artists to go out and paint on the spot, whether it is just to gather information in a few loose sketches, complete a painting or maybe something in between.

Whatever your intention, try to learn from the experience and you will find that your studio work will improve dramatically. It doesn't really matter where painting has been done, what does matter is the finished result. Stand back and look at your painting and ask yourself this: will the viewer feel what first inspired you to create the painting? Does it still have the feeling and expression that you first felt when you were inspired to paint that picture?

Working more quickly

Speed will come with confidence as you gain more experience. Working on a smaller scale will also enable you to complete a painting in less time. Using larger brushes will ensure that you cover the ground quicker and not fiddle in the early stages. Another aid to working quicker is to try to avoid putting in detail too soon as this will make you feel precious about it. Work on larger areas first. Do concentrate on your observational skills. Look for contrasts, negative and positive shapes, and be aware of spatial differences.

Dealing with changing light

Probably one of the greatest disadvantages of working outside is the fact that the light can change constantly. Typically on a sunny day, one minute the sun may be casting strong shadows, giving wonderful contrasts then the next minute, the sun can go, leaving everything looking tonally flat in comparison. So it is advisable to try not to spend more than an hour and a half on a painting as light and shadows can change so fast.

When painting outdoors, it is very tempting to chase the light. In other words, if you start your painting and the light changes dramatically, you must decide if you want to stick with your original concept or change it, but bear in mind, the light is likely to change again and you can't keep altering the picture. Clouds can move incredibly quickly. Make several quick pencil sketches in a sketchbook to use as the painting goes along.

You may start your painting with a cloudy sky and find there is not a cloud in sight as you finish so the sketches you made earlier will come in useful.

Try to visualize the finished painting in your mind and stick to that image. Shadows will move. Think ahead, will the scene look better when the sun has moved round? Where will it be? Would that building or tree look better if the sun caught only one side, leaving the rest in the shadow? Once you have made that decision, stick to it and place the shadows all at the same time. It is not unusual to see paintings that have been started in the morning with a tree shadow cast to the left and the painting finished in the afternoon with a telegraph pole casting a shadow to the right. I think you will agree that this is not very convincing to the viewer.

Another way around the problem of changing light is to take several canvases out with you. Monet was known to do this, working on a canvas for up to forty-five minutes at a time before working on the next one. This he would do over several days, working on each one at the same time of day until they were finished. This isn't always practical and so the answer would be to take the unfinished painting back to the studio to finish.

Another problem facing the *plein air* artist is selecting what to paint from the landscape around you. When you are in the studio working from a photograph, the scene has already been selected and cropped by the camera. When working outdoors, we are faced with a vast panorama. We have to select our subject from the larger scene in front of us. A good composition plays a very important part in making a good painting. This is where the viewfinder comes in handy. The viewfinder will help to crop the scene in front of you and help to eliminate the unnecessary.

Once you have decided on your selected subject, make two or three thumbnail sketches.

These don't have to be large or detailed but what is important is the placement of the main shapes. The thumbnails should also be tonal and stick to only three tones: dark, mid and light. This will help you to evaluate the composition as a whole and ensure that you have got a good balance.

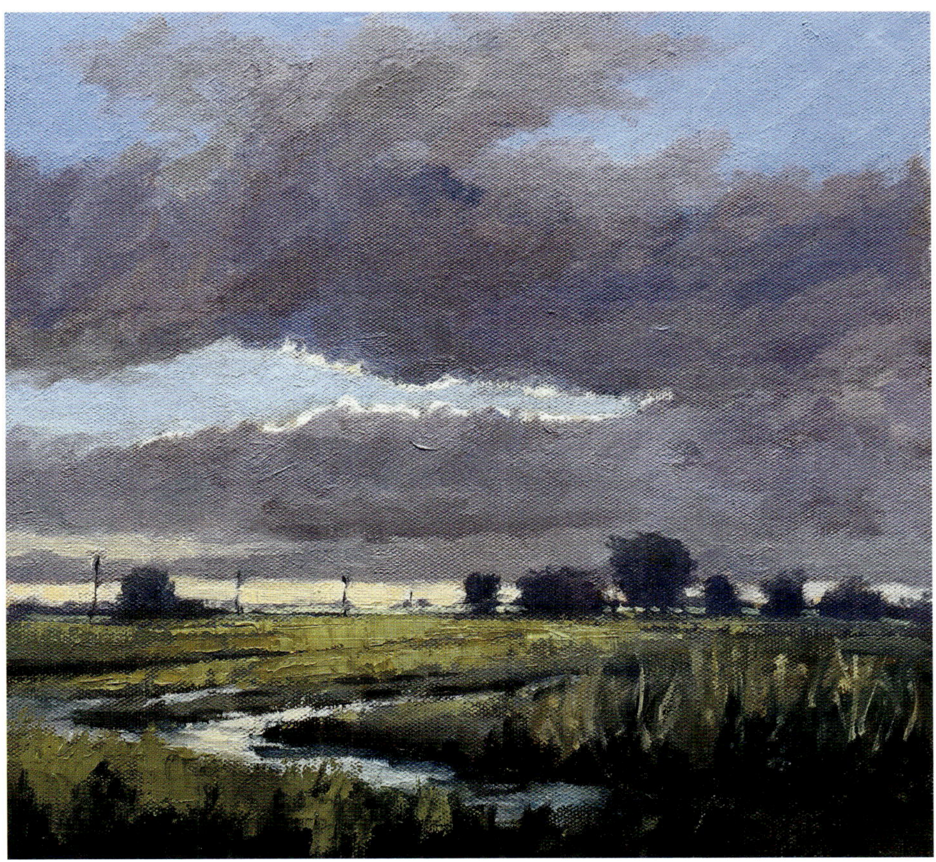

Dark Clouds and Stream.
This is an interesting composition that happened quite naturally. The shape of the clouds is almost a mirror image of the shape of the river. The dark foreground acts as a foil to the light of the water, reflecting the sky and leading us into the picture.

Thumbnail sketches are also useful for planning out cloud patterns and can be referred to if the sky suddenly becomes clear.

In the studio

When you have taken an unfinished *plein air* painting back to the studio to finish, you will have more time and there may be the temptation to overwork the picture, thus losing any feeling of spontaneity and freshness. Imagine yourself back at the location and try to give yourself a time limit. *Barge at Pin Mill* is a studio painting worked from a photograph and on limited time.

Working from a *plein air* sketch

Try to put yourself in mind of how you were feeling when you made your sketch and visualize yourself back there. If you are working from a *plein air* study, you should have already reached the stage where all details required for the painting have been mapped out. If the telegraph pole, post, distant trees and so on aren't in the painting then consider that it wasn't important to the picture in the first instance.

The advantage of having the painting back in your studio is that you have the time to consider what you have already painted. Stand back and take a good look. Looking at it in a mirror will help to see any compositional faults, as will putting it into an old frame.

Having a few frames in the studio is very useful. It is easy to overlook a crooked horizon or a building that might be leaning but once you put the picture in the frame, these faults stand out straightaway. Being in the studio means that you can work at a slower pace and also allows you to be more considered and analytical in the way that you apply paint.

PHOTOGRAPHS

American photographer Alfred Stieglitz took over 220 photographs of clouds between 1925 and 1934. He said:

> I wanted to photograph clouds to find out what I had learned in forty years about photography. Through clouds to put down my philosophy of life – to show that my photographs were not due to subject matter – not to special trees, or faces, or interiors to special privileges – clouds were there for everyone – no tax as yet on them – free.

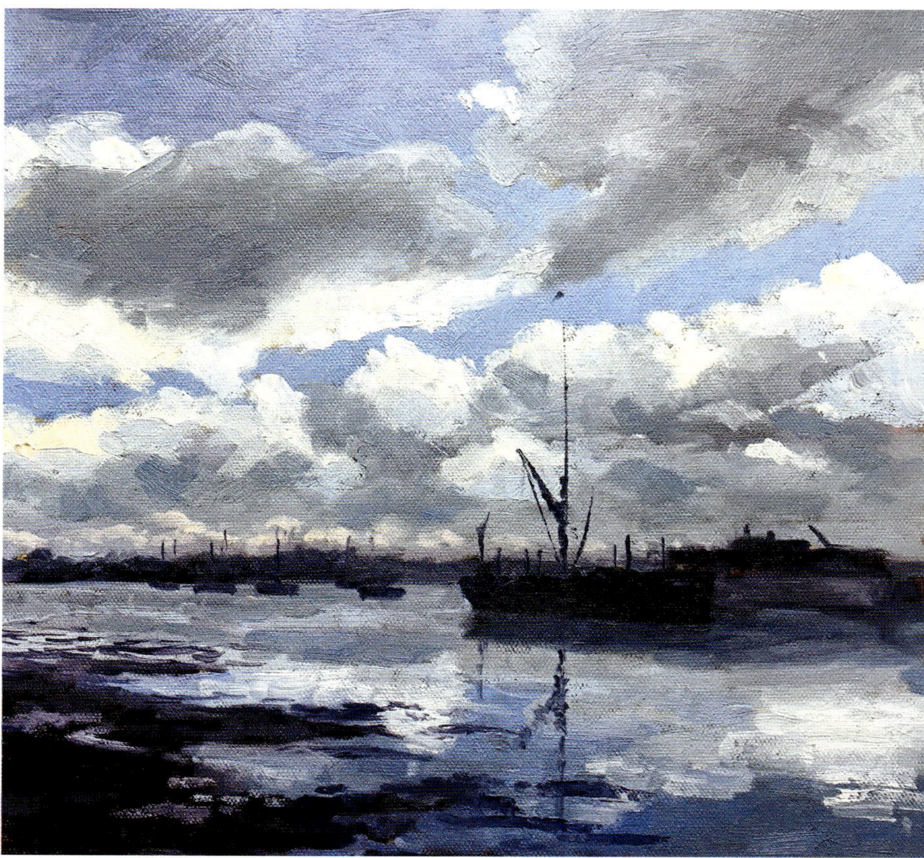

Barge at Pin Mill
(Painted over an old painting that had been sanded down.)
Warm Light Yellow
Cadmium Red
Kings Blue Deep
Ultramarine Blue
Blue Grey
12" × 12" Oil on canvas board

This painting took about an hour. I wanted to work quickly to avoid the temptation of blending too much. The photo reference showed the strong outlines and structure of the clouds, and I wanted to capture this with my brush strokes. I used a flat no. 6 brush from the Rosemary & Co Ivory range for most of the painting; this again inhibits the temptation to fiddle. The limited palette creates a harmony within the picture.

He was greatly influenced by the paintings of his wife Georgia O'Keefe. The early photographs featured some aspect of the landscape such as a tree or a building; later photographs were pure sky, with no points of reference. These photographs are recognized as some of the first abstract photography. He referred to the photographs as the equivalents because as he said, they were 'equivalent to my most profound life experiences.'

Through his photography, he was representing his feelings not necessarily through the subject but by the feeling he had about the subject.

At this time, photography was still comparatively new as an art form; filters, papers and developing techniques were still being advanced. Using the resources available to him, his photographs were very dark, sometimes the sky being almost black but that only served as a contrast to the light coloured clouds.

Photography has come a long way since then, especially with digital technology. Like Alfred, we can quickly capture a mood or feeling, our response to the subject. Without the camera, we would have to rely on a remembered image and later, as we try to recall that image, after the original stimulation has gone, details would fade and distort.

Working from photographs

These days, a lot of artists use reference photos for their studio landscape paintings. A good photograph is a useful source of reference, which can be used to create a captivating landscape painting. Choosing and using a good photo is an important step to the success of your finished painting. Problems can arise when the artist relies too heavily on a photograph for their emotional inspiration because photos lack the depth, value, colour and saturation of reality.

Photographs could never be a substitute for painting from life; they may capture a scene's beauty but the first emotional response will be a couple of steps removed. As an *aide-mémoire*, they are ideal and can be used for creative inspiration.

There are a lot of artists that rarely work from photographs, preferring to paint *plein air*, sometimes taking their oil sketches back to the studio to work up into a larger painting. This does of course mean working quickly to capture the moment. Working outside is not always practical for everyone and this is why photography is a great aid to the landscape painter as they can instantly catch a fleeting moment either in a single shot or a series of photographs. These photos can then be taken back to the studio and put

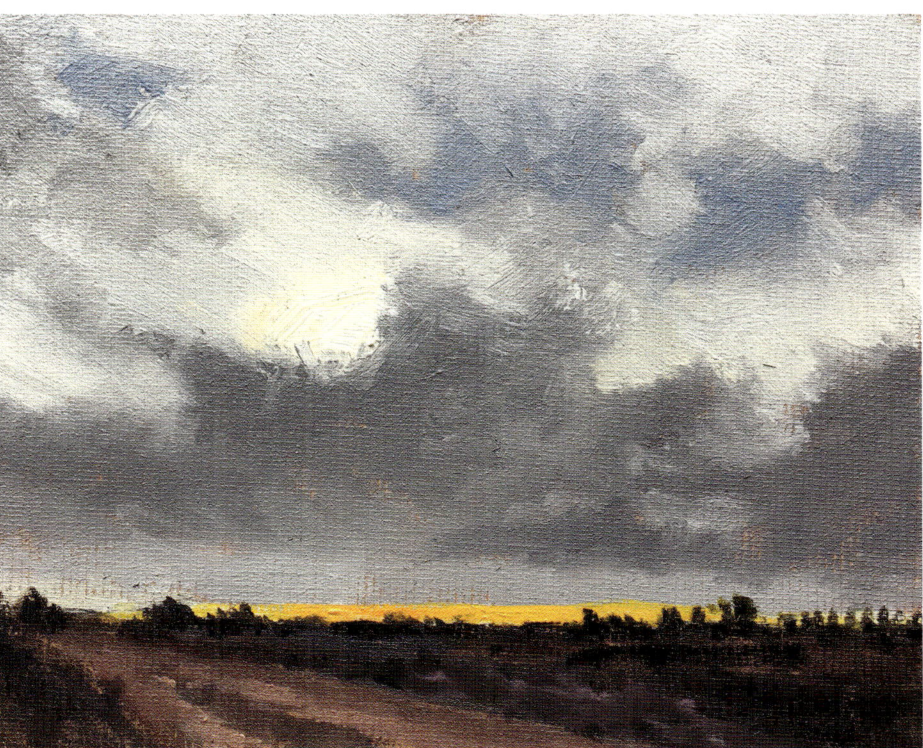

Lincolnshire Glow.
This painting was done from a photograph. The light in the sky was so fleeting that it would have gone by the time I had set up my easel.

For the sky I used:
Kings Blue Deep
Warm White
Blue Black
Naples Yellow

The light clouds were painted first, then the dark cloud was painted with Blue Black and Warm White. The blue of the sky was applied in between the still wet light clouds and then, working over the whole sky with a bristle brush, I softened all the edges, allowing some of the colours to mix. The glow on the horizon was first painted with white and allowed to dry. A thin wash of Cadmium Orange was laid over the white. By glazing like this, it allowed the white to shine through. Had I mixed the orange and white together, it would not have had the same glow.

onto a screen. However, as an artist, if you want to create a work that has feeling and mood, you really ought not to try and faithfully reproduce a photograph. A photograph is a great *aide-mémoire* but do not study it too hard or you will end up putting in a lot of unnecessary detail.

I always recommend when the student comes in with a photograph that they would like to use for a painting that they first make a tonal pencil sketch from the photograph. A softer pencil, for example a 5B, will give stronger darks and enable stronger contrasts in tones.

Once the sketch has been done, it is best to put the photograph to one side to avoid the temptation of referring to it and, as a result, adding more detail. You will find that in making your initial sketch, you will have picked out all the important elements of the design and less important elements will have been discarded. There are many advantages achieved by making a preliminary sketch. Firstly, making a sketch will help greatly in making for a better composition.

Bear in mind that you do not have to paint all of the photograph; maybe there was too wide an angle on the camera. If this is the case, you will be able to crop the picture if necessary. Cropping will help to focus in on the subject. For example, there may be too much foreground or sky and by reducing this, we are left without unnecessary detail. By careful placing of the different elements such as the horizon and main shapes, you will help to prevent any errors or issues that might have been made if you had started working straight from the photo such as the horizon, tree or building being in the middle of the painting.

It is much better to do this than to start the painting, realize that it is not right and then have to make alterations once the painting has been started.

A tonal study helps to see where the contrasts are going to be in the painting. It will help to plan where to place light that will make for a stronger contrast with the darks. Shadows can be used well for this.

By making a quick sketch, you will not be bogged down with finer details.

You tend to concentrate on the main shapes rather than how many fence posts and telegraph poles there are. You are instinctively picking out the most important elements of the photograph.

Once the sketch has been finished, it will obviously have no colour. Again, this can be an advantage as it enables us to plan our colour scheme rather than try to faithfully reproduce the colours from the photograph. Thought needs to be given as to the range of colours needed to recreate the atmosphere of that moment. Having a colour plan is a good idea. Is there a dominant colour in the picture? Do you want bright, saturated colours? Colour saturation refers to the intensity of a colour. When colour is fully saturated, the colour is considered pure. As another colour is added, such as

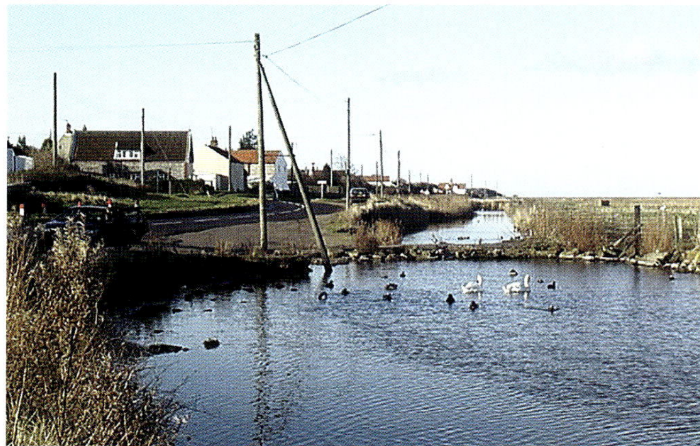

The photo reference for the *Salthouse* sketch.

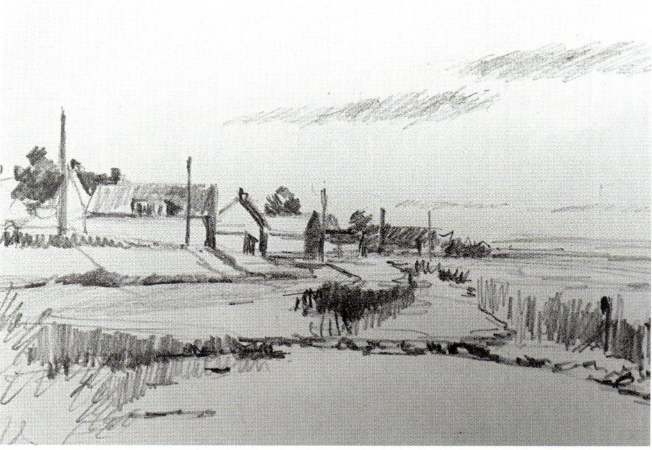

Salthouse sketch.

white, the saturation decreases and the colour appears to be more washed-out or pale: it becomes de-saturated. A neutral colour scheme might suit the subject better and a limited palette can be very useful.

Salthouse is an example of sketching from a photograph. You can see how the foreground has been reduced and details (such as the telegraph poles) have been left out.

The horizon is lowered because in the photograph it was at a midway point, cutting the picture in half; this is never a good thing compositionally. More has been made of the tree on the left so that the house can register light against the dark of the tree.

Tip: try out the same painting using different colours. You could try one version with cool primary colours and the same painting again with warm primaries. By experimenting like this, you will learn a lot and eventually be able to draw on your experience.

The camera is not able to capture the atmosphere and excitement that you could see and feel when you take your photograph. I have often taken a picture when I have seen a fantastic subject only to be disappointed when I look at it back home on my computer. Leading me to think, why did I take that?

If this happens then you have to think back, knowing that you were originally inspired by that particular subject and had therefore taken the photograph for a good reason. This is where making a pencil sketch from the photograph can be very useful. By making the sketch, you will be eliminating the extra details that the camera has captured, the details you did not notice when first seeing the scene. Even though the photograph may not be inspiring, by making a sketch, more often than not, you will be able to see your original inspiration.

Tips on using a camera

An automatic camera can take great pictures but such high levels of light from the sun can confuse it. Never look at the sun through a lens. Taking a photo *contre-jour* or towards the sun will create too much contrast between the sky or the ground. Either the sky will be completely white with no cloud detail or the ground will be entirely black. The best thing to do is to take two photographs but be careful not to change your sense of perspective.

A fixed lens camera can have a wide angle attached, such as a pocket camera or a phone. These lenses are always getting better and technology is still rapidly developing but it is a 'do it all' type of lens that distorts the reality of what your eye sees. Small details or distant objects can be hard to decipher once they have been printed out. Our eyes have a very forward focus and a relatively small scope of vision. If your subject is close and you have to turn your head to see it all then the lines of perspective will move. A wide angle lens is simulating what we can't see and bending it into one line of perspective, which is why images from photos can be unnaturally curved.

DSLR cameras are expensive but really good. A 50mm lens is the closest thing to what our eyes see; if you have one of these cameras you will see that there is a very narrow field of vision. It may be accurate but it can be limiting. If you are using one, try and get a good crossover between a wide angle and what the eye is seeing.

When editing a photograph digitally, be careful not to change the values too dramatically. Sometimes we need a little definition in the sky or the ground but by changing the light and dark values, the colours will also become either more or less saturated.

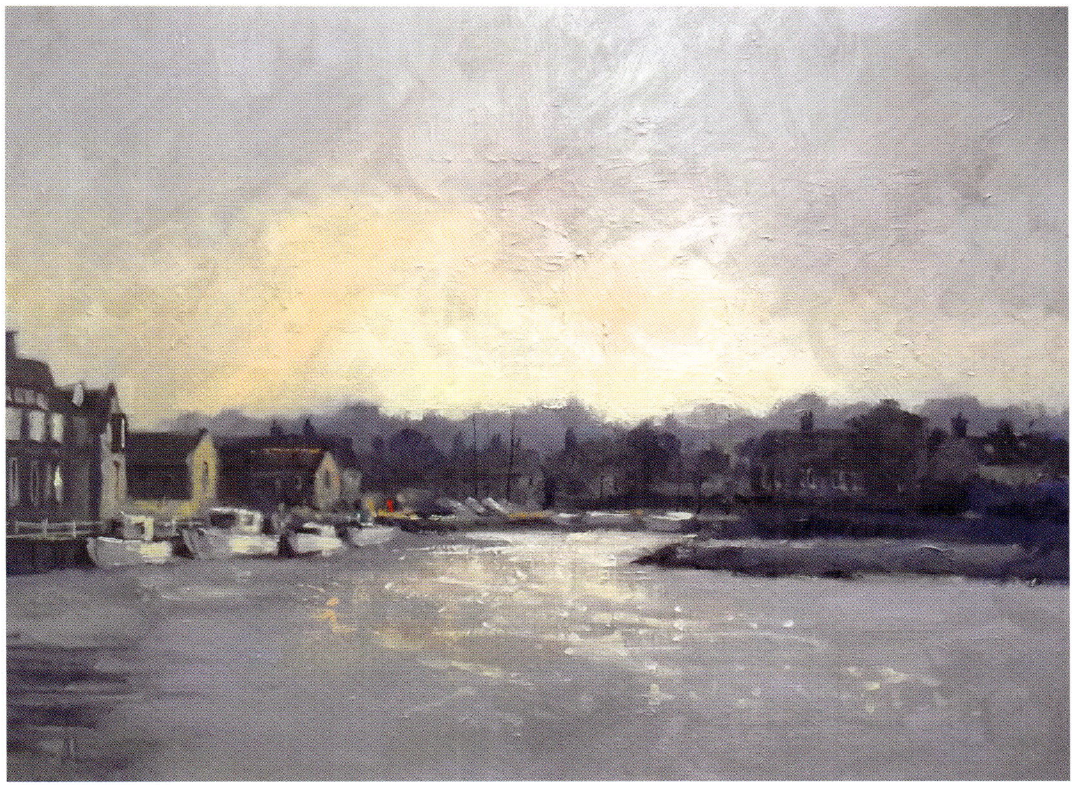

Evening Light, Blakeney. The tide at Blakeney comes in surprisingly quickly and often catches out unsuspecting motorists. On a high tide the water often covers the road. This particular tide was just right to capture the width of the creek and reflect the gentle colours of the sky.

If you are using a home printer, make sure all of your colours are working and you print onto good paper. Printing on copy paper you can lose a lot of tonal information. It's amazing how one manufacturer of ink can influence the colour of a print. I have often found my prints coming out too blue or too yellow compared to what I can see on the computer screen. I'm no expert when it comes to configuring printers and computers but it is certainly something to be aware of.

When we see a potential subject, our eye and mind can visualize the finished composition. The camera on the other hand will capture a larger area. Consider that the photograph may be a better composition if it were cropped. Of course, ideally, I should have made a sketch on the spot but as we all know, it's not always a practical alternative.

A main disadvantage of working from photographs and where the photograph fails us is that the camera tends to make everything look in sharp focus whereas in reality, the further the clouds and horizon are away from us, the softer they become. It is up to us as artists to interpret this.

Traps to avoid

A common mistake to be made when working from photographs is to work on the sky, maybe from one reference photograph and then to paint the landscape from a different reference. If not chosen carefully, two photographs will not make a complete picture. Imagine a beautiful summer sky with a few clouds; think how wrong the landscape would look if there were no shadows, or if the landscape was dull and not sunlit. Conversely, an overcast sky but the landscape bathed in sunlight would look just as wrong. That is not to say 'don't use two photographs for a painting'; do so by all means but choose carefully.

There is another trap to avoid in using two pictures. Make sure the sun is in the right place. The sun rises in the east and sets in the west. This means that if you were facing north when you took your photograph then it is very unlikely that the sun would be in front of you. This means that if you are painting a familiar landscape known to many, you will have to be mindful of the time of day, where the sun rises and where it sets.

Using technology

These days, many people have electronic tablets and phones with large screens that can store our photographs. This gives us easy access to our pictures wherever we are. These devices also take very good photographs, which is very useful for quick reference when working on location. For example, if while working on a painting outside, an interesting figure

ARTIST PROFILE

Mari French

I'm a full-time artist working from my studio, not far from the North Norfolk coast. As a keen mixed media artist, I enjoy experimenting with diverse materials, from acrylics and oils to ink, oil pastel, oil sticks, collage and paint pens, often in the same work – an unpredictable and exciting process.

Much of my artwork is inspired by the wild expanse of Norfolk's salt marsh coast, its sweeping shoreline and big skies, wind in the reeds, scribbled prints of waders on the sandbanks, light-filled marsh pools and the calls of geese. However, I'm not interested in achieving a true representation of the landscape, but in capturing a distillation of my experience and a loose, atmospheric evocation of place.

When painting in oils, I prefer to use Michael Harding, having a particular love of their Kings Blue Light which I find works so well for East Anglian skies, especially with a touch of Raw Umber and added white. I tend to work quickly, so I prefer to use Griffin Alkyd Titanium White, which helps speed up the drying process. Liquin medium is also useful for this.

Texture is important in most of my work, so I enjoy working impasto with a palette knife and I'll often finish a work in oils using the alla prima *method. Huge white clouds are often a feature of the Norfolk coastal skies and a knife helps to build up their bulk, giving them depth and perspective. With brushes, my choice is a 0.5 inch flat hog or a 1.75 inch soft hake. I rarely use smaller brushes, thus avoiding the temptation to 'fiddle' with detail.*

My painting mantra tends to be 'whatever works' and I'll use a variety of techniques to achieve the result I'm after, including painting with a rag, scratching through paint with the end of a brush (sgraffito), using the edge of my hand to smudge and blend, dripping thinners onto the paint, allowing it to run and bleed, dry brush technique – great for adding sparkle and light, and scumbling and glazing several thin layers of oil with medium to achieve depth, particularly in stormy skies. I'll also freely mix colours directly on the surface of the board or canvas I'm using, rather than on the palette first. All these help to give the lively and impressionistic result I'm after.

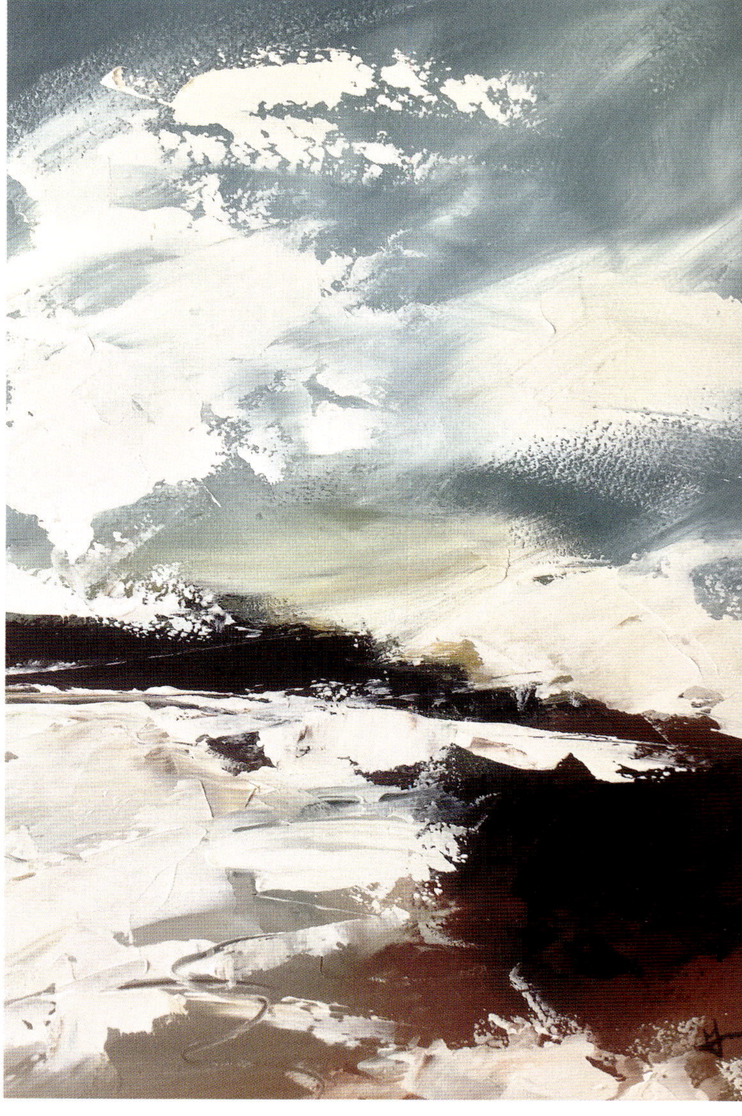

Blustery Day, Early Spring, Mari French.
Mari French works from sketches she makes out on location. This painting *Blustery Day, Early Spring*, in which she brilliantly captures the feel of the blustery sky, was inspired by one such outing in Norfolk.

may walk by that would enhance the composition or add extra interest. There is not enough time to paint them in as they are moving too fast but a quick photograph will give the information needed to place them correctly in the picture. Without that information, we may end up with the figure out of proportion because the feet or the head are in the wrong place.

Another useful trick when trying to decide on a decent composition is to take a photograph of the whole scene in front of you and then, by pinching the screen with two fingers, reduce the photograph and move it around the screen until you have a pleasing composition.

Consider holding the camera vertically. Sometimes a portrait shaped painting can make a better composition depending on the subject.

The electronic tablet is also useful back in the studio or at art groups. You'll have all your photographs at your fingertips. Your subject can be manipulated on the screen and then propped up to work from. It is sometimes easier to work from a printed version but you have to make allowances for the fact that a photograph may not reflect the colours accurately.

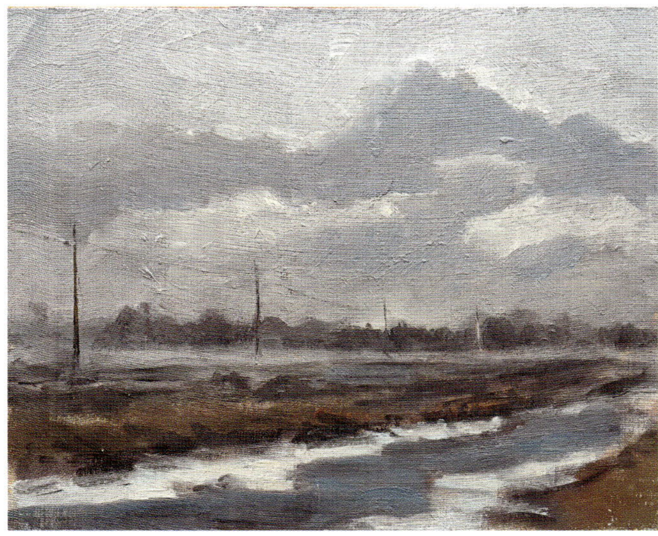

Sunday Showers.
This 6" × 8" painting was painted from memory. Driving home, I was taken with the colours following a quick rainstorm. While it was still fresh in my mind, I went straight into the studio and painted it. The warm ground makes for a break from the greys of the painting.

The experience of painting *plein air*

By painting out on location, you can get a feeling of how you want to respond to the subject. The more experience we have, the better our observational skills. We can put this to good use by committing a scene to memory as I did in *Sunday Showers*. This is a good example of how we can use our familiarity of the landscape in conjunction with studio work.

Tip: if your screen keeps going blank, go to your settings, look for 'display' and turn off the 'auto lock'. Most devices are set to turn off after a certain amount of time and it is useful to be able to override this when needing to constantly look at the screen.

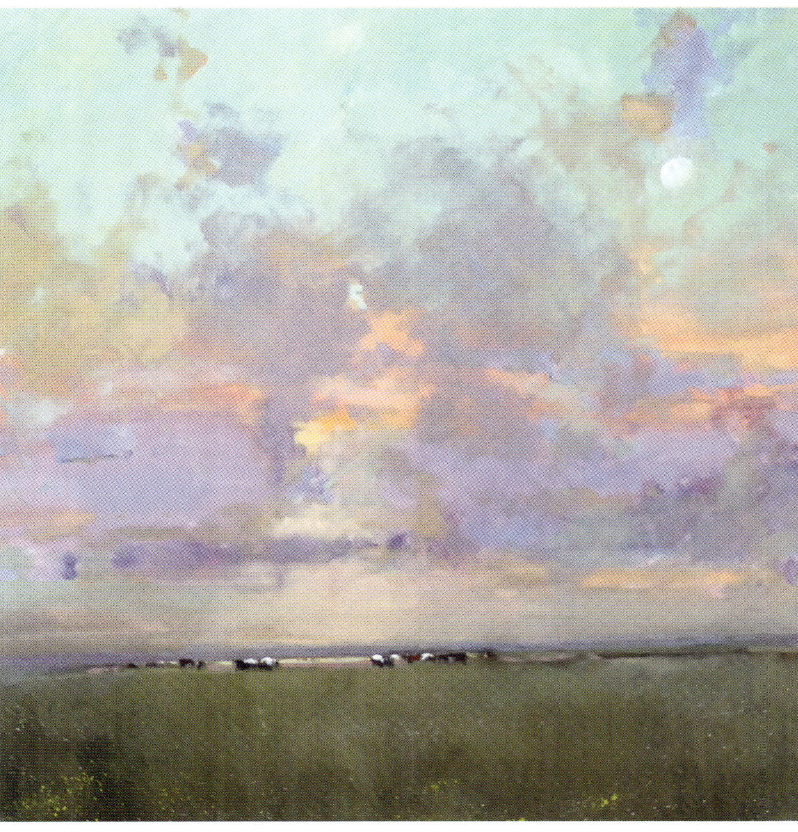

Clouds Over Cley, Brian Ryder ROI PPIEA.
Brian's fresh colourful painting here shows how we should not be afraid to use colour in the sky. He has picked up on the subtle changes of colour and exaggerated them to great effect.

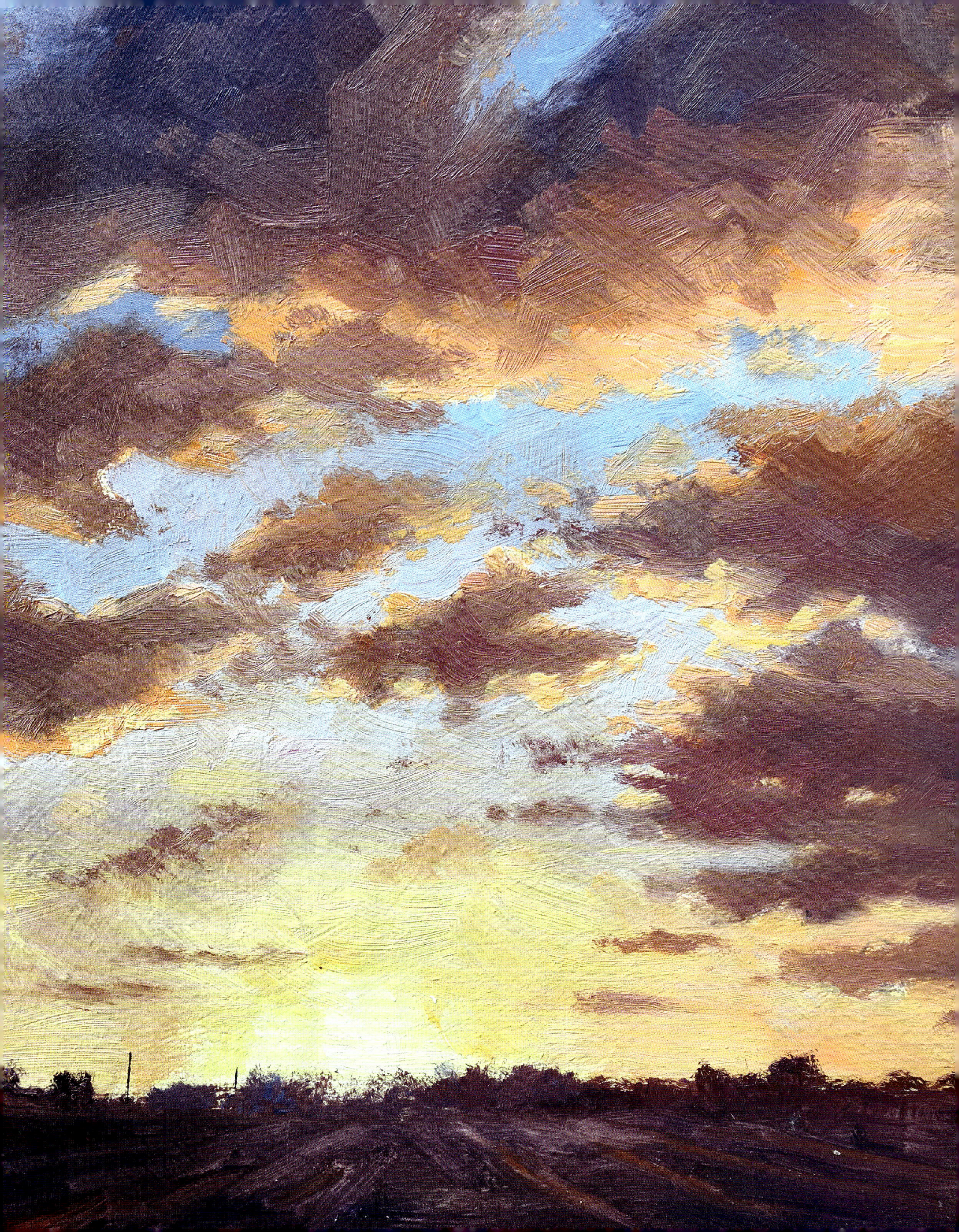

CHAPTER 8

Sunrises and sunsets

Almost all of us at one time or another have stopped to take in a sunset and some may have even witnessed a few sunrises. The wonderful display of reds and oranges are hard to believe sometimes. Many an artist has been heard to say, 'If I painted that, no one would believe it.'

You can see this wonderful show of colour anywhere in the world. The most beautiful sunsets happen in areas where there are more particles of dust or water in the atmosphere such as deserts and the tropics or after a volcanic eruption. These particles reflect the light in all directions; the more particles in the air, the more the shorter and intermediate violet, blue and yellow wavelengths are scattered, leaving the longer orange and red to reach the eye. High concentrations of salt are the reason why sunsets can be so red over the sea.

Both the sunrise and sunset are very transient. To paint them in *plein air* you do need to have had a lot of experience painting outdoors before deciding to tackle one on the spot. One dedicated artist who does just this most mornings is Dutch artist Roos Schuring (pronounced Rose).

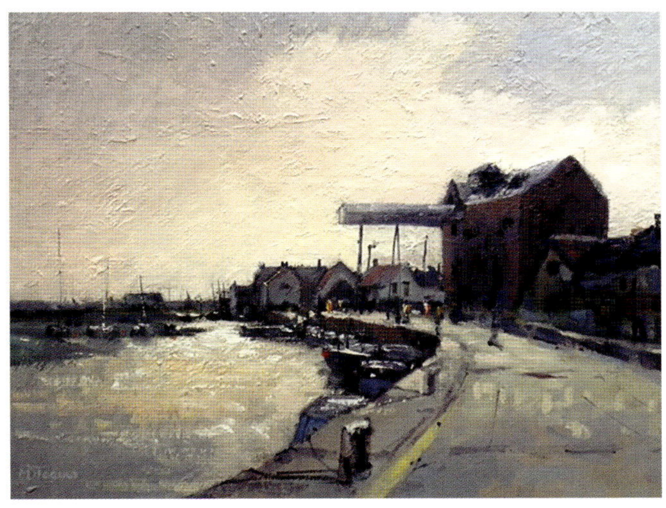

Wells, Morning Glow.
This is another early morning painting. The sun, hidden by clouds, gives the main building a strong silhouette.

Sunset Over the Fens, 12" × 14" (detail) on gessoed board, Mo Teeuw.

ARTIST PROFILE

Roos Schuring

Roos is an award winning contemporary *plein air* artist. She will paint regularly in rain, storms and snow to capture those rare and quick changing moments.

I witness the changes of each season in detail and I love each. I paint en plein air *all year round.*

There is really nothing more fleeting than a rising sun. Fire lasts longer, a rainbow might last longer even. So when painting the sunrise you'd probably be wise to return to it, again and again, to really get the hang of it. And the second part of difficulty is of course the ever-changing conditions, keeping it all a big surprise, as to what you'll find there, every morning. You can never know in advance and if you wait for the sky to turn pink indoors, then it may be too late to paint it. Sometimes you'll have to travel through darkness, set up all gear in twilight, to sometimes pack it all up again to return home, when there's just 'nothing there'. Very often a morning starts out grey. So what makes it all so very worthwhile? The getting up early, the morning haste to not miss out, the disappointment, the utter magic we can witness, the starting of the day; the rising of the sun is one of the most beautiful scenes we can encounter in nature. And painting it can be wonderful. Its beauty will probably overwhelm you at first, and screwing up the painting because of it, but if you are determined enough you will return and try again.

The materials I use are canvas, easel, palette, oil paint, brushes and knife. It's good to check your paint before you want to paint the morning sun. Your first tries will show you the colours you might have left at home, so you can bring them the next time around.

You might also find out a big size canvas does not really work, as the sheer haste doesn't let you fill big sizes in the little time you have. You will get better at finishing from memory, as you will have to, there isn't another way. Yes, there is photography but try it, you will see the camera having a very hard time recording this precious moment. Here is where you can immediately see that the camera can't record true colours. It's never so clear to see this as with a rising sun. All the more reason to go out and paint it from life.

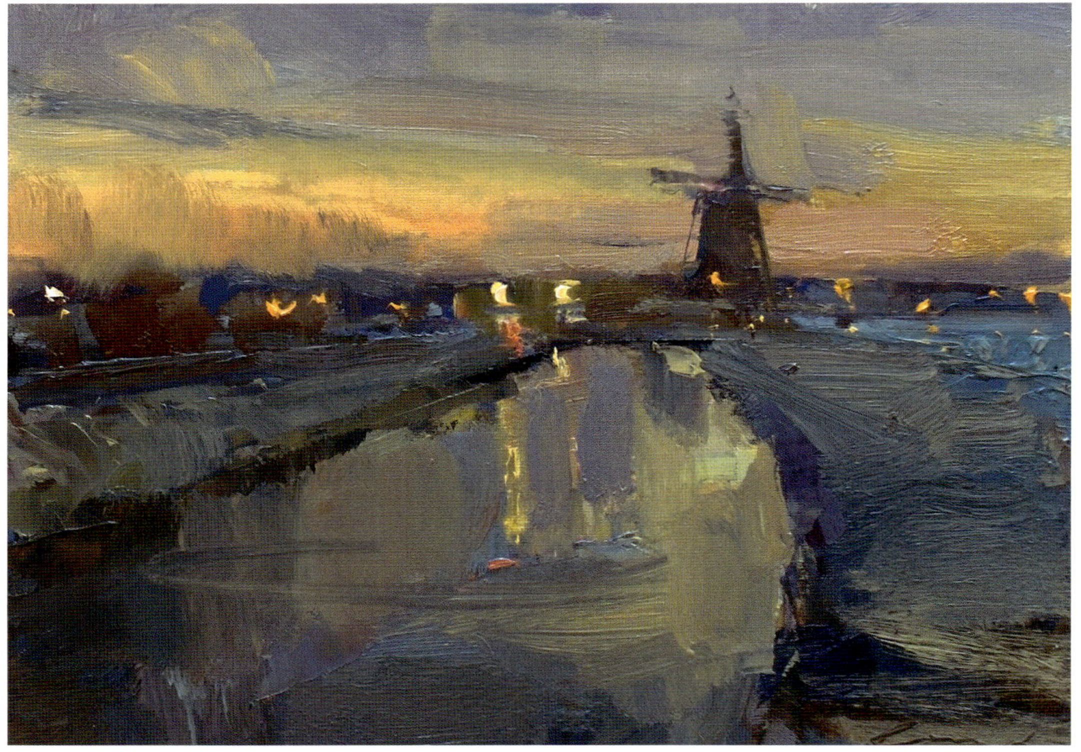

Landscape Windmill – Bright Morning and Frost, Roos Schuring.
Roos has chosen a higher horizon for this sunrise painting. We are left in no doubt about how cold it is. Even though there is frost on the ground, the foreground is kept dark, reflecting the distant lights and glow of the sun not yet risen. There is a wonderful array of complementary colours in the sky which are echoed in the foreground.

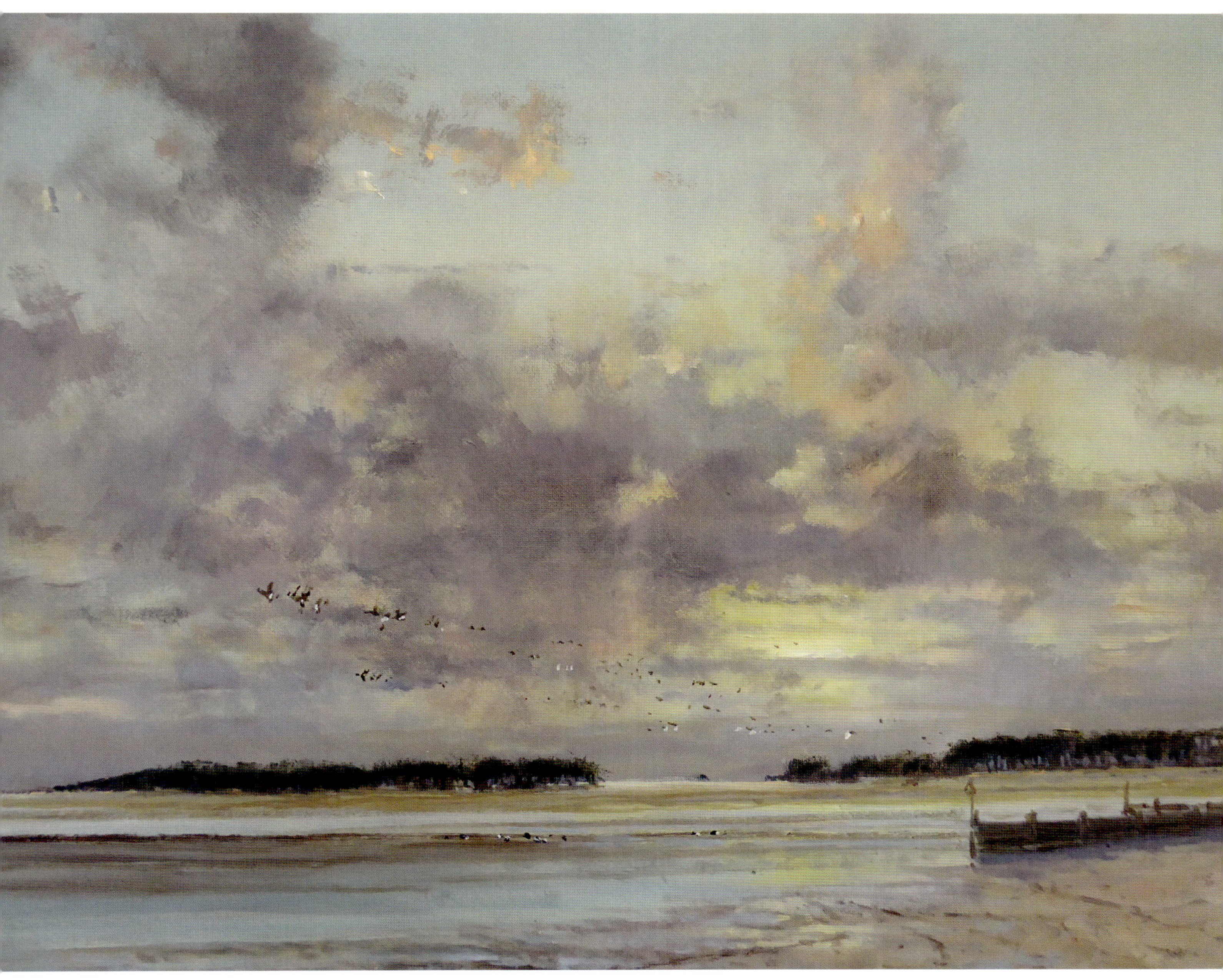

Winter Sunrise, Wells, Brian Ryder ROI PPIEA.
Although we cannot see the sun, we are aware of its presence rising up behind the clouds, creating a wonderful warm glow. This is very much a painting about the sky and Brian has played down any emphasis on the foreground.

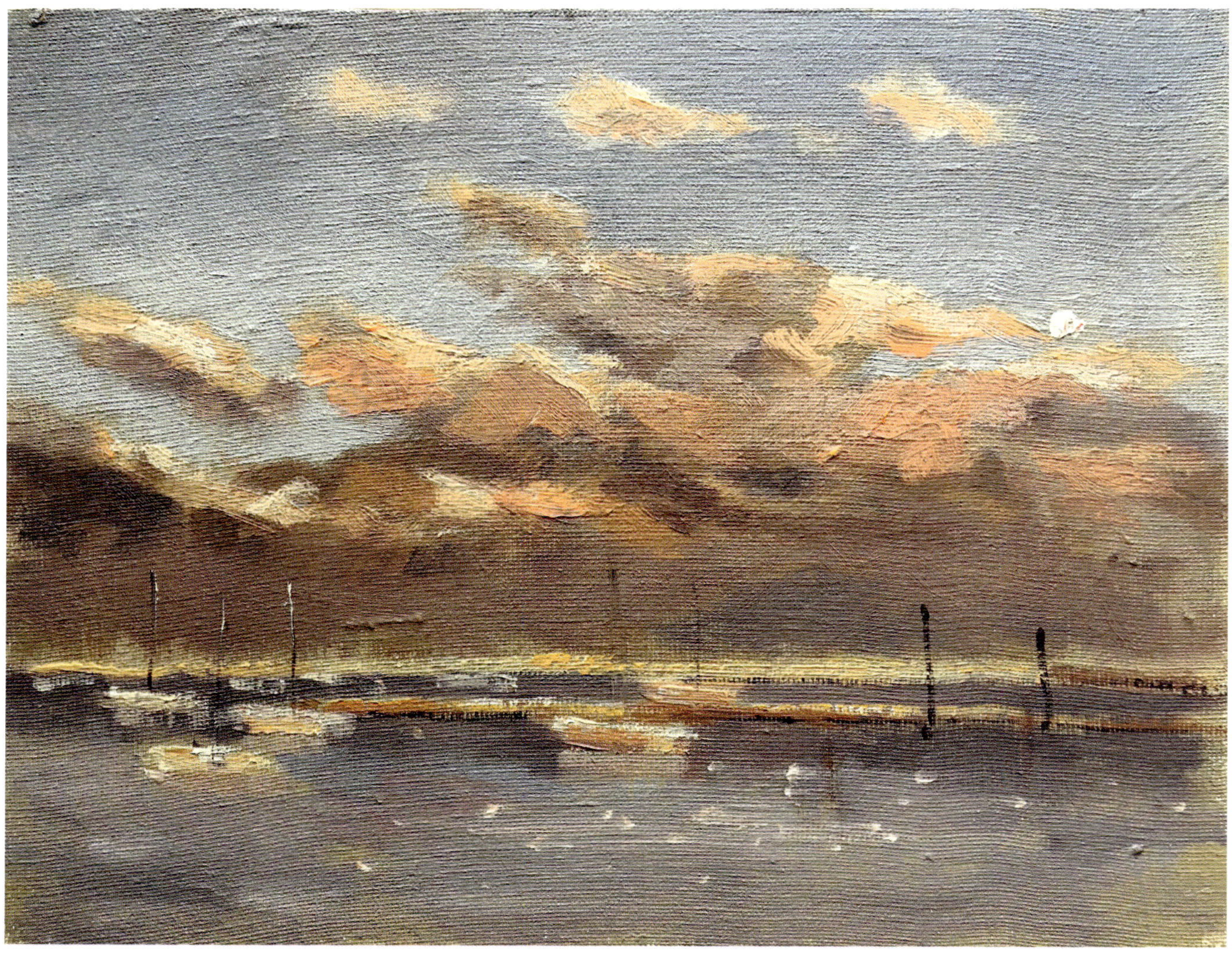

Afternoon Moon.

It has been said that you should always look behind you when painting outside. Many a time, on completing a painting, I have turned and painted the view that I had previously ignored by having my back to it. Afternoon Moon was one such occasion when I nearly missed a wonderful subject.

Titanium White
Lemon Yellow
Cobalt Blue
Cadmium Red
8" × 10" Butter Muslin on card
Yellow Ochre ground

This was a quick half hour oil sketch, made at the end of a busy day, painting with friends at Brancaster Staithe, Norfolk. I had been painting my favourite view and was about to pack up, when I turned around to see that there was a full moon and the clouds had turned the most wonderful pink colour. Knowing how quickly the sky can change at the end of the day, I chose a small panel and painted the clouds first. The low sun illuminated the distant marshes and they positively glowed against the darkening sky. The water too was registering dark against the marshes, emphasizing the sun's effect on the land.

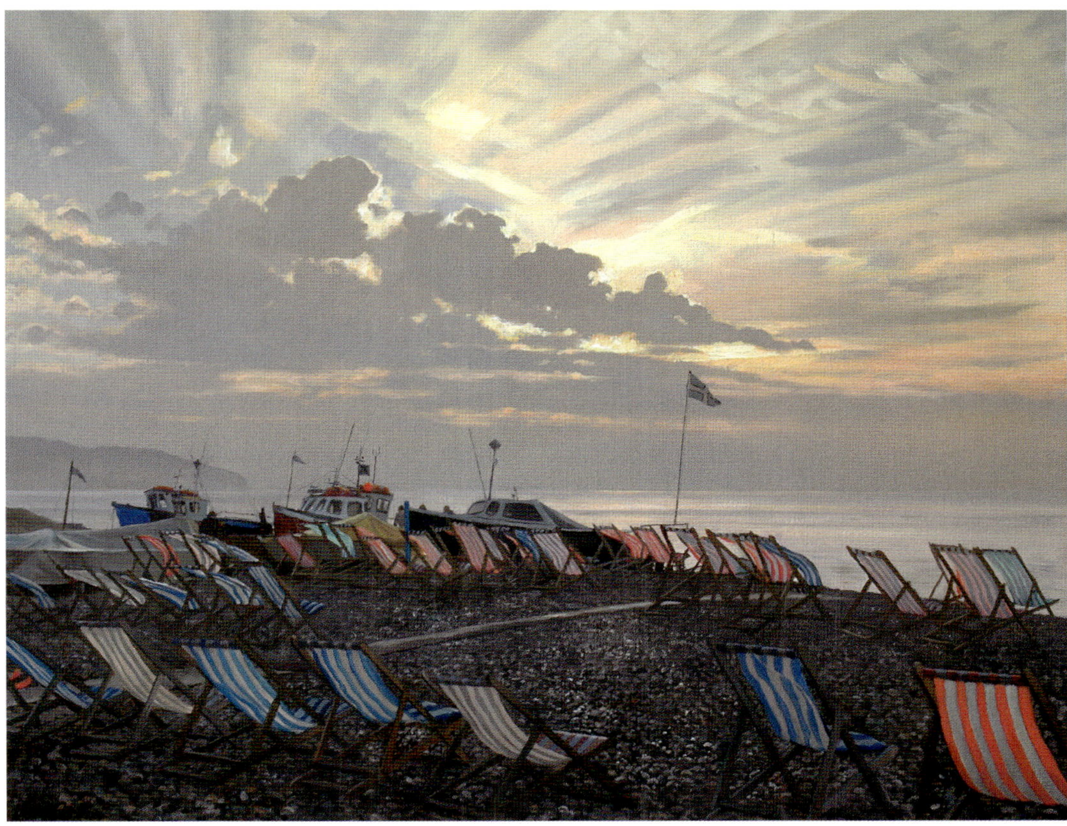

Sunset, Peter Barker.
In this lovely early evening painting, we are given the impression of the end of a summer's day with the deckchairs gently billowing in the wind. Peter perfectly captures the suns rays emanating from behind the clouds. He has used a pastel palette of colours in contrast to the painting *Sunset, West Beckham*, where I used much stronger colours.

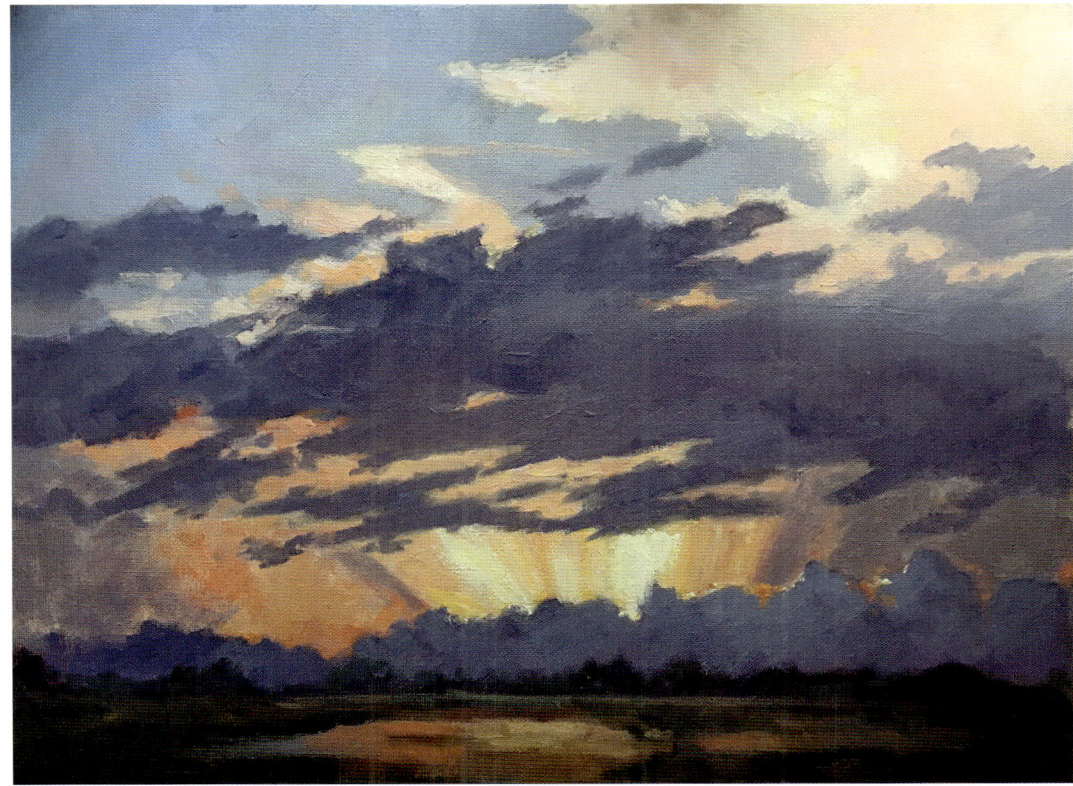

Sunset, West Beckham, 14" × 18". Oil on canvas. This was a particularly spectacular sunset in Norfolk. There was so much happening that I decided to work from a photograph. The sun was throwing out so many shadows from the clouds that it was behind. The sky was still the blue of the sunny day just gone and the sun illuminated the high clouds. A veil of dark clouds that were in the shadow of the sun drifted across, giving contrast to the light show behind.

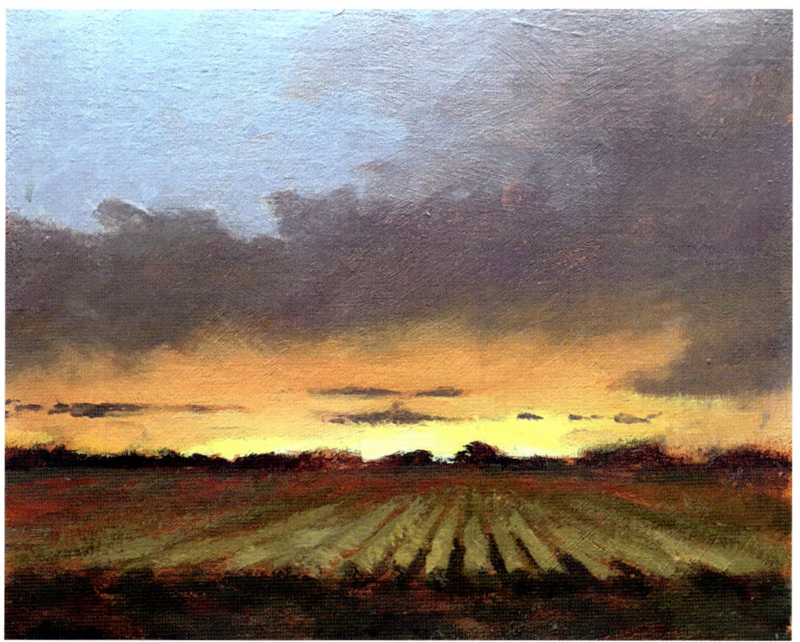

Fen Sunset.
Titanium White
Cadmium Yellow
Yellow Ochre
Cadmium Red
Permanent Rose
Ultramarine Blue
10" × 10" Gessoed card
Burnt Sienna ground

The dark of the Burnt Sienna ground was a good start for this dramatic painting. I allowed a lot of the ground colour to show through, which helps to make for a more harmonious painting. To make the sun setting on the horizon appear as light as it does, it was important to provide plenty of contrast, thus the rest of the painting is tonally quite dark.

The fading blue of the sky was painted first with French Ultramarine/Cadmium Red and a touch of Yellow Ochre. The clouds of Permanent Rose/Cadmium Yellow/French Ultramarine had a distinctive shape on the left and as the clouds came towards me, they blended into the sky. This effect is achieved by gently blending the cloud and the blue sky colour together with a softer brush. The same soft brush was used to blend the Cadmium Yellow/Cadmium Red glow into the clouds. Next, the tree outline was painted using an Ultramarine Blue/Permanent Rose and touch of Cadmium Yellow mix to give a complementary colour for the sinking sun, which was painted with Cadmium Yellow/ Titanium White.

The foreground was kept very simple so as not to distract from the sky. Ultramarine Blue/Cadmium Red/Yellow Ochre is used to indicate the furrows in the field with Titanium White added for the highlights.

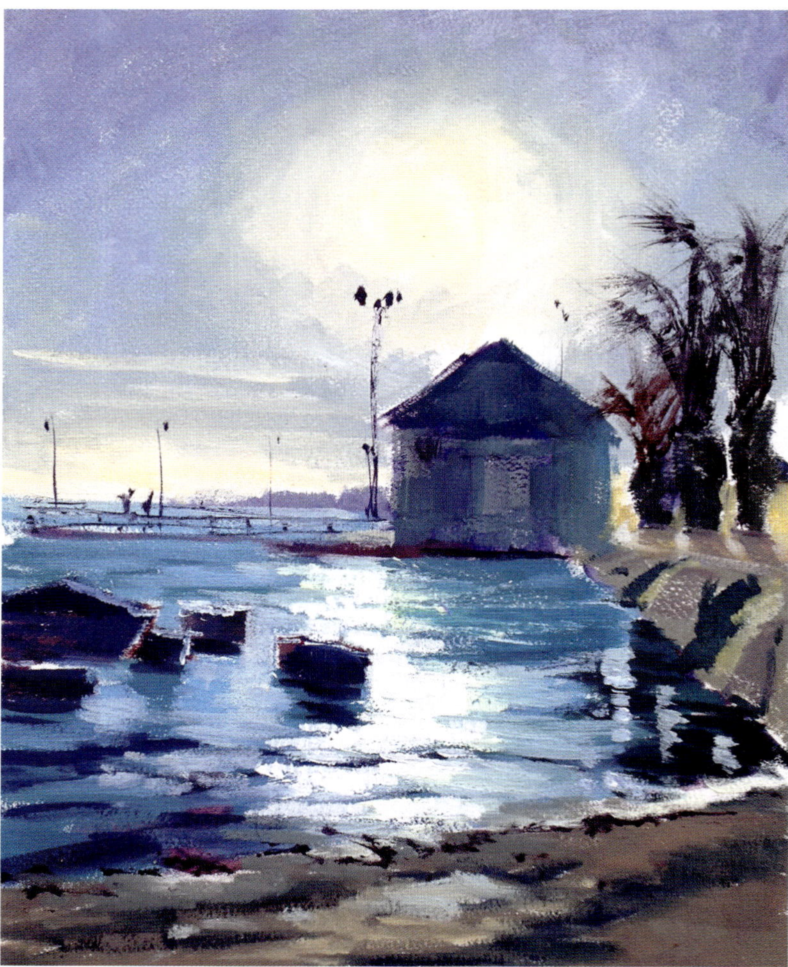

Olhao, Portugal, 8" × 6". Primed card.
The sea in Olhao was painted on a small panel at the end of a day. The sea was an unusual colour so I decided to try out Manganese Blue for this little picture. The sun was very bright in my eyes so I tried to give that impression by diffusing the light. There was a strong reflection of the sun in the water which silhouetted the boats.

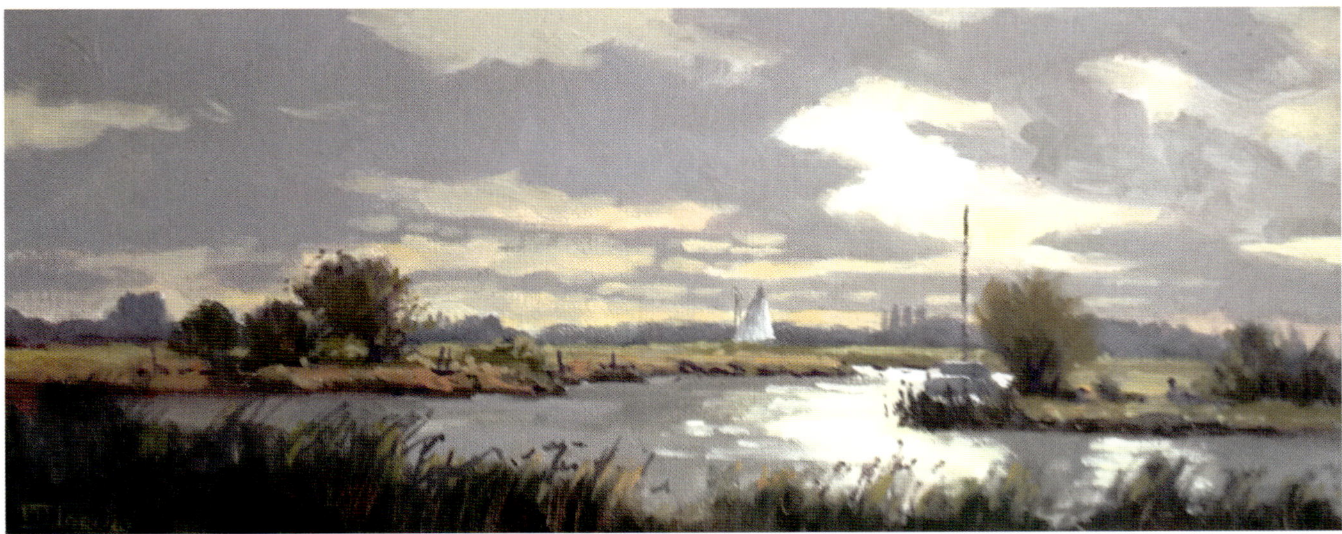

Norfolk Broads.
Titanium White
Yellow Ochre
Lemon Yellow
Burnt Sienna
Cadmium Red
Ultramarine Blue
8" × 20" Stretched lined canvas
Yellow Ochre ground

This dramatic sky was painted on the Norfolk Broads at the end of the day. Working fast to capture the light, I premixed my sky colours. Ultramarine Blue, Cadmium Red and Titanium White for the sky and water. Lemon Yellow, Cadmium Red and Titanium White for the clouds. Using a rigger and Burnt Sienna diluted with white spirit, I drew the outline of the banks, horizon and trees. With a darker version of the sky colour, the distant trees were blocked in. Next, the shapes of the clouds were blocked in, leaving the areas clear where the light was going at the same time the same colours were used for the water. Notice how the clouds decrease in size towards the horizon. I left painting the lightest, sunny highlights for later. The dark reeds in the foreground were roughed in with Burnt Sienna and Ultramarine Blue. They proved to be a useful compositional aid. Notice how they were elongated on the left to break up the horizontal line of the water and hold the eye in the picture. The dark trees in the middle distance were painted with Ultramarine Blue and Burnt Sienna. I needed the edge of the bank to provide a contrast for the water so I darkened the mix with Ultramarine Blue and Burnt Sienna. The lighter green in the distance is a mix of Yellow Ochre, Ultramarine Blue and Titanium White with Lemon Yellow in the lightest, central part. The light green is painted in between the trees to help with the suggestion of depth. The same green was flicked into the foreground reeds to give form to them. The highlight in the sky and water were put in almost last with Lemon Yellow and Titanium White. I left a dark area to represent the reflection of the tree. The final dark marks to add contrast were a few more dark reeds in the water against the reflection and the mast of the boat crossing the lightest part of the sky. Note how the eye is drawn to the area with the strongest contrast, the corner of the bank jutting out into the sunlit water.

Norfolk Sunset.
Titanium White
Cadmium Yellow
Burnt Umber
Permanent Rose
Ultramarine Blue
6" × 6" Linen covered board
Thin Burnt Sienna ground

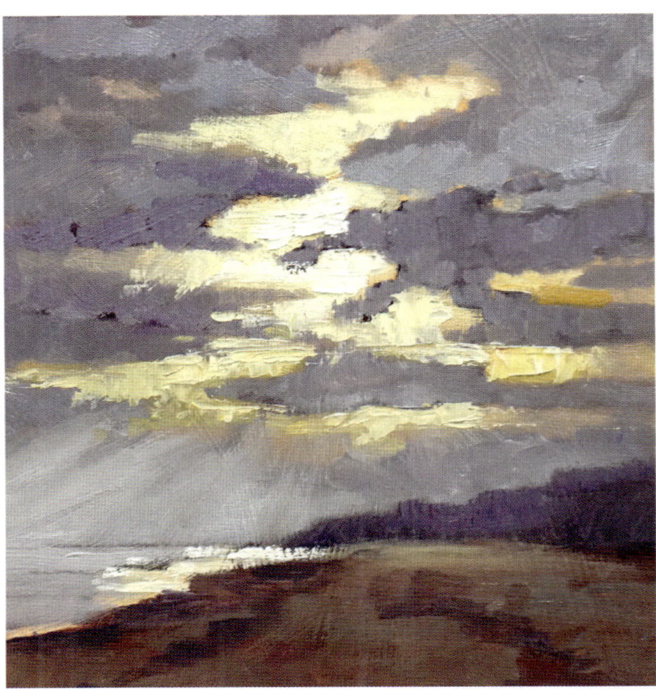

Painted on location, this Norfolk beach is a very simple subject. What makes this painting work is the use of complementary colours and strong contrasts. The dark clouds and cliffs were painted first with Ultramarine Blue/Permanent Rose/Burnt Umber then the mid tone of the sunlit areas with Cadmium Yellow/Titanium White and a very little Permanent Rose. Having done this, I could see that the original clouds were too dark so I lightened them by adding Titanium White to the first mix and painted over them but allowed some of the original dark to show through. A lot of the warm Burnt Sienna ground can be seen at the edges of the painting in the sky. This helps to concentrate the light in the middle. The Burnt Umber/Ultramarine Blue beach was kept dark in the foreground and lightened with Cadmium Yellow/Titanium White where the sun lights up the beach in the distance apart from next to the water, where I kept it particularly dark as a strong contrast to where the water is reflecting the sun.

A mix of Ultramarine Blue/Titanium White/Burnt Umber provides the colour for the sea and for the rays of light coming down from the sky. The final touches are the Cadmium Yellow/Titanium White areas in the sky and water.

STEP BY STEP DEMONSTRATION

Lincolnshire Sunset

This picture was taken late afternoon in the winter in the Fens of Lincolnshire. The soft cirrus clouds had just turned the most delightful pink and registered light against the darkening blue, giving a lovely contrast. Two minutes later, they had changed to a soft grey. It is worth waiting and taking a series of pictures when photographing sunsets, as you never know what will happen next.

Colours

- Warm White
- Yellow Ochre
- Cadmium Yellow
- Cadmium Orange
- Magenta
- Cobalt Blue
- Blue Grey

Support

For this demonstration, a 10" × 8" board was used. This was prepared by painting mount board with a coat of gesso. Whilst this was still wet, butter muslin was stretched over the surface and another coat of gesso painted on top. When this was dry, a turpsy pink was painted over to tint the board to give a warm ground. Sometimes when using fabric and gesso, the surface can be a little rough as the gesso hardens the loose fibres so it is advisable to give it a light sanding down for a smoother surface.

Brushes

All from Rosemary & Co. Ivory range

- No. 2 Filbert
- No. 2 Rigger
- No. 4 & 6 Flat

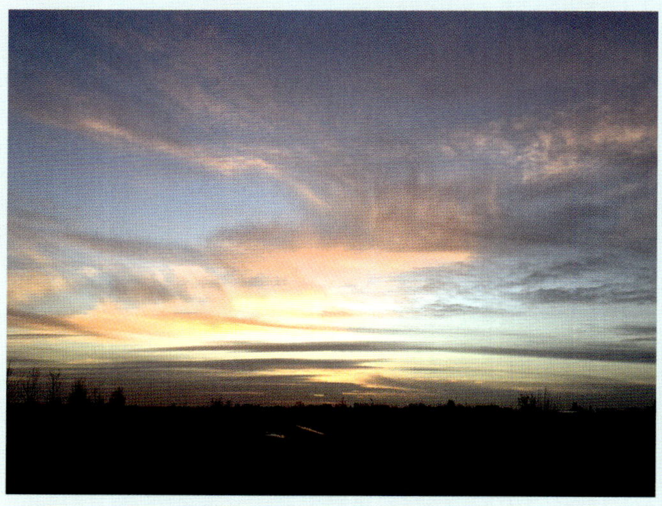

Lincolnshire Sunset.

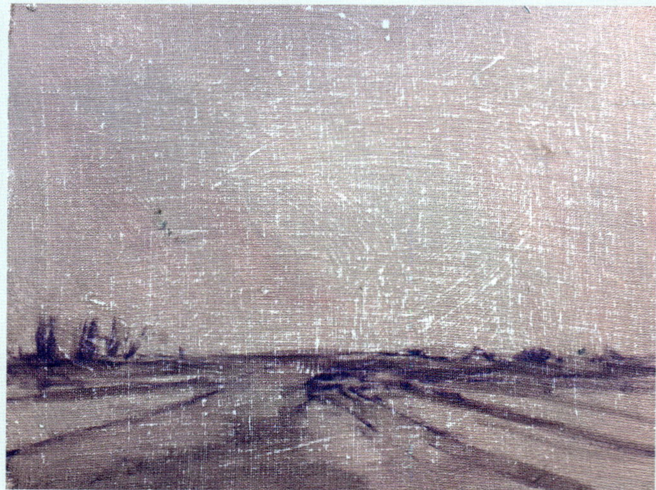

Step 1. Keep the drawing simple and draw it out with a rigger and Ultramarine diluted with turpentine. A low horizon and exaggerated perspective of the road help give this painting a feeling of depth and distance.

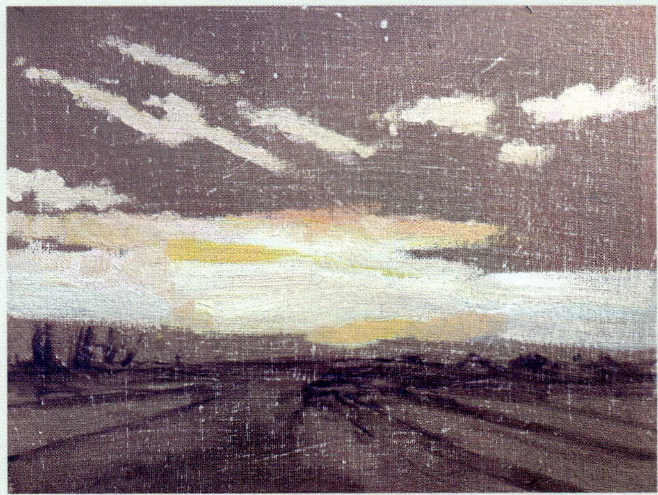

Step 2. Block in the largest light areas of the cloud formation first. These may well be modified at a later stage but for now, those areas need to be preserved. The dark ground of the board is useful as it helps to judge the tone of the blue that will be placed next to the lighter colours. Blend in the Cadmium Yellow and Orange clouds at this stage.

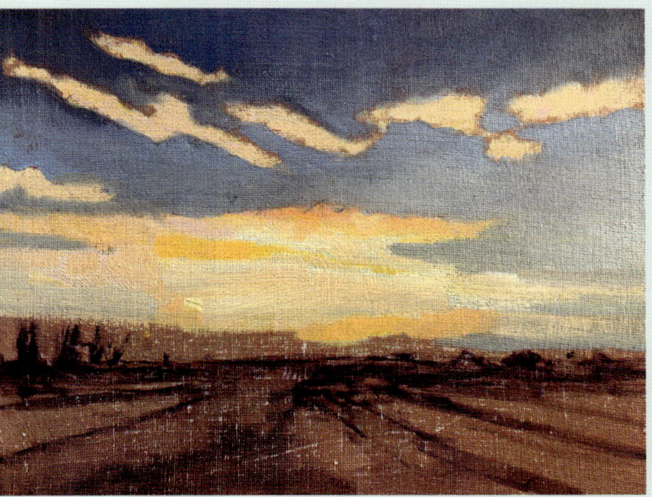

Step 3. Blue Grey, Cobalt Blue and a touch of Yellow Ochre make up the sky colour. Start at the top and work across the board, gradually lightening the colour with white and blending with your finger as you come down towards the horizon. Take care not to pick up any of the light cloud colour. It is best to leave a small gap between the two colours. They can be blended together later.

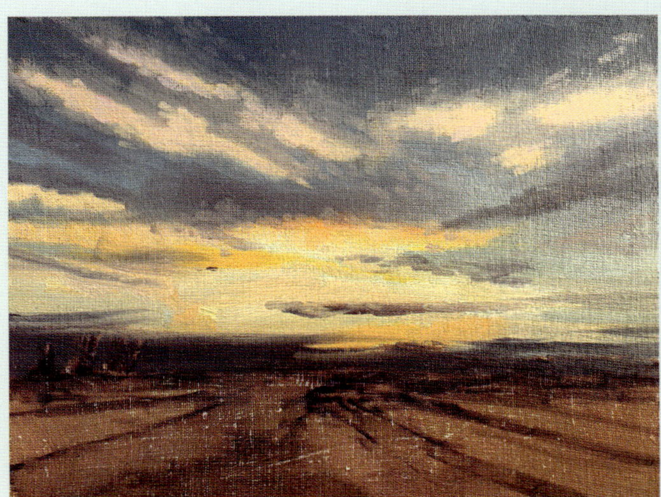

Step 4. Apply the dark clouds at the horizon with a no. 4 flat brush and use thin horizontal strokes, wet into wet. At the same time, blend the colours to soften the edges. When adding the dark thin clouds over the still wet sunlight area, it is important to wipe your brushes clean of any paint you pick up or you will lose the dark colour of the cloud. The pink clouds at the top are a mix of Cadmium Orange, Magenta and a lot of Warm White. Using the tip of a no. 4 filbert, blend and soften these clouds by taking some of the blue into the pink at the same time as some of the pink into the blue.

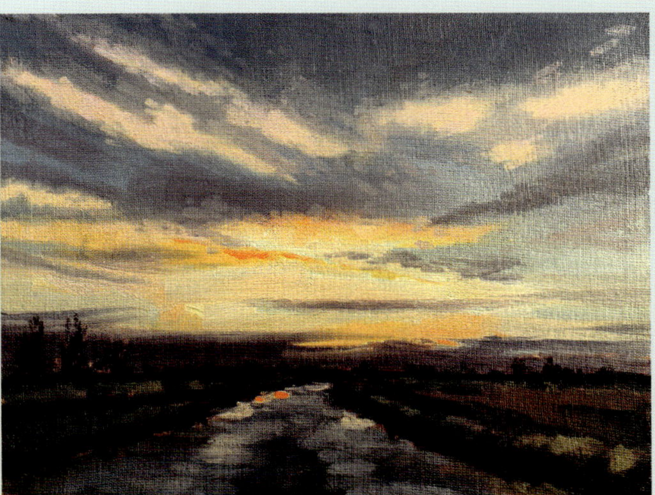

Step 5. The landscape was quite dark as it was silhouetted against the sky and the photograph gives very little information. If you have to invent a foreground, try to keep it simple. If the foreground was too fussy, it would end up as a very busy painting. Use the same colours on the wet road as were used in the sky: darker in the foreground and getting lighter in the distance, reflecting the light in the sky. Add some stronger colour to the sky with Cadmium Orange. This can be picked up in the puddle on the road, helping to unite the colours and composition and give a little 'pop'.

The dark trees in the distance are the darkest tone in the painting and are the last to be painted. Make sure that the tone of the trees is darker than the dark clouds behind them otherwise they won't stand out. To paint the trees, use the rigger and paint them in with a light touch, as you will be painting over wet paint. A few flicks of dark tones in the roadside verges will help to define the road and add a bit more contrast.

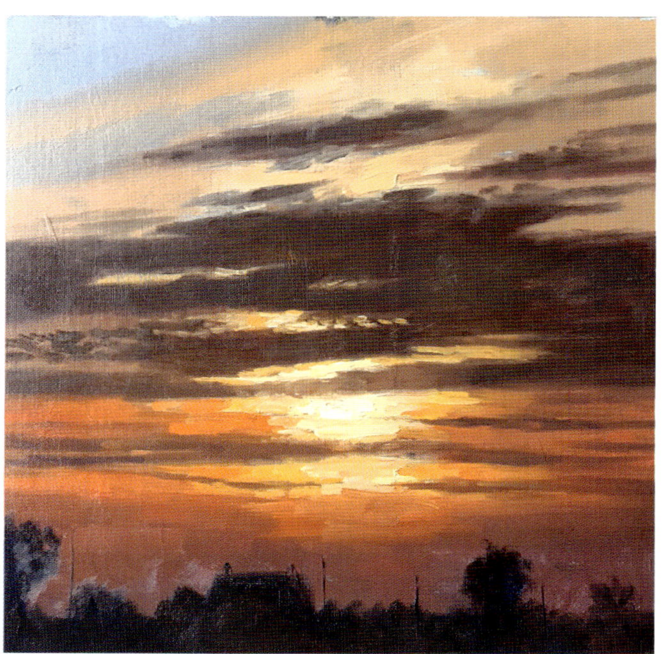

Sunset, Orange Sky, 12" × 12". Canvas board. Pale Umber ground.
This was painted on a particually cold day. The sky looked as if it was on fire. It was only 3 p.m. on a December afternoon. The sky was still blue above but the landscape in front was already dark in contrast to the sinking sun making silhouettes of the trees and house. The horizon was kept low as there was not a good deal of interest in the foreground but it does make a good foil for the sky.

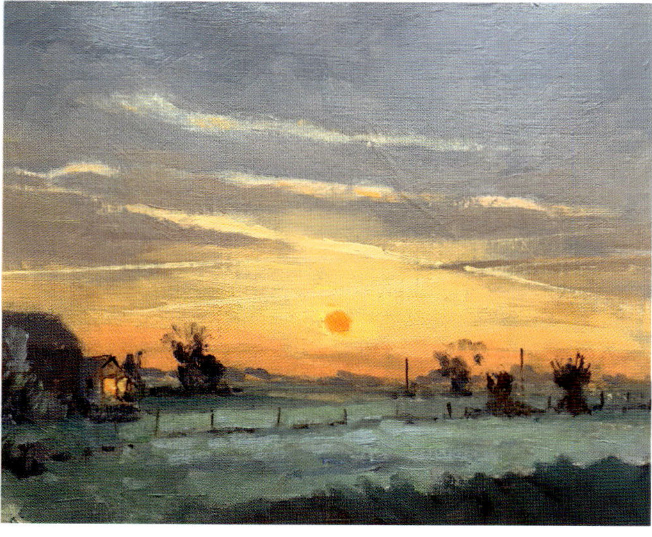

Sunrise and Frost, 8" × 10". Canvas board.
This was a joy to paint in spite of the cold. It was 7 a.m. and the temperature was minus two degrees. The sun was a deep red as it rose; what fascinated me the most was the reflection of the sun in the glasshouse. There were a lot more vapour trails in the sky than I have included. I decided that in this case less is more. I selectively chose the ones that would complement the painting both in colour and composition.

The time of year can have an effect on sunsets. When it is colder there is more of a chance of ice particles in the sky. When ice is present, light rays will reflect off them and they will scatter more. The painting *Sunset, Orange Sky* that has a really strong orange colour was painted on a day when temperatures had dropped to well below freezing.

The painting *Sunrise and Frost* was painted in December on a very cold morning. There would have been a lot of ice particles in the sky, which is why the vapour trails of the aircraft are so colourful. The light from the sun's rays are bounced around in the moisture of the trails.

It's quite difficult to distinguish between a sunrise and a sunset just by looking at a single image. The two occasions appear quite similar and you can't be completely sure of what you're looking at unless you can see if the sun is going up or down.

In general, the dawn or sunrise will have a clearer atmosphere, enabling more brilliant oranges and reds to make their way through to the observer whereas, at dusk, when the sun goes down, there is a thicker atmosphere as pollutants have built up during the day and light is more scattered. A sunset therefore tends to be more chaotic and a sunrise more orderly and calm.

When painting a sunrise, you may need to have more yellow on your palette, as well as bright orange, pink and blue, whereas when painting a sunset, your colours would probably be warmer with more saturated colours of red, orange, purple and magenta on the palette.

It also helps to position the sun a little higher in the painting for a sunrise and lower for a sunset, as this will help to make it clearer the time of day you are trying to depict.

There are of course no two sunsets nor sunrises the same, unless of course there are no clouds present; cloud formations will differ from day to day. Some days there will be less cloud than others.

In the painting *Sunset Over Moulton*, the dark diagonal cloud echoes the shape of the road leading us into the painting. The clouds nearer to the horizon are more horizontal and paler as they're further away. This helps to give the feeling of aerial perspective.

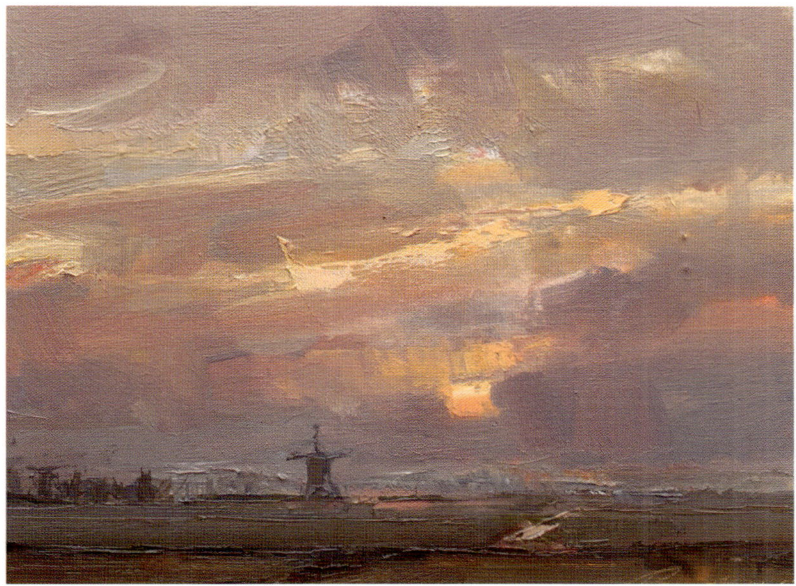

Roos Schuring, *Sunrise.*
The oranges, pinks and purples in this painting indicate that it is a sunrise. Again Roos has perfectly captured the moment of the sunrise with the windmill silhouetted against purple clouds on the horizon.

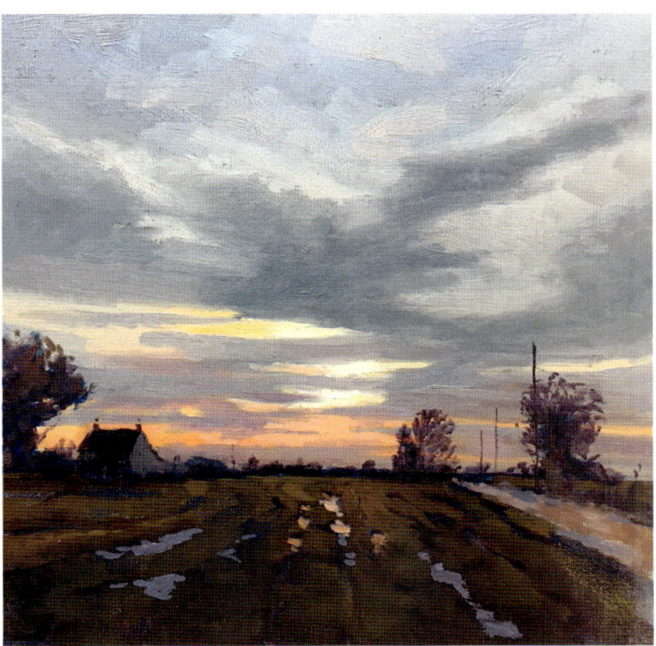

Sunset Over Moulton, 12" × 12". Canvas board.
The sun here is hidden behind a cloud, which gives good light and dark contrasts. The cloud covering the sun is slightly lighter as it is further away. The sun hasn't quite gone down, meaning that the sky in the top half of the painting is still showing blue of daylight. The cloud that comes towards us in front of the sun is dark because it is in shadow. Had it been further back in the distance, it may have turned red if the sun had been able to illuminate it.

Cadmium Orange was a useful colour to get the colour near to the horizon and is also reflected in the puddles, helping to lift the foreground and give the painting a 'pop'.

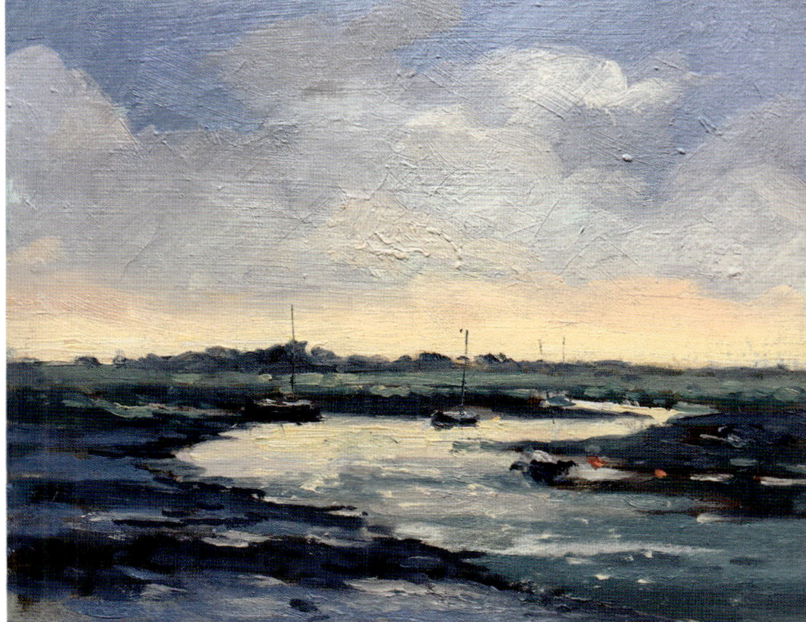

Brancaster Sunset, 10" × 12". Canvas board.
To emphasize the light in the water, the foreground and banks were kept dark. Cadmium Orange, Permanent Rose and white were the perfect colours for the glow on the horizon. Strokes of the Cobalt Blue sky on the exposed mud suggest that the tide has just gone out.

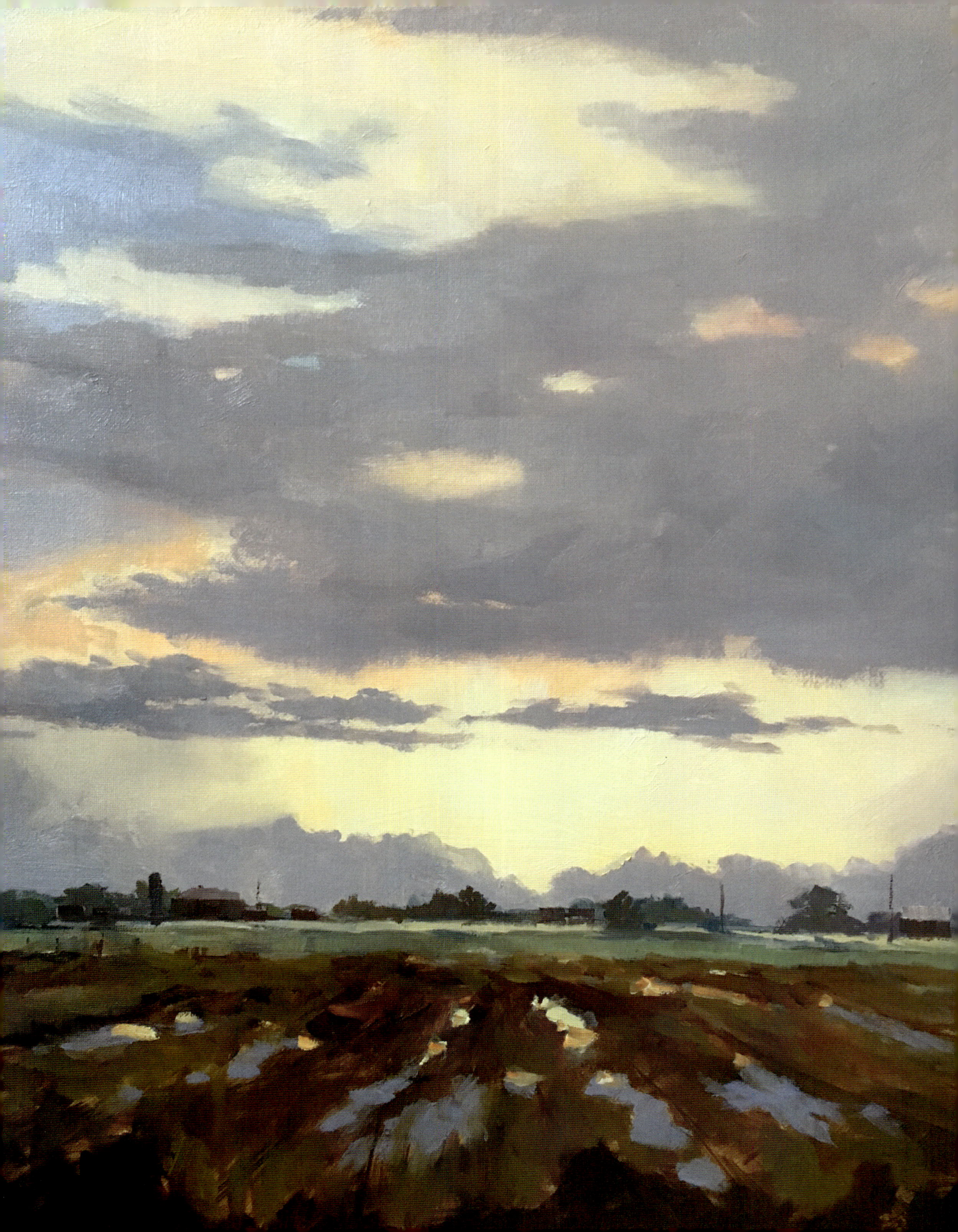

CHAPTER 9

Dramatic skies

Dramatic skies are those that have probably the greatest impact on us. Granted, sunsets and sunrises are very dramatic but there is surely nothing more powerful and dramatic than a sky full of clouds threatening a storm, or the sun lighting up a dark sky with the flash of light in the foreground, illuminating a focal point giving strong contrasts.

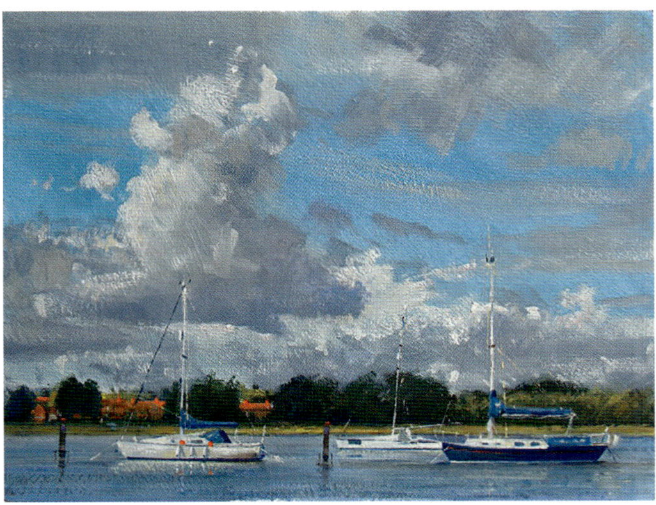

Moored Boats at Hamble, John Stillman.
This painting perfectly captures the atmosphere of a summer day. The clouds drift gently across the sky over the calm water. The clouds with subtle shading have soft and hard edges, giving a feel of realism.

Norfolk Sunset (detail).

ARTIST PROFILE
John Stillman

Epsom Downs is great for its big skies and on this day, it was not to disappoint. I started by mixing some Titanium White and Cerulean Blue to establish a base colour for the sky. Then I mixed some Burnt Sienna, French Ultramarine and Titanium White plus a touch of Alizarin Crimson, and proceeded to paint the stormy band of cloud in.

Using my finger, I blended the colours together to create the soft edges of the clouds. Then with a clean cotton cloth, I wiped away the paint to reveal the top highlights of the clouds. By mixing some Cerulean Blue with Lemon Yellow Hue, I painted the sky into the cloud from the top of the painting down to help indicate the shape of the cloud. A mix of Alizarin Crimson and Titanium White were then added to the top of the sky and blended into the darker band below to give more shape and warmth to the cloud. I then painted the horizon in, using the same colour mix as the dark band of cloud; instantly it gave the painting depth. The painting is very simple in composition: foreground, middle and the sky. Again, as in previous paintings, the grandstand, people and additional highlights were all finished back at the studio but the main objective of the day was to capture the humid afternoon of that oppressive sky.

I think every artist is fascinated by the sky, I know I have ever since I can remember, and to this day I am constantly inspired by the shapes, colours and vastness of our wonderful skies and clouds. Whether you are an abstract painter or a more traditional painter, it has always been there to offer inspiration and to challenge you in your choice of medium.

As a landscape painter, the sky really does determine the whole mood and atmosphere of the scene, and so it is important to get the main elements right when attempting to paint a convincing sky.

The best thing I ever did was to get outside with my paint box and paint directly from life. And it was the sky and clouds that I concentrated on, as I knew that if I could paint a credible sky with the right tonal values, then I would be on my way to achieve a more finished landscape painting.

It is always a scary prospect to paint in front of the subject and to deal with curious onlookers, but my advice to you is – if you do feel intimidated by this – to set your easel/paint box up in your garden or from a window of your home and paint a sky from there without any interruptions, and in time your confidence will grow.

If on the other hand time is against you, then try to carry a small sketchbook with you, and make quick colour notes and sketches to use at a later date. Whatever your preferred method of recording the sky, you can never have enough reference; it really is your biggest asset.

I would also recommend that you look at other artists' work that you admire; it goes without saying that the works of Constable and Turner are so important when considering painting dramatic skies. They truly were masters of their craft and you can learn so much from viewing their wonderful paintings.

I have for many years admired the work of Sir John Alfred Arnesby Brown RA (1866-1955), and for me he too is a master of painting atmospheric skies. As a painter from Suffolk, he was widely known for his paintings of cattle in the landscape, but his skies are truly wonderful and very inspiring.

One other artist that I simply must mention is the famous Norfolk painter Edward Seago (1910–1974). There are many illustrated books available of Seago's work and I would highly recommend them for you to view his paintings, as his style and technique made his skies look so effortless.

Another useful exercise is to paint the sky every morning for an hour from 7 a.m. till 8 a.m. for a week. Pick a small panel to paint onto like a 6" × 8" or 7" × 10" as you will be able to cover this quickly, and when you line your paintings up at the end of the week, I am sure you will be surprised with the results. The small paintings that you produce will become an invaluable reference, and if you continue with this exercise on a weekly basis then you will amass quite a collection of panels that you can use to refer to when working on future paintings.

When painting your sky, simplify the cloud shapes along with the tonal values. The clouds themselves need as much

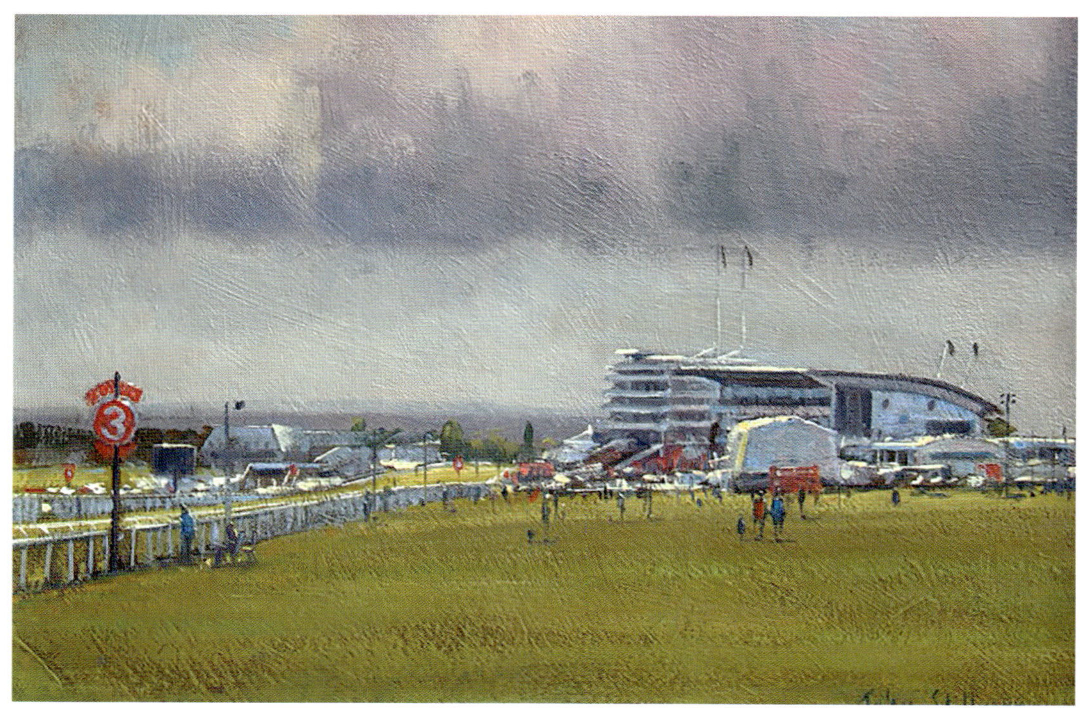

Heading to the Races, Epsom Downs, John Stillman. 10" × 14". Oil on board.

consideration in composition as the landscape itself, and in time you will know what to keep in, and what to leave out so that the sky looks balanced; it is all about getting a harmony not only in the sky but the landscape itself. By half closing your eyes, it will make it easier for you to 'block in' the shapes of the clouds. By doing this, the clouds will look more convincing and not 'overworked'. Choose a large brush when blocking in the main shapes, as this not only covers the panel quickly, but also keeps your brush work looking lively, and it will all add to the feeling of the sky, and give the impression that the clouds are light and airy within the landscape. It is also good practice to have a small part of the landscape in your painting, as this will help in judging the scale of the sky, and it will also add distance to your painting.

Do try to remember to add a touch of the colour from the sky to the landscape itself as this will help in linking the two elements together. One other important tip would be to try not to be stingy with the amount of paint you use, because as your confidence grows there is nothing better than 'sculpting' oil paint with your brush to create the clouds. I also use my forefinger to soften the edges of the clouds if needed, and unlike a brush it does not wear out.

The major difficulty I and many other painters have come up against is that the landscape is constantly changing, and the need to work fast becomes very evident early on when tackling a sky. That is why I would advise you to work on a small scale as you can cover the panel or canvas quickly and therefore, in time, be able to hold the image of the sky and clouds you are painting in your visual memory. The more skies you paint, the more experienced you will become at knowing exactly the colour mixes – but generally the base colour of clouds is always grey – and you will be able to determine what kind of grey. I tend to keep my colour mixes on the 'warm' side as opposed to being cold, as clouds generally are very warm in tone.

I would also recommend reading The Cloudspotter's Guide *by Gavin Pretor-Pinney. It is a good read, and it certainly opened my eyes to all the various cloud formations. Like all painting, you need to know your subject, so the more information you have to hand, the better.*

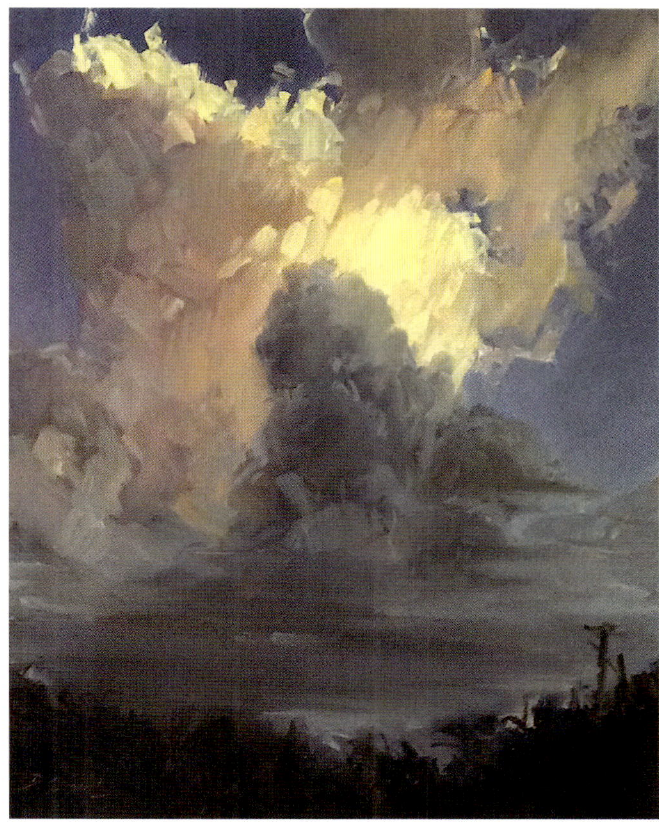

Dramatic Sky 1, David Simons.
Dramatic skies don't necessarily have to be stormy. What makes this sky by David Simons so dramatic is the sheer size and volume of the cloud. The main cloud dominates the picture with juxtaposition from the darker one. The contrast between the blue of the sky and the dark grey with the warm yellow of the sunlit area has a really strong impact.

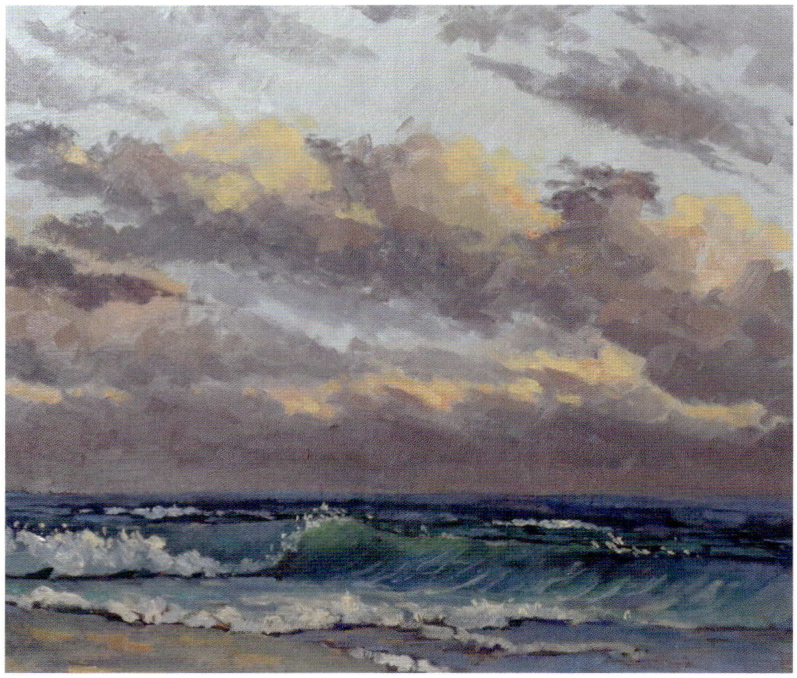

Wave
Cobalt Green
Cobalt Blue
Cadmium Yellow
Naples Yellow
Cadmium Red
Titanium White
10" × 12" Canvas board
Yellow Ochre ground

Painted from a photo reference in the studio. I liked the diagonal lines created by the clouds, which help give the painting a feeling of movement. The main bulk of the cloud shadow was painted first, then with a mix of Cobalt Blue, Naples Yellow and a touch of Cobalt Green and white, the main sky colour was painted up to the cloud edges. Next, Naples Yellow, Cadmium Red and Cadmium Yellow were added for cloud highlights. It was a rather busy picture but to tie it all together, I used the cloud highlight colour as reflections in the wet sand. The foam on the surf was a paler version of the cloud highlight.

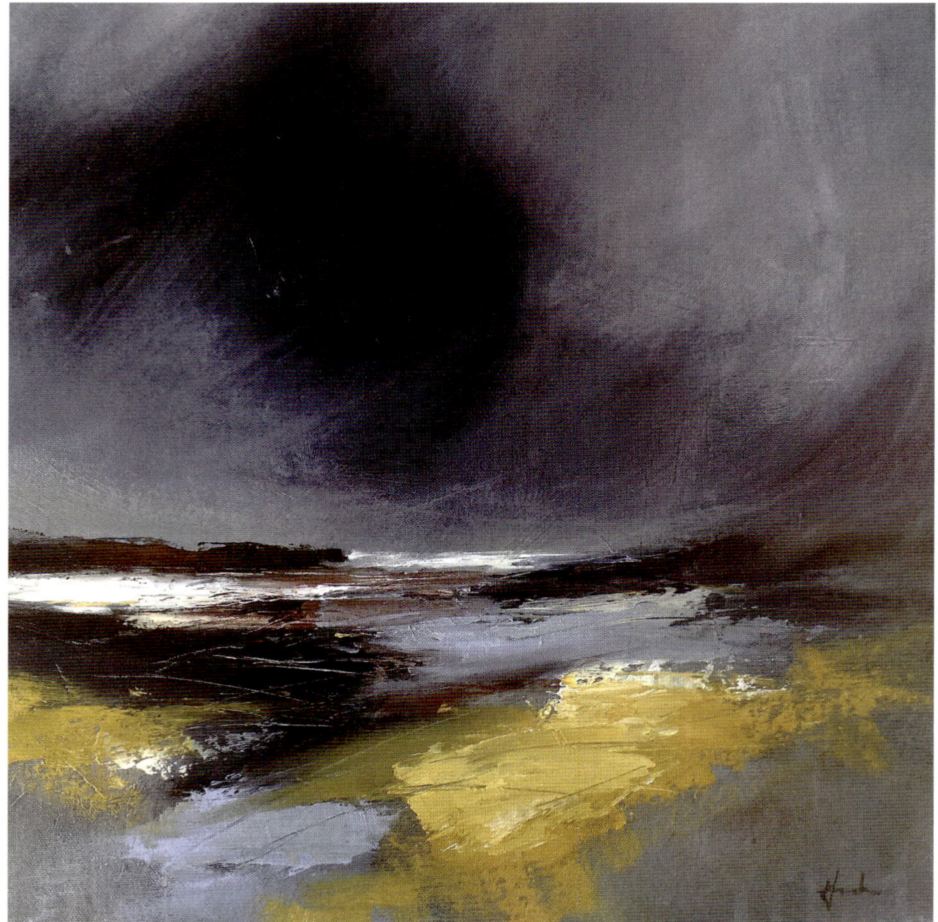

Storm Rolling In, Mari French.
When it comes to dramatic skies, Mari certainly has captured it in this one. You can almost feel the atmosphere in this painting. The strong dark of the storm cloud is a bold colour to use but works so well in this painting.

Cley Mill
Cadmium Red
Yellow Ochre
Cadmium Yellow
Burnt Umber
Ultramarine Blue
Titanium White
24" × 30" canvas
Burnt Sienna ground

This large studio painting was painted in two sessions. The sky was the dominant feature here with Cley Windmill providing a point of interest with the white sails contrasting against the dark sky.

The water in the foreground creek gives an interesting lead into the picture. The only detail in the reed beds is in the foreground, leaving the imagination to fill in the rest of the information. The sky was initially painted with Ultramarine Blue, white and a prick of Yellow Ochre graduating from dark at the top to a paler colour at the horizon. This was then allowed to dry.

Starting at the horizon, the clouds were applied by scumbling thin paint over the dry under painting, allowing the original colour to break through. By starting at the horizon, it is possible to give the impression of the clouds banking up and coming towards you, thus giving a strong feeling of distance.

The final whiter cloud has no pure white but subtle variations of grey (mixed with the blue, red and yellow) and the highlights Titanium White/Yellow Ochre were added last. When the sky was touch dry, the sails were added.

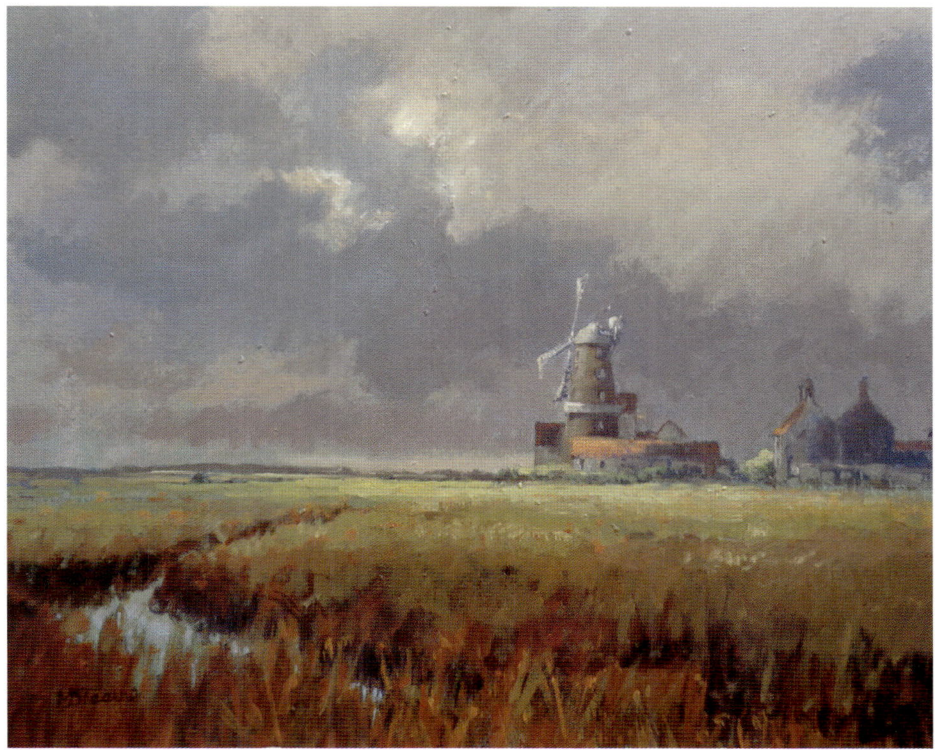

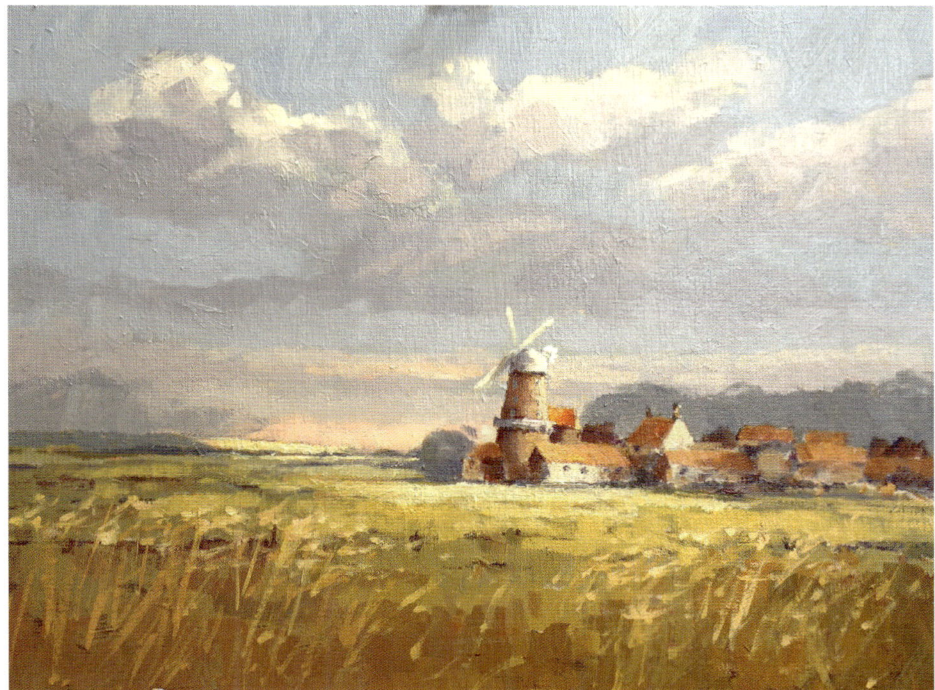

Summer Clouds, Cley.
This may be the same subject as before but whereas *Cley Mill* was painted in the winter, we can see the contrast that a different season can make. The sunny sky with a few drifting clouds makes for a completely diverse feel in this picture.

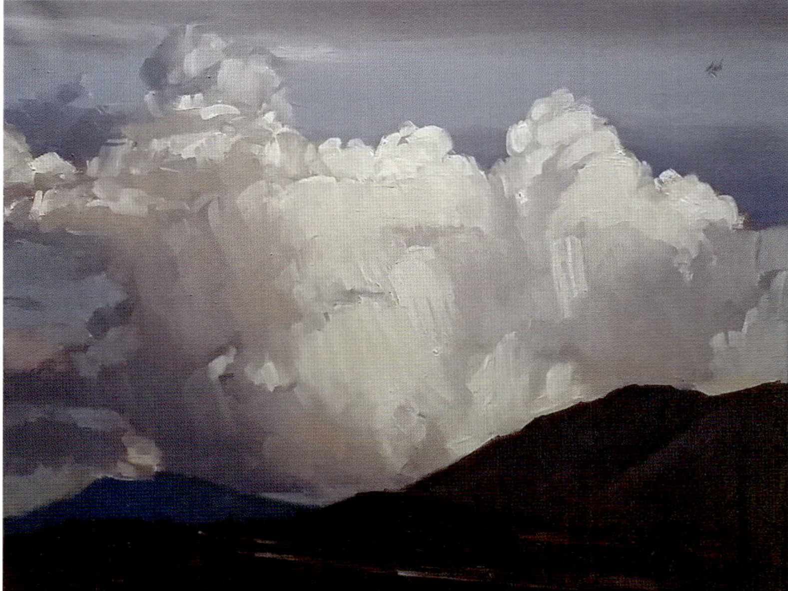

Looming Cumulus, David Simons.
This strong image uses minimal brush strokes to maximum effect. The cloud looms large as it blows over the mountain. The warm shadows help to give the cloud its form.

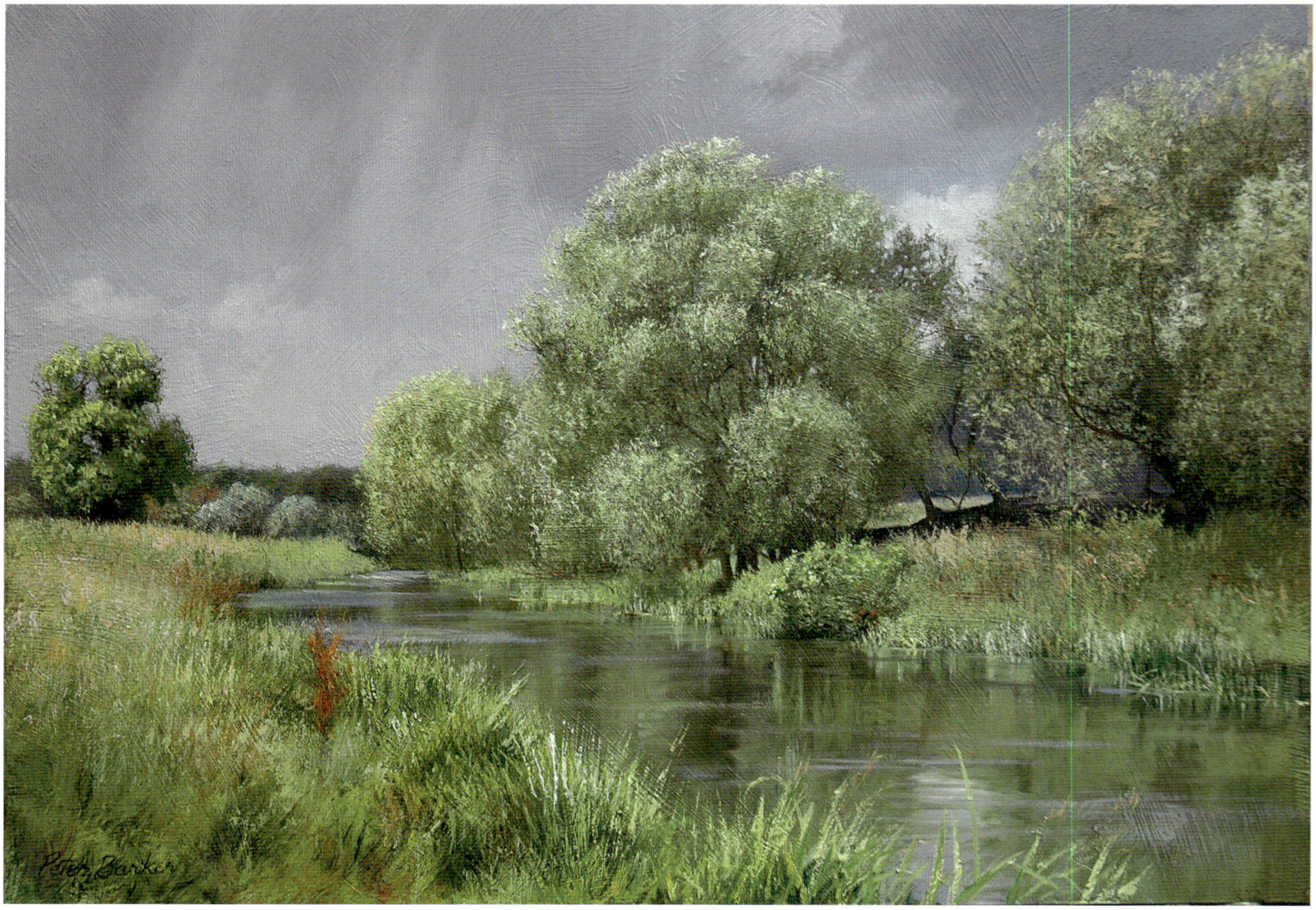

Grey Sky and River, Peter Barker.
The calmness of the water is in stark contrast here to the threatening sky. We are left wondering if the storm has just passed or if it is approaching. Without Peter actually painting it, we can see from the light reflecting on the top of the trees indicating that the sky above is much brighter than the sky in the distance.

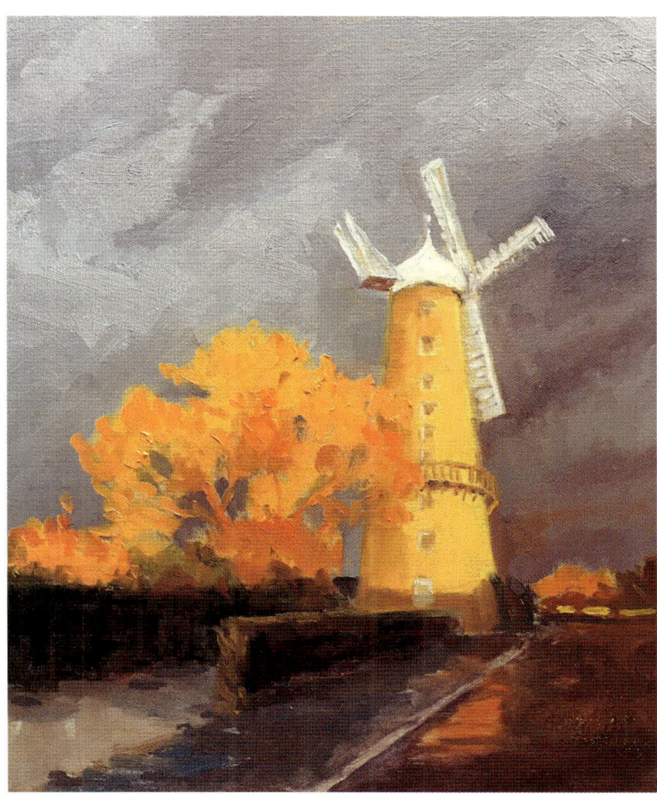

Moulton Mill. 12" × 10" cotton covered MDF. Pale Umber ground.
We have the tallest windmill in the UK by our house. The chestnut to the left is in our garden. From my kitchen window I can see the mill, which acts as my own personal weather vane. In this picture, the tail fin is missing, as it had to be removed for repairs. There had just been a terrific storm and the sun came out, illuminating the mill and emphasizing the dark of the passing clouds. The reflection of the mill in the wet ground helps to carry the colour through the painting. Cadmium Orange really came into its own for this painting. It was not only the perfect colour for the chestnut tree and the glow on the mill, but it also mixed in well for the dark clouds with Ultramarine.

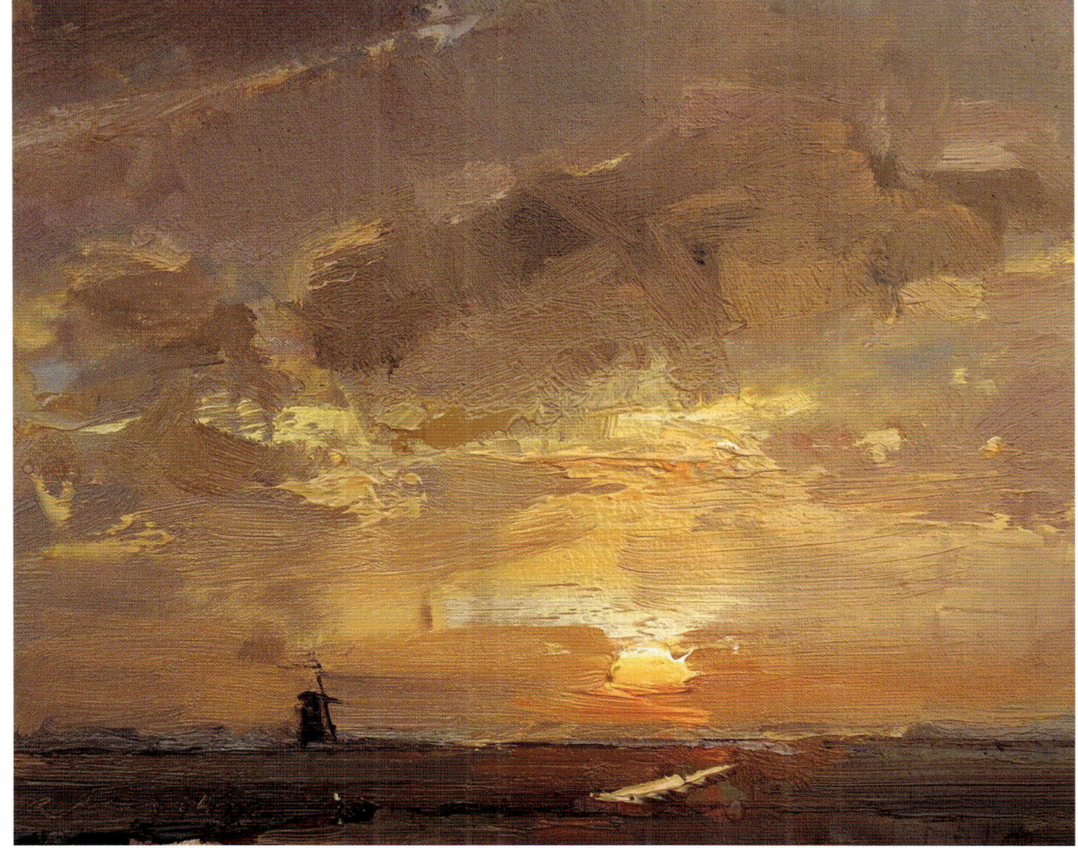

Just Before Heavy Rain, Roos Schuring.
This stunning painting certainly has drama. Roos has chosen a palette of warm greys, yellows and orange. There is a great unity of colours here. The threatening rain clouds allow the glow of the sun to shine through; the touches of blue grey are sheer genius. I like the low horizon as it heightens the vastness of the sky and although there is little foreground, we are given the feeling of distance because of the dyke leading away from us and reflecting the sun.

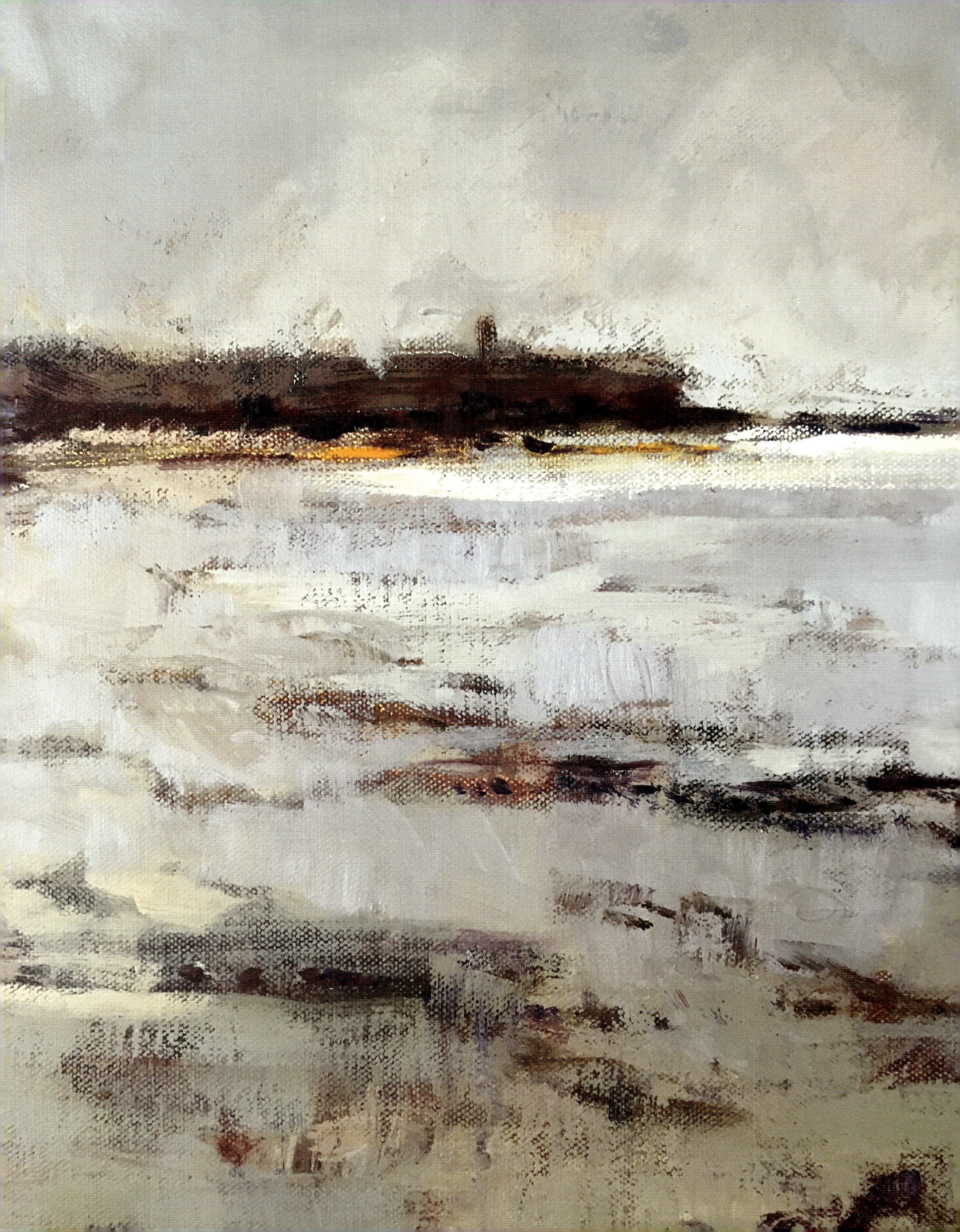

CHAPTER 10

Development of personal style

Having your own style is something that makes your paintings identifiable with you. Lucien Freud, Gauguin, Frans Hals, Rembrandt and Van Gogh to name a few all have a distinctive style and individual ways of mark making.

Brush strokes are like your handwriting – they are unique to you. It is not something that can be forced, but developed and evolved over a period of time. If you do a lot of painting, your style will automatically progress as you discover your own way of doing things. Don't worry too much about developing a style of brushwork. That too, like your style, will materialize in time. Do, though, try to use your brushes in the most expressive way you can.

Sometimes you need to be bold. The following examples by Louise Balaam show a great confidence of brushstroke. She has developed her own very definite style, which, although it may look simple would be very hard to emulate.

When you first take up painting, you probably have an idea of how you would like to paint. Maybe there is an artist whose work you admire and would aspire to emulate. This is harder than it would first seem. If you look at the seemingly simple brush strokes of Edward Seago, you might be tempted to think it would be easy to paint like that, whereas the actual truth of the matter is that this is a style of a master painter with great experience and each stroke is executed simply and confidently.

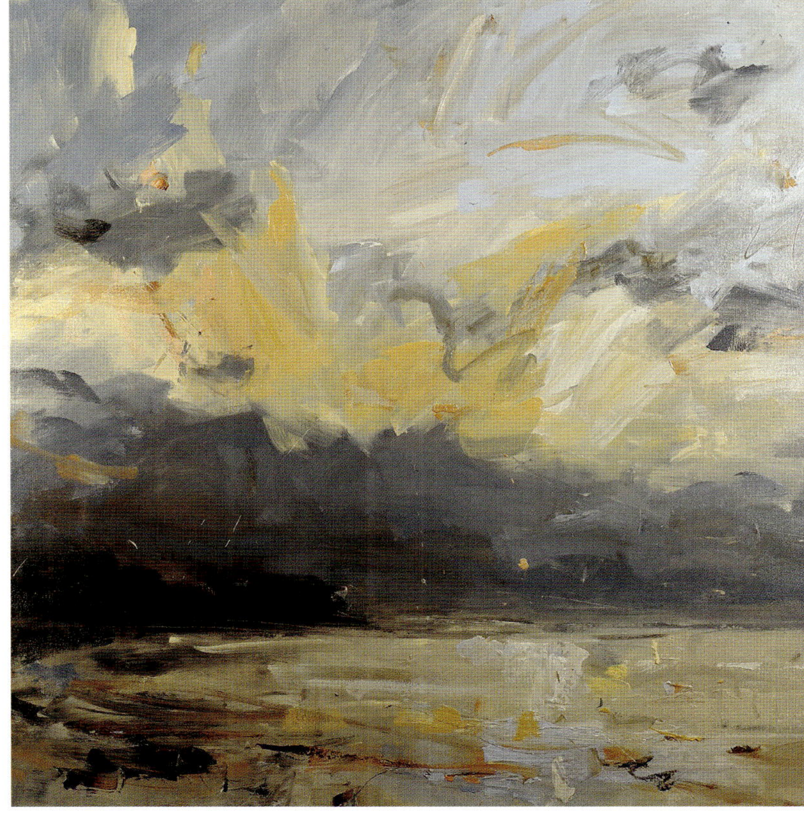

Low Sunset and Grey Clouds, Louise Balaam.
This impressive painting is larger than you may guess at. It is 51" × 51". Louise has used big brushes to enable her to cover the canvas with her loose, expressive brush marks. By keeping to a limited palette, there is a good harmony to the painting. The sweep of the bay leads us back into the picture and colours from the sky reflect back in the wet sand. (Photo: John Caruana)

Towards Hunstanton, Norfolk.

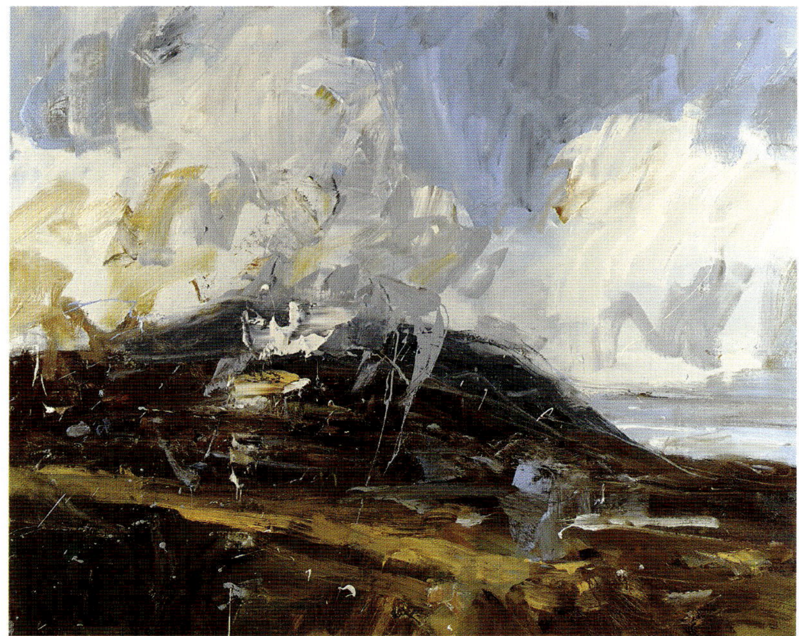

Early Summer, Skylarks Singing, Louise Balaam.
Another large painting, this is 43" × 51". We can feel the freshness of the blustery clouds coming up over the moor casting shadows. The flash of sunlight lifts the dark foreground and echoes the yellow in the clouds. Flicks and dashes of colour help to unite the two halves and soften the outline of the horizon. (Photo: John Caruana)

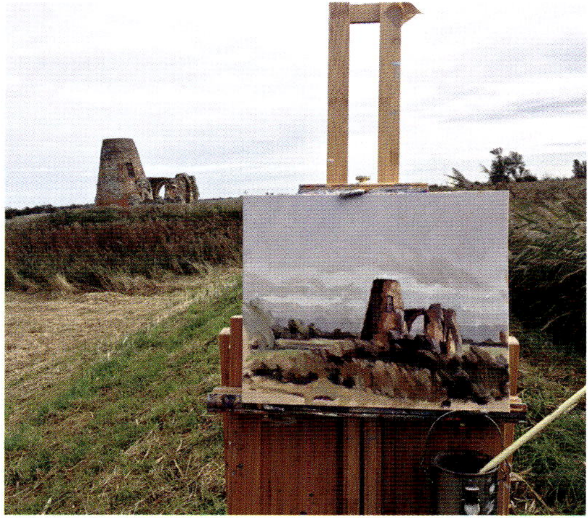

St Benet's Abbey.
This 10" × 12" painting of St Benet's Abbey near Ludham, Norfolk, is featured often in the paintings of Norfolk artist Edward Seago, well known for his East Anglian skyscapes.

Constant observation is essential to an artist. Whether you are travelling on a train, bus or walking, look around your surroundings and think, how would I paint that, which colours would I use?

I feel that anyone can be taught how to paint, the difficult part is the inspiration and the need to paint; a bit like learning an instrument, you can learn the technicalities but it's putting the passion into playing that makes it flow and stand apart. Be prepared for failures; most artists go through a period of self-doubt. If this happens to you, look at some of your past work and say to yourself, 'Yes, I can do it'. Don't get despondent and give up. Work through it, sometimes using a different medium for a while helps. For example, going out and doing a few watercolour studies not only is useful in that it is valuable source material but it can bring back the need to express what you have captured on a larger scale.

Study other artists

Go to art galleries to look at other artists' work, study their brush strokes and the colours they use, can you learn something from them? Is it something you can employ in your own work? If you particularly like a painting, ask yourself why. What makes it a good painting? What drew you to it?

I always return from a trip to an art gallery with itching fingers. I went to an exhibition at the Mall Gallery with a fellow artist friend, we stood at the top of the stairs and scanned the room, taking in the atmosphere and the feel of the exhibition and both of us simultaneously said, 'Wow, look at that one.' Right across the room there was a painting that stood out to both of us. We went across to study it and to ask ourselves why we were both so drawn to it. The conclusion we came to was that it had everything. Good composition, strong contrasts and a good focal point. I remember the impact it had and when I am working on a painting, I try to stand back and ask myself, does this work? Has it got the wow factor? It is hard to emotionally distance yourself from your pictures. Sometimes try to put them away for up to three months out of sight. When you see them again it will be like someone else seeing them for the first time, then you can better judge the impact it has on you.

I think of my painting as a journey, I am constantly learning, developing my style, always striving for a good painting. If it came too easily then I don't think I would have the same enthusiasm to paint.

ARTIST PROFILE

John Stillman

Tower Bridge is always a pleasure to paint, whatever the weather but on this particular day the sky was the centre of attention for me. The board I was using to paint on was prepared using Gesso Primer (Windsor & Newton) and had a light covering of Texture Paste (Daler Rowney) to give the board some texture to enable the paint to be drawn from the brush.

I started with a very 'turpsy' wash of Cerulean Blue, Alizarin Crimson and some Gel Medium (Daler Rowney) to advance the drying time of the paint. I then mixed a warm pink using Titanium White, Cadminum Red, plus a touch of Lemon Yellow Hue to give the sky the warmth. While this was wet, I used a clean cloth wrapped around my finger to 'wipe out' the highlights of the clouds and the intended buildings.

Using cloth to wipe out is a great way of indicating the direction of the light straightaway but this technique can only best be achieved when applying the initial 'turpsy' wash.

For the more detailed highlights, I use the wooden end of a brush and scratch away to reveal the white of the board. Where I had used the cloth to wipe out the highlights, I then mixed some Titanium White and Lemon Yellow Hue to accentuate the highlighted areas of the clouds. Again, use your finger to blend the highlights into the wet background. Once I had the light source indicated, it was time to start blocking in the buildings with a paint mixture of Burnt Sienna, Cerulean Blue and French Ultramarine. The boats were indicated with simple brush marks while working on site and any details were completed back at the studio. My on site work is all about getting the feel of the scene and the day and not about trying to complete a finished painting on site. I always like to complete my paintings back at the studio as it gives me time to consider any changes that need to be made to improve the painting. I like to do any changes a day or so after as I feel it is good to look at the painting with a fresh perspective.

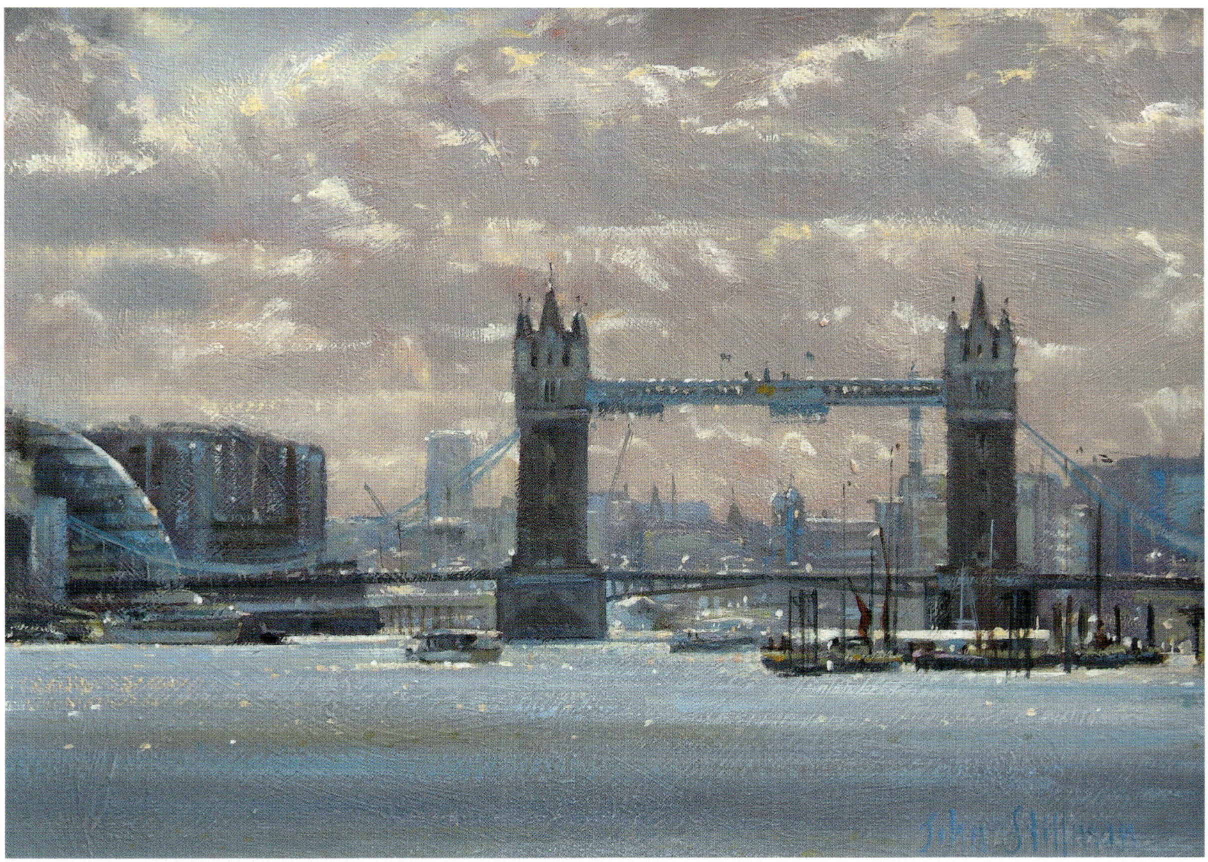

Afternoon Light, Tower Bridge, John Stillman, 9" × 12". Oil on board.

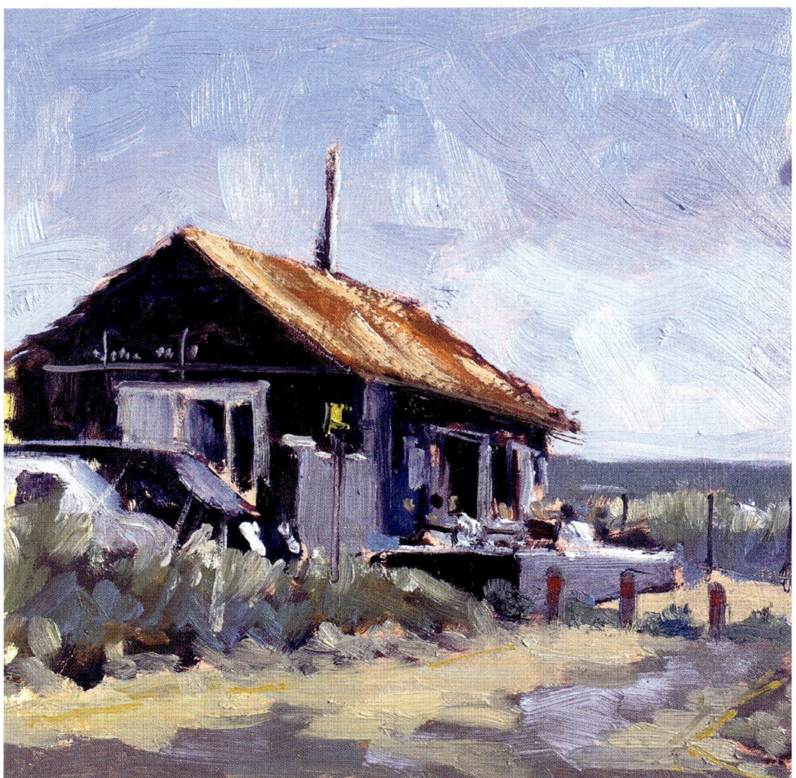

Winterton.
This 6" × 6" painting was painted as part of a *plein air* competition. No one was more surprised than me that it won first prize. It goes to show that the simplest of subjects can work.

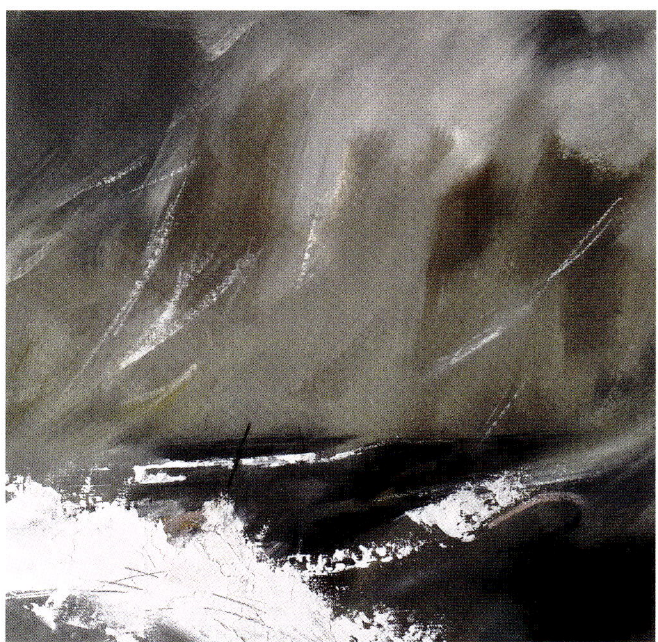

Wild Weather, Running Tide, Mari French.
Blended greys in the background convey a bank of all-encompassing rain whilst the bold sweep of white indicates the wildness and force of the wind sweeping up the waves. This is a painting full of movement and shows great confidence and a unique style.

Keep a scrapbook of artists that you admire and aspire to. Pinterest is a very useful online site where people create pin boards of things that interest them. Many an hour can be spent browsing other people's pin boards of artists. Consider what it is about these artists' work that appeals to you and what drew you to their work. Was it the colour palette, their use of light, an unusual composition or the way that they applied the paint or a combination of all?

When starting out painting it is hard to know what to paint. Many amateurs start off by copying the work of other artists, particularly those they admire. This is fine up to a point and you will probably learn a lot from the exercise but bear in mind that it is their inspiration and not yours, and certainly should not be presented as your own work. With so many styles, try to just focus on one at a time; to try out too many at once would be confusing and it would be hard to focus on the outcome.

Repeating a painting because it was successful or maybe because you sold it may be an enjoyable exercise, especially as we know what our final objective is but it will not further your progress as an artist. Try to improve on previous attempts and think how you can make it better.

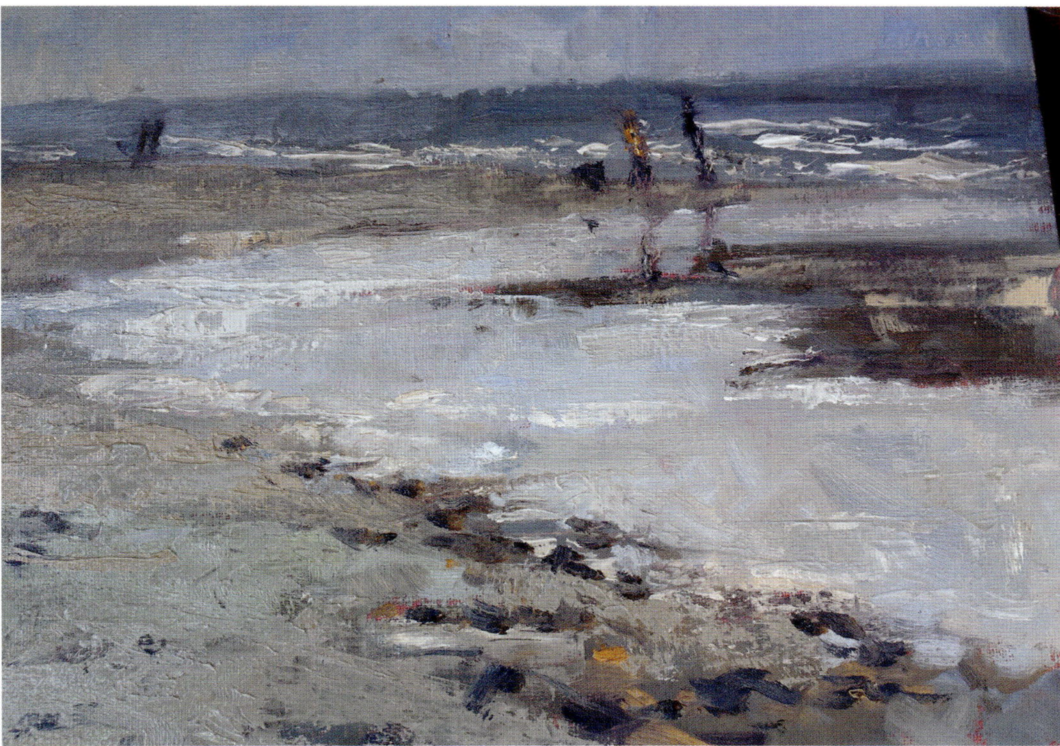

Sea and Sky, Holland.
This is an example of working with a limited palette. A large brush was used from the start to keep the painting simple with finer details added only at the end with a smaller brush.

Galleries

Galleries prefer artists who have an identifiable style. The more unique it is, the more it stands apart from other paintings in the same space. It also means that someone can walk into a gallery and immediately recognize the work of a particular artist. Working to a constant standard is something that a gallery owner and collector would like to see. Don't try to make up numbers by putting in inferior work; it will let your best work down.

If you are looking for gallery representation, it is a good thing to have a body of work and having a distinctive style certainly helps. It also helps to concentrate on one subject. Unless your style is very distinctive, it would be confusing and distracting for the gallery owner to see consistency if they have to look through different subjects such as portrait, still life, landscape and animal pictures.

Deciding on a subject that interests and inspires you and concentrating on that alone for a good period will certainly advance your progress to achieving a style of your own. It would be difficult to see any progress when you flit from subject to subject so decide on just the one to start with. It might well be landscape. Gather as much source information as you can that includes sketches and photographs. Try to keep it fairly simple and work on similar sized canvases. Prepare your boards and make a few preliminary sketches to check your composition.

Work in a series

Working on a series of paintings of the same subject is an excellent way to develop your style. It gives you a plan and the confidence to explore. Your series will evolve as you try different angles, colours and perspectives. With each one you should notice an improvement, in other words, it just gets better. A series of ten pictures would be a good start. Working with a limited palette will also be an advantage, as you will not have to keep stopping to think about how to mix your colours as you will be familiar with the colours you are using.

When you have finished the first painting, keeping it where you can see it is a very useful practice as you are able to make reference to it. As the series progresses and you have more paintings around you, you will be able to see your progress. Look back at the paintings already done and take the best from each one. Look at them critically, ask yourself why a particular area maybe doesn't work and how you can improve it. Stay with it until you can honestly say that you have a series of paintings that look as if the same person has painted them.

Once you have completed this exercise a couple of times, explore the possibilities of your subject. Analyze each one and decide where it could be improved. Keep an open mind and try different approaches. It is a good thing to push yourself out of your comfort zone because, sometimes if you are

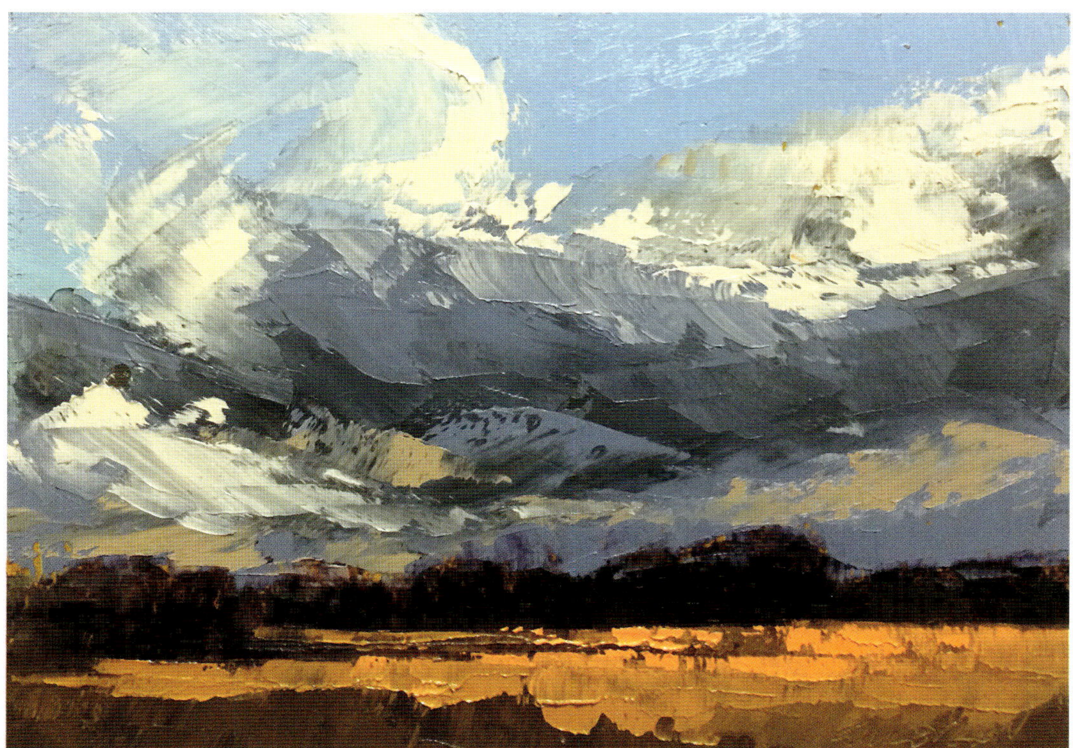

Spring Storm, Mary Bentz Gilkerson.
Many of Mary's paintings are painted on 5" × 7" pieces of card. Her style that she has developed with her use of the palette knife is immediately recognizable.

too familiar with a subject, you tend not to pay attention to the details. You need to closely observe the small nuances of colour and shape, and take time to really study the subject. Make a few notes to refer to. This helps to remind you of your objectives.

Try using a different palette of colours. Experiment with the way you apply the paint. You could try using a palette knife in some areas or change to larger brushes. The way paint is applied and the colours you use play the biggest part in making your style distinguishable. The tools you use to make these marks brushes are the tools used by most artists, and they come in all shapes and sizes; each one will make a different mark. It isn't just the shape and size of the brush we must consider but also the fibres it is made of. A softer brush is useful for applying paint over wet paint. A hog hair or bristle brush would only serve to scratch at the paint, probably removing more than you are trying to apply.

EXPERIMENTING

Every now and then it is fun to play. Oil paints are a very versatile and adaptable medium, which readily lend themselves to experimentation. By experimenting with colour, texture and different ways of applying paint you will not only gain confidence but, more often than not, you will make a few discoveries. You might well find that your experimenting takes your painting journey down a completely different road. Learning to take risks is an essential aspect of being creative with colour.

Put some time aside to play with colour, texture and style. Prepare a few small panels, gessoed card is good. Working on a small scale means that you will be able to cover the ground quicker. Another advantage of working on card on a small scale is that you will not feel precious about it.

One good way of experimenting is to step out of your comfort zone by choosing a subject that you consider difficult. It might be glass, a figure, a view from inside some woods or even a subject with difficult colours. You will have to solve the problems presented by these seemingly impossible subjects of how to achieve the effect you want. The problems and their solutions will help you approach a subject in a different way. You will be surprised at the outcome.

The following two paintings are examples of an afternoon spent in the studio. This was a fun session. It involved layering up dark colours through to light, lots of scraping back with a palette knife to expose previously applied colours which were then worked back into.

It can be a very useful exercise to repeat a subject using a different approach. In the second version of *Abstract Beach*,

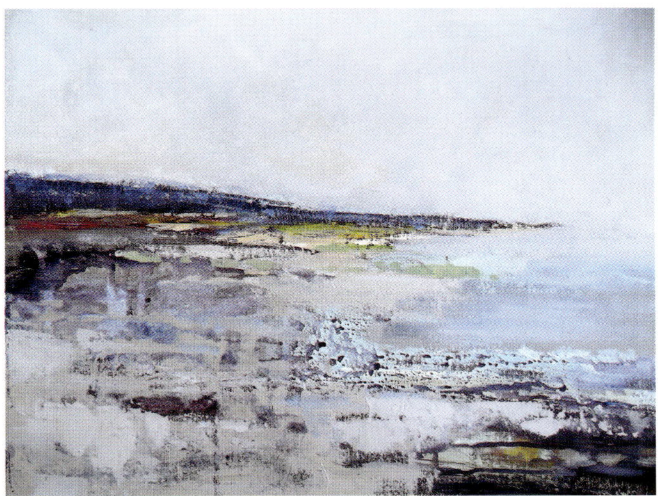

Abstract Beach 1, 6" × 8". Canvas board.
The sky and the sea are only defined in this little painting by the addition of the cliffs. There is no actual line dividing the two. The brain does this for us because we know it should be there. The sky needs to be simple in this semi abstract painting as the foreground is so busy. Lots of techniques were used, including scraping off, thin washes, impasto and flicking.

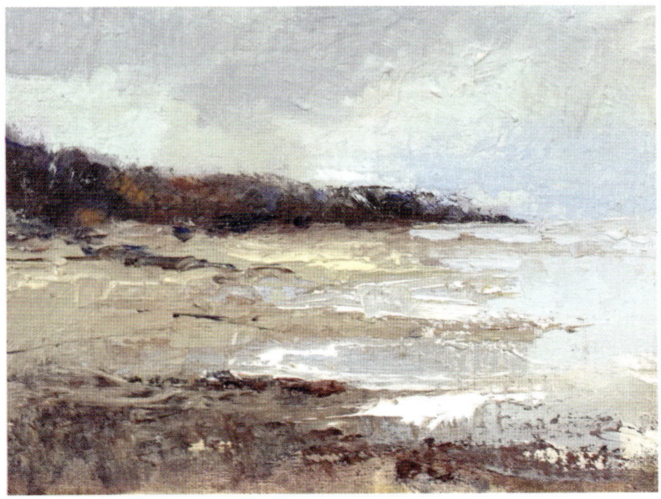

Abstract Beach 2, 6" × 8". Canvas board.
This painting started out in my mind as another abstract as in the painting *Abstract Beach 1* but as it developed, a feeling of realism crept in with the colours and the sky was more true to the original subject.

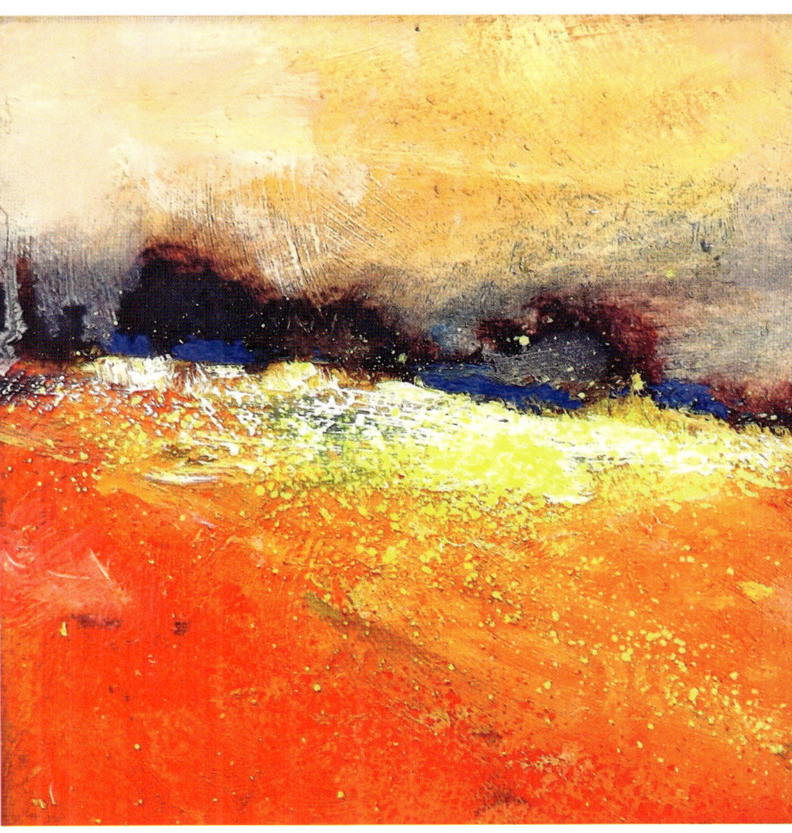

Poppy Field.
Lemon Yellow
Cadmium Yellow
Cadmium Red
Brown Madder Alizarin
French Ultramarine Blue
Cobalt Blue
6" × 6" Heavily gessoed MDF

This little painting came about as a result of breaking my wrist and was thus painted with the left hand. The sky almost has a Turneresque quality with the yellow being picked up in the landscape. Paint was applied very thinly to start with and rubbed back with a cloth, leaving a ghost of all the colours. The trees are a mix of Brown Madder Alizarin and Ultramarine, applied thinly and smudged into the sky. The colours were then built up, working from light to dark. The final touches were added when the paint was dry. This was done using a broad bristle brush and dragging it lightly across the surface, taking advantage of the heavy texture. Yellow and red splatters were added last, using an old toothbrush and paint diluted with white spirit.

although started in the same way with thin washes, the paint was built up and applied much thicker with the use of a palette knife. The colours were changed to a much warmer palette and pure white was used for the highlights.

The main thing here to remember is that when you are experimenting you are not aiming for a finished painting. By adopting the attitude that it doesn't matter what the outcome is, you will become less precious about the picture.

First you will need to have an open mind and a palette full of paint. The results can be very rewarding. Just remember the balance between experimenting and your goals as a painter.

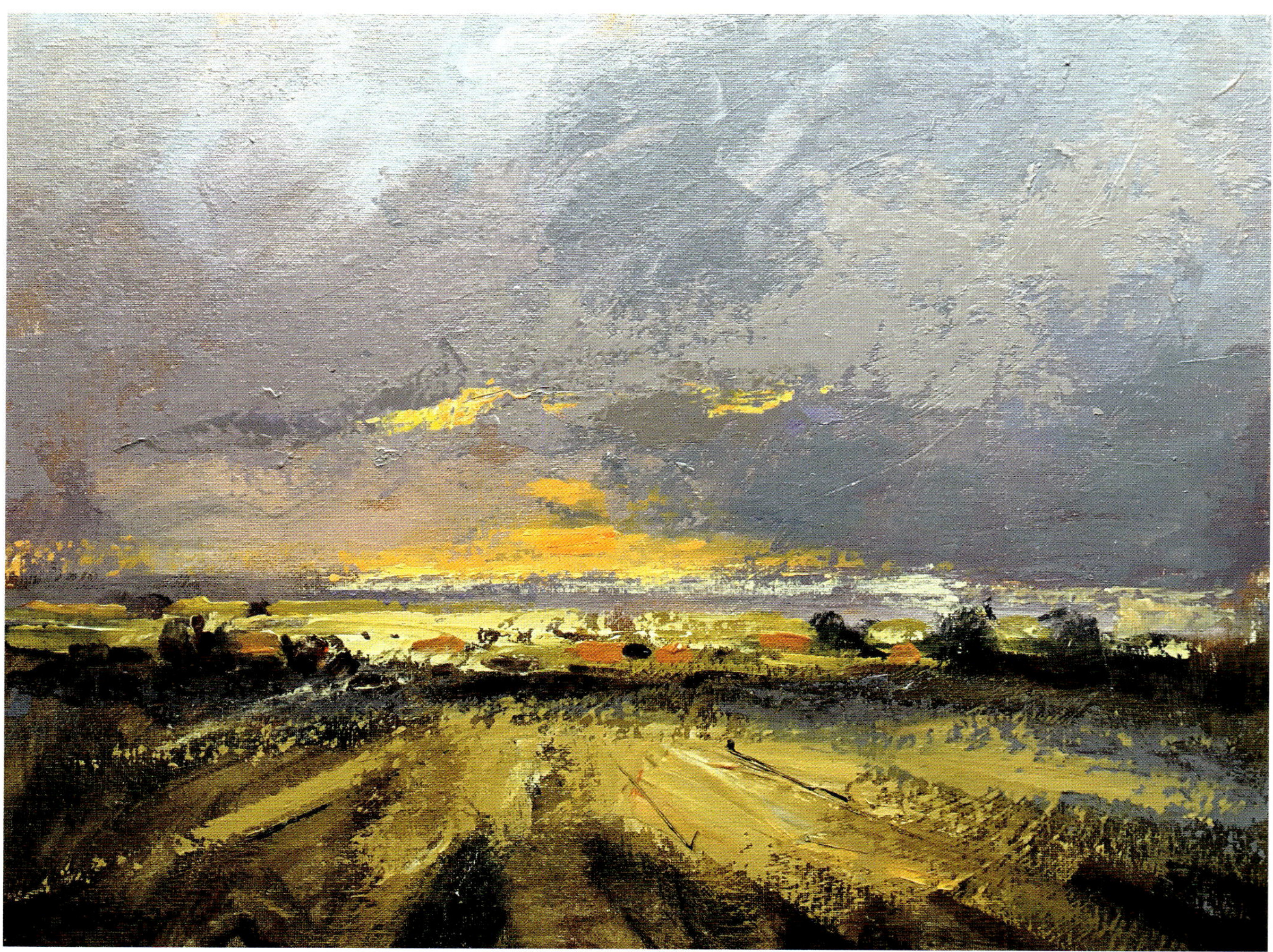

Across the Common.
Titanium White
Yellow Ochre
Cadmium Yellow
Cadmium Orange
Burnt Umber
Cadmium Red
Cobalt Blue
Ultramarine Blue
14" × 18" Gessoed canvas board
Permanent Rose/Yellow Ochre ground

This studio painting is a view across the common at Brancaster. It is a subject I have revisited several times using an oil sketch made on the spot as a reference. It is not my usual style or method of painting but I found it to be fun and liberating. Using a wide brush (no. 10 flat hog hair) I started with very dark, thin washes of Ultramarine Blue and Burnt Umber in the foreground and for the mid distant trees.

Using the same brush, the sky was started with a dark mix of Cadmium Red/Cobalt Blue on the right and warmer Cadmium Red/Yellow Ochre on the left. The original layers are still visible in places. Over on the right side I painted Cobalt Blue/Titanium White and Yellow Ochre and on the left, the same mix with more Titanium White. Going back to the foreground, I dragged a Yellow Ochre/Burnt Umber mix following the direction of the lines in the field.

To help tie top and bottom halves of the picture together, some of the sky colours were also dragged into the field. The strong perspective of the field lines helps with the impression of distance. The texture of the gesso on the board gives the broken lines, making it look less solid. Cadmium Yellow in the sky makes for a good contrast to the blue colours.

At this stage the painting has a lot of paint on it so I switched to using a palette knife. A bristle brush would tend to lift paint off. I wanted the strongest contrasts to be in the centre so for my highlight there is Cadmium Yellow/Titanium White. Cadmium Orange was added to the sky for more warmth and also for the rooftops in the centre. Yellow Ochre/Titanium White provides the highlight on the field. The end of a brush scratched through this gives some more directional lines.

Finally, using various mixes on the palette, some lighter colours were dragged across the sky to break up large areas.

Things to try

- Making a colour chart. This is a very good way to learn the potential of your palette. You will discover by mixing different colours together which colours mix well and which ones make 'mud'. There are many secrets hidden on your palette waiting to be discovered. For example, Kings Blue Light and Lemon Yellow make a wonderful soft green, especially with the addition of a little white.
- Different coloured grounds. If you normally play safe with a neutral colour, try a brighter colour.
- Dilute the first wash with turpentine and let it run down the canvas, this can have some interesting results.
- Dripping turpentine into paint that has just been applied and tilting the canvas can get colours to meld.
- Leave areas of thin paint. The contrast between thick and thin paint makes for added interest.
- Use larger brushes. This will also help to free up your brushwork. It is harder to fiddle with a large brush.
- Apply paint thickly. This is also known as Impasto. For this method of painting, you will need a surface with plenty of 'tooth'. Tooth basically means textured or rougher surface. The tooth is required to hold the paint onto the canvas but be aware, thick paint can take a long time to dry.
- Scraping back. If an area isn't working well, take the palette knife to it. It is surprising how effective this can be. There will be a residue of the original colours that can work well left on its own or be used as a base for another layer.
- Lay paint on with a palette knife. If applied lightly, the underneath layer will show through, making interesting contrasts, especially if you have used a complementary colour.

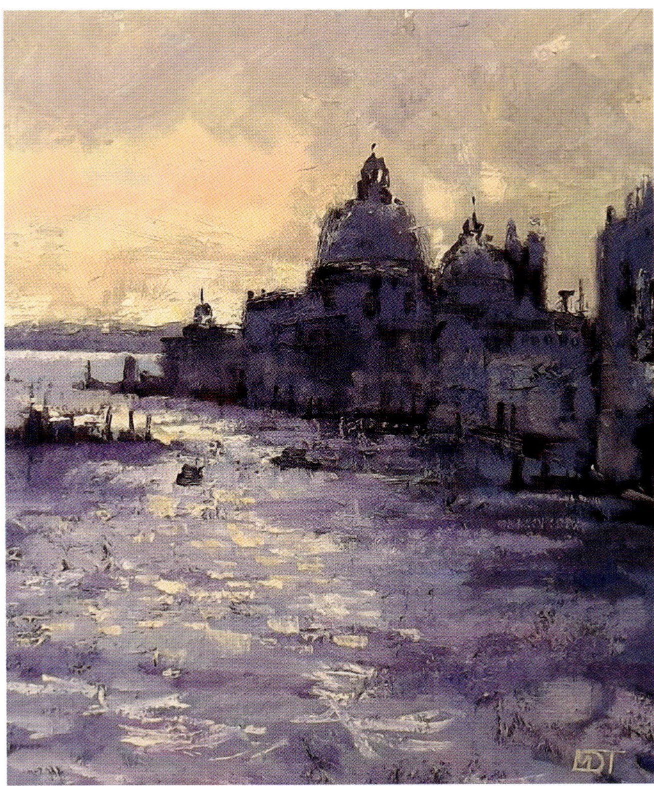

Venice Reflections.
Ultramarine Blue
Cadmium Yellow
Magenta
Titanium White
12" × 10" Gessoed board
Burnt Umber ground

This studio painting was painted from a tonal sketch made on location in Venice. Having a tonal sketch makes it a lot easier to imagine your own colours. I still had the impression in my mind of the moment I saw this early morning scene in Venice. The dark shapes of the buildings were blocked in with Ultramarine Blue, Cadmium Yellow & Magenta diluted with turps. The dark areas in the water were done at the same time. Staying with the purply mixes, I lightened the colours, building up the form and shapes of the buildings. The sky was a warm pinky yellow and the complementary purple helps the colours to glow. The paint on the buildings was still wet and I blended the edges of the buildings with the end of my brush to soften the outlines. The sky was painted from the horizon upwards, adding more Magenta towards the top. The final touches were the sparkles in the water using the lightest sky colour to pull the painting together.

Surfaces

Different surfaces are another way of experimenting. The following examples are painted on rough watercolour paper that has added texture and has been gessoed. An advantage of working on paper is that it can easily be cut to any size. It is inexpensive, especially if you are painting over an old watercolour. It can also look very effective mounted onto mount board and framed with the edges exposed.

Adding more texture to your support can be fun. There are several texture pastes on the market or you could make your own. Try adding sand or fine grit when painting gesso onto the surface.

Different textures on the board or canvas can give a wide range of effects. Try as many different surfaces as possible. Each one will give different results and eventually you will find one that best suits your requirements.

If you are after fine detail then a smoother surface is best. This could be anything from a pre-prepared fine linen canvas to a gessoed board, sanded down between coats. Watercolour paper that has been primed with gesso or gelatin to seal the surface makes for a very good surface to paint on. Not only is this inexpensive, it is light to transport if painting outside. It would need to be fairly rigid, at least 300gm weight to prevent too much bending.

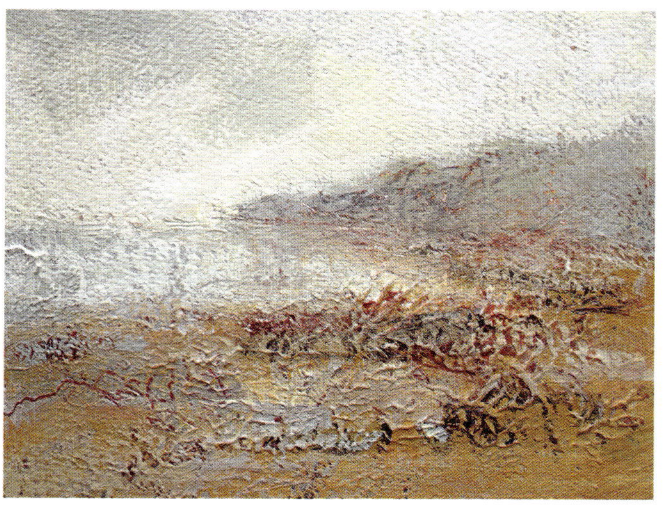

Arches 300lb rough watercolour paper; two coats of gesso.

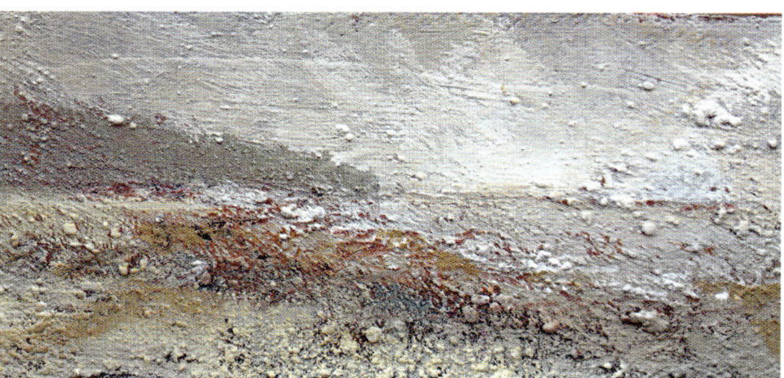

Arches 300lb rough watercolour paper. Builders sand was added to wet gesso then a second coat of gesso applied. In both these paintings, strong colour was laid down first and layers were built up by dragging successively lighter colours over it, leaving the under layers showing through to give depth and interest.

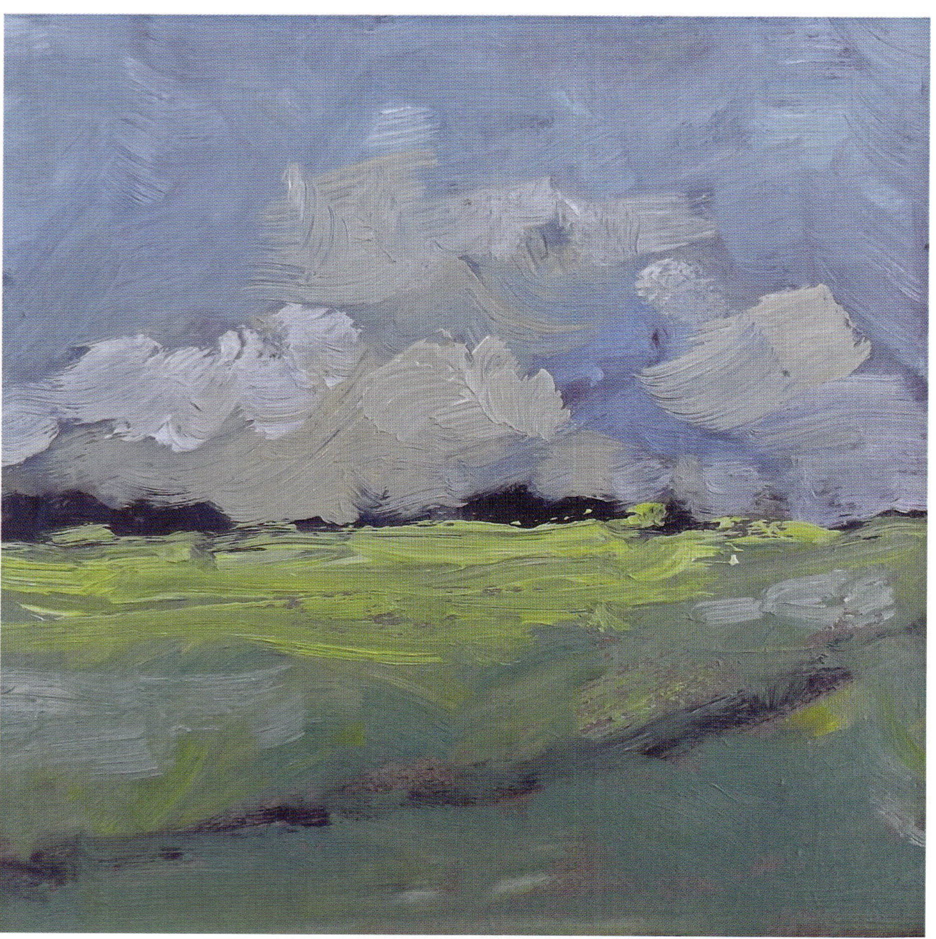

Mustard Field.
Ultramarine Blue
Cadmium Yellow
Burnt Umber
Titanium White
6" × 6" Gessoed board
Burnt Umber ground

This was a very swift rendition to capture a moment. I used a big brush and resisted any temptation to fiddle. The clouds were warmed with Burnt Umber and a touch of Cadmium Yellow, and applied confidently to convey movement. There is something a bit Van Goghish about the sky with the swirling brush strokes. This hadn't been my intention. The under painted trees on the horizon gives scale to the picture whilst the Cadmium Yellow scumbled across the green field for the mustard seed flowers gives a splash of colour.

Towards Hunstanton.
Cobalt Blue
Burnt Umber
Cadmium Yellow
Cadmium Red
Titanium White
14" × 18" Gessoed MDF
Diluted Cobalt Blue ground

The main dark shapes of the cliff and beach were blocked in with Cobalt Blue and Burnt Umber and allowed to dry. The darker blue in the sky was a mix of Cobalt Blue with the smallest amount of Burnt Umber added to knock back the brightness, then with white to lighten the mix. Towards the horizon, more white was added and a touch of yellow. I formed the clouds by painting the negative shape. This meant that I could work on the clouds and not pick up wet paint from underneath. The first clouds are a mix of white, yellow and the tiniest touch of red. This mix was darkened with blue and red and laid wet in wet over the first layer. This gives nice soft edges. All of the cloud colours were used at the same time to paint the sea with only a hint of an horizon. The sea colours were dragged over the dried paint to give broken colour, as was the sky over the cliffs. The final touch was to flick diluted white in the foreground.

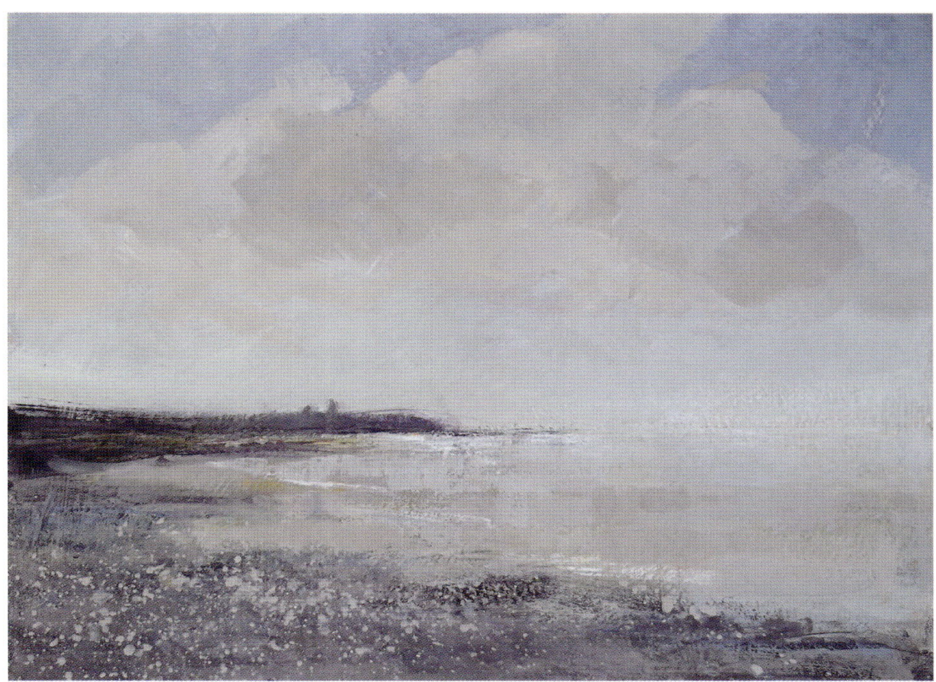

Path Through the Field
Titanium White
Cadmium Yellow
Burnt Sienna
Blue Black
6" × 8" Gessoed 300lb Arches rough water-colour paper

This simple, semi abstract painting shows a very simple sky. It was a grey day and the sky was very flat in colour. Blue Black is a very useful colour, not only for skies but also for mixing greens. Here it was mixed with Cadmium Yellow and varying amounts of Titanium White. Because of the texture of the watercolour paper, some of the Burnt Sienna under painting shows through to break up the foreground and indicate the fields. The end of the brush made a useful tool for scratching through the paint. The sky was painted last with Titanium White/ Blue Black. By dragging the paint across the distant trees, it softened their outline.

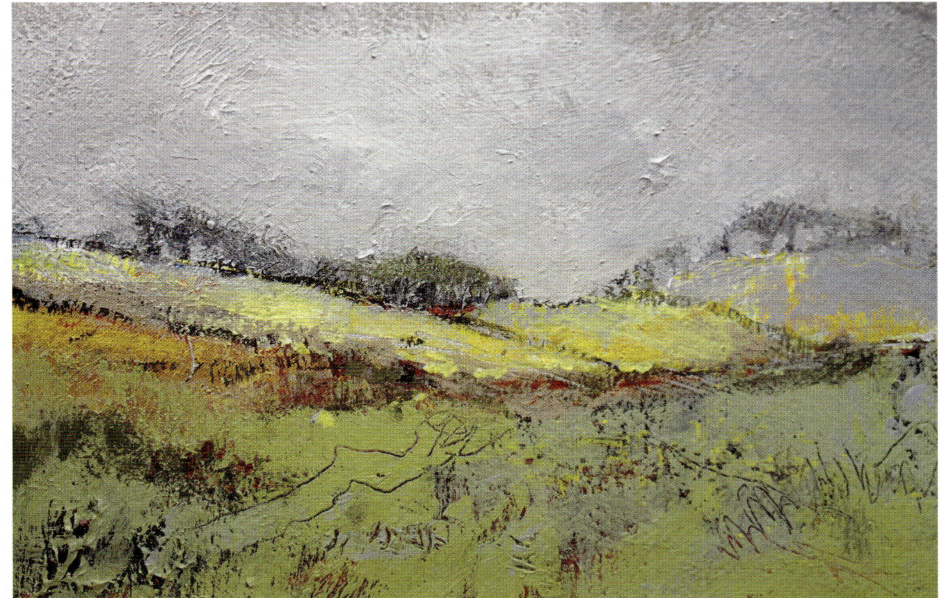

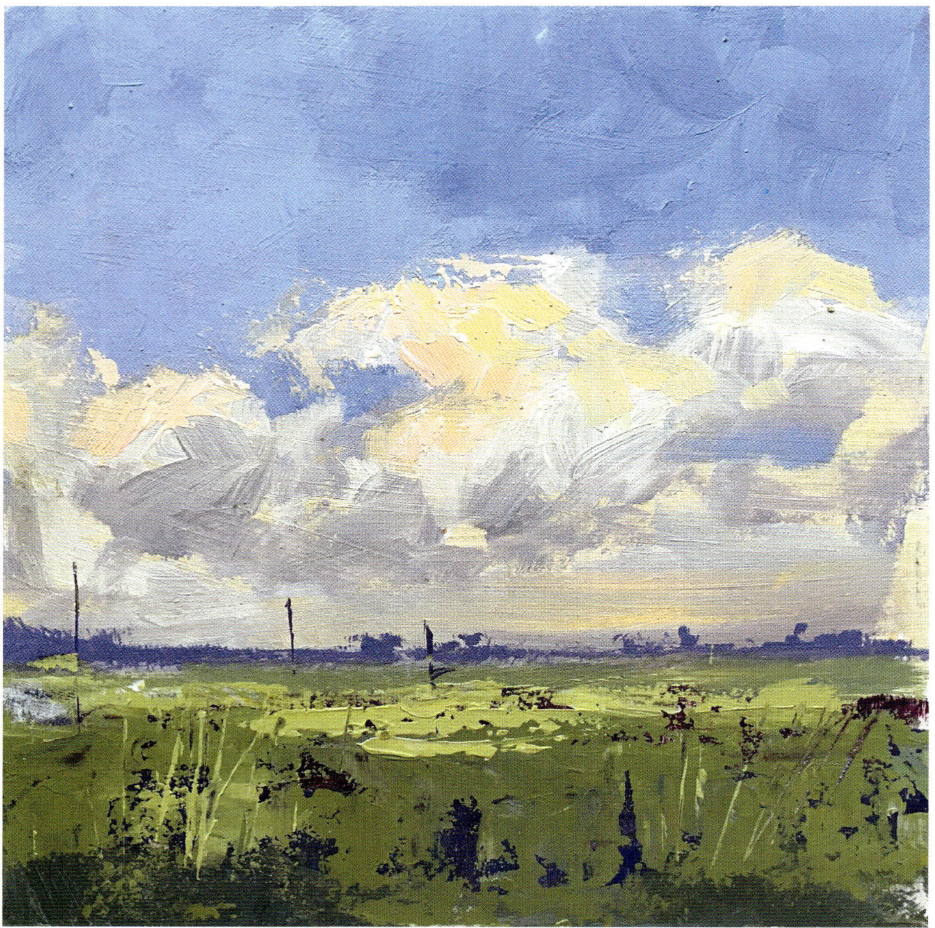

Summer Clouds, palette knife, 6" × 6". Gessoed MDF. This was painted first with a large brush. Some layers were scraped back and impasto paint laid on with a palette knife.

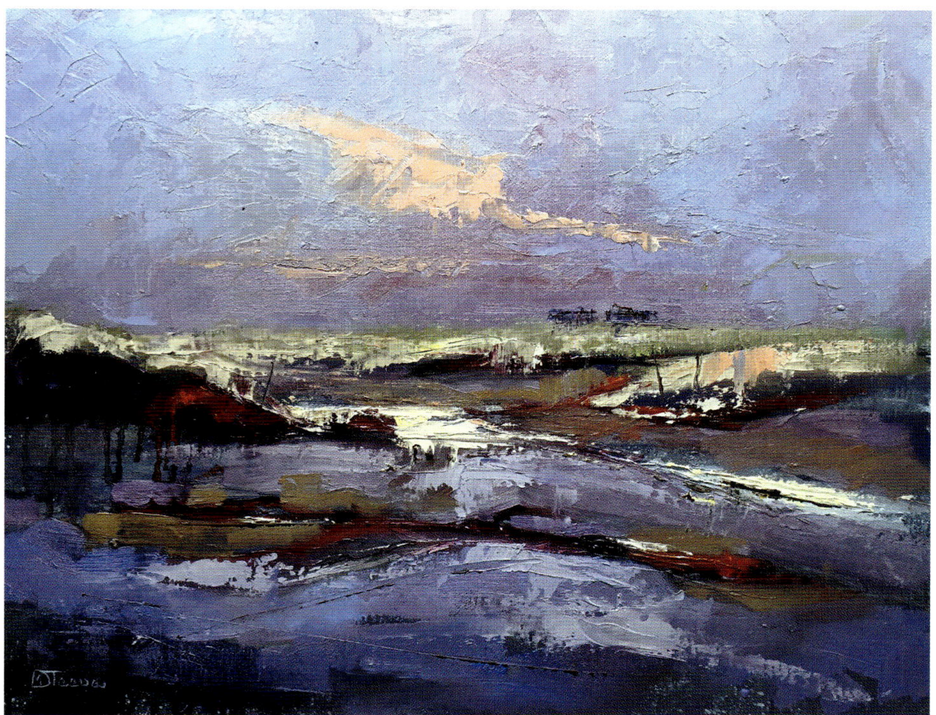

Brancaster Staithe.
This was painted using various techniques from thin paint dribbled on to thick impasto paint applied with a palette knife. Both *Summer Clouds* and *Brancaster Staithe* were both painted with a 'let's see what happens' attitude. The fact that they are both small paintings means that they don't take so long to do. Another consideration is that they did not take a lot of paint. Taking time to experiment like this is a good break from the normal routine of painting, it takes you out of your comfort zone and at the end of it, you have nothing to lose but you will, more often than not, have gained a great deal.

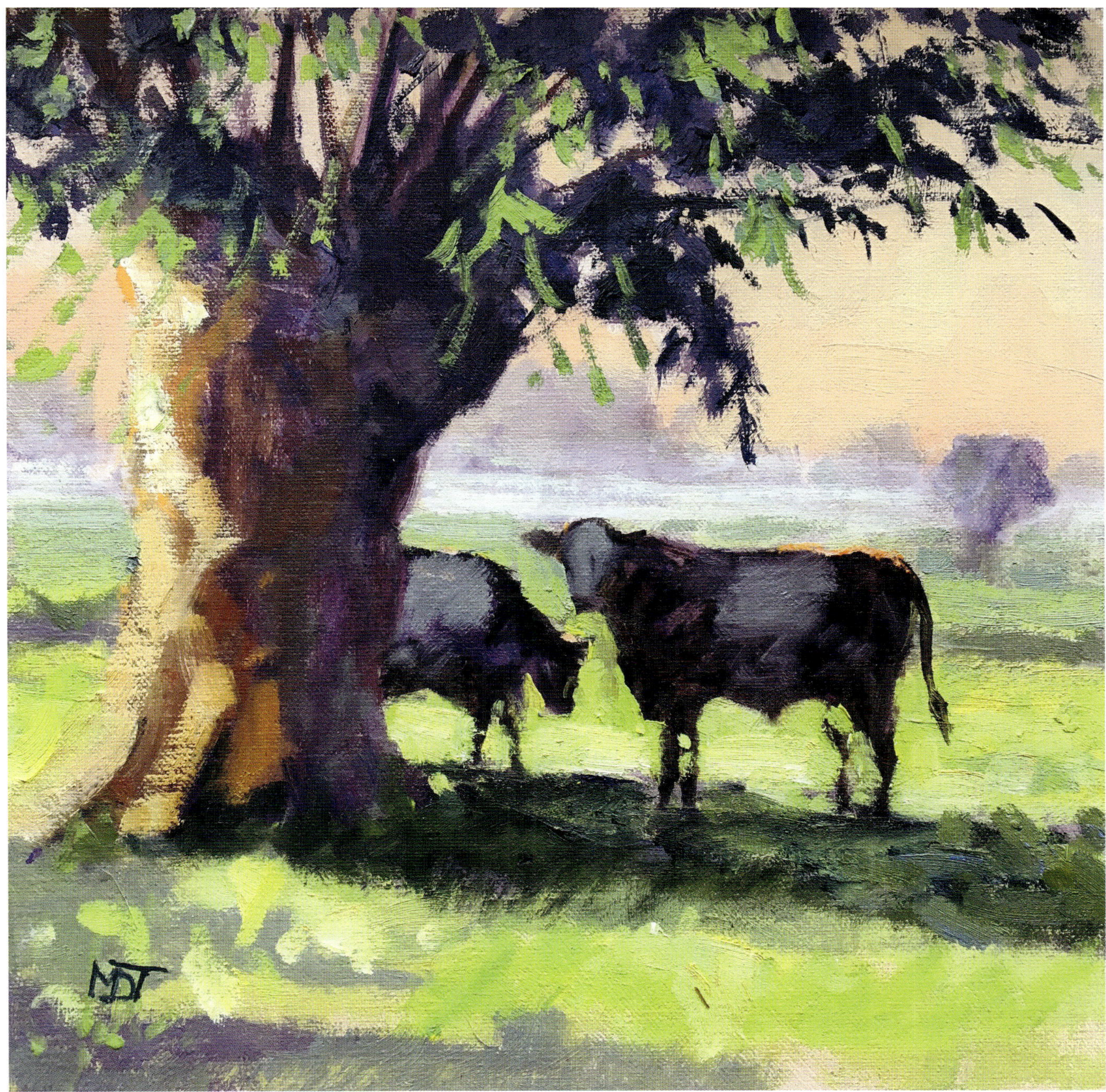

Cows
Titanium White
Cadmium Lemon
Burnt Sienna
Cadmium Red
Ultramarine Blue
6" × 6" Canvas board
Burnt Sienna ground

Another painting undertaken in experimental moment is *Cows*. It is an example of how the colour of the sky can change the whole mood and feeling of a painting This was a quick *plein air* study at Dedham. Suffolk. I chose not to have a blue sky. If I had been too literal and painted the sky blue, it would have given the whole painting a completely different feel. The orangey glow makes for a warmer painting. The strong darks of the willow trees are carried across the painting in the shadows to balance the picture. The strongest contrast here is in the centre of the painting, giving focus to the cows.

Butter muslin, cotton or linen can be applied to a surface with PVA glue and then given a coat of gesso or gelatin to seal the surface. If the surface is not sealed, the oil will soak in and the resultant painting will be dull.

Wood panels were often used by the old masters, as were other surfaces like stone and tin. These would take little preparation other than making sure they were clean and free of grease.

STEP BY STEP DEMONSTRATION

Backlit Clouds, Pin Mill

This photo reference was taken whilst painting on location at Pin Mill in Suffolk. The clouds were perfect for painting and I did several studies while I was there, but needed more time to capture their form properly.

Colours

- Warm White
- Cadmium Orange
- Magenta
- Cobalt Blue

Support

For this demonstration, a cotton covered 10" × 8" board was used. This gives a comparatively smooth surface but still has enough tooth to prevent the surface from becoming slippery. The board was prepared by gluing cotton sheeting to the board using PVA. When the glue dried, two coats of gesso were applied. To give a warm ground, diluted Burnt Umber was painted on. Finally this was given a light sanding down with fine sandpaper.

Brushes

All from Rosemary & Co. Ivory range

- No. 2 Filbert
- No. 2 Rigger
- No. 4 & 6 Flat

Step 1. Mix a turpsy wash with Ultramarine and Magenta, and block in the cloud formations and the distant tree line on the far shore and mid distance.

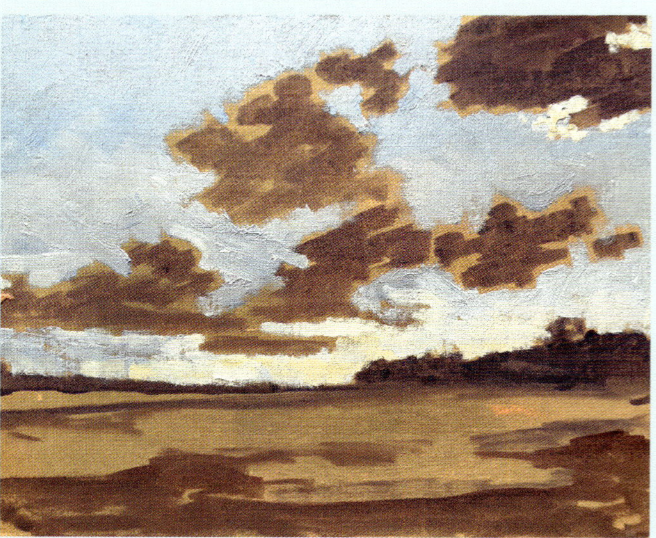

Step 2. Using Cobalt Blue toned down with Cadmium Orange and Warm White, the sky is painted in around the clouds. Leave a space between the two colours, as the highlights will go in there next. In the top right corner, you can see how the lightest areas have started to be put in with Warm White and Cadmium Orange.

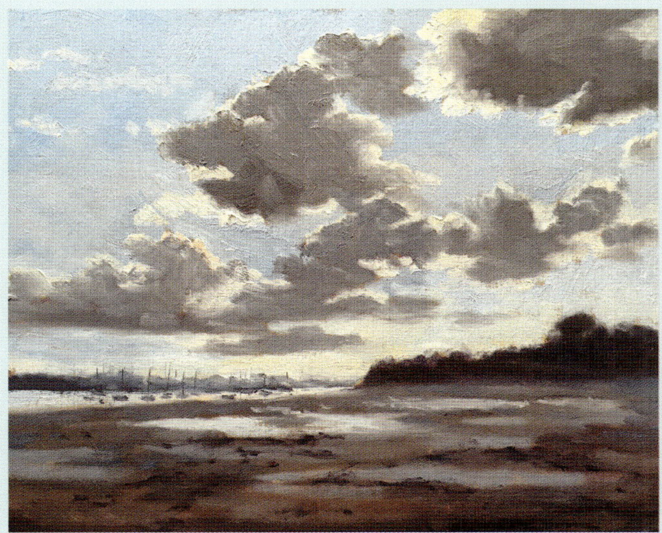

Step 3. Continue to paint the highlights around the clouds with white and orange. White on its own would look too cold but the touch of orange in the mix helps to warm the highlights.

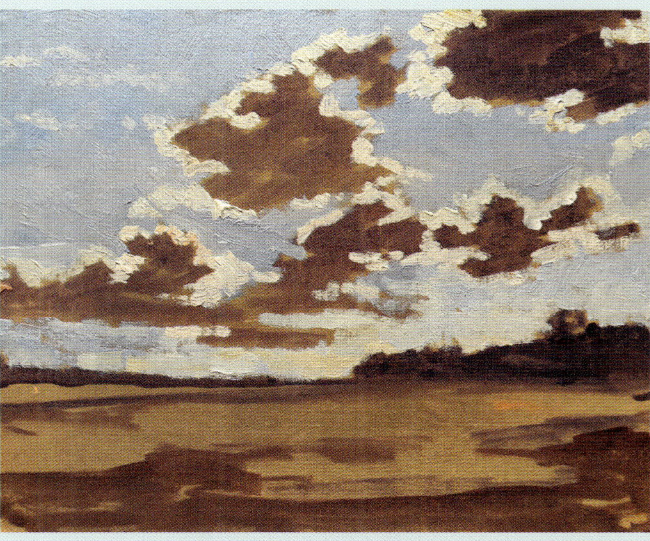

Step 4. Various mixes of Cobalt Blue and Cadmium Orange are used in the foreground of the wet mud, leaving the space for the wet sky reflections.

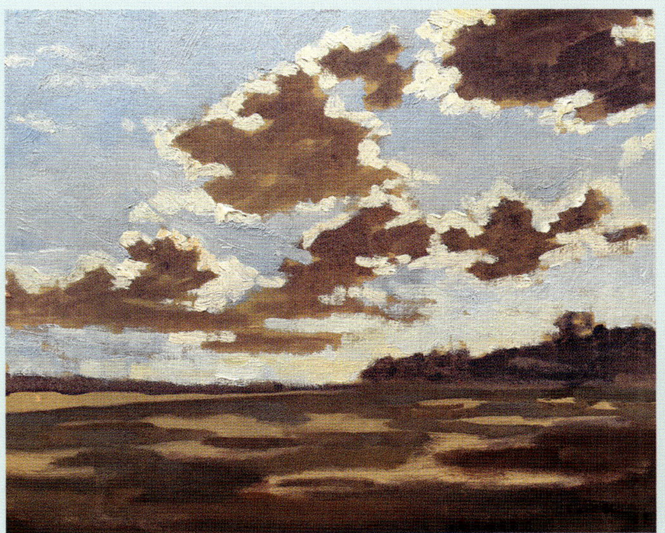

Step 5. On looking at the painting and the source photograph, it can be seen that the underpainting for the clouds needs to be not only paler but softer and blended in.

Prepare a few mixes of grey with Cadmium Orange and Cobalt Blue. These two colours make a surprisingly good range of warm grey and with the addition of white, the range of greys can be extended even further. Using these mixes, use the tip of the brush to push paint from the centre of the cloud to the edge. This pushes the white back to make a thinner edge. It would be difficult to paint a line as fine as this. The resulting line will have a comparatively hard edge. The clouds have a combination of soft and hard edges. To soften some of the edges, use a bristle brush and draw the paint out using a stippling action.

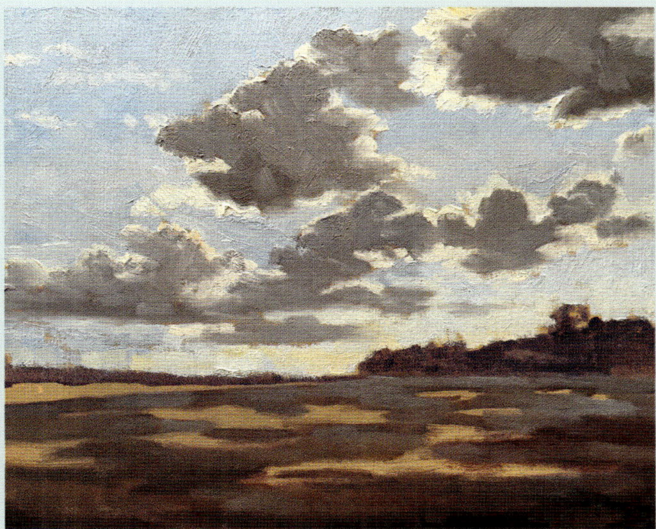

Step 6. Using the Warm White and Cadmium Orange mix that was used for the highlight on the clouds, paint the water in the estuary. You will find a rigger useful for this as you can get a fine point on it. Keep the lightest area central, this is where we want our focal point to be. The contrast between the highlight on the water and the dark of the trees will draw the eye in.

Add a small amount of Cobalt to the mix for the water to start painting the puddles. The light reflected in the distance in the puddles left from the receding tide needs to be a tone darker than the highlight of the water so as not to lessen the effect.

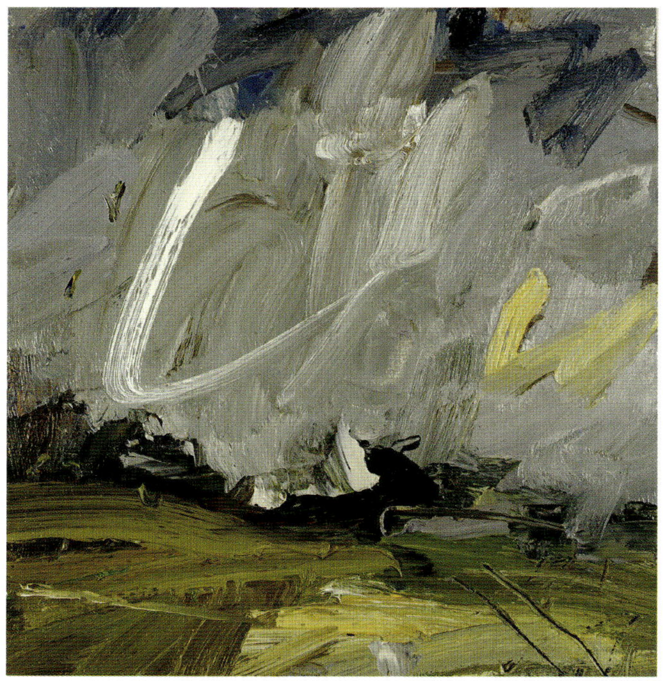

Dark Skyline Across the Downs, Louise Balaam.
This painting is a fine example of a style that has grown and developed. Louise's bold loose brush marks show great confidence and skill.

Painting looser

A lot of artists aspire to paint in a loose style. Unfortunately, it doesn't just happen this way.

Before being able to paint in a loose way, we must first learn to paint in a controlled manner. We need to acquire the skills to put down the correct colours and tones, and our drawing skills are also very important. One brushstroke can speak volumes but drawing skills enable the control and confidence to make such marks. By acquiring all the skills needed, we will gain the confidence about the strokes we put down. If we are unsure, that will lead to reworking and fiddling which will spoil the effect we are aiming for.

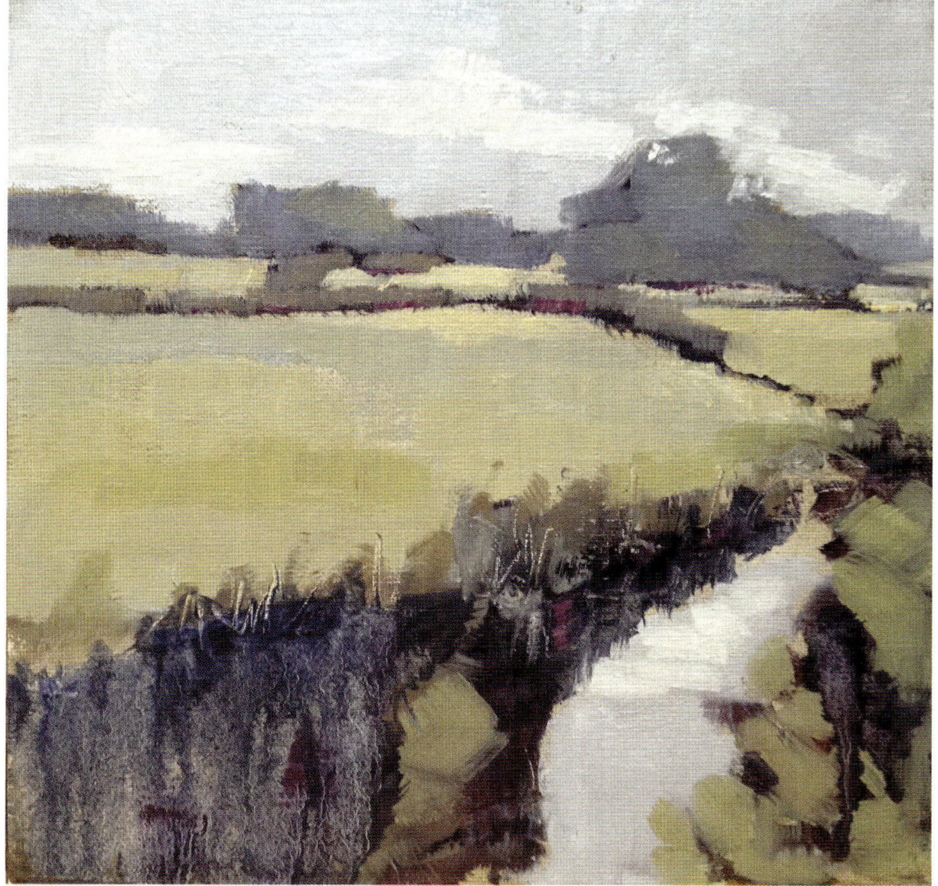

Burnham Overy Fields, 10" × 10".
Canvas board.
Cadmium Yellow
Magenta
French Ultramarine
Titanium White

Thin dark washes of Ultramarine and Magenta were applied over most of the canvas, these dried quickly and thicker opaque paint was painted on with a size 8 flat brush. The large brush prevented any temptation to add detail. The very limited palette helps to give this painting harmony. The sky reflecting in the river balances the picture whilst the original dark wash defines the field edges and in the foreground, it works to give the impression of the shadows of the reeds.

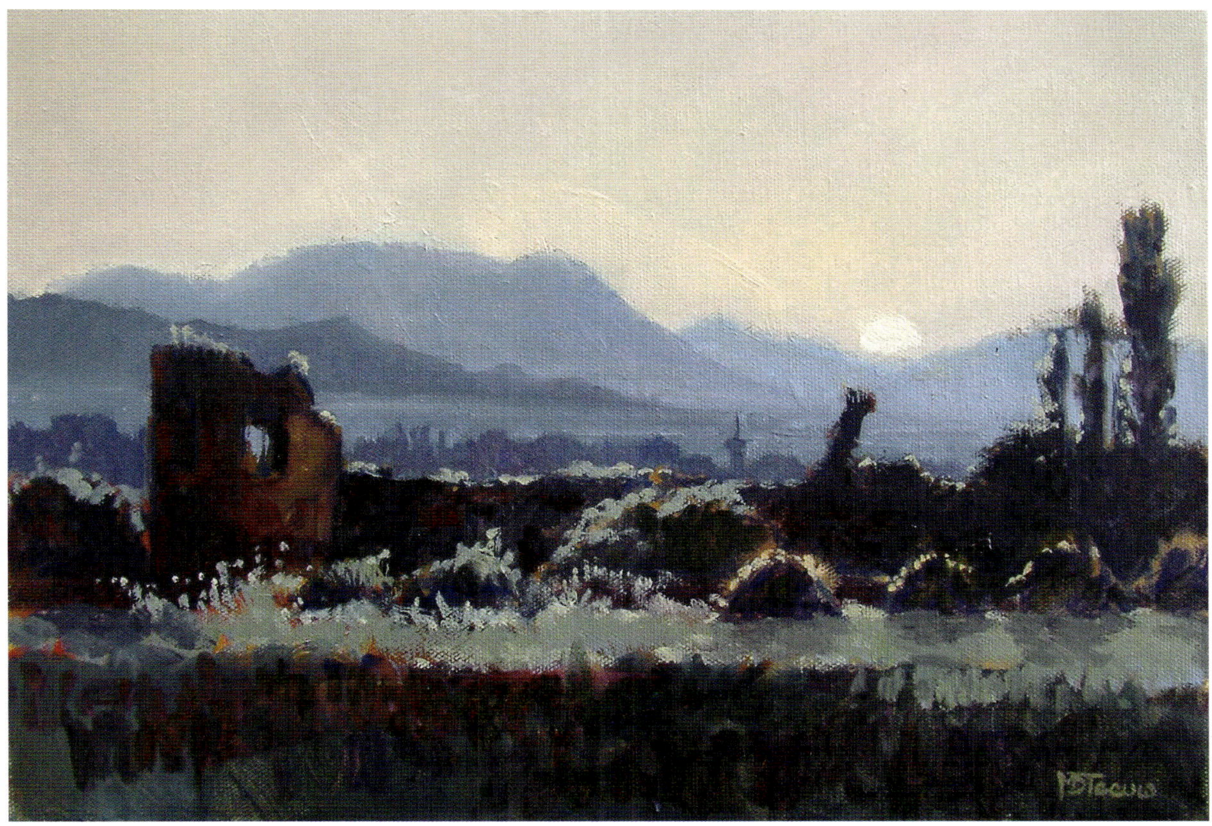

City Wall, Iznik.
Titanium White
Cadmium Yellow
Alizarin Crimson
Burnt Sienna
Ultramarine Blue
10" × 14" Canvas board
Burnt Sienna ground

This was painted at sunrise, just outside the town of Iznik in Turkey. The sky had a warm hazy glow as the sun rose over the distant hills. I kept the hills soft and pale, strengthening the colour as they came forward to give the illusion of distance. The silhouette of the town was also kept in blue tones. Warmth was added to the old walls with Alizarin Crimson, Burnt Sienna and Ultramarine Blue.

I was careful not to make the green in the foreground too bright as I wanted to keep the harmony of the blues so I used the Ultramarine Blue with only a little Cadmium Yellow and Titanium White.

The light on the stooks make a good contrast against the dark wall and gives the picture a lift. The Burnt Sienna ground stops the painting from looking too blue.

There is a big difference between paintings that are painted in a loose style and paintings that are hastily put together. It is all very well to be relaxed about our painting but each brushstroke needs to be considered and expressive.

One of the first steps to loosening up a painting style is to use bigger brushes. It is often an idea to start a painting using a brush bigger than you think you will need. This will not only help to keep it simple and not feel the need to add extra detail but it will make your brushwork look bold and more expressive.

By keeping it simple, you can focus more on colour and good tonal values and by doing this, you will say more. You will need to have a very firm idea in your mind of what you are trying to accomplish and the process you are going to go through to achieve that effect. For example, plan the painting out. Block in the shapes and lose the blank canvas. By covering it in general colour and values, the basics will be there. Squinting your eyes helps you to see the larger shapes and the general colour.

Sadly, painting in a loose style does not come naturally to most of us. If in the past you have been painting your pictures in the style where they represented a photograph, you are going to find it a very difficult challenge to depart from that style.

A loose painting is not contrived or forced. You should not just try to paint loosely. Painting in a painterly and masterful way will only come as your confidence grows. The answer is to practise, practise, practise.

Tip: hold your brush at the end of the handle, not at the ferrule. This will enable you to use your whole arm, not just your fingers.

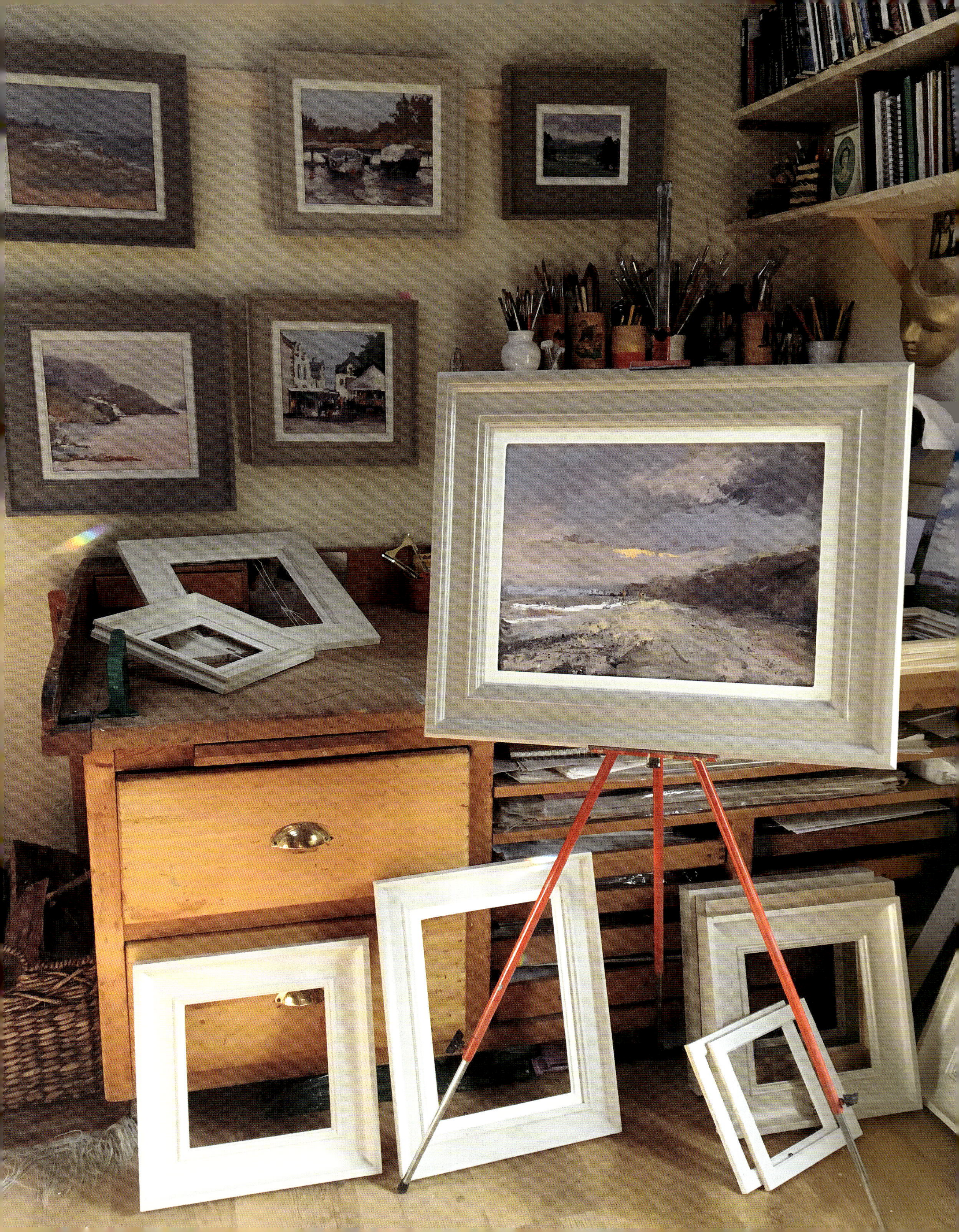

CHAPTER 11

Finishing and presenting your paintings

Have I finished? Have I done all I set out to do? Is there anything else I can do to improve the painting? These are the questions asked by many an artist. Deciding when the painting is finished is a common dilemma. Starting the painting is the easy part, knowing when to stop is the difficult part. Sometimes it is obvious, you instinctively know when the picture is finished.

First of all, you must ask yourself, have I achieved what I started out to do? An artist will usually have an idea in mind; they will have planned the picture out and will have a vision of the completed painting.

It is very easy to get sidetracked as you go along. An area of the picture may not come out as envisaged; the original concept changes and this can change the feeling of the whole painting. We continually learn as we paint, find different colours as we mix, maybe apply paint in a different way so the original concept will inevitably shift slightly.

Sometimes we may stop too soon, resulting in a painting that looks unresolved. And other times we may take the painting beyond its limits and overwork it. Overworking a painting will cause you to lose any spontaneity you may have had in the picture.

Finishing off frames in the studio.

Review your painting

It is always a good policy to keep an overview of your original plan in mind while painting. Try to step back from the picture at regular intervals and view your work from a distance. By stepping back, you will view your painting as a whole. Ask yourself if this is what you had intended with your original idea. When working close to the canvas, it is easy to just concentrate on one area at a time and therefore not see the painting as a whole.

A painting executed swiftly out in the landscape will have all the right elements but often, when more time can be taken, it can be easy to fall into the trap of working on one area at a time and not seeing the painting as a whole.

Try to keep the painting going by working your way round the canvas; if a colour is mixed, where else can it go? Could you put some of the sky mix in the foreground?

Try to be subjective about your painting; it is easy to fall into the trap of not seeing clearly what is in front of us. We have become so involved in the painting that often we only see what we were trying to achieve and not what we have actually painted. Glaring mistakes don't readily jump out at us.

Don't just look for the negative parts of a painting. In assessing the painting, you must also look for the positive elements. There will be parts of the painting that you are pleased with. It's easy to get so caught up in thinking about how you could improve the picture that you forget to appreciate the things you're doing well. But this aspect of the process is just as crucial – you need to know your own skills

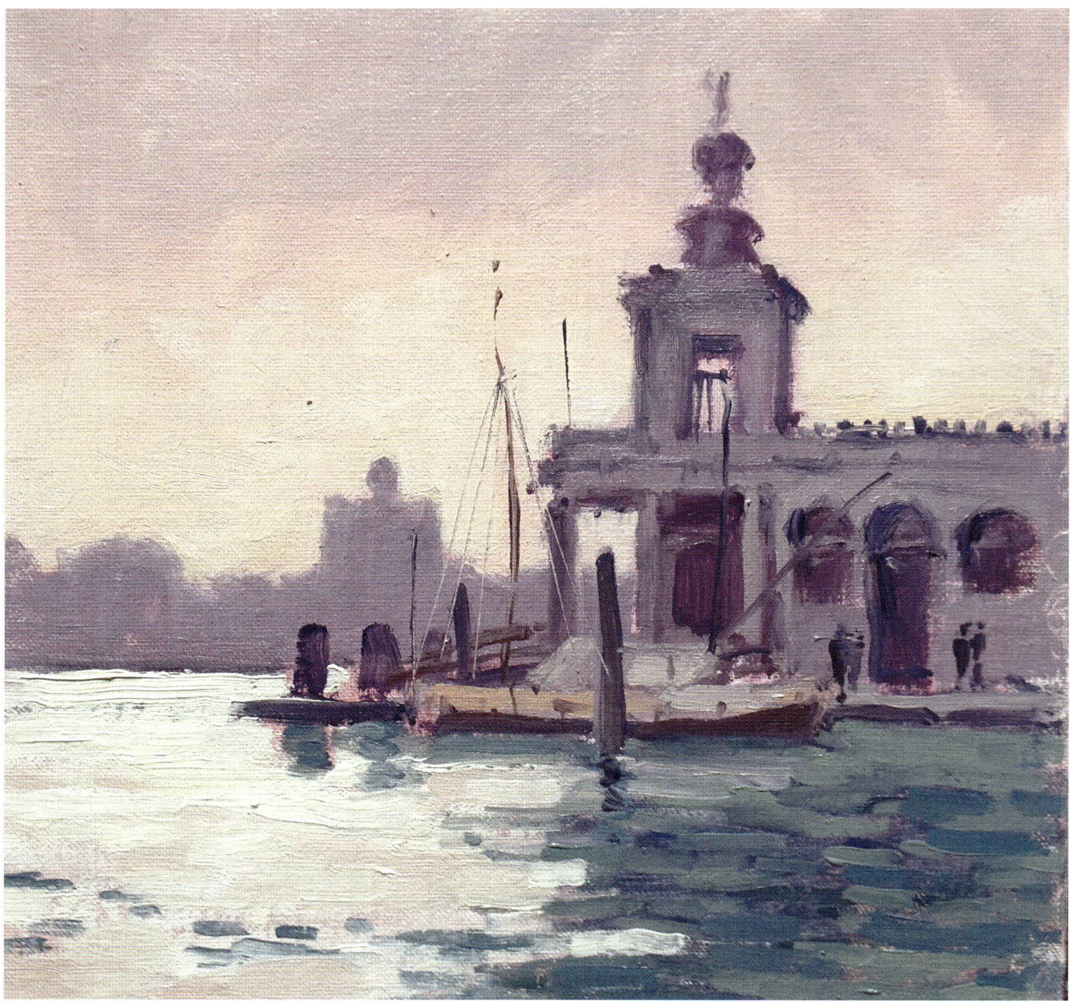

Pink Sky, Venice, 6" × 6". Primed card.
Painted on location in Venice early one morning. The sky had a pink glow to it which was echoed in the water and the buildings.

and abilities to have a realistic understanding of what you're capable of. This has an impact on your direction as an artist, and on your future works. Draw on these components and learn from them. Remember that as artists we are continually learning.

Before rushing with what you think to be a finished painting off to the framers, it is a good idea to 'live' with it for a while. Prop it up somewhere where you can keep having a look at it. Stare at it from a distance.

If you are still not sure, avoid the temptation to go back and fiddle with it. An overworked painting can look very dull and lifeless.

Try putting the painting away for a few weeks; when you get it out again you will see it with fresh eyes. Sometimes, time away from your work can be invaluable, and you will be more able to assess your work. We can get too familiar with our painting and tend not to see glaring errors, so seeing it from a different aspect is a good way to help decide if it is finished.

Adjustments may have to be made to make the whole picture hang together. It is not uncommon to revisit a painting for five minutes and then before you know it, you have repainted the whole thing in order to tie everything together. Never is this more true than with paintings involving a sky. The colours in the sky need to be reflected in the landscape and vice versa.

Brushstrokes need to be consistent. A sky painted with broad brush strokes and a landscape painted in detail with a small brush just would not work. It would probably look like two paintings joined together.

Another trick employed by many artists is to look at your painting in a mirror. If you are over familiar with your painting it is hard to see mistakes. Looking at it in a mirror is like seeing the painting from a different angle and is almost as if you are seeing it for the first time but through different eyes.

You might also try turning the painting upside down. This will bring to light any compositional errors, such as the balance of the painting.

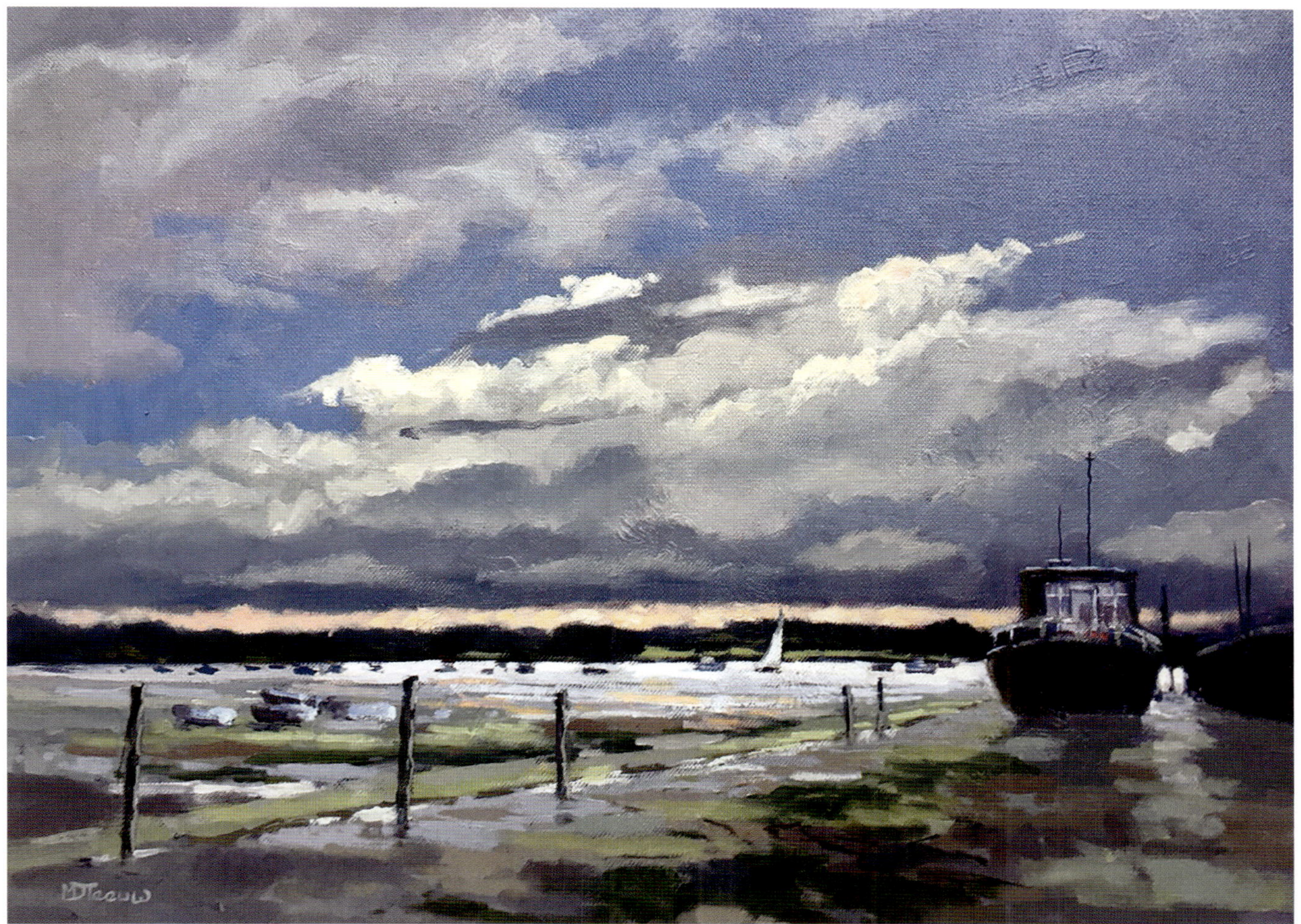

Spring Clouds, Pin Mill, 16" × 20". Canvas board.
There is always something interesting to paint at Pin Mill. However many times you visit, it always looks different with the movement of the boats and the different seasons. This spring day was very fresh with plenty of cloud movement. This painting was worked in the studio from a 10" × 12" oil sketch. The small painting was too busy which is why I opted for a larger canvas.

Some areas may have gone a bit dull where paint has dried flat. A coat of retouching varnish will bring it back to life. Artists' painting varnish should not be applied for at least six months to allow the paint to dry completely. It is perfectly OK to paint over retouching varnish if you do find you need to make any final adjustments. The main points for consideration are:

- Does my focal point work? Is the eye drawn to it?
- Is the colour balance right? Is there a harmony within the colours? Is the temperature right?

A common mistake is to work on the sky, maybe from a reference photograph and then the landscape from a different reference. Imagine a beautiful summer sky with a few clouds, think how wrong it would look if there were no shadows, or the landscape was dull and not sunlit. Conversely, an overcast sky but the landscape bathed in sunlight would look just as wrong. When you feel you have got all these elements right, stand back and have a good look at your painting. Putting it in an old frame will help to show up any discrepancies, and the trick of looking at the painting in a mirror also helps.

Get online help

As artists at any level, we all need feedback and critiques to improve our work. It always helps to get a fresh set of eyes on your artwork because others tend to see mistakes that you've completely overlooked. Attending a painting class will provide you with a lot of advice but who can the solitary artist turn to?

Getting an honest critique on our work can be quite tricky. Friends and family tend to be encouraging and are very quick to praise. Receiving useful constructive criticism about your art can be difficult – by asking those close to us, we are putting them on the spot. They will be afraid of hurting your feelings or offending you and therefore they are probably not the best people to go to for help. Even fellow artists may not really give their true opinion for fear of offending you.

There is help out there on the Internet. There are very many arty groups on social media. Facebook is a good example of where a lot of artists come together to share their work. But even here we cannot be sure if the feedback is honest enough. If you look at the average comments, they are all positive, even when you have asked for criticism. People even here are afraid to offend. The way to go would be to find a place where everyone can retain anonymity.

Most blogs allow for anonymous comments to be made. By being anonymous, acquaintances will be more readily prepared to offer a truer criticism and opinion of the painting.

Do remember that you should not ask for advice unless you are prepared for the comments you may get back. Remember, it is only some other person's opinion. You do not have to take it all on board. Take note of the useful advice and don't take detrimental comments personally.

ONLINE PRESENCE

If you want to be recognized as an artist then you will find it very beneficial to have an online presence. People need to know who you are and what you do. There is no point painting away in solitude, wondering why no one has ever heard of you. The public won't come knocking on your door if they don't know who you are or what you do, or even if your paintings are for sale.

Galleries will want to see a website or images of available work but you must keep it up to date. Gallery owners will not be interested in seeing artwork that was done years ago. They want to see recent work.

There are many ways to achieve an online presence, the main ones being blogging, your own website and social media.

Blogging

The word 'Blog' comes from the term 'Web Log'. It is a form of online journal or diary that is regularly updated. It is a place to share your thoughts and your passions. It can be anything you want it to be. Your blog is your online presence that you are going to update on an ongoing basis.

A blog is normally a single page that may contain pictures along with your dialogue. When the author adds a new entry, it appears at the top, and all the older entries are pushed down, which are then archived in reverse chronological order from the latest entry to the oldest. People can scroll back through older posts but it is usually the top page that they are interested in.

Originally, people used blogs to write about their day-to-day lives, a sort of online diary. Slowly these bloggers began to gain a following and the hobby of blogging was born. Not everyone chooses to publish their blog over the Internet and they keep their blog just for their own purposes or they may just share with a chosen few.

How you use your blog is up to you. A lot of artists like to share their paintings with the public, others will give a detailed account of the colours they use or even post short videos of work in progress. However you decide to use the Internet, it is a very useful way of reaching the general public.

You may be wondering where to start. Since blogging has become so popular, there are many more options open for us and it has become much simpler to start your own. Two very popular ways of starting a blog are through blogger.com and WordPress.

You will need to select a name for your blog that identifies you as an artist. Make it easy to be found, don't try and go for fancy 'arty' names as it makes it harder for search engines to find you when people type in your name.

It's all very well writing your blog but how to direct traffic there isn't easy at first. Until you have built up a following, you will need to write your blog and then share the link for it on social media.

Encourage visitors to your blog to enter their email address and sign up for latest updates. This is the way to keep your audience engaged and in touch.

Websites

Websites, unlike blogs, have several pages that people can navigate through. The first page of a website is referred to as the home page and this is where visitors will find links to other pages within the website.

If you decide to have your own website, the first thing you will need is your own domain name. A *domain name* is the key part of your online address, and this is what search engines and visitors will use to find your website. As with the blog, make it easy to be found, try to use a name that is unique to you.

When you own your domain name, you can use it for your email address. For example, with the website www.moteeuw.co.uk, the email could be info@moteeuw.co.uk, or sales@moteeuw.co.uk or any other prefix that is relevant to your site.

Setting up your email and getting your own domain name isn't difficult. It is worth doing a bit of research or asking friends who they use to host. You can buy your own unique domain name online from as little as 99p per year. Be aware, though, that certain domain names will have been snapped up years ago.

These days, there is such an abundance of website hosting sites that it can be very confusing. The best advice here would be to avoid sites that offer free hosting. Nothing is free. Many of the free sites will probably have pop up adverts and flashing sidebars, which can be very distracting to visitors. There may be links to other websites; these are best avoided too as it will only take people away from your site and they may not come back again.

1&1.co.uk is a very good hosting site and they are also available to talk to on the phone whereas a lot of companies only communicate by email. The software for building your site is also easy to use, enabling you to build different galleries and links within your site.

The main thing to bear in mind is to keep it simple. Do avoid the use of flashing banners, and lots of different fonts and adverts, as these can be very distracting.

Make sure your site is easy to navigate. If it is confusing or has dead ends, you will lose your viewer very quickly.

Present your work as if it was in a gallery with clean, simple layouts. Give information about each image such as size and title. If you are already represented in a gallery, the prices should be reflected on the website. A buyer would not be best pleased to see a similar painting on the web at half the price they paid in a gallery.

Each page should link back to the main pages, such as home page, galleries and contact information, otherwise visitors will get lost.

You need to be able to change content and update the site regularly and easily. More and more people are using mobile phones and tablets to access the Internet and that number is only going to increase. It is important that your website is compatible with these devices; you will want your website to look at its best in whatever format it is being viewed in.

Social media

Since the advent of sites like Facebook, Twitter and Instagram to name but a few, the use of social media has rocketed and is growing daily. We can share our artwork to thousands with the click of a button.

To really get the best out of this method of communication, you have to decide what you want to get out of it. Do you just want to meet like minded artists, share ideas, meet up with people to paint with, gain recognition as an artist or do you want to sell online and reach galleries?

We have to consider who the target audience is. It is all very well posting your pictures and getting 'likes' on them but are they the buyers and galleries? Whichever route you decide to take, you will need to build up your network. Nearly everyone has a social outlet they use; by connecting with people that have the same interests and by following galleries, you will gradually build up a following.

Most social networking sites will have groups that you can join to share ideas. It is important to find a few of these groups. There are a lot of art forums on various sites. A word of warning: if you are not sure about protocol, don't jump straight in. Start by following conversations to see how they run. When you feel comfortable in following a thread then join in the discussions; if you are passive, no one will notice you.

If you have an art page, for example on Facebook, try to keep it professional. Galleries and buyers don't really want to see pictures of what you had for dinner last night or your new puppy, however cute it is.

Tip: beware of over posting. If you bombard the Internet with images, people are more likely to 'unfollow' you.

Social media is really a numbers game; the more followers you have, the more you will gain and the more likely we are to find mutually beneficial relationships.

When someone does take an interest in your work by following you, do take the time to follow him or her back and to thank him or her for their interest in your work. It is possible to build up a following by sharing and retweeting other people's work. If people see you doing this then they are more likely to reciprocate.

Linking accounts is a good idea so you don't have to multi post. In settings it is easy to link your Twitter and Facebook accounts so that each time you put something on the Internet, it is duplicated on the other site.

We can announce exhibitions and the more people who see and share it, the more followers we will get.

Often, it is a case of knowing the right people. Through social media you can find other artists with advice, or connections to a gallery. If you are aiming to show in a particular gallery then it will be easier to get an introduction if you know an artist already exhibiting there.

FRAMING

Now the painting is finished, all it needs is the finishing touch – the frame. The main purpose of the frame is to make the painting stand alone as an individual work of art and to unify it as a whole.

All too often, artists fail to select the correct frame for the painting, not understanding the importance of the right frame. A carefully selected frame can make all the difference to a painting. Do not underestimate the importance of framing your artwork in the most suitable and visually attractive way. Taking your time over making this decision will certainly pay dividends. Think of the frames as an investment.

Framing tastes like all fashions tend to come and go. Think back to Victorian times and the gilt frames. They were often heavy and very ornate. These days, with more minimalistic décor, people prefer a more simple style but even still, trends shift.

It is a good idea to visit large exhibitions of some of the different major societies to see what people are using. Look carefully at the paintings on the walls and try to envisage your work in the different frames, is there one that would particularly suit your work?

This is where a good framer is worth knowing. He or she will know what people are looking for and should be able to select a frame to show your work off to its best advantage.

Generally, oil paintings are not glazed. At one time, glass was put in the frame as protection against pollution and smoke damage but these days, it is not necessary as people don't smoke so much indoors and homes are not heated with open fires.

Elaborate frames can make a painting look more important and a lesser painting can benefit hugely by being placed in a good frame. Conversely, a poor frame can have a detrimental effect on a good painting.

Artists can use their frames to create their own visual identity. This means that their work can be identified as much by the frame as by their painting style. Unfortunately, if it looks good and really shows the painting to its best advantage, as soon as the painting goes on public display, the frame is open to being copied and often is.

Hand finished frames that have been painted are very much in vogue at the present but these have the disadvantage of being rather on the expensive side. It requires a great deal of time.

Consider carefully the width of the frame. A good framer will be able to offer advice and various options. A moulding that is too thin can look like an afterthought whereas a moulding that is too wide may dwarf a small painting. A moulding with a bevel or 'spoon' shape will help draw the eye into the picture. A liner, or small inner frame, painted a different colour, can often help to complement a painting.

Several small moulding shapes can be multi-layered to create a unique shape that would be more difficult to copy but might also prove to be more expensive.

Having a few frames made at the same time is a good idea, especially if you want to play with colours. Try painting six frames in differing colours and see the various effects each one has on one painting. It really is surprising how just the right colour can complement a picture.

Hand finishing a frame

The best way to create an individual frame that is unique to you is to make your own. Unfortunately not everyone has the time, skill or equipment to do this. A good option is to visit a framer that stocks plain, bare wood moulding and to ask for frames to be made up to your requirements and then for you to hand finish the frame yourself.

This involves a couple of layers of white gesso which are applied over the profile then sanded to leave a smooth surface; this will not only take off sharp, crisp edges but also hides the mitred joints.

Emulsion or clay paints selected to suit your painting are then painted in a couple of layers. Farrow and Ball have a large range of colours that are ideally suited for this purpose. The more layers, the deeper the colour.

Finally a clear wax is applied to protect the finished frame from scuffs and scratches. Try to keep it simple, an over fussy frame can detract from a painting as can a strong colour. If you are unsure as to which colour to use then it is safest to stick to neutral colours. Try and work to a standard size. This will enable you to change paintings around and guarantees that you have a frame to fit your painting.

If you are making your own supports by covering boards with either canvas or gesso, it is a good idea to have the boards conform to sizes of commercially bought canvases. By having standard sizes, it offers more opportunity to buy off the shelf frames.

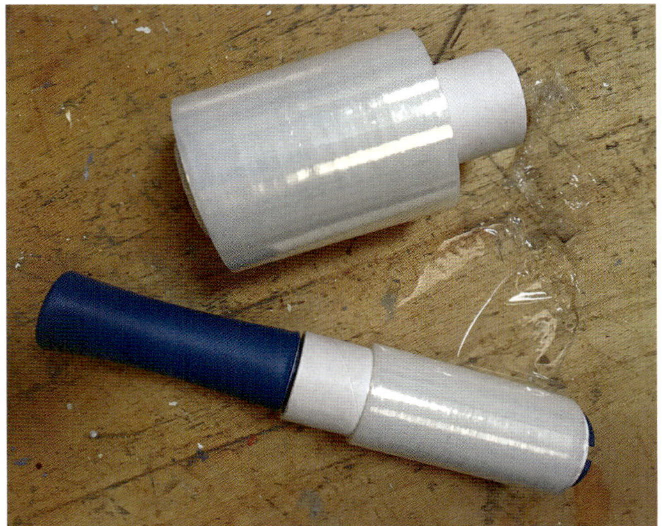

Protecting – wrapping and stacking. This handy wrap is a form of cling film, available from Lion, and is easy to put around the frame. Replacement rolls slip onto the blue handle.

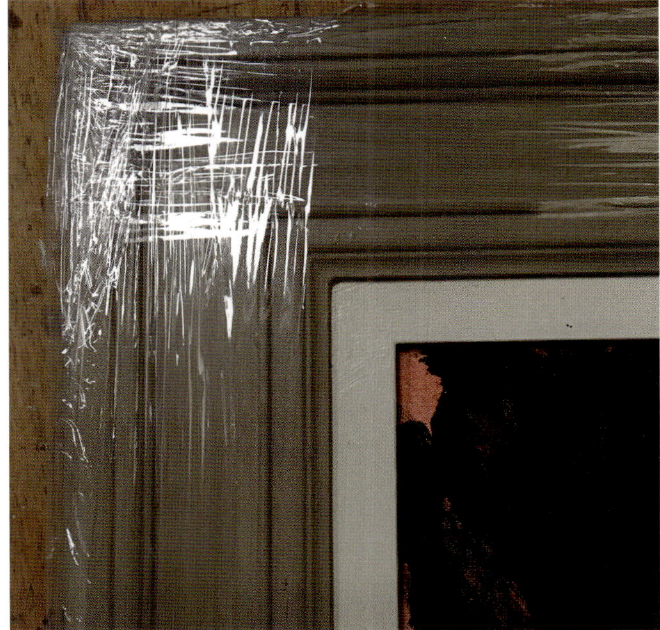

This picture shows the film once it has been applied. I usually wrap it around two or three times. Whilst it will not protect the frame from knocks, it does prevent scratches. It sticks to itself, which means that frames can be stacked up in transport and will not slide around. Another big advantage is that if you are submitting work for consideration to a gallery or art show, then you won't have to take off all the protective wrapping.

A general guideline is that a small painting looks better in a wider frame whereas a large painting is probably better in a simple narrow frame.

GALLERIES

So now we have finished and framed our painting. It is natural to want to share our work by displaying it to the public and hopefully selling our work too.

A word of advice here is not to be too hasty. You wouldn't want to go on stage and play a concerto to a large audience after a few months of piano lessons. Make sure you are happy with the work you are producing. Go and visit exhibitions and be really honest with yourself: is your work up to this standard?

Before even considering approaching any gallery, you will need to build up a body of work. A gallery would want to see this and to know that your work displays consistency.

A well-designed, eye-catching business card gives a good impression, especially if it has an image of one of your paintings on it.

When you finally feel that you are ready and have plucked up enough courage to approach galleries, it is important that you do a little research first. Optimistic artists looking for representation are constantly approaching galleries. Don't make the mistake of walking through the door into a gallery with a bundle of paintings under your arm. You will see the barriers go up straightaway.

First you must choose your gallery carefully. Make a couple of visits to see different exhibitions, look at the work on the walls and ask yourself, 'would my work fit in here? Is it of a similar style to the other work they sell?' It would be pointless taking traditional work into a very contemporary art gallery.

Research the gallery, find out how many exhibitions they hold per year and which artists they represent.

Finally, having decided which is the gallery for you, approach the owner. Find out and use their name as this shows that you have taken the time to do your research.

Ask if you can make an appointment to see them and leave them all your contact details including a brief biography and web details. If, having been granted an interview, the answer is 'no', don't be afraid to ask why and what might have made a difference. This way you will be better prepared for next time.

CONTRIBUTING ARTISTS

Louise Balaam RWA NEAC
www.louisebalaam.co.uk
Louise is a member of the New English Art Club and the Royal Watercolour Association. With her loose Impressionistic style, she captures the emotional impact of landscape in her paintings.

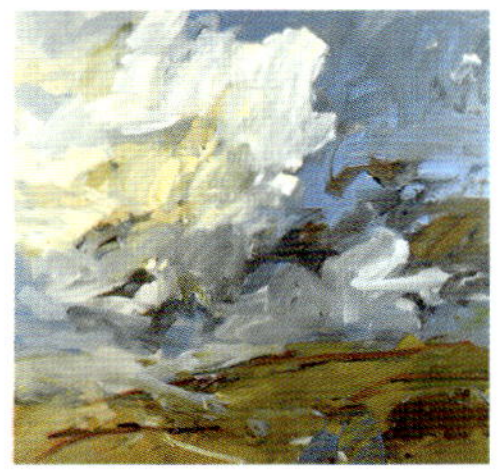

Peter Barker RSMA
www.peterbarkerpaintings.co.uk
Peter, who is a member of the Royal Society for Marine Artists, has been a professional artist since 1983. He paints both *en plein air* for smaller panels in oils, and in the studio for larger works. He owns and runs a gallery, Peter Barker Fine Art, in the village of Uppingham.

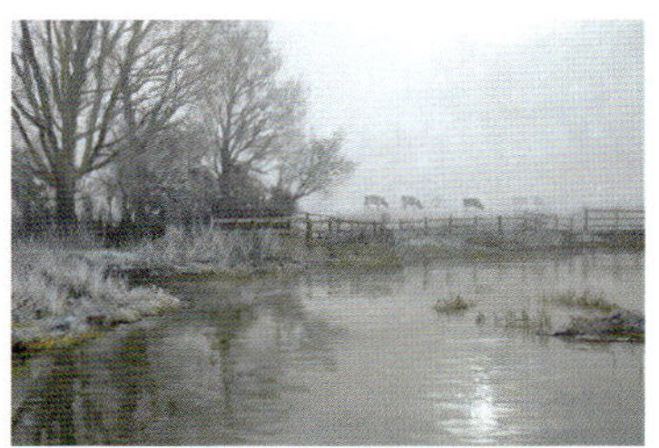

Mari French
www.marifrench.com
Mari French's energetic, yet intimate works are inspired by Norfolk's saltmarshes. She studied art and design at Stockport College before working as a graphic designer. She now works full-time as a contemporary mixed-media artist in Norfolk.

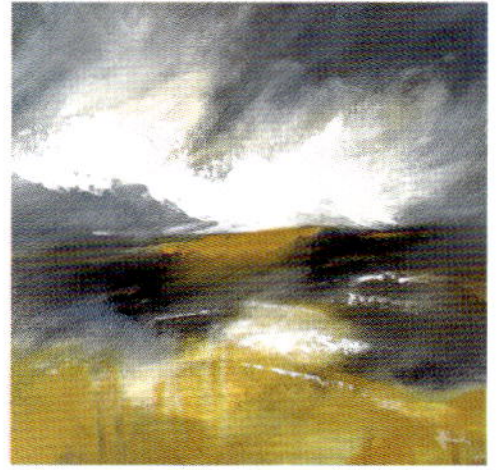

Mary Bentz Gilkerson
https://marygilkerson.com
Mary Bentz Gilkerson is a contemporary artist and art teacher who is passionate about landscape, the environment and sense of place. She draws inspiration from the landscapes in the area of South Carolina where she lives. Her work is in many collections.

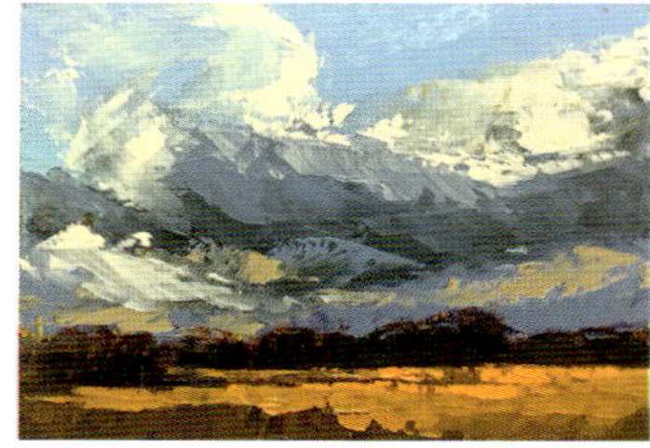

Roos Schuring
https://roosschuring.com
Roos Schuring, who works solely *en plein air*, is passionate about painting. She received a degree in graphic design from the School of Fine Arts in Utrecht. She won the Netherlands prestigious Rembrandt Painting Award in 2004, and is represented by many galleries.

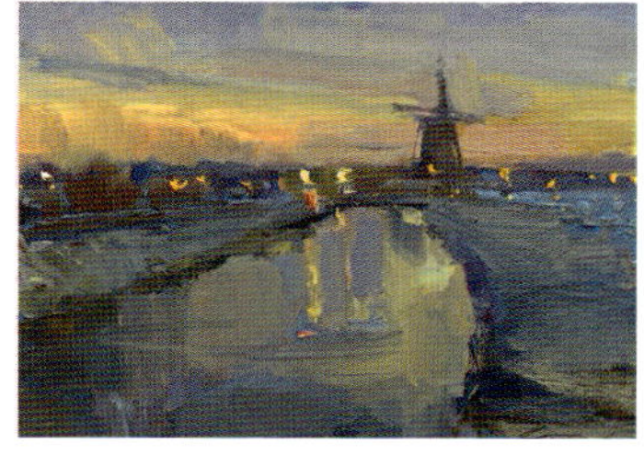

David Simons
www.davidsimonsfineart.com
David, who is a member of Oil Painters of America, is primarily a landscape artist. Self taught, his work which shows loose and confident brushwork has won acclaim in the southwestern United States. He is also a distinguished Artist Member of the Tucson Plein Air Painters' Society, and is one of the founding members of PASSA (Plein Air Painters' Society of Southern AZ).

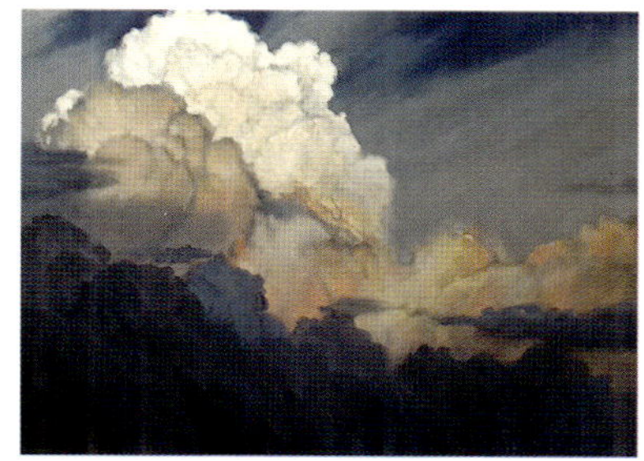

John Stillman ARSMA
www.johnstillman.co.uk
Before becoming a professional artist, John had worked as a book illustrator and a graphic artist. Completely self taught, he is a member of the Royal Society of Marine Artists and the Wapping Group of Artists. His paintings capture the atmosphere of the events that he visits to paint.

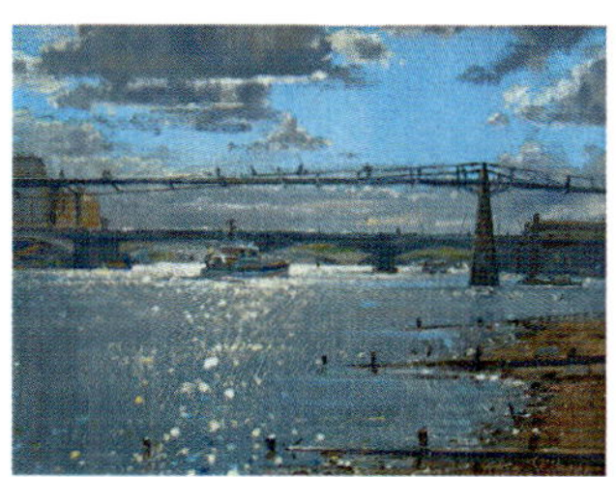

Brian Ryder ROI PPIEA
www.brianryder.org
Brian is a member of the Royal institute of Oil Painters and is the Founder of the IEA (the Institute of East Anglian Artists). He trained and worked as an architect before turning professional. His lively, colourful work is studio based, drawing on his experiences of the landscape.

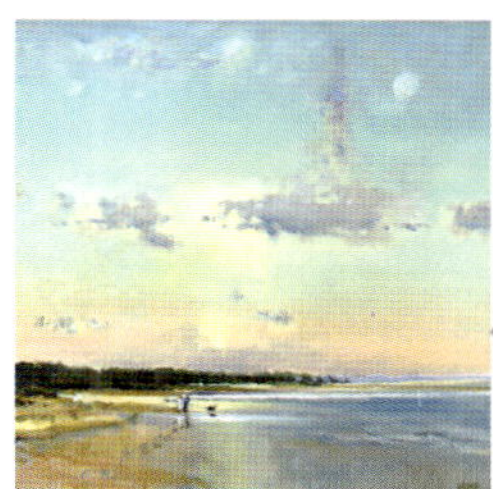

Mo Teeuw
www.moteeuw.co.uk
Mo is a member of the East Anglian Institute of Artists and East Anglian Group of Marine Artists. Mostly self taught, Mo works primarily outdoors, learning from observation, this is the main contribution to her lively, loose and fresh paintings.

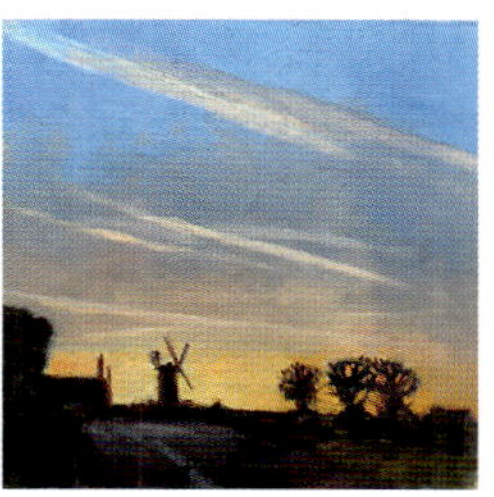

SUPPLIERS

Michael Harding Paints
www.michaelharding.co.uk
High quality handmade paints using techniques which date back to the days of the Old Masters.

Winsor & Newton
www.winsornewton.com
Makers of Artist Quality oil colours, Watermixable oils, Winton Oils for large volumes, Griffin Fast drying oils and oil bars.

Mussini Paints
www.schmincke.de
Mussini artists' natural resin-oil colours are unique throughout the world based on the oil paint formulations of the Old Masters. There are 108 colours in the range.

SAA
www.saa.co.uk
Online suppliers of Artist Materials from the world's largest art community with discounts for members.

Lion
lionpic.co.uk
Suppliers of picture frame mouldings, mount board, materials, equipment and display/hanging systems to professional picture framers.

Rosemary & Co brushes
www.rosemaryandco.com
The finest quality artists' brushes, handmade for 30 years.

1&1 website
www.1and1.co.uk
Domains, website building, hosting.

Open M box
www.openboxm.com
Quality, lightweight and portable *plein air* easels and equipment. Handmade in the USA for almost 30 years.

Strada easel
www.stradaeasel.com
Strada *plein air* easel is a versatile aluminium pochade box made for travel.

INDEX

Related titles from Crowood

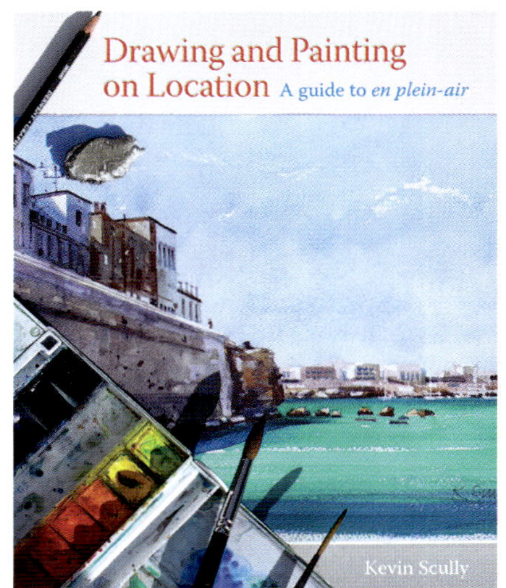

978 1 78500 240 3

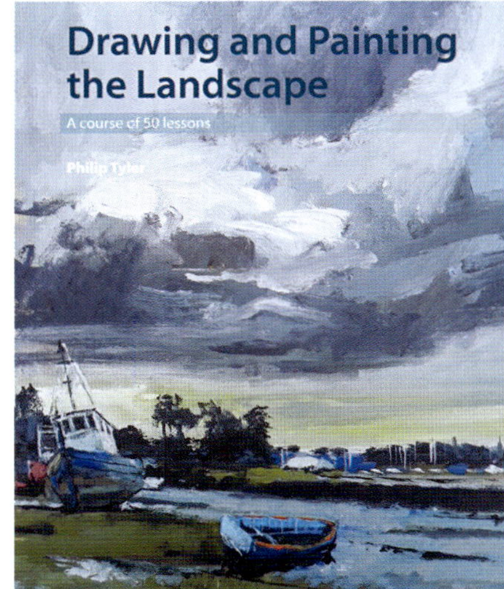

978 1 78500 324 0

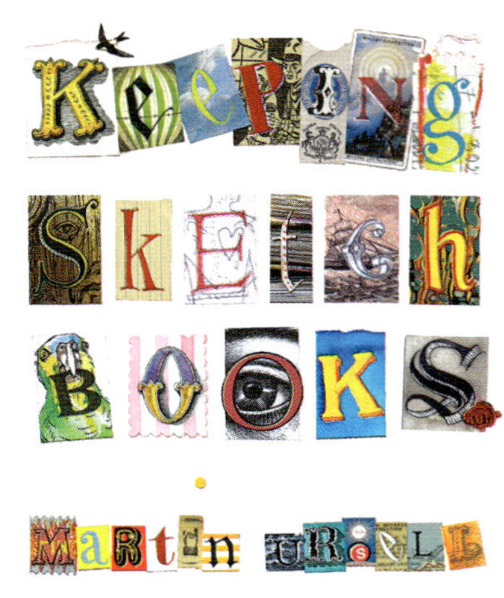

978 1 78500 108 6

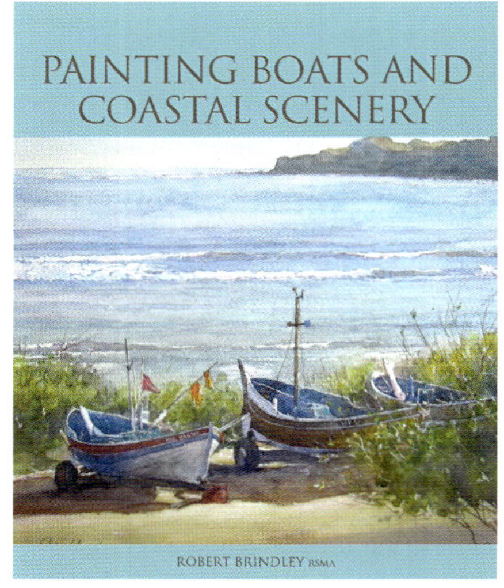

978 1 84797 119 7

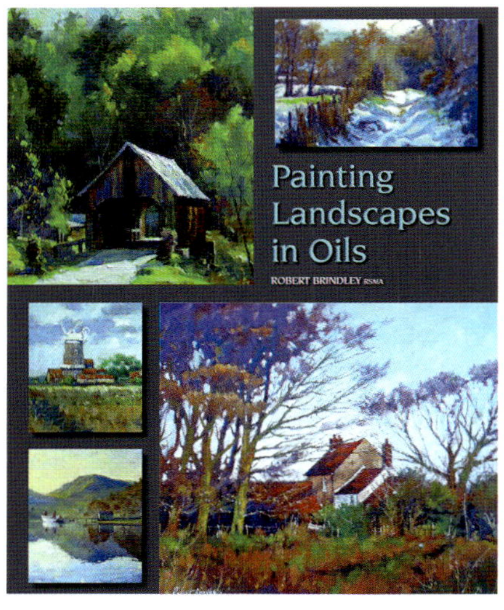

978 1 84797 314 6

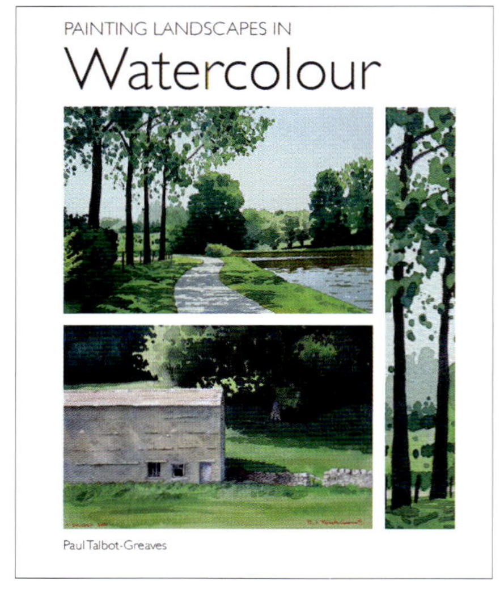

978 1 84797 085 5

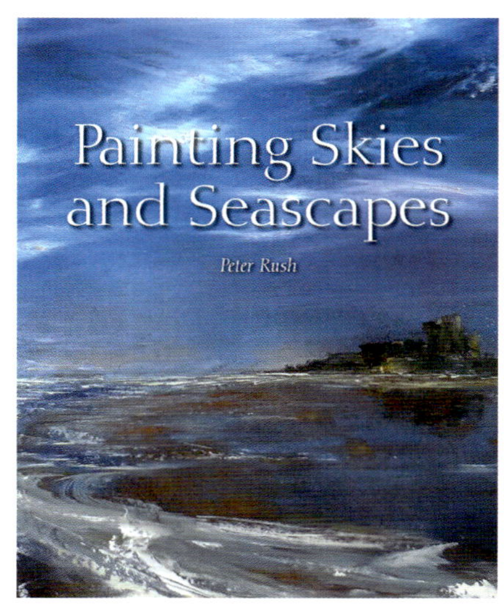

978 1 84797 621 5

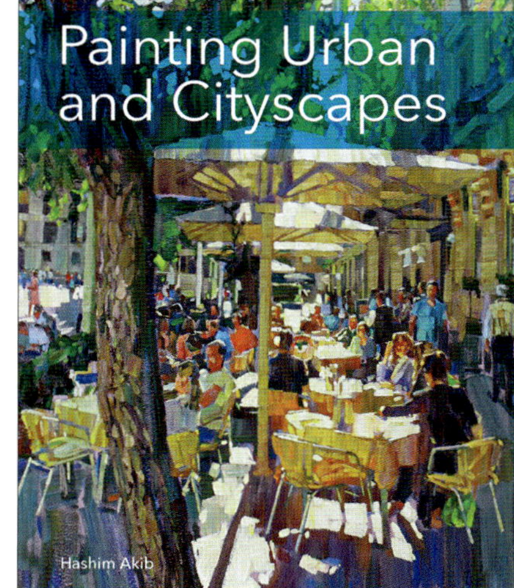

978 1 78500 268 7

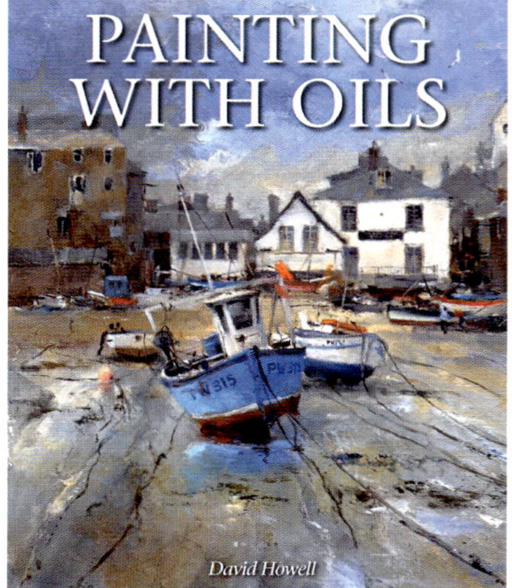

978 1 84797 715 1